TOO REAL

A HOLLYWOOD MEMOIR

DALE WHEATLEY

For the cast and crew of Don's Plum and indie film fans everywhere

PREFACE

Everything in this book is true. I did not seek the opinions of lawyers, publishers, publicists, or agents before publishing *Too Real* because telling my story without restraint or legal white-washing mattered more to me than any so-called protection they may have offered. The story in this book is my Hollywood experience completely uncensored, and I'm entitled to it. I do not fear litigation from anyone because I have only written what is true and not a word of it with any ill intent. If anyone is displeased with the way I have portrayed them, perhaps they should have behaved differently.

Separate from the facts, the opinions in the book are my own, and I've done my best to distinguish them from each other to avoid conflation. I've combined some events and conversations for the readers sake, but every major event in this book happened as described and without embellishment. If anything, I have toned down some of the events in order to remain focused on their purpose in the story. I've changed a couple of names, including that of TV star "Emily Foster." If Emily wishes to come forward with her perspective, she can, but I will never share her name publicly for reasons explained best within the book itself.

I wrote a lot of dialogue for this book, but I approached it much differently than I do fiction. When I was deposed in

Stutman v DiCaprio, the lawyers asked about conversations from our past and I was hesitant because I was under oath and I couldn't possibly be sure of exactly what everyone had said. So one of the lawyers explained the legal understanding of the term "sum and substance." He said the dialogue I provide in my sworn testimony isn't meant to represent exact quotes but rather the spirit of the conversation and what was said by each person. The dialogue in this book represents, to the best of my ability, the spirit of the conversations I witnessed and participated in. I did my absolute best to represent each person as authentically as possible and with every respect for their character, but this is certainly a book from my perspective and that includes the dialogue I have written for all the people who appear in it.

In 2019, the New York Post published a three-part documentary series called *The Curse of Don's Plum* in which I sat for a long interview. In response to the series, Leonardo DiCaprio's publicist made a statement publicly calling me a liar and accusing me of " an effort to gain publicity and unlawful financial gain." Both statements were deliberate lies clearly meant to damage my credibility and reputation. Leo and his representatives have never had access to my finances and could not have known anything about my sources of income. They just made up a lie and put it out in the world with impunity because they've got an endless flow of money and influence to fight off or buy whatever they need to escape accountability.

Their lies inspired me to write this book, and it's been an arduous journey, but after four years of combing meticulously through my archive and digging deep into my memories, I ended up creating something much more than a candid response to a bully. I wrote a book about the tenacity of our dreams and the enormous will we possess to keep them alive, and I'm proud to share it with you now.

PART I

1

LIT only by a dim shop light dangling above his head, an older, rugged man fastened a blow torch to a shelving beam in the interior of a large grip truck using a ratchet strap and a large wrench for a spacer. His friend, a younger disheveled guy with a neglected goatee, sat leaning over a large equipment case and meticulously rolled up the last of nine balls of Gold Seal black hash between his fingers and placed it on the cover of a pack of cigarettes along with the others. With a disposable lighter retrieved from his front pocket, the older man lit the torch and heated the tips of two butter knives in the blue of the flame until they were red-hot. Using one of the knives, he dabbed up a single hit of hash. A faint wisp of deliciously fragrant smoke rose in the air as the hash sizzled to the blade. He brought both knives up to within a few centimeters of his lips and pressed them firmly together, vaporizing the hash in between. A thick explosion of smoke burst from the knives like a magic trick, and the older man inhaled all of it. His eyes bulged and teared, his chest heaved and rolled, but he successfully held in the smoke for a solid minute. I was impressed.

"Wow! Do you guys do this shit all day?"

The older man exhaled the thickest cloud of smoke I had ever seen. "We do this shit at the end of the day," he said without even clearing his throat. He put the knife tips back in the yellow and red torch flame. "Let's go, eh," he said to me. "It's your turn."

I shook my head. "I'm gonna pass. That'll destroy me."

"You're not gonna take a hit?!" He said it like I had just slapped him in the face. "Come on, man—I didn't even cough."

It was my fourth or fifth visit to the *Hideaway* movie set, and each time I found myself increasingly drawn to the grip department. I'm an admirer of simple ingenuity and a few weeks earlier I watched these same men rig up a perfectly good car with pipes and wires and clamps and camera mounts, and then launch it all into a river in the middle of the night. They worked fast and smart, and they also happened to be the coolest people on the set. So when the older guy invited me onto the back of the grip truck for a hit of hash, I couldn't refuse. Not until I saw the size of the hash balls. "If I take one of those, I'll end up in the hospital," I said. "They're so huge."

"You want me to make yours smaller for you?" said the younger guy. "I can do that."

"Nah, fuck it," I said with a wave of my hand. "I can handle one hit, I think."

"Attaboy!" said the older man as he dabbed a ball of hash from the top of the cigarette pack with a red-hot tip.

I leaned in slightly as he raised the knives close to my lips. The heat was intimidating. One slip by either of us and I'd be scarred for life. He pressed the tips together and the smoke came thick and fast. I sucked up about half of it before my throat and lungs quit. I spiraled into a coughing fit that was so brutal it gave me lower back pain. At least I was amusing. Both men were nearly in tears laughing while I struggled for a single painless breath.

"You want another one?" said the older man like it was a punchline. The younger man laughed.

"Oh yeah," I said with red, stinging eyes. "Make it a double."

"That's what I'm talking about!" said the older man with a raised fist. Something outside the truck caught his attention. "Look who's here!" he said, acting suddenly paternal.

I turned to see Alicia Silverstone perfectly framed by the open

4

truck box. She had her hands on her hips and an adorable grin. She pointed to me, "I've been looking all over the place for this guy."

"Me? What's goin' on?" I wiped more of the stickiness from my eyes. "Is Jeremy finally finished with his eyeball close-up?"

Alicia giggled and beckoned me with a wave. "It's a surprise. Jump down."

"Aww," the older man whined. "You're gonna steal our new buddy?"

"Just for a little bit," she said. "He can come back."

Alicia took me by the hand as I hopped off the truck. She led me along a cable-covered path. "I think you just saved my life," I said. "Those dudes can smoke some hash!"

She looked back at me, grinning. "You should see them chug beer."

I was nearly clothes-lined by a low tree branch as she pulled me to the right along a new path of bound cables. "Where the hell are you taking me?"

She giggled adorably. "You'll see."

The path veered left and we followed it until we came upon a huge lot with an expensive travel trailer parked alongside a couple more modest ones.

"We're here." Alicia approached the small metal steps that led to the trailer door. She knocked a couple of times and a moment later the door opened from the inside.

And there stood Jeff Goldblum, crouched slightly in the door-way, grinning. He batted his big sleepy eyelids and smiled warmly at Alicia, then glanced at me. I gulped.

"Alicia, sweetheart," he said. "Hello. Please, come in. Come in, please. And bring your friend of course." Jeff Goldblum beckoned me with an elegant wave. I followed Alicia inside.

"Hello," said Jeff Goldblum as he stepped in behind me. He offered his hand and I took it. "I'm Jeff Goldblum." We both knew I knew his name, but I was glad he said it anyway.

"Hello, Jeff," I said, "I'm Dale."

He tilted his head slightly. "Dale, Dale?"

I chuckled nervously. "No, no. I'm sorry. Wheatley. Dale Wheatley."

"Ah!" His eyelids closed and opened very slowly before focusing on me again. Then, he raised his index and middle fingers to his temple and began tapping rapidly while repeating my full name to himself, "dalewheatley, dalewheatley, dalewheatley, dalewheatley, dalewheatley." He took a deep breath, flashed the most charismatic smile I'd ever seen, and said in that perfect tone, "Very nice to meet you, Dale. Please sit down." He gestured to a horseshoe bench where a couple of mutual friends sat. "Make yourself as comfortable as you can in such a little booth. I'm sorry I can't be more accommodating."

Jeremy Sisto, who was playing Jeff's evil nemesis in *Hideaway*, and Jeremy's stand-in, a lovely Canadian guy named Trevor, shuffled over so Alicia and I could squeeze in next to them.

"So, how do you two know each other?" Jeff Goldblum asked as he lowered into the love seat across from us.

Jeremy told him about how my roommate hooked up with one of their co-stars, and how that eventually led to all of us hanging out together one night. "And that was it," said Jeremy. "We've been friends ever since."

"They're inseparable," said Alicia.

"What was the main attraction between the two of you?" Jeff's eyes shifted to mine.

I glanced at Jeremy and then back at Jeff. "Oh, me? Yeah, it was a few things, I think. Jeremy is very kind, as I'm sure you already know. He's very funny, and likes good music..." Jeremy fidgeted uncomfortably, so I laid off. "Honestly, I love all of you. You're like the nicest people I've ever met."

Jeff laughed, "Well, coming from a Canadian, that's quite a compliment." He looked at Jeremy, charm oozing out of every pore, and raised one brow. Jeremy took his cue.

"Dale is very talented. I told you about us playing some acting games and how he became possessed by this homeless guy we met earlier."

Jeff's eyes swung from Jeremy to me, "I remember the story

6

well. I prefer Meisner's method personally, but spirit possession is certainly a valid approach..."

We all laughed.

"I'm kidding, of course." Jeff smiled. "I'd love to know how you did it."

"Oh, now I'm embarrassed."

Jeff laughed. "Why?"

"What am I gonna tell you, Jeff Goldblum, about acting?"

He smiled graciously. "You're too kind. I would just love to know how you were able to recreate this character in such a short time. If you'll share."

I shrugged. "Yeah. We came across this homeless guy, and I was immediately fascinated by him. I think we both were. This dude had survived ungodly cold temperatures, rain, snow..."

"Loneliness," said Alicia.

"Jeremy bought him some food and we hung with him for a bit while he absolutely destroyed a chili burger... I couldn't stop thinking about him the whole night. Back at Jeremy's hotel we started playing around with acting games or whatever, and the guy just kind of popped into my head, like a lucid dream almost. I focused on his hands at first, I don't know why they were interesting to me—they were thick like my father's so maybe that was it. His fingers were like pipes. I observed everything—his breathing, his posture, the muscles on his face, that sort of stuff. And then at one point, I just kind of stepped into this loop of him in my mind. The pictures of him went away and I started responding and being him I guess you could say." I laughed at myself. "I sound ridiculous."

"No, not at all," said Jeff.

"You channelled his spirit, Dale" said Alicia. "Oh my god I just got goosebumps all over. Look." She held up her arm to prove it.

Jeff smiled. "That's incredible. I love playing acting games. I think your story put me in the mood for some." He checked his watch with a grin. "I've still got plenty of time before my car arrives, anyone interested?"

We all were of course, and for the next several hours we

7

played a variety of acting games with one of the greatest living actors on the planet. It was an indescribably wonderful experience.

"Thank you, everyone," said Jeff as he bowed his head. "This was such a wonderful way to end this production. You're all so talented."

Jeremy cleared his throat. "Speaking of, Jeff, mind if I ask you something real quick?"

"Please do."

"I'm just curious, if you were Dale, would you move to LA to pursue acting, or stay here in Vancouver?"

I adjusted in my seat, uncomfortable and excited by the question.

"I don't know, Jeremy." Jeff furrowed his brow. "That's a difficult question. If you're asking if I think Dale is talented enough, then, yes, he seems to be." He turned to me, "Half the battle is finding some sense of truth in all of this..." he gestured to the world around him. "You'll do well in Los Angeles, or Vancouver, or anywhere you choose to be."

"That is a very nice thing to say, thank you, Jeff." I said, trying desperately not to burst into little screams for joy. Jeff Goldblum just told me I was talented, and I didn't care if he was just being nice. I was more than happy to believe every word.

"If you decide to come to LA, Dale, you're welcome to study at Playhouse West. I teach there occasionally. We play games there all the time."

"Thank you, Jeff, that's very kind. We'll see what happens."

When Jeff's car arrived, he hugged each of us goodbye and walked out the door forever. I sat there dumbstruck.

Alicia raised her brow at me. "So? What are you going to do?"

I shook my head. "I don't know. I can't even think straight right now."

Jeremy grinned, his eyes young and playful. "What would Tony Robbins do?"

I grinned back at him and sighed, knowing full well that my life was about to change forever.

"What's the purpose of your trip?" asked the stern-faced US Immigration Officer. He held out an expectant hand, palm up.

I handed him my documents: a British Columbia driver's license, a customs declaration form, and a bus ticket. I could barely hear his voice over the thudding of my own heart.

"What brings you to the United States?"

"Visiting a friend." I steadied the tremble in my voice.

"What's your current home address?"

"1011 Beach Ave, unit 1204, Vancouver." He didn't take his eyes off me as I recited my postal code.

"How long have you lived there?"

"About two years. Just under."

"What's your friend's name?"

"Jeremy Sisto." I half expected him to know who I was talking about.

"Where does he live?" He inspected my bus ticket, front to back.

"Los Angeles. I have his address written down in my bag. I don't remember it by heart."

"Your ticket's only going to Seattle." His eyes narrowed on mine, and a shot of anxiety ripped through me.

"I got a cheap flight out of SeaTac. Would you like to see the ticket?"

"Are you staying with your friend in LA?"

"Yes."

"How long are you planning to visit?"

"Two weeks." *Or the rest of my life—I haven't quite decided, Mister Immigration Officer, sir.*

"How much money are you bringing with you?"

"Three grand. American."

He checked my ID again, typed something into his computer, then searched me with his eyes one last time, looking for any reason to send me back to Canada. A nervous grin crept onto my face. I held my breath.

"OK, Mr. Wheatley," he said with a dutiful smile. "Enjoy your visit to the United States."

———

I CALLED Jeremy Sisto from a payphone at SeaTac airport and confirmed my arrival time at LAX. I had some time to kill before my flight so I walked over to a magazine rack and perused the covers, looking for something to keep me occupied. Interview Magazine caught my eye because I recognized the rising star on the cover, Leonardo DiCaprio. He was clutching a red Mylar balloon shaped like lips with "kiss me" printed across the top. His hair was tussled and messy, his expression unabashedly seductive. I recognized him from an article in one of the Vancouver papers when he was in town shooting *This Boy's Life*. His career was inspiring to me, particularly his life-changing audition with Robert De Niro.

If I recall correctly, DiCaprio, who was up against several actors for the part, improvised his scene with De Niro, shouting his lines just inches from the legendary actor's face. He then dropped to his butt and glowered through the rest of the scene. He took a big chance because none of that stuff was in the script. From the reaction in the room, he thought he'd blown the audition, but instead he impressed De Niro so much that he would later fight for DiCaprio to get the role. The rest, as they say, is history. I, too, wanted to be bold and impressive enough to be worth fighting for. I snatched up the magazine and headed for the cashier.

LOS ANGELES WAS SUCH an epic sight from a thousand feet in the sky. The concrete and steel went on as far as the eye could see. There were at least five huge downtowns, all with bigger skyscrapers than any in my hometown. I strained every muscle in my neck for a glimpse of the Hollywood sign but couldn't find it anywhere. The plane swung over the Pacific coastline and glided in for a smooth landing and all the passengers applauded, which I found odd.

There were thousands of people buzzing around inside the airport, eating in restaurants, shopping at kiosks, sleeping on chairs and on the floor. A few rushed through the crowd, presumably late for their flights. LAX was incomprehensibly enormous. I must have walked a mile indoors to get to the baggage claim where Jeremy was waiting for me.

"What's up, Jeremy Sisto?"

"Good to see you, my man." He looked great despite his messy hair and over-sized clothes.

"I can't believe I made it!"

We hugged. Hugging was still a very strange thing to me. I could probably count the number of times I've hugged someone, family included, on both hands before meeting Jeremy.

"How many bags do you have?"

I held up my backpack, "This is it!"

"Let's go then," he said with a beckoning wave toward the parking deck. "You must be hungry!"

Just the word turned my stomach into a creaky hardwood floor. "I'm starving."

"How long have you been traveling?"

"I left my apartment at five."

"This morning? Jesus! Why?"

I shrugged, "I saved like a hundred bucks flying out of Seattle."

Since Jeremy was working with the likes of Jeff Goldblum and Kevin Kline, I just assumed he'd be driving something luxurious, something immaculately detailed and smelling of expensive air fresheners, so I was very surprised when he guided me to an old, dirty, Toyota 4Runner.

"My air conditioning is on the fritz, so roll down your window."

I opened the backseat door to discarded fast-food wrappers, water bottles, cigarette boxes, unopened mail. The car was trashed. I tossed my bag in the back and jumped into the passenger seat. Jeremy pulled out and began navigating our way out of LAX.

"Just to give you a sense of direction, when we're on this side of the Hollywood Hills..." Jeremy pointed out his window. "Those hills right there are to the north. If we were on the other side, the valley side, they would be to the south, of course. The rest of LA is mostly a grid."

"OK, cool," I said. "So, we're headed east."

"We are driving east, correct."

"It's funny how just knowing what direction you're going makes you feel better somehow."

"Oh no, are you freaking out already?"

I laughed. "No, no, not at all—the opposite. I'm thrilled."

"That's great!"

We were silent for a moment. I turned to the open window and watched LA go by like a kid watching Saturday morning cartoons. I loved everything I was seeing, from the diverse crowds on the streets and in their cars to the trash in the gutters. I was thrilled to be there. "I have such a good feeling about this," I said quietly.

"Just remember what I said about the competition around here," he said.

"I'm not worried about that stuff. I'm not here to compete against anyone."

"Well, they're gonna compete against you."

"That's fine. I'm cool with that. I bring people together, Jeremy —I'm literally trained for it."

"You gotta be careful who you trust, though. This is Hollywood."

"I don't know what that means..."

He chuckled, "It means it's really fucking competitive. I'm not trying to freak you out, I'm trying to help you. You should assume everyone you meet is out for themselves. Hundreds, sometimes thousands of people, are competing for every fucking role in this town and you might be what's in their way."

Jeremy's advice seemed misplaced, like a parent telling their kid not to smoke while a cigarette dangles from their lips.

"Why trust me then?"

"I don't know. Probably because you're a Canadian."

WE STOPPED at a cool retro diner below the Beverly Hotel called Swingers. Inside, we were greeted by a stunning young woman who sat us in a booth by a window. The entire staff looked like models plucked from the pages of a 1960s issue of Life Magazine.

"Do any ugly people work here?" I asked.

Jeremy nodded. "They're in the back."

I burst out laughing just as a pretty-boy server approached our table. I was probably just overly tired, but I couldn't stop laughing.

"You guys need a minute, or?"

"No, no," I said as I pulled myself together. "Sorry, he ah—he said something very funny. Could you recommend something for a vegetarian?"

"Veggie club. It's probably the best thing on the menu."

"Easy decision then. Thank you."

He scribbled on his pad. "And you?"

"Cheeseburger, please," said Jeremy. "No tomato. And I'll take an unsweet iced tea as well."

The waiter headed off as my thoughts drifted back to Canada.

"What are you thinking about?"

I chuckled, "I'm thinking... what the hell am I doing here?"

"What do you mean?"

"It's so far from Winnipeg, dude. I mean, look at that." I pointed out the window. "That's a palm tree, motherfucker."

Jeremy laughed. "Yes, it is. I keep forgetting you're not from Vancouver originally."

"No, man. I'm from snowbanks and minus-fucking-thirty degrees, and that's a goddamn palm tree right outside this window."

"You're very funny right now."

"I'm serious, this is so fuckin' crazy to me—I can't believe it." I chuckled. "You wanna hear something else totally crazy?"

"Sure."

"You remember my roommate?"

Our waiter returned with two waters and Jeremy's iced tea.

Jeremy nodded. "I do, yes. Kevin?"

I nodded back. "Yeah, he reads the newspaper every day—always knows what's going on in Vancouver and on the island, and one day, out of the blue, he tells me Jeff Goldblum is coming to town to shoot a movie."

"This is before we showed up, I take it?"

"Yes, by weeks. Maybe even longer."

"OK."

"And for some reason, and this has never happened to me before, but for some reason I got this overwhelming feeling that we were going to meet."

"You and Jeff?"

"Yes."

"You're shittin' me."

I flashed my eyes. "As soon as I heard Kevin say his name, the thought popped into my head like it wasn't even mine."

"What do you mean?"

"I don't know—like it was put there."

Jeremy laughed. "How?"

I shrugged. "I know it sounds ridiculous, but it's true. Kevin blew it off, of course. But then a few weeks later he hooked up with Mara, who introduced me to you, which of course led to finally meeting Jeff Goldblum."

"On his last day in Vancouver, too." Jeremy shook his head. "That's so nuts."

"I still can't believe it."

"I can't believe you didn't tell me sooner. I would have introduced you guys."

"I mean, it's a little fuckin' weird. Besides, I figured the whole thing was really all about meeting you. Feels like a lifetime ago."

"You weren't expecting all this, huh?"

I shook my head, "God, no. I was going to live in Vancouver for the rest of my life. Probably would have stayed in sales, or maybe started a business."

"Yet here you are."

"Here I am, lookin' at palm trees."

"Well, then..." Jeremy raised his glass of iced tea. "Here's to destiny!"

We clinked glasses.

"Here's to Jeff Goldblum," I said.

Our meals arrived and my sandwich was one of the best I ever had. When the bill came, I snatched it up and slipped a hundred-dollar traveler's check in the fold and handed it to the waiter.

WE DROVE east on Beverly Boulevard to Jeremy's apartment, talking about one thing or another when, rather nonchalantly, the Hollywood sign slid out from behind a building and into view. I must have gasped.

"Oh shit! The Hollywood sign!" said Jeremy. "Do you want to drive up and see it?"

"We can drive up to it?"

Jeremy nodded. "Do you have a camera?"

"I don't. We can do it another time." I watched the sign for as long as I could. I thought about all the people who have lived and worked beneath it. Chaplin, Bogart, Cliff, Heston, Brando. Marlon Brando was probably still up there somewhere. The dark side of my mind remembered the story of Peg Entwistle. She committed suicide back in the 30s by diving headfirst off the letter H. I guess Hollywood's not always champagne and strawberries.

WE PULLED up in front of an old, dingy apartment block decorated with weathered Asian moldings and a sign above an archway that read "Pagoda." Jeremy jammed the 4Runner into first, killed the motor, and pulled up on the parking brake all at once. He retrieved a long ratcheted metal rod out from under his seat and fastened it to the steering wheel with the turn of a key.

"You really need that thing? For this car?"

Jeremy grinned. "I'll try not to be offended—"

I laughed, "That's not what I mean..."

"This car would get stolen in a minute."

"Really? Damn..."

"Welcome to Los Angeles, my friend."

THE APARTMENT HALLWAY smelled like low rent. I've lived in bad neighborhoods most of my life, and there's a certain smell to them, something between musk and mold. The hallway was dark and the textured walls were stained with dust and nicotine. We arrived at an apartment door. Jeremy tried the knob but it was locked. Just as he pulled the keys from his pocket, the door opened.

"Hello! Come in." Jeremy's roommate, Bill, had the most perfect smile and big blue eyes. We entered, and Bill took a moment to look me over. His smile grew as he pulled back his shoulder-length hair with two long fingers, then offered his hand for a greeting. "I'm Bill."

We shook hands. I was relieved he didn't want to hug—I'd had enough of that for one day.

"We're so happy you're here, Dale. Jeremy told us so much about you."

"Jeremy said a lot of great things about you as well."

Bill shot Jeremy an under-the-brow, what-did-you-tell-him look.

"Thanks so much for letting me crash here," I added. "This is great."

"As long as you don't mind the mess. It's not always like this."

"Not true." Jeremy giggled. "It's been like this since day one."

"How would you know? You barely live here."

The apartment looked like Jeremy's truck. Trash scattered everywhere: fast food bags, cigarette boxes, cans of Dr. Pepper, and loads of unopened mail. A half-wall with a laminate countertop divided the living room from the kitchen and served as a drop-off spot for dirty dishes and trash.

Bill turned to me. "I thought about cleaning, but then I just sort of... didn't." His laugh was loud and throaty.

I set my bag against the wall and took a seat on their couch that looked a lot like my grandmother's from the '70s. There was something familiar about Jeremy's run-down apartment and his old, cluttered 4Runner, something comforting. Perhaps if misery loves company, so does struggle.

"I'm gonna go check up on Marisa and my sister. I'll call you guys in a while." Jeremy had me assure him more than once that I cool before finally leaving me and Bill, two complete strangers, alone together.

I felt suddenly anxious. Not because I was uncomfortable or afraid to be alone with Bill, it was the sudden realization that I didn't really know anybody in Los Angeles, that I was, in effect, completely alone.

"So, Dale, what's your first impression of Los Angeles?"

"Really fucking big."

Bill laughed. "I know, it's so ridiculous."

"Not what I expected. It's a lot less—I don't know..."

"Sexy?"

"Yes! Sexy. Vancouver is so beautiful, I guess I'm comparing it too much to that."

"My family used to vacation in Whistler, so I've been to Vancouver a bunch of times. It's one of the nicest cities I've ever visited." Bill paused for a moment as a grin slowly widened his face. "Can I confess something to you?"

"Yeah, sure."

"You're nothing like we expected."

"Oh, no?" I laughed.

"Not at all."

"Is that a good or bad thing?"

"No, it's a good thing." He tucked a few stray locks of his hair behind his ear. "Yeah, no, we were convinced you were going to show up in like a cowboy hat with a pair of big old Canadian shit-kickers on—"

I laughed, "Cowboy boots? Why?"

"Yeah, and like, we pictured your shirt would have all this country embroidery across the chest and shoulders with, like, those white pearl snap buttons—Meadow pictured you in the shirt, actually. You're going to love her, by the way—Jeremy's sister."

"That's hilarious."

"The cowboy boots were mine."

"What about you?" I said, hoping to change the subject.

"What about me?"

"Yeah. What do you do? What do you like?"

The phone rang and Bill walked over to the half wall where it sat. "OK, sure. I'm a trained opera singer, but my true love is Broadway. Stephen Sondheim is a god to me. Technically, I'm gay, but really I'm asexual. And I fucking hate talking on telephones." He held up his finger, "One sec." He lifted the receiver, "Hello? Meadow. Hi." A big smile stretched across his face. "Yes! He's in the bathroom... Yeah. Do you remember how we pictured him? No, he can't hear me—he's in the bathroom I said... Meadow, just listen to me before he—yes! He looks just like that, I swear to god." Bill guffawed. "No, no cowboy hat—but he is wearing an embroidered cowboy shirt... No, it's brown. He's wearing cowboy boots, Meadow! I swear, the really, really pointy ones. OK, he flushed, I gotta go... We're leaving now." He hung up the phone and belly laughed. "That was Meadow. I had to fuck with her."

"You were very convincing."

"Where were we? Oh yeah, you wanted to know more about me. What else is there? Nothing, really. I'm pretty boring. Oh, well, I work at Tower Records and can give you my employee discount if you want."

"Nice little perk."

"Retail sucks, but it's fine. We should head over to see the ladies, Dale Wheatley. Everyone is dying to meet you."

BILL LEANED into his red Corolla and swatted a bunch of stained, crumpled up Tommy's Burger bags off the passenger seat so that I could get into his car.

On the drive over, the Hollywood sign was outside my window, which meant we were heading west to get to Jeremy's sister's place.

THE GIRL'S apartment was a major step up. For one thing, it was clean. The private entrance opened to a spacious living room and dining area with beautifully aged hardwood floors throughout. The ceiling was high with fans and gorgeous crown molding. There was a long hallway toward the back of the apartment that presumably led to bedrooms, closets, and a bathroom. An open doorway from the dining area led into a nice sized kitchen.

Marisa and Meadow greeted me with big eyes and curious smiles. Bill had mentioned they were both beautiful women. Stunning is the word I would have used. They invited me to sit down on their old sagging sofa.

Jeremy appeared with a couple of beers and offered me one. I took it gratefully. He twisted the top off the other and handed it to Marisa, then turned to his sister, Meadow.

"You want one?"

"Yes, sweetheart, if you're going back for more."

"I am. How about you, Bill?"

"No, I'm good."

"You sure?"

Bill shrugged and rolled his eyes, "OK, fine. I'll have one."

"We're so excited to meet you, Dale," said Meadow with an enormous smile.

"I'm excited too. And a little overwhelmed."

"I'm sure. Is this your first time in the United States?"

"Second. First time in LA."

Jeremy returned with the beers.

"How long are you planning on staying?" said Marisa.

I shrugged. "I'm not sure, I—"

"He's staying," said Jeremy as he handed out the bottles. "He moved here." He took a seat on the floor near the window and grinned at me. "You can't defy Jeff Goldblum, Dale."

"What does that mean?" said Meadow. "What does Jeff Goldblum have to do with it?"

I waved it off. "We were messing around with some acting games in his trailer, and he was just being extremely nice to me–"

"That's not true," said Jeremy. "He said you were talented and that you should move to LA."

"No. You asked him if he thought I was talented enough for LA, and he sorta' kinda' said I was, but that's because you put him on the spot."

Jeremy giggled. "No. He said you found truth in the make-believe. That's more than just being nice."

"Wow," said Meadow. "That's high praise."

I scoffed. "What was he going to say, I'm fuckin' terrible?"

Meadow shrugged. "Who cares why he said it. I wish Jeff Goldblum would say something nice about my acting. He has an acting school, you know?"

"Yeah, he mentioned it."

"I've heard good things. You should check it out."

I nodded and took a sip of my beer. "We'll see what happens."

We hung out for several more hours, drinking and smoking weed and talking about everything under the sun and eventually the moon. When the night ended, we hugged each other good-night and everything felt wonderful.

I TUCKED some sheets into the sofa cushions, fluffed up a pillow and tried to make myself comfortable. Bill finished brushing his teeth and stuck his head out the door frame that separated the living room from the bedrooms.

"Dale, you look uncomfortable. Your feet are hanging over the edge. Just sleep in Jeremy's bed."

"Nah, I'm OK."

"Why? It's a lot more comfortable. He hasn't slept here in months."

"I'm good. Really. I'm comfortable—"

He shrugged. "If you say so…" he shrugged and smiled. "Good night, Dale." He went into his bedroom and closed the door.

I stretched out and fixed my eyes on the popcorn ceiling. I had no idea what was going to happen next, but Hollywood sure felt good on me.

———

I SPENT the next several days hanging out with some combination of Marisa, Meadow, Bill, and Jeremy. I loved Marisa's pragmatism, Meadow's wit, Bill's drama, and Jeremy's wide-eyed wonderment for the world, and I loved sitting around in their Detroit Street apartment listening to them go on and on about the Hollywood life.

"I'm not saying luck isn't a part of it," said Jeremy. "I'm saying that luck alone isn't enough to make it in this business. You have to be talented as well."

"That's complete bullshit," said Marisa. "Give me one film Keanu Reeves is good in?"

Bill's jaw dropped.

Jeremy stiffened up. "He was great in Little Buddha."

Marisa guffawed. "Oh, come on, Jeremy. You're just trying to piss me off at this point."

"No, why would I do that?"

"What about Point Break?" I said with raised eyebrows. "He was awesome in that."

She rolled her eyes at me. "He played a surfer!"

"I thought he was good in My Own Private Idaho," said Bill.

"None of you are being serious right now, you can't be." Marisa shook her head. "Patrick Swayze is why Point Break worked. And River Phoenix carried My Own Private Idaho. Keanu's movies work despite his talent, not because of it."

"So you're admitting he has talent," said Jeremy.

"Yeah, barely enough to get to the set." We all laughed as she continued. "Keanu Reeves is luckier than he is talented. That's what I'm saying. And if you can't see that, then you must be blind."

Meadow sat up on the edge of the sofa, her eyes narrowed. "What about bad luck? Is bad luck enough to stop a career?"

"No, I don't think it is," said Jeremy. "I think people just give up."

"Really? I don't agree with that at all," said Meadow. "You're a wonderful, talented actor, but the difference between our careers is that you got your break with Lawrence Kasdan and Grand Canyon, and I got mine with Captain Ron. You landed an amazing role, and now you're working all the time. I got cast in a mindless family film, and I struggle to get auditions, let alone actual jobs."

"They're very different movies," said Jeremy. "But they're both huge opportunities."

Meadow shook her head. "Don't be ridiculous, Jeremy."

"Captain Ron was a big deal, it's not unlucky."

"Stop, please."

"How much have you made in residuals this year alone?"

Meadow held up her hand. "Stop it, Jeremy. It's not about the money, you know that."

Marisa chimed in. "You're being ridiculous, Jeremy."

"No! Why?"

"Because there's such an enormous difference between Grand Canyon and Captain Ron. They shouldn't even be mentioned in the same conversation."

Jeremy doubled down. "Captain Ron is a huge family film. Working with Martin Short and Kurt Russell is a big fucking deal."

"Yeah, that's why I took the job. And I love Kurt and Marty—Marty was like a father to me, but I'm not talking about any of that."

Marisa jumped in, "Jeremy, she played the daughter with nothing going on. You played a character with a beautiful arc in a screenplay that was nominated for an Academy Award. Come on! You know better."

Meadow's eyes narrowed again. "Jeremy, pay attention." She flared her nostrils and turned to me. "Dale, do you know who Lawrence Kasdan is?"

"He wrote Empire Strikes Back, right?"

"Yes. And he also wrote Grand Canyon. Do you know John Dwyer?"

"He wrote... Captain Ron?"

"Ha ha, Dale. Very funny. I'm trying to make a point here, and you're not helping. You're a little too new around here to be pissing people off, don't you think?"

There was enough bite to make me wonder if she might be mad at me. "OK, I didn't know John Dwyer by name," I said. "But I liked Captain Ron—quite a bit, actually."

"No, Dale! You cannot be serious right now."

"It's a good movie for what it is—"

"You are walking on very thin ice."

I chuckled. "I'm not saying it's a work of art."

"Right!" Meadow swung her attention back to her brother. "Did you hear your new friend? Grand Canyon is a work of art, Jeremy. Captain Ron is fun for the whole family. Do you understand the difference?"

"I do. It just seems weird to consider Captain Ron bad luck."

"If it ends up being the only notable thing I do in my career, what would you call it?"

"It was a good job," Jeremy said with a shrug. "But your break is coming,"

"Oh, is it?"

"Yes, of course. You're a brilliant actress. You'll get your 'Lawrence Kasdan,' or you'll land an amazing independent film. It's gonna happen, you just gotta keep the faith."

"Yeah, whatever. I'll just ride your coattails like Julia Roberts did. Worked out pretty well for her."

2

ON MY FIRST Friday night in LA, Jeremy and the girls picked me up to go to a house party in the valley. Marisa was in the front passenger seat of the 4Runner, so I jumped in the back seat next to Meadow.

"Yo, can we stop and grab some beer?" I said as Jeremy pulled away from the curb.

Jeremy found my eyes in the rearview mirror. "We could, but we don't need to. There'll be plenty to drink at Jay's house."

"Really? I don't think I've ever gone to a party empty-handed before."

"It's totally fine," said Meadow. "He'll have a keg and a fridge full of beer."

"Would it be bad to bring some anyway?"

"You're struggling with this, huh?" said Meadow.

"I am, yeah."

"What's that about?"

"Where I'm from, if you drink beer that isn't yours, you get hockey punched in the face."

Meadow threw her head back and laughed. "Hockey punched?! What in the hell is that?"

"You pull the back of someone's shirt over their head, which

24

kind of chicken-wings their arms so they can't hit back or defend, and you just start fuckin' punching them as fast as you can."

Marisa laughed, "Wait a minute, I don't understand—I thought Canadians were nice people."

"We're a very nice people, Marisa."

"Punching people in the face is not very nice, Dale."

"Neither is drinking someone's beer."

"You're being ridiculous, but if you insist, we can make a stop." Jeremy laughed, but I got the feeling I was testing his nerves.

We stopped at a 7-11. I was in and out in no time with a twelve-pack of Miller Lite under one arm and a couple of packs of Marlboro Lights jammed into my front pockets. We jumped on the 101 and headed for the valley. When we got to the house party, Jeremy suggested I leave the beer in the car.

"I'm annoying," I said. "I'm sorry."

"No, not at all." He chuckled. "No need to apologize. It's just that you'll be the only person walking in with a case of beer, and I just didn't think you'd want the attention."

He was right, I didn't. I followed Jeremy to the house empty-handed.

THE FIRST PERSON I saw as soon as we walked through the front door was Shannen Doherty from *Beverly Hills 90210*. She was leaning up against a wall with a cocktail in her hand, people watching. I was surprised to see her but managed not to stare. I wasn't star struck. I had never watched her show or followed her career, but she was a big TV star and I did not expect to run into her in this lifetime. She was looking sidelong at a group of five or six guys sitting in a circle on the floor to her left.

One of those guys caught my eye because he looked a lot like Leonardo DiCaprio. I convinced myself it couldn't possibly be him. These were connected people, but it seemed too coincidental that I had just read about the kid in the airport a week ago and, out of all the actors in Hollywood, he'd be the one sitting a few feet away from me dangling a bottle of beer between his knees.

25

Jeremy led us into the kitchen where he opened the refrigerator door like he owned it, grabbed a beer and offered it to me. I refused, so he cracked it open for himself. Meadow rolled her eyes, reached in and grabbed two beers, twisted one open and handed it to me. "That's the only one I'm getting for you. You gotta take care of yourself, Dale."

I smiled and thanked her.

"I'm gonna check out who's here," said Jeremy. "You good?"

"Yeah," I said. "I'm great."

Jeremy walked off. Meadow and Marisa recognized someone, and they got talking, so I wandered back into the main room.

Shannen Doherty was still there, leaning against the wall like a vixen. We made eye contact and I smiled. She smiled back.

I glanced over at the group of guys on the floor. Everyone was dialed into the kid who couldn't possibly be Leonardo DiCaprio. He was highly animated about something. I listened in as best as I could. He said something about working with someone named Jean. They did some kind of gun scene together and he, this kid, had a hard time learning how to spin a gun on his finger. The gun kept slipping off. Then one of the guys asked about Jean again, but this time he said his last name: Hackman. Gene Hackman? The Academy Award-winning, Lex Luthor, *Mississippi Burning*, Gene fucking Hackman? It was Leonardo DiCaprio, it had to be.

Jeremy found me eves-stalking DiCaprio and invited me out back for a smoke. There were a bunch of people hanging out on a small, paved deck that was lit by warm string lights and a couple of tiki torches. A few meters away, a rectangular pool rippled and glittered like a giant sapphire.

Jeremy got absorbed in a conversation with a small group of people. I waited awkwardly at his side for an introduction, but it never came, so I spotted an empty chair at an umbrella table and took a seat.

"Hey, bro. How you doin'?" said a shaggy-looking guy with a neglected goatee and long unkempt hair hanging over his bloodshot eyes. My first thought was, *what's up, Jo-Jo the Dog-Faced Boy?*

He smiled at me through wire-thin lips and said, "I'm Tobey Maguire, what's your name?"

"I'm Dale. Dale Wheatley. How are you?"

"I'm doin' all right, thanks." His head kept nodding, but he stopped talking as he looked me over. "So, who do you know here? Who are you with?"

"Oh, yeah," I said. "I'm friends with that guy right there." I pointed at Jeremy just as he swooped into the conversation.

"Tobey, what's up kiddo?"

"Jeremy. What's up? Welcome back, baby." Tobey stood and the two of them embraced.

"Good to be back."

Tobey returned to this seat. "I was just getting to know your friend here."

"Yes, this is Dale. We met while I was shooting Hideaway."

"Oh, cool," Tobey turned back to me. "Are you Canadian?"

"I am."

"Oh, that's cool, eh?" I didn't laugh. He continued. "Did you meet on Hideaway?"

"No, no. I'm, um, I ah—we actually met through an unusual set of circumstances, I guess you could say."

Tobey laughed.

"We met through a mutual friend," said Jeremy. "Hey, you know who Tony Robbins is, right?"

"The Unlimited Power guy? That Tony Robbins?"

Jeremy nodded. "Dale was working for him when we met."

"Really?"

I nodded.

"I love that dude. I read his book, it was great. Very fuckin' powerful. What did you do? Did you work with him directly?"

"I worked with one of his franchises in Vancouver. I facilitated a little, but I mostly helped people get through the program. I love his stuff. It's changed my life in ways I don't think I've fully realized yet. But yeah, I did a lot of follow-up work with clients and that sort of stuff. Sales. Lots of sales."

Tobey sat up in his chair more attentively. "Very cool. I'm into all kinds of that stuff, like philosophers and yeah, even like Tony Robbins, and what's that habits guy?"

One of the dudes who had been sitting with DiCaprio inside the house came out and took a seat at the table next to Tobey.

"Steven Covey," I said.

"Yes! The seven habits–or like ten habits." Tobey turned to the new guy at the table. "What's up, baby?"

"What's up—don't let me interrupt." He looked at me, "Continue your conversation."

The guy's blue eyes were the most stunning I had ever seen on a human or animal. They were utterly mesmerizing, like white-blue glaciers. I forced my attention back to Tobey.

"The seven Habits of Highly—"

"—right, right, right, of Highly Successful—Effective, I mean... Effective People. Jesus!" Tobey laughed at himself. "I'm extremely high at the moment. I can barely remember my own name."

The new guy caught me with his blue tractor beams. "I'm Scott. How are you?"

"I'm Dale. Good to meet you." We shook hands over the table, nearly starting a domino of spilling beer bottles and cans.

Scott opened a fancy pack of cigarettes like a jewelry case and retrieved a thin, elegant cigarette rolled in chocolate brown paper. "It's nice to meet you too, Dale," he said with the filter held lightly between his teeth. "Yes indeed. What are you guys, ah—what are you discussing right now, at this moment? What's the topic?"

"Dale works—or worked? I don't know your status."

"Worked," I said

"Yeah, whatever, he worked for Tony Robbins. Do you know who that is?"

"Yeah, the guy with the big teeth?" said Scott.

We all laughed.

"Are you from San Diego? Isn't that where he's from?"

"No, I worked in their Vancouver office."

Scott grinned. "You're Canadian?"

"I am."

"I'll spare you the 'eh' jokes."

"Thanks, on behalf of all Canadians."

"So, you're into that whole mind manipulation stuff? You're into fucking with people's minds?" Scott was grinning, but he sounded serious.

Tobey jumped to my defense, "No, bro. It's not like that at all—Tony Robbins is totally cool."

Scott shrugged. "If you say so." He flashed an enigmatic grin, then took a long draw off his dark cigarette. He inhaled half the smoke, letting the rest twist and tease off his lips like a charmed snake. "I'm just messin' around with you. I like Tony Robbins too, I suppose. What was your name again?"

"Dale. Dale Wheatley."

"I'm Scott Bloom."

"Well, I think it's cool as hell that you worked for Tony Robbins, bro," said Tobey. "I thought his book was, like I said, powerful. I would even go so far as to say important."

Scott flashed a grin. "Unlimited Power. What even is that?"

Tobey reached into his pocket and pulled out some weed. "Do you partake?"

"I do," I said.

I did a double take on another guy who exited the house because, at first glance, he looked a lot like DiCaprio. He was taller and fuller, with similar bone structure, and blue eyes. He noticed me and nodded and said what's up.

"Hey, what's up," I said.

"I'm Jay."

"Oh, cool. This is your house!"

"Yes, it is."

"I'm Dale. I'm a friend of Jeremy Sisto's."

"Where is that boy?" Jay's eyes searched around until he found Jeremy, who had drifted over to another nearby circle. "Oh, hey, what's up Sisto? I didn't see you come in. Welcome home, brother."

"Jay! It's good to be back. Thank you for all of this." Jeremy held his beer up in salute. "You're amazing."

"Of course!" Jay returned his attention to me. "Nice to meet you, bro. If you need anything, just help yourself. There's plenty of beer in the fridge."

"Thanks, man." I glanced over at Jeremy, knowing there would be a "told you so" grin waiting.

Leonardo DiCaprio came strolling out of the house, lanky and disjointed, with his hair held back in a hairband. He was holding a basketball in one hand and a lit cigarette in the other. He noticed Jay's attention lingering on me, so his eyes shifted to mine. He nodded at me, "What's up?"

I nodded back. "What's up."

Jay poked Leo in the ribs playfully, causing Leo to lose grip of the ball. He recovered and dribbled over to the hoop nearby where he completed a layup. Leo began goading Jay into a game of one-on-one. Jay refused at first, but eventually caved and the two of them shot hoops while the rest of us drank and smoked Tobey's weed.

After a few minutes, Leo returned to the table victorious. He and Jay grabbed a couple of empty chairs and joined the rest of us.

"I'm too good for you, bro," said Leo.

Jay shook his head, "Dude, I've been drinking since three in the afternoon."

"Excuses!" chided Tobey.

"Oh, really? Let's see you play, Tobey."

"I don't want to play—I want to sit here and talk to my new friend here," he gestured to me with his chin, "and smoke some weed."

"Excuses," mimicked Jay.

"It's a preference, Jay. Big difference."

Jay nodded at the joint between Tobey's fingers, "Areyougonnapassthatshitorwhatbro?"

Tobey leaned forward with the offering. Jay took the joint and started puffing on it aggressively.

Leo stood up, fanning the thick, skunky smoke. He nodded at me, "Yo, you shoot hoops?"

"Yeah, a little."

"Care for a little one-on-one then?"

I nodded. "Let's do it." I took a quick swig of my beer and rose from my chair.

"I'm Leo, by the way."

"Hey, Leo. I'm Dale. Good to meet you, man."

We shook hands and headed toward the hoop.

"You wanna go to eleven or..."

I nodded. "Eleven is good."

Leo bounced the ball to me. "Challenger goes first, bro." He lowered into his defensive stance and held me at arm's length.

I made my first move to the hoop for a clunky, unsuccessful layup. Leo hit his first shot and the next two or three after that, all of them unanswered. He never relinquished the lead.

When the score reached 9-3, he asked if I wanted to concede.

I scoffed. "I'm not gonna give up, dude."

He chuckled, "Suit yourself."

He made another quick move for the basket, but I intercepted the crossover and dribbled the ball back to the line.

"Nice play. Three–Nine." He stressed the nine.

I faked him out and laid in a quick basket that surprised us both. I hit a couple more shots, but it wasn't enough. Leo beat me easily.

"Good game, bro."

I chuckled, "You fucking destroyed me, dude."

I spent the rest of the night on could nine. It was hard to believe that I had just arrived in LA, and I was already ballin' with an Oscar nominee and getting to know a bunch of incredibly interesting people in the business. I overcame my issue with drinking the host's beer, and even graduated into grabbing rounds for others. I returned from the kitchen and handed Leo and Jay each a beer as they continued an intense conversation.

"It's the same thing, bro," said Jay. "You basically stole my career."

Leo shook his head. "That's such bullshit—"

"Maybe not stole it, but you changed it. You altered its direction for the worst."

"I did the same thing as you, bro. I went to auditions. I went to my call-backs, just like you did. The only difference is I booked the jobs, and you didn't."

"Oh!" Tobey nearly fell out of his seat. "Bro, he just bitch slapped you so hard, bro."

Jay ignored Tobey and pressed Leo further. "I would have killed that fucking role, and you know it."

"Yeah, you probably would have," said Leo sweetly. "But you didn't. I did."

"You know what I'm sayin', though."

Tobey sneered at Jay. "Are you talking about Gilbert Grape?"

Jay squinted and nodded. "Yeah."

Tobey shook his head dismissively. "No way, bro. Did you even get a call back?"

"Yes, but I didn't get to do it because they fell in love with this fucker, and that was it."

Scott sniggered, "You didn't even test."

"Because Leo fuckin' scooped it up. That's what I'm saying right now."

"The audacity to make this argument." Scott's response was slathered in disgust. "You didn't even test for god's sake. You don't know if you would've gotten it in the end. Do you even hear yourself right now?"

"Dude, Gail Levin called my manager and told her they were waiting on Leo and if he passed, the role was mine. All I'm saying is, had it gone my way, I would be where he is right now."

Scott sneered. "You can't say that—that's ridiculous."

"I'm pretty sure I just did."

"You're entirely different people, man." Scott pointed at Leo with his thumb. "What happened for him wouldn't just happen for you because you got the role instead of him. Do you think you would have booked Basketball Diaries too?

"OK, whatever you say, Bloom."

"Answer the question."

"No, I'm not saying that..."

Scott sipped his beer triumphantly. "OK then. That's all I'm saying."

When this conversation ended, another one just as entertaining began. And it went like that until the wee hours of the morning. When the party ran out of beer, I became the unlikely hero with my 12-pack of warm Miller Lites in the car and I got high-fives from my new friends Jay, Scott, Tobey, and Leo.

3

I WOKE up the next morning on the couch with a nasty hangover. After making some coffee, I sat on the stool next to Jeremy's beige Touch-Tone phone and picked up the receiver. I had three difficult calls to make, one to my mom, one to my brother, and the last one to my boss back in Vancouver.

"MOM."

"Hi. How are you?"

"I'm good. You?"

"I'm OK. Where are you?"

"That's why I'm calling. I gotta tell you something... I got some news."

"Oh yeah, what's that?"

"I don't want you to get upset, OK?"

She didn't respond.

"I moved to Hollywood, mom."

She was silent at first. Very still. Then came a very long, audible exhale. "Are you being serious with me right now, because—"

"Yes, I am."

"You're there? Right now?

She was upset, but I couldn't help but smile.

"When did this happen?"

"I came down to visit a friend and decided to stay."

"When? Why didn't you tell me you were going?"

"A week ago. I didn't want anyone talking me out of it."

"Dougie-Dwayne-Dennis—oh, Jesus Christ, you got me so flustered I can't even say your name right now."

"It's Dale."

"I know your name, smart ass, I'm the one who gave it to you. You're supposed to tell your mother when you're going to another country."

"I'm sorry…"

"Are you smiling right now?"

"No."

"Don't lie to me. I can hear it."

I dropped the smile. "I'm not smiling, Mom."

She sighed again. "What are you going to do down there? How will you survive?"

"I'll be fine. I met some people. I think I'm going to be an actor."

"Oh god, Dale. Why?"

"I think I can pull it off."

"What about your job? What about your apartment?"

"My roommate took it over, and I don't care about that job. I'm doing this for me."

She let out another deliberately loud sigh into the receiver. "Well, I'm really mad about this, Dale."

"Why?"

"What do you mean why? Because now I'm going to worry about you all the time. That's why."

"Hank?"

"Dale Wheatley?"

"Yes. How are you, Hank?"

35

"Dale, where the hell have you been?" Hank's voice was deep and soothing even when he was upset.

"It's a long story…"

"We thought you were dead somewhere on the island. I've been worried sick about you. You're OK?"

"Yes, I'm fine. I'm so sorry. I've just been going through a lot lately—nothing bad, but…"

"It's been more than a week."

"I should have called sooner."

"Am I that bad to work for?"

"No, you're phenomenal, Hank."

"Well, not even a phone call, Dale."

"I know. There's no excuse. I got a lot going on and didn't handle it all that well."

"What's happening?"

"This is gonna sound ridiculous, but… it's been my dream to be in entertainment. I want to make movies, Hank, and I met some people who can help me do it. It's crazy, but this could be my big chance."

"Hollywood movies?"

"Yes."

"Well, that sounds interesting. Come into the office and let's talk about it."

"I'm already in Los Angeles, Hank."

"Wow, that's dramatic."

"Yeah, it happened fast."

"What are your plans? Acting?"

"Yeah, I think that's it."

"That a tough racket, don't you think?"

"I don't really care." I chuckled. "It's reckless, I guess, but—"

"It's fuckin' bold, kid."

"I wanted you to know how grateful I am to you, Hank. I loved working with you and everyone else you brought together. You changed my life. I'll never forget that."

"You don't have to say that…"

"It's true. I would have never left, but I'm in a once-in-a-life-time situation here."

He took a moment and then sighed. "Well shit, Dale, I'm proud of you."

I chuckled, but unexpected tears welled up. "Really?"

"Yes. It's what we teach, isn't it? It's certainly what Tony Robbins is all about. You're young, you gotta chase your dreams. Just be careful how you go about it."

"I will, Hank."

"Call up Debbie and she'll send your check. I wish you the very best, kid."

"Thank you for everything, Hank."

"Mom's really upset, Dale."

"Yeah, well, what can I do?"

"Why didn't you tell any of us you were moving? I don't understand."

"Because I didn't know it was going to happen for sure. My life is crazy, Doug. It's like it's being swept up in a gust of wind.

"A gust of wind, eh?"

"I met this American in Vancouver, and we got really close. He was in Van shooting a movie with Jeff Goldblum..."

"That's pretty cool. Did you meet him?"

"Yes, and he said he thought I was talented enough for Hollywood. Jeff-fucking-Goldblum said that shit about me, Doug. He even invited me to study at his school here in LA."

"How would Jeff Goldblum know if you're talented?"

"We played a bunch of acting games in his trailer for a few hours."

"So, you moved to Los Angeles because Jeff Goldblum said you're good at acting games? Is that what you're telling me?"

"I mean, he's a fucking legend, Doug—and they were Meisner games, not... never mind. No is the answer to your question. Not entirely anyway. I can't explain what's going on except that it feels like I am supposed to be here. It's not about any of the Jeff Goldblum stuff, that's just a fun story. I'm talking about me and my life. I feel like I belong here, Doug. With these people. Do you know who Leonardo DiCaprio is?"

"No."

"He's an actor—a really, really talented actor. He was nominated for an Oscar for a movie called What's Eating Gilbert Grape with Johnny Depp."

"Yeah, OK, what about him?"

"I met him last weekend at a party and, I don't understand it, I don't even know if it's real, but I have this very strong feeling we're going to work together."

"You're gonna work with this Leonardo guy?"

"Yes. It's probably just nonsense, but everything is so weird right now—in a good way. LA is so strangely comfortable. I've been here less than two weeks, but I feel like I've lived here my whole life."

"Maybe because you've been watching it on TV your whole life."

"No, wait until you see it, Doug. It's nothin' like on TV. Not even close. Doesn't matter. What's important is that I think I finally found my thing in life. My place. Finally. It wasn't hockey, or the band, or fuckin' stand-up comedy. I'm supposed to be in films, Doug. I can feel it in my bones."

"Well, fuck, Dale. I was calling to tell you you should come back home, but now I don't know... I mean, you pretty much have to go for it."

I laughed.

He sighed again. "What am I going to tell mom?"

"Tell her what you just said to me."

I WENT for a walk to let it all sink in. Los Angeles had become my home, as impossible as that was to believe. I didn't really love the city itself. The air stunk like sweat and piss most of the time. The smog was so bad it stung my eyes, it was dirty and oppressively hot. Despite all of those things, I was absolutely crazy about being in Los Angeles, around all of these incredible, creative people. I couldn't get enough of it.

When I got back to the Pagoda, I did some accounting. I had a total of $2600 in American Express Traveler's checks and whatever cash was in my pocket. I stuffed my envelope back between Jeremy's mattresses as pangs of anxiety burned and twisted in my guts. $2600 wouldn't last very long.

I noticed a screenplay sitting on the nightstand. It had a red cover with a white logo on the bottom that read CAA. I leaned over, grabbed it, and opened it to the title page.

No Worries
written by
Amy Heckerling

I TURNED to the first page and began reading.

4

I PICKED up a Sunday LA Times and fumbled through the classifieds, looking for a job. Telemarketing was my best bet. They'd hire just about anybody, and if it was a half decent gig, I could make good money working part-time. After a few calls, I landed an interview for the following week at a company on Hollywood and Vine.

———

JEREMY PICKED me up to catch a double feature at one of the local cinemas. The sun was just beginning to set as we walked up to a couple of guys standing beneath the theater's marquee.

"Sisto, what's up bro?" said one of them as he and Jeremy gripped hands and pulled it in for a hug.

"What's up, baby, what's up?" said Jeremy.

"Hey, Jer," said the other while glancing sidelong at me. "Where's Marisa?" He and Jeremy gripped hands and pulled it in for a hug.

"She and Meadow are coming from an audition—No Worries, as a matter of fact."

The dude waved his hand dismissively. "I booked that shit easy, bro."

"I know! Congrats. I'm so happy for you."

"Yeah, baby, I'm gonna be fucking huge."

Jeremy giggled, "Damn straight you are."

The first guy introduced himself as Blake Sennett, who I later learned was an actor and musician. The second dude, the one who was going to be "fucking huge," was RD Robb. He didn't introduce himself, instead he acknowledged me with a rather dickish flick of the chin, said "what's up," and left the introduction to me or Jeremy.

"Yo, Sisto," said RD, "You wanna grab some seats, or my balls maybe?"

Jeremy laughed. "What?!"

"I'm kidding, don't grab my balls. I'm straight. We should grab some seats, though."

"I'm gonna wait for Marisa and Meadow. You go ahead—save us something in the middle."

Scott Bloom and Leonardo DiCaprio casually rolled up from around the corner.

"Bloom, 'Nardo, what's up?" said RD.

"What's up, RD Robb." Leo and RD shook hands and did the bro-hug thing. "Congrats on No Worries, man."

RD puffed up proudly, "I'm gonna be huge like you, bro."

Leo chuckled as his eyes shifted to me, "Hey, what's up?"

"What's up?"

Scott nodded in my direction. "Dale, right? The Tony Robbins guy?"

"Yeah, I guess so." I said and shook his hand. "Good to see you again, Scott."

"Do you know this director?" Scott pointed up at the marquee. It read: *Two by Mike Leigh.*

I shook my head, "Never heard of him."

"Me either. Until recently." He took a drag of his cigarette. "I'm curious to see what all the hype is all about. Did you get your ticket?"

"Not yet."

Scott butted his half-smoked cigarette in the pedestal ashtray. "Come on."

The New Beverly Cinema, or the "New Bev" as it's affectionately known, had an old-school ticket window, the kind with the hole cut in the glass for transactions. This had the added effect of billowing the mouth-watering smell of sweet, buttered popcorn straight into your face while you paid for your tickets. I paid the criminally low price of $5 for both feature films and followed Scott inside.

From the outside, the New Bev looked old and dilapidated, but the inside was warm and charming with a little concession kiosk packed with candy and chocolate that was dwarfed by a giant popcorn machine behind it. The old plaster walls were adorned with vintage movie posters that spanned decades of cinema. I grabbed a large popcorn and drink and headed into the theater.

The auditorium was small, maybe a couple of hundred seats, with a modestly sized silk screen above a shallow black stage. There were old, retractable red-velvet seats with very strong springs, which was great if you had three hands, two for your large popcorn and beverage, and a third to pull the damn thing down. Lacking the extra appendage was a predicament that several people found themselves in, and we all navigated it in pretty much the same way. I reversed my butt into the seat back, arched my lower back a little to help grip the lip of the cushion with the tuck of my ass, and then dragged and pushed the seat down while sliding into it slowly. My quads were burning by the end of the maneuver, but I pulled it off without losing a single kernel of popcorn. Others were not so fortunate.

The rest of the gang, including Jeremy, Marisa, and Meadow, joined us just as the lights went down to applause. Americans applaud the oddest things, like planes that land and movies that start.

The trailers alone were worth the price of admission. They played original prints for films like *Faster, Pussycat! Kill! Kill!*, *Sid and Nancy*, and *Repo Man*. The prints were dusty and scratched, with audio pops and taped splices. The theater felt electric. The audience hooted and hollered through every trailer, elevating the experience even more. I knew then that I would see as many movies at the New Beverly Cinema as I could afford.

We finally got to the first feature of the evening, *Life Is Sweet.* I was caught off guard by the strong and varying English accents of the cast, but before long I had fallen in love with the film and every one of the characters in it. It was as if there were a little bit of me or someone I knew in every one of them. I found myself thinking about my uncles, aunts, and cousins, the friends I went to school with and the ones from my neighborhood. Everything about *Life Is Sweet* was magnificent.

Nearly everyone in the theater remained seated through the entire crawl of the end titles. The film felt so powerful, but it never really did all that much. It was just about people and their lives, all twisted up in the confusion, misfortune, misery, and joy of being born into something. It was extraordinary.

We piled outside for the intermission and stood beneath the marquee smoking cigarettes. Everyone had a similar look of reverence on their face.

Leo nudged Blake's shoulder. "That was fucking brilliant, bro. Thanks for the invite."

"He's a fucking genius, right?" Blake took a drag off his hand-rolled Drum. "Wait til you see Naked."

"Don't over-hype, bro," said RD.

Blake leaned to within inches of RD's face. "It's fucking genius, bro—it's the best film ever."

RD swatted him away.

Meadow was off to the side, leaning against the stucco exterior wall, looking a bit dejected. I approached her.

"Hey."

"Hey." She sounded as down as she appeared.

"Did you like it?"

She nodded tentatively. "Yeah."

"You alright?"

"Yeah, I'm fine. Thanks for asking."

"You seem upset."

"I don't know. I guess... Sometimes when I see films that are so fucking amazing, it makes me feel a little sad, or something. It's strange."

I nodded. "I get it. I feel that way all the time."

"Oh, yeah?"

"Yeah. It's like... envy, maybe. Or maybe not, maybe it's more like... like a longing for it."

"Yes. That's it exactly."

"Like, that's what you want to do with your life, you feel like it's something you were born to do, but you don't know if you'll even get the chance."

She took a long drag on her cigarette and inhaled. "That's it exactly."

"I think your brother's right. I think you just gotta believe in it, you know?

"Faith?" She curled her lip skeptically.

"Yeah."

"Do you have faith?"

"In you? Absolutely, yes."

"No, dummy. Do you have faith it'll happen for you? Whatever it is you came all the way down here for."

"I believe it with all my heart, Meadow."

The ticket clerk gave us a five-minute warning before the next film. We took a last pull on our cigarettes, pushed them into the crowded pedestal ashtray, and headed back inside.

At about the midpoint through *Naked*, completely awestruck by the work, I felt that familiar longing creep into my own heart.

"WHAT MAKES THIS PLACE SO FAMOUS?" I said as we waited with the others to be seated in Jerry's Famous Deli.

"It's not famous, it's just a regular deli declaring itself famous," said Scott.

"Like most of Hollywood," Marisa cracked with a half-cocked grin.

We were given a giant corner booth. Blake, Meadow, Scott, and

44

Leo piled in one side, and Jeremy, Marisa, RD, and I slid into the other.

The hostess handed me a menu that had to be two feet long and probably a foot wide, all covered in fine print. "Are you sure they're not famous for having a ridiculous menu?" I flipped it over using both hands. "How does anyone decide what to eat at this place?"

"The menu is so ridiculous," said RD. "I just get the matzo ball soup, but I'm a Jew, so..."

"What's good for a vegetarian?" I said.

"Get the veggie burger," said RD.

I felt strange eyes on me from somewhere, and when I looked up, I noticed a couple of people checking out Leo from across the restaurant. Their eyes shifted to mine and I looked away.

"Do you eat sour cream?" said Meadow.

"Yeah, I eat dairy."

"Get the latkes, they're amazing," she said.

"What the fuck is a latke?"

"Potato pancakes, fried in schmaltz," said Scott. "They've been around for hundreds of years."

I chuckled. "OK. What the fuck is schmaltz?"

"Rendered fat from various animals," replied Scott.

"Various animals..." Meadow scrunched her nose. "Gross."

"I've been a Jew my whole life," said RD, "and I did not know that shit."

"Well, shucks," I said. "No schmaltz for me."

A server arrived at our table and greeted us blandly.

"Hi. Yo, do you fry your latkes in schmaltz?" asked RD.

"I'm not sure what that is, but I can ask for you." replied the server.

I waved it off. "Nah, don't worry about it–he's asking for me. I'll just have the veggie burger."

"Actually," said RD. "I still want to know if they use schmaltz."

"No problem, I'll find out for you, babe."

The rest placed their orders. I watched as the server went to the next table. It was another booth filled with a bunch of young friends fucking around in the middle of the night just like us.

"How genius were these films, bro?" said Leo.

"Mind blowing," said Scott.

"I still can't believe it," I said. "It was like real life. How did they do it?"

"David Thewlis was on another fucking level," said Leo.

Meadow jumped in. "What amazed me is that Mike Leigh could write Life Is Sweet, about a normal British family with tons of quirk and wholesomeness or whatever, and then go from that to Naked. It just seems impossible to me."

"Well, there's an explanation, actually," said Scott. Everyone waited for him to continue, but he didn't. He just let it hang there.

"What the fuck, bro?" said RD.

Scott shrugged. "What?"

Leo chuckled. "You're not going to finish what you were saying?"

"I'm not just going to assume you want to hear the whole story."

Meadow laughed. "Why are you so weird, Scott?"

"I respect your time, what's weird about that? Maybe that's what's wrong with the world. No one is considerate of other people."

"Would you just tell us what the fuck you're talking about, please?" said Leo.

Scott shook his head at us. "Mike Leigh writes his films using improvisation, so it's very authentic. It's basically real dialogue."

"Through the whole film?" said Leo.

Scott nodded. "I believe so."

"How would that even work?" Meadow looked perplexed. "So, he used the actors to write with? You're saying David Thewlis came up with all that brilliant dialogue on his own? Mike Leigh didn't write any of it?"

"Yes. I believe so. The whole cast worked that way," said Scott.

"It's true," said Blake. "I read this somewhere too—The Weekly, maybe. I think it's fuckin' cool."

Meadow furrowed her brow even deeper. "Then why is Mike Leigh the only one credited as the writer? That's a little weird, don't you think?"

"Well, apparently, it's his story and his characters, and they work through the dialogue together," said Scott. "Whatever he does, it seems to be working well."

"What was Naked even about?" said Marisa to no one in particular. "I love slice-of-life, but I'm just trying to piece it all together."

"Maybe it's about the nakedness of humanity on display, or something?" I laughed at myself. "No, that's stupid."

"There was that whole pre-apocalyptic vibe goin' on," said Scott. "I think it was just a slice of life film, exposing the dark side of London from the perspective of a, you know, a guy who's probably depressed, maybe even suicidal." Scott smiled confidently. "Maybe something like that."

"A two-hour existential crisis?" said Marisa.

Scott nodded. "Maybe. I'm just talking shit like everyone else here." His eyes drifted over to me for some reason.

"I just love how it was so dark and disturbing, but also funny as fuck," said Leo. "That shit is hard to pull off."

"It's fucking genius," said RD.

"I'm gonna grab a smoke before my food comes," I said. "Anyone care to join?"

Meadow raised her hand. "Yeah, I'll join you."

"I might come out in a minute—I might not." Scott flashed a grin. "I haven't decided for sure, yet."

Meadow laughed at him. "Are you at all aware of just how weird you're being tonight?"

"I wasn't, no. But thank you for telling me. It's a good thing to know."

We disrupted half the group scooting our butts out of the booth. I followed Meadow outside.

I LIT Meadow's cigarette with my Zippo. Her face glowed from the flickering flame.

"Thanks."

"No worries."

She took a drag, "You liked those films a lot, huh?"

"You didn't?"

"Why don't you answer my question first, Dale."

"I'm sorry. Yeah, I did. Very much."

"I did too," she said, smiling.

"That's great. So, you feel better?"

"Yeah, I guess. I'm just frustrated with this business." She shrugged. "I don't know if I want to do it anymore."

"Why?"

"A bunch of reasons. Mainly because I'm not booking anything. I haven't had an audition I actually care about in weeks, maybe months. It's all shitty roles written by a bunch of clueless men. No offense."

"None taken."

"It's just... what's the point, you know?"

"Do you love acting?"

"I do, but—"

"Then, that's the point, Meadow."

"But I don't love the business, Dale. Do you understand what I'm saying?"

"I do, I really do. But I don't think there's such a thing as a truly perfect situation. There's always gonna be someone or something fucking things up and making things harder than they need to be. Even when we're living the life of our dreams."

"Yeah, so what then? Move to the forest?"

"Or just do what you truly love and learn to live with the shit that comes with it."

"Shut up, Dale, OK?" She grinned playfully.

I chuckled. "Why?"

"Because I don't want to listen to reason or get any advice right now. I don't want anything. Thank you, though." Her eyes were smiling.

"For whatever it's worth, I think you're brilliant."

"Oh yeah, how would you know?"

"Some people just have it. It's intangible so it's hard to describe, but you got it."

She chuckled, "You should tell my agent."

"And I rented Captain Ron."

"Oh God, Dale. No." She buried her face in her hands.

"Yeah, I did. I wanted to see it again—check out your work."

She looked up at me, her cheeks were flushed. "Why, Dale?"

"It's a great movie. And you did a fucking great job."

"Don't be ridiculous."

"It was a shallow role maybe, but that's what was impressive. You brought a lot to your character that wasn't in the writing. Your brother, on the other hand, not so much."

"Jeremy?"

"No, no—"

"Oh, Benjamin. Ben's great. It was his first thing, he'll be fine."

"Meadow, you're young, beautiful, and so fucking talented. You just gotta be patient."

She drew on her cigarette. "So I've heard." Then her eyes brightened a bit and she looked at me so sweetly that I had to look away.

MEADOW and I returned to our food cooling off on the table. We shuffled back into our seats and spent the next few hours laughing and talking together, but the conversation always found its way back to Mike Leigh and those two wonderful movies.

JEREMY DROPPED me off at the Pagoda sometime after 2 a.m. I was tired but couldn't sleep, so I just laid on the couch with my eyes fixed on the ceiling, dreaming about my life. I wanted to make movies that were different, movies that provoked people into long discussions at late-night diners. I wanted to inspire people the way Mike Leigh had just inspired all of us.

5

WORKING on Hollywood Boulevard sounded exciting to me, but Hollywood and Vine turned out to be a foul smelling dump. I was bummed about it. And the telemarketing office wasn't any better. It was small, maybe five hundred square feet. The walls were badly stained from nicotine. Three of the five people working on the phones were puffing cigarettes, creating a yellowish haze that glowed under the fluorescent light.

A disheveled middle-aged Asian man emerged from a back office and greeted me. "Hi, I'm Terry. Come with me."

Terry was a Korean immigrant with a thick accent. He was a short, unassuming dude with shaggy black hair that hung just above his shoulders. He had a slight bend to his upper back, and his belly hung over his waistline like a full sack. He wore an unbuttoned yellow and white floral-patterned shirt over a tucked-in wife-beater stained with coffee and condiments, wrinkled khaki shorts with too many things in the pockets, and sandals that showed off yellow, cracked toenails. Terry was a bit of a mess.

On our way to his office, I made eye contact with a woman who was probably in her thirties. She had her phone pushed to her ear with her shoulder to free up both hands. Her make-up was thick, her hair stiff and shiny from cheap hair products. She took a deep drag off her cigarette, and her tongue folded the smoke into the back of her throat, where she sucked it all into her lungs. She smiled at me, revealing teeth that matched the walls. Her eyes were tired, but kind. She swung her chair around and faced the photocopy of the pitch and the photos of her family all taped and tacked up in front of her, and began pitching.

"Hi, Karl, it's Karen O'Hara here with the Police and Sheriff's Association. Just calling to personally thank you for your continued support over the years..." She had a singer's rasp that was pleasing to the ears. "Oh, you didn't donate last year? Well, no worries, Karl...that's only part of the reason I'm calling today—"

Terry took me into a little corner office that looked like it belonged to a hoarder.

"Please sit down." He gestured to a metal framed chair with a vinyl seat held together by aged, once-clear tape. I sat down across from him.

"Have you done phone sales before?"

"Yes," I said. "Lots of sales."

"OK, that's good. The hours are from 8 a.m. until noon, OK? That's twelve o'clock every day. I pay every Friday in cash, OK? You make twenty-percent of your sales—technically they're donations. We are getting donations for Police and Sheriffs, and we send the donors these decals." He held up a couple of stickers. They were solid black with large white letters that read, I SUPPORT MY LOCAL POLICE & SHERIFF. "The job is easy," he said. "It's good to have this decal on your car if you get pulled over. The cop might look the other way. But you can't say that to the people you call, OK? Because I will get in big trouble and lose my contract. I will fire you if I hear you use those words, OK?"

I nodded. "No problem."

"You have to be subtle about it," he said with a wry grin. He handed me a photocopy of some text on a page. "This is the pitch. Read it real quick if you want."

Someone had apparently used it as a coaster for their coffee at some point. I glanced over the pitch. The gig was a straightforward numbers game. If I made enough calls, I would make enough money. "Yeah, I can do this," I said.

"OK, so you want to give it a try?"

"Sure. Yes."

"OK, I need to make a copy of your social security card and your driver's license."

"Oh, ah, yeah. I don't have those right now."

Terry stood up abruptly and closed his door. "You're not American?" he whispered as he lowered back into his chair.

"No." I tried to whisper back, but it came out more like a prepubescent crack.

He leaned forward and whispered, "Canadian?"

I nodded.

"Fuck. Shit. You don't have a work visa?"

"Not yet, but I'm sure I can—"

"You're supposed to have a work permit, man." He sighed and combed his fingers through his shiny hair. "This is not good."

"I can get one. I'm sure it's not a problem—"

"It's hard to do, man. It can take years." He chuckled nervously. "Trust me."

"Really? Even for Canadians?"

He hissed. "Listen to me—are you a stupid or something?"

"What?"

"You can't just move here. You have to go through immigration if you want to move to another country, dumb ass."

I knew the guy for ten minutes, and he was already comfortable calling me a dumb ass. "I didn't realize it was a big deal."

"You will have a hard time finding work, my friend. I can get in big trouble if I hire you."

I swallowed a ball. "I won't tell anyone."

"You promise?"

I nodded. "Yes."

He leaned back in his chair and caressed his sparsely stubbled chin. "I pay cash on Fridays."

"Yes. Great." I paused to give him a chance to offer me the job, but he didn't. "When can I start?"

A smile crept onto his face. "8 a.m. tomorrow. Don't be late."

"I definitely won't."

52

"Keep your mouth shut about what we talked about."

"Not a word."

Terry walked me out into the phone room and announced me as the newest member of the team. The crew each acknowledged me in their own way before Terry escorted me to the door.

I exited the office building and turned east along Hollywood Boulevard. I didn't get very far before coming upon a seedy little watering hole called Frolic Room. I didn't know anything about the bar's fabled history; that it dated all the way back to the days of speakeasies and prohibition, or that its next-door neighbor, The Pantages Theatre, was once the venue for The Academy Awards, making it a hot spot for stars like Frank Sinatra and Judy Garland. I didn't know any of that stuff, or about Charles Bukowski's affinity for the place. It was the buzzing neon sign and the stink of stale beer that drew me inside.

As my eyes adjusted to the dark interior, it felt more like I had time travelled and stepped into an elaborate speakeasy in the 1930s. Everything from the light fixtures to the barstools looked like genuine antiques.

I took a seat at the bar a couple of stools over from an old man with watery eyes and a cigarette burning between badly stained fingers. I ordered a beer and lit up a smoke of my own.

The bartender grabbed a bottle from the cooler and popped off the cap.

"Glass?"

"Bottle's good."

He set the frosty beer down on a cardboard coaster. I slid a fiver across the bar, and he snatched it up. The first swallow stung the back of my throat, conjuring quick, sticky tears. The bartender continued his rant about the Paula Jones lawsuit against President Clinton. Old Stained Fingers said a few things about it, and that got me going. I told the bartender I believed the president, even going as far as to call Ms. Jones, a stranger to me, an opportunist. Old Stained Fingers didn't like Clinton one bit, and he didn't hold back his opinion about him, he called the president one of the worst things that ever happened to America. The old man and I never said a word to one another directly, but we still managed to carry on an argument through two rounds of beers by using the bartender as our conduit. The debate ended in a stalemate. I took my last swallow, left a tip on the bar, and headed outside into the blinding California sunlight.

MEADOW PICKED me up at the Pagoda later that afternoon in her white Civic. She nodded at the screenplay I set down on my lap. "What's that?"

"It's a screenplay..."

"I know it's a screenplay. Do you have an audition or something?" She pulled away from the curb.

"No, this is Jeremy's. I'm writing something on the back of it."

"Cool! What? You don't have to tell me if you don't want to."

"No, you're fine. It's about nothing at all... It's just a long conversation between a few people at a bar. I'm just fucking around a little."

"Good for you. I'd love to read it when you're ready."

She pulled up to a parking meter on Melrose. "We're here. This isn't my main dealer. This guy only sells joints, it's kind of expensive."

"I'm just happy to get some weed."

"Oh my god, did you hear what happened to Tobey? You know who I'm talking about, right? Tobey Maguire?"

"The shabby stoner dude? Yeah, I know him. What happened?"

"He was arrested at an airport in Texas. I don't know all the details, but he got busted with a bag of weed."

"That's not good. How much did he have on him?"

"I'm not sure, but he's in big trouble."

"What was he thinking?"

"He was on his way to shoot Empire Records and I guess he forgot he had it. Or maybe he thought he could get away with it." She shrugged. "I don't know, but it's probably going to be expensive and he's gonna have a record." She pointed out the wind-

54

shield. "That's where we're going—that beauty salon right there." She pointed at a store sign that read, *Gabriel's Beauty Salon* with the motto, *Specializing in Long Hair and Getting You There,* written in cursive along the bottom.

I shook my head and chuckled. "A hair salon? That's hilarious."

"Yeah, he calls a joint a bottle of conditioner. You just tell him how many you want."

"OK. Weird, but hey, whatever."

"Don't say weed or joint, or he'll throw us out."

"Your story about Tobey got me all paranoid. I'd be so fucked if I got busted right now."

"I'll get them for you if you want me to."

"Really?"

"I'm going up there anyway. How many you want?"

"Three bottles, please. For permed hair if he has it."

———

"*THIS IS A COLLECT CALL FROM:* Dale. *Do you accept the charges?*"

"Yes, I accept. Dale, are you there?"

"Doug!"

"Hey, how's it going?"

"Are you watching TV?"

"No, why?"

"Turn it on. I'll wait."

"What's going on?"

"Go turn it on right now. Are mom or dad home?"

"No. Just any channel?"

"Yeah."

I was on the couch at the Pagoda. My eyes were glued to the TV where breaking news was playing out on the seventeen-inch tube screen. A breathless reporter was reporting by mobile telephone from a stationed news van while a chopper filmed a car chase from above.

"We can only assume that he plans to get off at Sunset and go towards, perhaps, his home..."

Doug returned to the phone call. "I don't understand."

"It's not on?"

"What, Dale? I don't know what I'm supposed to be looking at."

"It's OJ Simpson. He's not on your TV right now?"

"No. What about him?"

"He's being chased by cops!"

"What the fuck are you talking about?"

"He fuckin' killed his ex-wife and her lover."

"I don't know anything about this."

"Put it on channel twelve."

Doug let out a big sigh. "OK, hang on."

I couldn't take my eyes off the screen. I was completely captivated by nothing more than a white Chevy Bronco being chased by a half a dozen cops at a top speed of 30mph.

"OK, yeah, I see it now. What's this about?"

"They think he killed his wife—this is happening right here, Doug. In Los Angeles! How fucking crazy is it that I live in a city where OJ Simpsons get chased by cops down freeways?"

"This is near you right now?"

"Yes! Like I could be on any of those freeways inside an hour, depending on traffic."

"OK. This is why you're calling me collect?"

"Yes!"

He paused. All I could hear was his breathing.

"Who cares, Dale?"

"What do you mean? This is big news!"

"Yeah, OK, what do you want me to do about it? You want me to react a certain way, or?"

"No. I just think it's crazy that I'm here right now and, you know, that shit like this happens where I live."

"Dale, I honestly don't understand why you're calling me about it, though. I really don't. It's good to hear from you, you're my brother and I love you, but I don't care about OJ fucking Simpson.

OJ has problems? I have problems too. Mine just aren't on the news right now."

"Did you kill someone, Doug?"

"Yeah, hilarious. This is costing money, I gotta go. I'm working on my portfolio right now. If you're still in LA next year, we can probably meet up. I'll be in San Diego for Comic Con."

"For real?"

"Yup. One hundred percent. I booked my hotel yesterday. And my portfolio is looking pretty darn good, so...it's gonna be a good Con, I think."

"Doug, how crazy is it that we're doing all this at the same time —you comin' down here to break into comics and me livin' in LA chasing movies?"

"I don't know... What else were we gonna do?"

6

I MET Jeremy for lunch at a dope little café and music venue called Highland Grounds. We grabbed a table for two overlooking their quaint courtyard.

We were talking about bands and I told Jeremy I was bummed about missing Pink Floyd in Vancouver. I gave up 8th row center tickets to a show coming up that weekend, and I was grieving a bit.

"Well, my friend, today is your lucky day."

"Oh yeah? Why is that?"

"Do you remember Gina? I introduced you guys at Jay Ferguson's house? She's dating that dude Jeremy London, with the twin brother, Jason."

"Yeah, yeah, I think so."

"She grabbed a room for Friday and Saturday night at The Mirage in Las Vegas for the Grateful Dead. She said we can crash on her floor for free. You wanna fuckin' go?"

"What's the Grateful Dead? And yes, I want to go."

Jeremy gasped. "You don't know the Grateful Dead?"

"Never heard of them."

"Are you sure?" Jeremy cocked his head like a dog trying to decipher speech.

I chuckled. "Nope."

Jeremy started bobbing his head and humming and singing,

"*Truckin' got my chips cashed in—Keep truckin'*," He stopped singing, but his head kept bobbing.

"Yeah... that sounds a little familiar."

"Oh my god! I just assumed everyone on the planet knew the Grateful Dead. You are in for a treat, my friend."

I woke up bright and early for my first day on the job, tucked my screenplay under my arm, and walked the 2 miles from the Pagoda to Hollywood and Vine.

My training at the new gig consisted of sitting with each telemarketer to listen in and get familiar with how the pitch flowed.

The first guy I sat with was Jim, a Vietnam vet who looked poisoned by alcohol. His skin was dry and pockmarked, his eyes were sunken, cloudy, and yellow. He spoke with a deep, slurring authority. I liked him, I could tell he had a warrior's spirit. His sales pitch, however, was god-awful. I wondered how he could possibly be surviving on commission alone.

I moved over to Skip, a chatty actor in his late 40s who was originally from Chicago. He said he preferred performing in theater where he had worked the most, but he'd take a TV or feature film gig if one came his way. Skip's breath stunk like booze, probably vodka. Later in the day, I caught him spiking his coffee from a secret flask.

Kathy, also a Canadian, moved to Los Angeles four years ago with her band. They broke up not too long after landing in Hollywood, but Kathy stayed behind to pursue her dreams. She was in between bands but writing a lot of great songs. Her eyes were bright and hopeful despite success seeming so distant.

The last two people I sat with were Lance and Marvin, whom I later learned were close friends from South-Central Los Angeles. Things were inexplicably awkward between us. I said what's up, and we exchanged names, and then I sat there for five or ten minutes without interacting with either of them. I didn't take it personally. We were only there to make a little money.

I finally got to my table and started dialing. My first pitch was full of nerves, but after a few more, I started getting the hang of things. I nearly closed one call, but in the last few seconds the dude wriggled away and ended up in the call-back pile. I hung up the phone and sighed. The gig was going to be harder than I thought.

Terry came out of his office and made us hang up their phones. He wanted to do some training because everyone was "sucking bad."

"First, and you guys know this already, so this is really for Dale here, OK?" Terry's eyes found mine. "Don't use your real name, OK? It's not cop sounding. Your name is Dale Wheatley, and that doesn't sound, you know, like a cop, does it? You're not going to see a TV show with a cop on it called, you know, Dale Wheatley. I'm not picking on you. My name is Terry Myeong, and trust me, OK, that will never go over with anyone." Everyone chuckled with Terry. "So, I change my name on the phone to Michael Callahan—"

I had to stop myself from laughing. Absolutely no one would possibly believe that Michael Callahan was his real name.

"There aren't any Rs in Callahan." Jim roared at his own joke until he started coughing.

"Or in Michael," added Skip.

That set the rest of us off. Terry's eyes narrowed. "Very funny, Skip."

"You know what you sound like to me, Terry?" Jim puffed up for his punch line. "You sound like a Korean."

"Fuck you! I sound as American as you. Give me the phone. I'll show you how it's done." Terry yanked Jim's receiver from the cradle, grabbed a lead, and dialed up the number on the Touch Tone keypad. The first call was a wrong number, but he got someone on the very next dial. "Hello, can I please speak with Calvin Newton? Oh, hello there, Mr. Calvin. This is, ah, Michael Callahan—"

Somehow, I kept it together, but Jim, he didn't even try. He laughed so hard he nearly fell off his chair. Terry batted him away with the lead sheet while he continued to pitch.

"I'm calling from the police and sheriff's association. How are you today?... Good to hear, Calvin, that's really great to hear. I'm calling to thank you for your past support, you know, for your generous donation last year, and to ask that you once again get behind the boys in blue here in 1994 and help with another small tax-deductible donation. Can we count on your support once again this year, Mr. Calvin, for our police and sheriffs?... Oh, great, that's great—that's really great! Last year, you helped with twenty dollars. Can we count on you to help with a little more this time around, you know, to help with all the inflation?" Terry listened for a few seconds, then his eyes relaxed into a smile. "That's great. How's fifty dollars sound this year? Can you handle that? The guys at the precinct would really appreciate it, Mr. Calvin... That's wonderful! Thank you very, very much! I'm going to include an extra decal this year, for the missus..."

Terry closed up the call and slammed the phone down triumphantly. Jim waved him off while the rest of us laughed and applauded.

"I call bullshit," garbled Jim.

"No, fuck you, you cocksucker. I just closed him in one call, OK? First call I made. Pay attention, and maybe you can make some money for once, you fucking bum."

"Fuck you, Terry, that was fake and you know it!" The playful argument seemed to have accelerated Jim's buzz because he started swaying on his feet.

Terry shook his head. "No, no, it was real, Jim. I'll show you the check when it comes in. Now get back to work." Terry turned his attention to the whole room. "You should be smiling and having a good time on the call, OK? They can hear when you're smiling, and they can hear when you're not, so at least pretend like you're having a good time—"

"Smile and dial, baby," I said, as turned around to face my phone.

We all settled back in and started dialing, everyone except for

Jim. He stumbled out of the office and didn't return for a good half hour. While he was gone, I closed two donations, one for $50 and another for $100.

The shift finished at noon. Jim ended up passed out under his table and no one said a word about it, like it was an everyday thing. Terry came out of his office grinning at me.

"You did good today," he said. "All of your donations verified and one of them paid by credit card."

"Thank you," I said.

"We'll see you tomorrow. Don't be late, OK?"

INSTEAD OF HEADING STRAIGHT BACK to the Pagoda, I slipped into the Frolic Room and took a seat at an empty table tucked away darkly near the front of the bar. I ordered a beer and opened my screenplay and began sketching out a new scene.

7

"I WANNA DO ACID!" Meadow shouted out the back window, her sunkissed hair whipping around in the driest, hottest air I had ever inhaled. We were surrounded on both sides of the highway by scorched earth, mutant weeds, and the occasional cluster of man-sized cacti.

Meadow flopped back onto the seat next to me. "Jeremy?"

"Yes, Meadow?"

"Will you do acid with me tonight, honey?"

"I'm not doing acid, no." Jeremy replied without taking his eyes off the road. When Jeremy refused things or when he was highly opinionated about something, he would often slip into this dad mode with a deep voice, a principled expression, and his chin tucked deep into his neck. "I am drinking copious amounts of vodka tonight. You are welcome to join me if you like."

"Ew," said Marisa from the front seat, her nose crinkled. "Why vodka?"

"It's The Grateful Dead, Jeremy. You do mushrooms or drop acid for the Dead." Meadow crossed her arms and sat back. "You drink vodka for The Rolling Stones."

"I don't think I should, Meadow. One of us should be seeing the world as it actually is... as a precaution."

Meadow laughed. "God, you are such a dork!"

"I am not!"

Meadow flapped the front of her blouse to get some air in. "Jeremy, can you please explain to me why you didn't get your air conditioning fixed when you knew damn well you would be driving through Death Valley?"

Jeremy cackled. "I'm sorry!"

"Death Valley, Jeremy! You're a working actor, you can afford air conditioning. What is wrong with you?"

"I'm sorry. We could have taken your car."

"My car has too many miles." Meadow pouted. "Why won't you do acid with me?"

"I already told you, sweetie."

"What about you, Marisa?"

"Me? On acid?" Marisa looked over her shoulder at Meadow in the back seat. Her hair was just long enough to be blown over her eyes and into the corners of her mouth. She pulled the hair away with her fingers, but it went right back in. "Yeah, I might do a little —can you do that?" She made the universal sign for tiny with her thumb and index finder. "A little?"

"I don't know, maybe. It depends on how it comes. With liquid, you can—for sure."

"We can cut up blotter," I said.

"Yeah, that's true." Meadow's eyes narrowed on me. "What about you, Dale? LSD, or vodka with Jeremy?"

"Hmm. That's a great question. I'm going to go with..."

Jeremy did a drum roll on the steering wheel.

"Acid!"

"Yeah, baby." Meadow hit me with a high-five. "We're going to have some fun this weekend."

I could see a tiny Las Vegas blinking and flashing miles and miles ahead, which was remarkable in the bright sunlight. I looked out my window at the desert, it was dotted with wildflowers, or maybe it was cacti that looked like flowers. Whatever it was, it was beautiful. There was something foreboding about the desert though, something quietly powerful, like a calm ocean. My mind drifted back to Canada, to the cold and windy plains of Manitoba and the bone chilling misty rain of southern British Columbia. I had only been gone for a month, but it all felt so distant.

JEREMY LONDON OPENED the door to their Mirage Resort and Casino hotel room and greeted us with a stressed smile. "No one's here yet—except you guys." He let us in with a gesture.

The room was elegant without being gaudy. There were two beds and lots of space on the floor for people to crash on. Gina was sitting cross-legged on the end of one of the beds. She was warm to us, but I got the feeling we were intruding.

"Where's Jay and Lisa?" said London.

"Luxor," said Marisa.

"I thought they were staying in Old Vegas? Is anyone staying with them?"

"Yeah... Shelley. Lynn too."

"Cool. It looks like it's going to be pretty tight in here. And guys, you know we're happy to have you, but we're going to want a little privacy as well."

"Of course," said Marisa. "Let me call Jay and Lisa and see what they're doing. Can I use the room phone?"

"Yeah, no problem."

The third wheel vibe was thick, so I was happy to hear Marisa make plans for all of us to meet up with Jay and Lisa at the Luxor.

We grabbed a cab and headed north on the boulevard. Las Vegas was so much more spectacular in person. I couldn't believe how massive the hotels were and how bright everything was. On TV, you see the Las Vegas lights, in Las Vegas you're bathed in them.

The vibe in Jay's room was much more festive. They were passing joints, drinking beers, and doing shots. A groovy Dead tune started on the boombox, and Meadow clasped her hands together and closed her eyes in prayer. "Jerry, please play this song tonight," and then started singing along. *"Drivin' that train..."*

Everyone else joined in. *"High on cocaine..."*

Jeremy took a shot of something stiff and shuddered. "I want to hear them play Ramble On Rose," he said. "If I have to go to all three shows, I will. I just want to hear that song live."

"Are you guys doing anything other than weed and alcohol tonight?" said Jay.

"Me, Marisa, and Dale want to drop acid," said Meadow.

Jay's face lit up. He glanced over at Lisa, who had a mischievous grin. "Acid sounds like fun."

Meadow flared her eyes. "Would you like to partake, Jay?"

"One hundred percent, yes."

Meadow giggled. "Are you sure?"

"I'm sure." He turned to Lisa. "What about you, baby?"

"I'll do acid. Fuck yeah," she said.

"Yeah, baby!" said Meadow. "Is anyone decent opening tonight by the way? Does anybody know?"

"Traffic," said Jay. "It's their twentieth anniversary tour. How crazy is that?"

"Wow," said Meadow. "That's amazing."

Jeremy tucked his chin in and announced, "Just a quick PSA, remember to drink water out there." His eyes shifted to mine. "It's a hundred and ten degrees outside right now—the heat can literally kill you."

WE SHARED a taxi to Sam Boyd Stadium. The sun was on its way down, but the heat refused to break. The taxi dropped us off a fair bit away from the venue. Jeremy suggested we split up to find tickets and meet up at the front entrance afterward. He and Marisa headed off in one direction, Meadow and I went in the other.

"What's with all these 'I need a miracle' signs?" I asked while scanning the milling crowd.

"They're Deadheads hoping someone will gift them tickets."

"Deadheads? Does it work?"

Meadow shrugged. "I don't know, I never tried. Deadheads follow the band to every show. It's strange. And beautiful."

It didn't take us long to find a scalper with four tickets before returning to our group. Jeremy, as it turned out, also picked up four tickets, so we both had a surplus. Jeremy spotted someone nearby holding up a miracle sign with one hand and the two-finger peace sign with the other. He walked up and offered the guy his extra tickets. The dude squealed with gratitude, his eyes shining on Jeremy like he was looking up at Jesus Christ himself.

Meadow asked what I was going to do with my tickets.

"I got an idea. I'll be right back."

I headed into the crowd and moments later came upon a lovely hippie couple, each holding up a sign. The dude looked at me pleadingly and tilted his sign so I could read it. I smiled and tapped my tongue with the tip of my finger. He scurried over, kicking up a little desert in his wake.

"I have five hits of blotter and fifteen dollars," he said. "I need two tickets." His eyes filled with pure joy as I retrieved the two tickets from my pocket.

I grinned. "Just give me the blotter."

I weaved my way back through the crowd, until I spotted my friends.

"Well?" Meadow smiled. "Did you give someone a miracle?"

I smiled and nodded. "I found a miracle of my own."

"Shut the fuck up!"

I bounced my eyebrows.

"You really got some?!"

I held up the foil envelope. Meadow spun around gleefully, flaring her skirt in the late desert sun. I unfolded the foil, revealing five tiny paper squares, each with a blue happy face stamped on it.

Meadow peered over at them like a child looking at candies. "Oh, they're so cute! We should do it now, right?"

We all looked at each other awkwardly for a second, like we were deciding who was going to jump out of the airplane first.

"Let's do it." I took one of the squares and stuck it to my tongue.

Jay, Lisa, and Meadow dropped their tabs between flirty looks and giggles.

. . .

THE ACID KICKED in about midway through Traffic's set. Time slipped into its truer, quantum state, and life and existence became blocks, like sandboxes connected by footprints. I wandered through the pulsing crowd, feeling every single thing around me all at once.

The desert heat became too intense. My throat was cracked from the dry heat. It felt like I was swallowing knives. I needed water. I scanned the area for a vendor, but all I could see were twirling bodies, swaying back and forth like leaves of sea kelp. I walked toward the bleachers, hoping for any sign of a vendor.

As I got closer to the bleachers, I heard strange chirping sounds swirling around me like an eddy. I looked all around and caught something scurrying beneath the bleachers, deep in the shadows. I couldn't make out what the hell it was.

Then suddenly the sun dipped below the horizon and the night swallowed the sky. Anxiety rushed through me like a river, and time shifted into darkness. It occurred to me that I was likely dehydrating without even knowing it. I needed water or I could die, but I couldn't stop thinking about what was under those damn bleachers.

It moved again just as the chirps picked up volume and tempo. My eyes adjusted, and I could finally make out men and women, maybe five or six of them, yipping and chirping as they hopping from one foot to the other, like an ancient ritual. I made eye contact with one of them and it was too intense a gaze to hold.

A hot gust of wind hit me in the face, reminding me of my urgent quest for water. I weaved in and around the crowd with renewed purpose. The music bubbled and rippled in the background but there was something suddenly different about it. It had changed and become lighter and more beautiful somehow.

I turned to a dude undulating nearby and spoke with a raised voice. "Hey, man."

"Hey, what's up, my brother?"

What a very nice smile. He must be a truly happy person. "Is this still Traffic?"

He leaned closer so he could hear me. "Say again?"

"Traffic, is this still Traffic playing?"

"No, man!" He pointed to the stage. "That's Jerry Garcia, right there."

I had no memory of Traffic finishing their set whatsoever. There must have been a transition, but it was as good as deleted from my memory. *You mean displaced, you fool! What is time? What is all of this for? Is it even really happening? Has it already happened? Or is it all just the routine death of another star in an infinite and overflowing universe of dying stars?*

My eyes wandered to a cluster of large oval screens on the side of the stage and suddenly everything else seemed to dissolve and merge into a prismatic luminescence of extreme beauty. Tendrils of light slithered out of the ovals and wrapped around me, embracing me with warm love. Dust devils danced. Humans surrendered. I witnessed pure music pouring out from the ovals down onto the crowd like a waterfall made of all the colors of the universe, translucent and beautiful. Everything felt so perfect and true. My attention drifted to the thousands of heads bobbing and swaying like sea anemones. I closed my eyes and started swaying to the music. The energy of the moment consolidated into a tiny ball of enormous power within me. It moved through my body, into my head, and the pressure expanded until I could feel it pushing hard against my skull, trying to find its way out. *I'm gonna leave my fucking body. I'm finally gonna leave my body!*

And just then, I swallowed the knives again and the slicing pain pulled me back from the ether of creation to the pressing situation of survival on a burning, dying earth. *Water.*

I navigated through another section of the crowd and spotted a vendor truck. It looked suspiciously out of place, like someone had just flicked the switch for the vending truck hologram in their little life simulation. There was a long, slow line, and I could feel eyes on me, too many eyes, so I closed mine and started rocking on the balls of my feet. Jerry Garcia's sweet voice and guitar twirled and twisted around me, rendering everything but the music untrue and unimportant.

I opened my eyes to find myself at the vending truck window.

Time isn't fucking real. We don't need it anymore. I bought six bottles of water, which were too many to carry. I cradled them in both arms and shuffled off to the side, beneath the truck's flickering fluorescent light. I shoved one bottle in each of my front pockets. The cold wetness sent shocks through my entire body, taking my breath away. I managed to hold one bottle between my knees while twisting the cap off with my free hand. I guzzled the entire bottle at once, instantly healing my throat and my soul. The ice-cold water rushing through my insides brought instant, ephemeral rapture. I opened a second bottle between my legs, raised it high above my head and poured it down, all over me.

Hallelujah!

Fully rejuvenated, I moved through the crowd with the speed and grace of a jungle cat. I needed to share the miracle of ice-cold water with my friends.

I spotted Jeremy, so tall and handsome, then Marisa, Lisa, Jay, Meadow, and all the others. They all looked dazzling, glittering in the reflection of the light show. I ran up to Jeremy and hugged him at the waist.

"Where the hell have you been?" He laughed. "Why are you soaked?!"

"I found water!" I said breathlessly. "I brought some for you." I grabbed a bottle from my back pocket. It was dented and the label was wet and torn.

He smiled gratefully or maybe sympathetically, "I'm good, actually."

"But... but we're in the desert, Jeremy. And it's so hot, like you said."

"I'm good though." He laughed and held up a half-full bottle. "I have plenty. Enjoy the show!"

I turned toward the stage, closed my eyes, and gave myself back to the Dead. It wasn't just a show, it was a life altering experience. I began undulating unconsciously, twisting and turning my hips like a rogue belly dancer. I opened my eyes and looked up at Jerry Garcia. He was silver and beautiful. His guitar was as sweet as his voice. He hit a perfect note and rolled forward on his feet and, in that instant, a gust of wind blew in from behind him. Jerry's long silver hair whipped the music toward the swaying crowd. It was as if the wind were a part of his instrument and he used it to literally touch us with his music. *Jerry Garcia can control the elements! Like a fucking god.*

"What?" said Jay with a cocked lip. "Jerry can what?"

Oh no! I said it out loud!

"Nothing, nothing. He's so amazing," I gripped hands with Jay. "I can't believe I'm here, bro."

"You're fucking tripping," he laughed.

I closed my eyes again, and fell headfirst back into the beautiful, beautiful music.

"DALE!"

I opened my eyes and Jeremy was right there above me lit in an angelic halo. His teeth were so straight, white, and perfect. *God, how can teeth be so perfect?*

"Hi, Jeremy."

"What are you doing?"

"I'm resting in this curious grass. It's so refreshing."

"That's because it's wet. Look at you—"

"What?"

"You're soaking wet, Dale." He laughed. "Why are you laying in the middle of Las Vegas Boulevard? You're gonna get arrested."

Suddenly, I could hear all the honking and motors running. I heard people talking and laughing, maybe some were crying.

"Jeremy, have you ever looked closely at this grass?" I pulled a few blades from the bed and offered them like a bouquet. "They feel like plastic. Here, take them—"

"I don't want your grass, Dale. Thank you."

"Why?"

"I'm good. Come on." He pulled me to my feet.

"How did they grow grass in the desert in the first place, Jeremy? It's horrifying!"

"Let's go."

We crossed the strip and headed toward the Mirage hotel.

"Don't wander off again, OK?" Jeremy put his arm around me. "Not until you come down a little bit. I looked away for five minutes and you were gone."

"Jeremy."

"What?"

"You're the best person I ever met."

I SPENT most of the following day by the pool at The Mirage, dozing in and out of consciousness. Blissful, euphoric, sacred.

The Sunday show was another glimpse into the heavens. None of us dropped acid or did anything crazy. We just smoked a little weed and drank whatever booze we could smuggle in. Jeremy's wish came true, The Grateful Dead played "Ramble On Rose." It was magical. The very next weekend, the four of us drove up to Shoreline in San Francisco for three more shows right in the Dead's backyard.

It was a perfect summer.

8

WHEN I STEPPED into the telemarketing office on Monday morning, the room was tense and densely quiet. I was fifteen minutes late, so I was expecting a tongue lashing, but Terry barely even glanced in my direction. He and Lance were engaged in a heated conversation.

"Don't be so naive," Terry said condescendingly. "He's obviously guilty, man."

"How do you know, Terry?" said Lance. "Were you there that night?"

"No, I wasn't there, but I know, OK. Because I'm not stupid."

"Oh yeah? The fuck you know?"

"He beat her, dummy. There are pictures."

"Yeah, I saw the pictures. So what?"

"So what? You're fucking crazy, man. So what." Terry turned to me just as I was taking my seat. "Can you believe this guy? He thinks OJ Simpson is innocent. Look at this... What a fucking idiot."

I shrugged. "He's innocent until proven guilty, right?"

"Oh, bullshit." Terry pointed at Lance and Marvin. "You're just like one of them."

"The fuck you mean one of them?" Lance stood up, and I got a look at his graphic t-shirt, the apparent cause of the argument. It had OJ's mugshot blown up on the front with *FREE OJ* across the top, *NOT GUILTY* across the bottom, and written on the side, in an absolute catastrophe of a design choice, was *Let The Juice Loose* in ugly white cursive "Tell me what you meant, Terry?"

"Sit down, OK." Terry waved his hand dismissively. "You don't scare me."

Lance moved closer, until he towered over the shorter man. Terry puffed his chest out.

Lance clenched his teeth. "What do you mean *them*?"

My heart rate jumped. Lance looked ready to strike.

"I meant you and him," Terry pointed down at Marvin, who sat at his station with his eyes front.

"You're a fuckin' racist motherfucker, Terry—"

"Hey, fuck you. I'm Asian, OK? Don't try to play that race shit with me, motherfucker. You think being Korean is easy around here? You think I don't have to put up with all the same bullshit as you? Go fuck yourself, OK? We don't need this shit."

Lance threw up his arms. "Fuck you, Terry."

"Hey, if you don't like it, get out of here then, OK? This is a place of business. We're here to make money. Get on the phone or go home." He waved a hand as if to shoo Lance. "I don't care what you do."

"I quit, Terry. Fuck you." Lance walked out the door.

Marvin remained in his seat for a moment, his eyes still fixed on the wall in front of him. Then he heaved a sigh, took a last pull on his cigarette and crushed it in the ashtray. "Why the fuck you do that, Terry?"

"Do what?" Terry hissed, "I didn't do shit. He's crazy."

"Yeah, you know what you did." Marvin shook his head and stood up. "Now I gotta go too." He scooped up his cigarettes and Walkman and headed for the door. "Peace, y'all."

Marvin left and the crew all turned to face their phones, but no one picked up the receiver.

Terry snapped at me, "Why are you late?"

"My bus was late."

"Take an earlier bus then. We start at eight."

74

I held up my hands like it was a stick-up. "OK, Terry, Jesus. I'll do my best."

I walked over to the coffee machine and poured a cup while Terry lingered, trying to read the room. It was as dead as a morgue.

"Alright, listen up." Terry centered himself in the room. "I'm going to put up a special bonus for today, OK? For the first one-hundred-dollar donation."

"How much?" gargled Jim.

"Ten dollars."

Jim rolled his eyes. "Jesus Christ, can you spare it?"

"It's free money—what do you care anyways? You're just going to pass out under the table."

Jim sneered at him. "Make it a decent amount and I'll win the fuckin' thing."

"Oh yeah? You're going to win it, huh?"

"If it's worth my time, you fuckin' right I will."

"Oh, I have to see this. OK, let's see...yeah, OK. The first, yeah, so the first hundred-dollar donation—that gets confirmed, OK? So don't try and write a wood order—the first hundred dollars confirmed gets fifty bucks in cash today, at the end of the shift."

Jim's eyes popped wide open. He spun his chair around and picked up the phone along with the rest of us.

"I'm losing money, so don't say I'm not a generous boss." The room filled with the familiar sounds of punching phone numbers and mingled voices selling hard. A big smile opened on Terry's face. "I'll buy everyone lunch too, OK? There's no limit to my kindness today."

"McDonald's?" Jim asked with another sneer.

"Yeah, McDonald's. You don't want it?"

"I didn't say that."

"If you don't want any, no problem..."

"No, no," chuckled Jim. "If you're buying, I'm eating. I'll take a Big Mac and some—"

Terry waved his hands to shut him up. "Write it down, please. Everyone write down what you want and I'll pick it up in a couple of hours. Skip, you want the fish sandwich?"

Skip turned, grinning. "Yes, I do, Terry, thank you."

"Write it down, please."

I returned to my table, took a deep breath, and picked up the phone to make my first call of the day.

About half way into the shift Skip won the big money. He was so happy, I thought I saw his face spasm from grinning so hard. Jim grumbled and complained, but eventually congratulated Skip. Jim left shortly after that, even before the free lunch. I ordered two cheeseburgers with no meat and extra pickles, and they were delicious.

LATER THAT AFTERNOON, Jeremy came by the apartment with a screenplay in hand and asked if I would help him rehearse before his audition later that day for a film called *Fast Sofa* and then grab some food afterward. We read through the scenes a few times and talked through some of his choices. It was so much fun breaking down the scenes and giving him notes and ideas and then seeing those ideas brought to life in our reading. I could have done it all day. I could understand why he loved the craft of acting so much, it's an endless sea of creative choices, and each choice can alter the scene and the character in infinite ways.

JEREMY PULLED up to the security gate at FOX Studios, and after a quick exchange with the guard, we were permitted entry onto the lot. We found parking and walked toward an unremarkable building when RD Robb exited and headed right for us.

"Jeremy, what's up, bro!"

They gripped hands. "RD! Good to see you."

"Are you reading for Fast Sofa?"

"I am."

"Jack?"

"Yup..." Jeremy anxiously combed his fingers through his hair.

"I just read. It was kind of a disaster." RD looked at me for a second, then returned to Jeremy. "They're all over the place in there, for a change."

Jeremy gestured to me. "Do you remember Dale?"

RD acknowledged me with a flick of his chin. "Yeah. What's up, bro?"

I flicked my chin back at him. "What's up?"

"Are you reading for Jack too? You look more like a Rick to me."

"No, no. I'm just tagging along with this guy."

"To his audition?" RD chuckled. "Why the fuck would you do that?"

"We're grabbing something to eat afterward," said Jeremy. "You're welcome to join."

"No, I'm good, bro. I gotta deliver fuckin' breakdowns for my mother. Yo, did you get an audition for No Worries?"

Jeremy cringed like he was about to be smacked. "Yes."

"For Elton?"

"Yes—I'm so sorry."

"Fuck!"

"I'm so sorry, RD."

"Fuck me right in the ass, bro."

"What the hell happened?"

"I'm getting fucked in the ass, bro. They moved it to Paramount, and now they're re-casting the whole movie."

"I'm so sorry," said Jeremy. "Are you auditioning again?"

"Yeah, I'm testing. But they already made me an offer, bro. I was cast."

"I know, that's horrible. Why did Fox drop it?"

"Fuck if I know. I heard they're changing the name, too."

"Yeah. It's Clueless now."

"Yeah, *they're* fuckin' clueless."

Jeremy couldn't help but laugh. "I'm sorry, dude. I'm—I'm not laughing at you, you're just so funny. I feel terrible, RD."

"It's cool. You gotta do your thing, bro. I'd say break a leg but, you know, you're basically taking food right out of my mouth—"

"No, don't say that!"

RD chuckled. "I'm just fuckin' with you." He nodded in my direction. "Good to see you again, bro."

"Yeah, man, good to see you too."

"I'm gonna go home and shoot myself. I'll catch you guys later." RD walked away while we laughed.

"That dude's a trip," I said.

"He's a funny guy."

"Does he know he walks like Charlie Chaplin?"

Jeremy laughed. "I think he might."

———

A FEW WEEKS LATER, RD Robb learned that he indeed lost the role of Elton in *Clueless* to Jeremy Sisto. It must have been crushing for him but at least his good friend got the part.

Re-casting for Clueless was almost complete, but there was one role they were struggling to fill: the role of Cher's stepbrother, Josh. I was physically right for it, and Jeremy managed to get me an audition with the producers and the director, Amy Heckerling.

"Oh my god, Jeremy! That is so fucking huge."

"It's just an audition."

I stood up and started pacing. "Can you imagine if I booked it? That would be the craziest sequence of events ever, right? You, me, and Alicia in the same movie together." I shook my head in disbelief. "It's crazy!"

"Well, look, it's a long shot..."

"Yeah, yeah, of course. But I got a chance..."

"You get a crack at it." Jeremy chuckled. "Come back here. Sit down. You're making a scene."

We were having lunch at The French Quarter in West Hollywood, and I could feel eyes on me. I sat back down and Jeremy handed me a piece of paper with a phone number on it.

"Call the casting director at that number. Her name is Marcia Ross. You're not going to speak with her directly, just talk to the person who answers and they'll set it up for you. I'll give you the script so you can start preparing."

"I've read it. I got it."

"Really? How?"

"You left it at the apartment ages ago." I glanced down at the number Jeremy just gave me and was overwhelmed with gratitude. "I feel stupid just saying thank you. It seems so insufficient but thank you, Jeremy. Thank you so much."

"No worries, my friend. Break a leg."

THE AUDITION WAITING room was narrow and windowless. The walls were a dull clay color with scuffed white wainscoting. A stained, threadbare rug covered most of the floor. There were a few other guys in the room, but no one I recognized. We were all bent over our scripts, going over our lines in our heads. Now and then, one of them would make a sound or gesticulate, causing their chair to whine and squawk. I wondered if their hearts were beating as ferociously as mine. I felt light-headed and thirsty, but at least I wasn't sweating.

A young woman came out of the audition room and called my name. I followed her through the door, my heart beating in my head like a kick drum.

I smiled at some of the many faces in the room until my eyes landed on Amy Heckerling. The magnitude of the moment hit me hard. I was about to audition for the woman who directed *Fast Times at Ridgemont High*.

"Hello," she said.

"Hello," I said.

"Thanks for coming in today," said another woman, likely the casting director, Ms. Ross.

"I'm so glad to be here." My voice quivered and cracked.

A man in the room, presumably a producer, told me he heard good things about me from Jeremy. He meant well, but all it did was sink the knife in deeper. I expressed my gratitude awkwardly, and Ms. Ross asked if I was ready. I said I was, even though I wasn't, and then with a deep breath, I began.

I do not have the words to adequately describe the disaster

that followed. My mouth dried up instantly, which caused my lips to stick to my teeth. I was making a smacking sound with my mouth that was so loud it sounded like someone was stirring mac & cheese behind me. I could feel that white gooey shit forming in the corners of my mouth, but I was too afraid to lick it with my bone-dry tongue and gross everyone out. I locked my eyes downward on my script sides, even though I had memorized my lines days earlier. I was too nervous to look any of them in the eye. The entire process lasted all of three minutes, but it felt like forever.

"OK, well thanks for coming in today," said Ms. Ross.

My eyes drifted over to Ms. Heckerling and she offered a sympathetic smile. I returned my attention to Ms. Ross. "We'll let you know," she said.

"Thanks," I said and then turned and walked out the door.

WHEN I SAW Jeremy later that evening at the Pagoda, I couldn't look him in the eye either. He tried his best to make me feel better, telling me I would get better at auditioning once I got a few under my belt.

"How do you do it?" I said. "How do you manage your nerves?"

He shrugged, "I don't know. It just got a little easier with time... And vodka helps."

9

TERRY CALLED me into his office and handed me a white envelope. "That's your pay," he said.

I opened it, removed the cash and counted it with a tightening chest. "There's only two-twenty-five here, Terry? I was expecting two-eighty-five."

"There's no commission slip in there? You had two cancellations yesterday after you left... the two-hundred dollar one changed her mind." He fumbled through some papers on his desk and then handed me a commission sheet with my name at the top. "I still got her for fifty bucks, so you got something at least."

My eyes skimmed down the cancellations. "Dammit."

He shrugged. "It happens."

"I can't live on this, Terry."

He sighed. "You just have to get more donations, man. You can make good money here."

"What's good money?"

"Five hundred a week. Easy. Seven hundred if you come in every day and kick ass. You're almost there now. After a year, you'll have a book of business—you'll see."

"I hope you're right."

"Come to karaoke tonight. It's my treat. You can drink and eat for free. Get your mind off your worries."

"Thanks for the invitation but I've got other plans already."

———

IT WAS another gorgeous afternoon in Los Angeles, so I chose to walk the two miles from the Pagoda to Meadow's apartment. I enjoyed walking through the posh neighborhood of Hancock Park where the homes were all enormous and beautiful. I was walking east along 1st street when I noticed a heavy branch sagging over a high fence and what appeared to be a big piece of fruit dangling from it. I couldn't quite tell what it was at first, but it looked like an orange. Apart from crab apples in the outskirts of Winnipeg, I had never seen a fruit tree in real life. It looked fake to me. As I got closer, the scent grew stronger. Water flooded my mouth. It wasn't an orange after all. It was a beautiful, perfectly ripe peach!

Can I pick it? Are there peach protection statutes in the state of California? It's hanging over the fence into the public domain—is it not the people's peach?

I peeked through the pickets and didn't see anyone. I reached up for the peach, but it was much too high. I crouched low and jumped as high as I could, but all I got was a handful of leaves. A running jump didn't get me any closer, so I gripped the top of the fence and pulled myself up, scraping my belly along the way. It took a moment to get my balance, but I eventually found the footing I needed to launch and capture the fruit with my outstretched hand.

I rinsed the peach with water from my bottle and sat on the sidewalk with my back against the fence. I held it up with my fingertips to admire all its beauty. It was flawless, like a Malibu sunset. I rubbed the soft fuzz against my cheek. I took in a deep smell from the navel. It was so sweet and sublime that my eyes rolled in their sockets and my mouth filled with saliva. I bit softly until the nectar spilled out like warm water. The sticky juice ran down my arm to my elbow, and I licked it up like melting ice cream. I wanted to savor every bit of it, but I ended up gulping the peach down in big, luscious bites instead.

82

I sucked on the pit all the way to Detroit Street and then tossed it into a bush with the hope it would one day grow into a healthy tree and bear fruit for those lucky enough to pass beneath it.

"WHAT'S UP, GUYS?" I said from behind the screen door.

"Come in, Dale," said Meadow from out of view.

I let the flimsy screen door go behind me, and it made a couple of sharp thwacks. Everyone looked up at me.

"So sorry!"

Jeremy laughed, "Canadians really do apologize for everything." He was sitting on the corner of the coffee table, messing around on his guitar.

"Yeah, sorry about that."

Jeremy giggled, "Did you just apologize for apologizing?"

Marisa let out a little snort from the couch and then returned to writing in her notebook.

Meadow was in the dining area painting something impressionistic at an easel. "What took you so long, honey?" she asked. "Did you walk?"

"I did. It was nice."

"That's good you got some exercise."

"I smoked two cigarettes on the way, but yeah, I feel great."

She chuckled. "Can you tell me how a vegetarian is also a smoker? That doesn't make any sense to me."

"I'm an activist. I'm not doing it for health reasons."

"Yeah," she said thoughtfully. "Yeah, OK, I get that... "

"Mind if I wash my hands?"

"Of course, sweetie. In the kitchen."

Marisa hollered to the kitchen from the couch. "Dale, I'm writing a short, and I wrote you a part, if you're interested."

"Are you serious?" I was nearly shouting over the running water.

"Yeah. It's small, so don't get too excited. It's an improv in the vein of Christopher Guest."

I returned with damp hands. "Who is that?"

83

"Christopher Guest? He wrote This Is Spinal Tap—he also played Nigel."

"Oh, neat, I saw him play live! Spinal Tap played all of Canada on Canada Day. They toured the whole country in one day."

Marisa furrowed her brow. "Are any of them Canadian?"

"I don't believe so."

Meadow laughed. "Why would they play Canada Day, then?"

I shrugged. "Maybe they were making fun of us, because they were fucking awful."

Marisa laughed. "Well, they're actors. You wanna hear about this or what?"

"Yes! I'm so excited."

"It's simple, but I think it could be really cool. You're gonna sit for a short interview and then a little b-roll around the apartment and that's it. We'll shoot here at the apartment for one day."

Jeremy flared his eyebrows. "On Super 16!"

"That's awesome!" I was faking it. I had no idea why that was a good thing.

Marisa continued. "We'll have a couple of rehearsals, but it's going to be improvised. Do you want to know about your character?"

"Yes!"

"He's a super flamboyant gay man named Chad who's in love with a conservative older man."

"Have I introduced you to Danny from Two-Faced Theatre Company?" asked Jeremy.

I shook my head, "No, we haven't met."

Marisa chuckled. "Danny's wonderful. You guys will go through the themes and some character-building stuff and we'll give you direction based on what you give us."

"Are you two directing together?"

"I'm directing, Jeremy is producing. Officially."

"Yeah, we're pretty much wearing both hats," said Jeremy.

"True. What am I forgetting?" Marisa looked at Jeremy for help, but he just shrugged.

"I don't know what to say," I said. "I'm blown away and so flattered. Thank you."

"We're excited too." Jeremy stood up and stretched. "And since you're always here, we can work on it a lot beforehand..."

I felt my cheeks flush. *Am I here all the time? Is that bad?*

———

JAY FERGUSON THREW another backyard party at his house in the Valley. Pretty much everyone was there from the first time, except for Tobey Maguire. I heard he quit *Empire Records* because of his drug arrest and entered a treatment program of some kind.

Jay rested his arm on my shoulder. "Dude, you were so fuckin' high at the Dead. I don't know if I've ever seen someone that fucked up before."

We were all on the deck again. "I was trippin' hard," I said.

"Jeremy found him rolling around on the grass in the middle of the strip." Meadow laughed. "Did you know that?"

"Are you serious?" Jay laughed with her. "That's so funny."

I was shrinking by the second. "I wasn't rolling around. I was just lying in. It felt amazing."

"That acid was so lovie-dovie," said Lisa.

The guy across from me acknowledged me with a nod. "What's up, bro, I'm Kevin." We shook hands.

"I'm Dale. Good to meet you."

Kevin chuckled. "Did you guys drop?"

"Yeah," I said.

Jay gestured at me. "This guy was so high—he was fuckin' dancing like a gypsy or something."

"I did not realize I was such a spectacle."

Jay shook his head, "It wasn't a bad thing, bro."

Meadow chuckled. "You were fine, Dale. You brought us water, which was very sweet and caring. Don't listen to these guys."

"That's why I won't do acid," said Kevin. "I don't trust myself. I feel like I'll end up fucking naked and shivering in fetal position on some random person's front lawn fuckin' suckin' my thumb."

Meadow laughed, "And then you end up on the sex offender's list—"

"Exactly, fuck that nonsense. I'll just stick to weed and alcohol, thanks. I might do mushrooms under the right circumstances."

"Yo, Kev," said Leo.

"There's no difference between mushrooms and acid," said Meadow. "Very little, I would say."

"Yo, did you guys hear the story about Johnny and the pool table incident?" Kevin laughed and nodded in Jay's direction. "You were there. You remember? With the fuckin' Cheetos—"

"Kevin-Fuckin-Connolly!"

Kevin looked up at Leo incredulously, "What, bro? Jesus Christ."

"Well, I've been trying to get your attention, but you keep blabbering on about nothing. You wanna shoot some hoops before I split, or not?"

"I'm obviously in the middle of a conversation right now."

Leo sighed. "You guys are a bunch of drug addicts." Leo and I made eye contact. I thought he was about to recognize me, but instead, he offered me his hand. "Hey man, I'm Leo."

We shook.

"Yeah, yeah, we met a few weeks ago," I said. "Right here, actually."

"Really?"

"We shot some hoops."

"Oh, rightrightright, I think I remember. Did I win? I won, right?"

I chuckled. "Yeah, you embarrassed me, actually."

Leo smirked, "Sorry about that."

"No worries," I said. "I'm Dale, by the way."

"Good to meet you again. You want a rematch?"

"Yes. I do." I emptied the contents of my pockets onto the table and trotted over to the hoop.

Leo bounced the ball to me. "Challenger goes first."

"Ready?" I asked. He nodded and I did a quick fake to my left. He bit on it, and I went in for an easy right-side lay-up.

"Nice one," he said.

I passed him the ball.

"Zero – one," he said and passed it back.

I scored four straight baskets before Leo made me miss.

I passed him the ball and he turned his back to me, protecting his low dribble, then he pressed in toward the hoop. He planted his left foot and pivoted back around to face me. He pulled off a beautiful crossover dribble through his legs, but missed the hook shot with my hand in his face. I grabbed the rebound and dribbled back to the check line. I hit him with a crossover of my own on the very next play, but mine was behind the back. It was sloppy as hell, but my hook shot didn't miss. Leo never held the lead once in the match. It was my night.

"Good game, bro," he said.

"That's one a piece," I said.

"We'll play the rubber match next time."

More people arrived. RD Robb, Blake Sennett, Scott Bloom. I recognized a girl from a soap opera I used to watch with my grandmother. Her name was Christy. She was Kevin Connolly's roommate.

I played the spectator for most of the night, admiring all the creative tension and dialogue flowing between them. Everyone seemed so carefree and happy. Back home, everyone I knew was worried about rent or money for gas, but these people didn't have any of those problems. They drank each other's beer and laughed about their troubles.

As the night went on, the booze grabbed a hold of us with a slippery grip. Leo and Meadow ended up off in the corner, flirting and whispering. He took her by the hand and led her languidly to another room where they remained for the rest of the evening.

10

JEREMY and I were having lunch at Caffe Luna on Melrose before heading to the New Bev to see two by Kubrick.

"Do you remember RD?"

"I do."

"He's directing a short film with Leo, Tobey, and Kevin Connolly. I'm pretty sure Scott Bloom's in it as well."

"The whole crew."

"The whole crew." He raised his eyebrows, "There's a role you're perfect for..."

"Really." I tried to temper my excitement.

"It's pretty cool, too. It's about a group of friends who gather at an abandoned hotel to pay their last respects to a friend whose body they just stole from the morgue."

I leaned back. "And I would be the dead friend, I take it."

"Correct."

I chuckled. "Only a couple of months into my illustrious acting career, and I'm already the go-to dead guy in Hollywood."

A couple of weeks earlier, Marisa directed a play on Theater Row, and she cast me to play the dead guy. "Dead Guy" was even my character's name in the playbill. The show opened with me collapsing lifelessly to the floor, where I remained until the closing curtain.

"You were amazing, you didn't move an inch for over an hour!" Jeremy laughed. "In this thing, you're in a bunch of flashbacks, so you're only dead for part of it. And you'd be working with Leo, so there's that.

"That's crazy."

He smiled. "It's a good opportunity. RD's gonna give you a shot."

"You're unbelievable. You really are."

He chuckled kindly. "It's just an audition. You're gonna have a thousand of them."

"I thought you'd be done with me after Clueless."

He handed me a piece of paper. "That's RD's number. Give him a call and he'll send the script over."

"You're an angel in my life, Jeremy."

"I'm always happy to help."

———

BEFORE SHOOTING Marisa's short film, Sessions, she asked the whole cast to see Clerks. The only thing she would tell me was that the director financed the production on his credit cards, and the movie made it into theaters all over the country. I was excited to see it, but I didn't end up liking it all that much. I didn't hate it either, but I thought the cinematography was more distracting than charming. The writing was fine—something between Hal Hartley and a medicated John Waters—but it just didn't resonate with me for some reason. But I could see why Clerks changed the game forever. Those guys opened countless doors that were otherwise closed to independent filmmakers. Suddenly, all a dreamer needed was a good idea and a few credit cards, and they could make it big in the movies.

WE SHOT Sessions in less than a day, but it thoroughly changed my life. Watching Marisa work experimentally was more like watching a painter or sculptor carving and layering the piece until it's finally revealed to them. Her approach was the opposite of traditional filmmaking, where everything, down to the finest detail, is planned out before a single frame is exposed. I loved the freedom, but I think what got me most excited was the enigmatic nature of the technique. There was no right or wrong way to do anything, and there was no telling how the work would turn out. I don't know why, but I thrive in that kind of environment. I crave it. In Winnipeg, I used to get up on the stage at the comedy club without a single written joke and had some of the best nights of my life creatively. *Sessions* was supposed to be about my acting debut, but instead I stumbled upon a whole new world behind the camera that excited me like nothing else.

————

RD ROBB and I traded messages a few times but we finally connected, and he had a script for his short film sent over for me to read. The writing was awful. The plot was thin, though service-able. It centered around a bunch of guys stealing their friend's corpse for a final reunion, which was interesting, but the charac-ters were indistinguishable, and the dialogue was trite and riddled with exposition. I called RD after reading it again for a third time.

"Hey, RD, it's Dale."

"Yo, what up?"

"I just read Last Respects, man."

"Awesome, dude! What did you think?"

"Really fuckin' great, RD." If it's good enough for Leonardo DiCaprio, it's good enough for me.

"Nice."

"Reminded of that movie with Jeff Goldblum... What the fuck is it called—"

"The Big Chill?"

"The Big Chill! I love that movie."

"We're getting that a lot. I guess that's a good thing."

"For sure, dude. I'd love to audition for Jason whenever you're ready."

"Yeah, yeah. We will for sure. We don't have dates right now, we're still working through schedules and shit, so I'll just call you when we're all set. It shouldn't be too long, though."

I DIDN'T HEAR from RD for weeks, but I made good use of the time by working obsessively on my character. I was determined not to blow another audition. RD called and asked if I would be interested in playing the role of Jason in a table read along with the cast for some potential investors. I accepted. He wanted me to read a couple of scenes with him first, not as an official audition, just to make sure I could handle the role in front of his investors. In exchange for picking me up all the way in Koreatown, I agreed to join him on some deliveries he had to make for his mother.

RD's tires chirped as he pulled away from in front of the Pagoda.

"After we deliver these fuckin' breakdowns, we'll head to my place, read a few scenes, and then maybe grab some food if you're down. I can bring you back to your place after that."

"Yeah, cool. What the fuck are breakdowns?"

"They're a service for casting film and TV roles... and some theater too, although that's mostly New York. My mom's a talent manager and these envelopes are filled with headshots and resumes of her shitty fucking clients. She submits them for pointless roles on TV and shit. She's too fucking cheap for a delivery service, so that means I gotta drop them off for her." He stuck his jaw out in a crude sneer. "I fuckin' hate it so much, bro." He cranked on his wheel to make a sharp right turn. He had a heavy foot and nearly caused an accident circling the block. After another car beat him to an open spot, he lost his shit. "FUCK, BRO!"

I jumped in my seat. "Jesus!"

He kneaded at the back of his neck. "I fuckin' hate LA sometimes. I can't fuckin' EVER find parking in this town. Can you do me a favor, bro? Before I lose my shit and kill everyone."

I chuckled, "Sure."

"It's easy." He reached to the back seat and grabbed a stack of large white envelopes and handed them to me. "Just take these and go through those doors, and on your right maybe—yeah, on your right, there'll be a bin or box or fuckin' whatever—it'll be down the hall outside a door, probably filled with more of these fuckin' things. Just drop them in there."

"That's it?"

"Yup, easy."

"Sure. Be right back."

I ran that and several more deliveries over the next couple of hours before we finally drove into the valley for my audition.

RD's split-level, two story condo was simple, with off-white walls, dirty gray carpet, and white cabinets in a small open kitchen. The whole place was beige except for this gaudy 1980s green glass octagonal dining table surrounded by five S shaped chrome chairs. There were a couple of stained black sofas in the adjoining room that served as an office for the management business. RD's walls were decorated with showbiz memorabilia from the silent era up to the present. Most impressive to me was an actual *A Christmas Story* theatrical release poster.

"No shit, you're a Christmas Story fan."

RD nodded, "Oh yeah, I'm a big fan of that movie."

"That's so cool. It's my favorite holiday movie of all time."

"Maybe we'll watch it together sometime. You ready to do this?"

"Let's do it!"

I guess running around in a hot car for several hours was good for my nerves because I nailed the audition. I got into a flow and didn't come out of it until RD cut the scene.

"Nice fuckin' work, bro."

"Thanks, dude. That was fun."

"I think you could definitely be him. That was really good."

"Are you saying I'm playing Jason? Seriously?"

"Yeah, for the table reading. I can't offer you the role officially until my partner checks you out. But you're in for the table read, and if Artie—have you met Artie Glackin yet?"

"I don't know who that is."

"He's cool. If he and everyone else likes you, then yeah, bro, the role is yours."

I struggled to find words. "I'm floored right now. Thank you, RD."

———

THE FOLLOWING WEEKEND, RD invited me to a party. He wanted me and the guys to hang out and build up some chemistry before the table read.

There had to have been a hundred people crammed into a small house somewhere deep in the valley. There were famous people everywhere. Doogie Howser was in one circle, Punky Brewster was hanging in another with the daughter from *Rosanne*. RD and I made our way through the crowd toward some familiar faces.

"What's up, bro!" said Kevin Connolly as we approached.

"What's up, bro." RD pulled Kevin in for a bro-hug.

I nodded, "What's up?"

"Dale, right?"

"Good to see you again."

"Yeah, man, good to see you too."

"Yo, I just read Dale for Jason," said RD. "And he fuckin' crushed it."

Kevin looked me over and nodded, "Yeah, yeah, you'd be perfect, actually."

"We'll see," I said with a shrug. "I hope so."

"What do you mean? RD didn't offer you the role?" Kevin turned to RD. "Bro, you just said he nailed it."

Tobey Maguire chimed in. "He can't just cast him, bro. He's gotta test with all of us." Tobey smiled at me gently. "No offense. I'm sure you'll be great, but you gotta go through the process, you know? See if the chemistry is there and shit like that."

"Yeah, of course," I said.

"Have you even met Artie Glackin?" said Scott Bloom.

I shook my head. "I don't know who that is—oh wait, yes, I do. He's the other writer. We haven't met, no."

"Dale's gonna do the table read," said RD. "They'll meet then. If that goes well, then, yeah, I think we found our Jason, boys."

Kevin grabbed RD and shook him by the shoulders. "Dude, I'm so fuckin' stoked for this film."

"It's gonna be fuckin' awesome, bro—"

DiCaprio busted into the circle with, "Whatthefucksgoinon-mydudes!" in a slurry lisp.

We all laughed. Kevin and Leo embraced. Leo made the rest of his rounds before pausing on me and smiling. "Hey, what's up, bro. I'm Leo."

"Seriously?" I said, grinning.

Leo chuckled. "What?"

"We've met twice, dude. Recently. We shot hoops both times— like recently-recently."

"Oh. I think... I remember..."

"He was at Naked too, dude," said RD. "You literally hung out with him at Jerry's for multiple hours. How do you not remember him?"

"Make that three times, then," I said. "My bad."

Leo just stood there with a dumb smile, staring at me blankly.

"I'm not telling you my name again. There's no point."

He started laughing. "You're not gonna tell me your name?"

"Why? You don't need it."

"What am I supposed to call you?" he said, still laughing.

I took his hand and started shaking it cartoonishly. "Hi, Leo. I'm Bobby..."

"No, you're not."

"Bobby McGee. Pleased to meet ya!"

There were some laughs and then Kevin bailed him out.

"His name is Dale, dude."

"Dale! That's right. Dale. I'm sorry, bro. I meet a lot of people, you have no idea. I do absolutely remember you, though. We're all tied up, one game apiece."

"That's right."

"We'll play the rubber match the next time we're at Jay's." We gripped hands for another shake, but instead of letting go he pulled me in for a bro-hug. "Good to see you again, bro. I remember you now."

"Dale might be playing Jason," said Kevin.

Leo's eyes narrowed again, "Jason..."

"Last Respects, dude." Kevin laughed. "What the fuck is wrong with you tonight?"

"Oh yeah, right... Last Respects. I'm losing my mind or something."

"He's playing Jason at the table read," said RD.

"Fuck yeah, that's awesome," said Leo. "I'm looking forward to working with you, bro."

I couldn't believe my ears.

———

RD CALLED one morning and invited me to see *The Adventures of Priscilla, Queen of the Desert* with everyone at The Vista Theatre. He picked me up, and we all met up at Leo's house in Los Feliz. I was surprised that Leo lived in such a modest, albeit nice bungalow with his mother. He introduced me to his mom, Irmelin, who was very sweet. Leo's Rottweiler, Rocky, didn't seem all that interested in any of us, but he was still a good boy.

Tobey, Scott, and Kevin were already hanging in Leo's room when RD and I showed up.

Tobey jumped off the bed, "We ready?"

Leo shook his head. "Emily's on her way."

Tobey huffed. "Why, bro?"

"What do you mean, why? She wants to see Priscilla, Queen of the Desert."

"You're just leading her on."

Leo shook his head, "That's ridiculous, we're just friends."

Tobey nodded. "Tell her that, not me."

Just then, the doorbell rang.

When Leo said we were waiting for someone named Emily, I didn't know he meant Emily Foster, one of the biggest TV stars on the planet. She was part of an ensemble cast on a hit sitcom and she quickly became the standout talent on the show. Her face was all over billboards, magazines, and entertainment shows. I was a little intimidated meeting her, but she ended up being very nice. I don't know whether Leo was intentionally leading her on or not, but everyone wants someone to look at them the way Emily Foster looked at Leo the whole time we walked to the theater. She was crazy about him.

I loved *The Adventures of Priscilla, Queen of The Desert*. It's a beautifully crafted movie. We were living in such a remarkable time for film. A week after *Priscilla* we saw *Natural Born Killers* at Mann's Chinese on opening night, a little while after that, it was James Mangold's *Heavy,* and then came *Welcome to the Doll House, Leaving Las Vegas, Swingers,* all at the Sunset 5. Film after film was a mind-blowing experience, and I got to see them all in some of the best movie theaters in the country. I couldn't believe my luck.

———

THE *LAST RESPECTS* table read was held in an office building in a part of Los Angeles I hadn't been to before. The space was dull, with filing cabinets lining a windowless wall and an old couch along another. A long folding table surrounded by metal folding chairs dominated the middle of the room. A couple of the guys were already at the table—Scott and Kevin, or maybe it was Tobey and Kevin, I was too nervous to remember. I said hello and saw their lips move, but all I could hear was my heart pounding in my head.

RD approached and introduced me to his partner, Artie Glackin.

"So, you're the Jason everyone's been talking about," said Artie. He was tall and lanky, with kind eyes. He was a good five years older than the rest of the guys. I thought he looked rather tired and lonesome.

"Good to meet you, Artie," I said. "I've heard a lot about you as well."

"We're super excited you're reading today."

"Me too, man." I lied through my teeth.

RD introduced me to the important people on the couch, but I was too busy managing my anxiety to retain their names. I knew if I didn't get a hold of myself, this could turn out worse than my audition for *Clueless*.

When it was time to begin, Artie stood at the head of the table and spoke on behalf of himself and RD. He thanked the cast and the producers for coming and mentioned how excited he and RD were to have me reading the role of Jason, which just piled on the pressure. Then Artie sat down and RD opened the script and began reading the narration.

"Fade In. Over Credits. Exterior graveyard, night. We float past a row of headstones until we come to a window and move through it to..."

I don't know what happened to my brain, but suddenly, I couldn't remember anything. Not my lines, not my emotional choices. It was all gone. And it disappeared right at the exact moment I had to open my mouth and deliver my first line in the script.

"What's up, my brothers?!" The words shot out of me like hot vomit under pressure. My volume was so out of control I jump-scared myself. I noticed a grin sneak its way onto Leo's face just before his eyes dropped to avoid mine.

"This is the old Canyon Hotel," I said, attempting to sound all slick, "otherwise known as, The Place." I put too much emphasis on *the plac'* and sounded ridiculous. I was fucking terrible, no question, but the dialogue was even worse. My character rifled off useless facts about the history of the abandoned hotel and its famous patrons. I had lines like. "It was open to anyone who had the juice and the digitosis to get in." Who the fuck uses the word digitosis?

That was when I learned that raw talent was not enough to make it in Hollywood. You gotta have iron balls and a good script, and I didn't have either. An opportunity like this would have been all I needed to land an agent or manager, but instead I blew it again. Horribly. As I performed each of my lines, I could sense the others in the room shifting physically to the discomfort of my performance.

Leo finally delivered the final line in the screenplay, and it felt more like a eulogy to my dream of becoming an actor in Hollywood.

"And even though we'll be climbing those mountains without him, Jason will always live within us... and The Place... Our Place."

The two investors stood and clapped obligatorily. Their smiles were big and fake. They told lies about how much they enjoyed the script and our performances. They shook everyone's hand, and then left the room. They hadn't gotten twenty feet down the hall before we started moaning about how badly the reading had gone.

"What the fuck just happened?" said Kevin.

"That didn't go well at all," said Tobey.

Scott muttered something under his breath repeatedly that sounded like, "That was terrible," or "We were terrible," his eyes landing on me more than once.

I just sat there, quietly dying inside.

Leo put his arm around RD. "R, can I talk to you, bro?"

They walked to the corner of the room but I could still hear what they were saying.

"RD, bro, I love you. You know that. And I want to make a film with you and the rest of our friends, but I can't do this. I can't make this film, bro."

"Why?" RD said with big eyes.

"RD, come on. You know why."

"What?"

"The script is terrible, R. Nobody did well today, not even me."

"I mean, we're not done yet."

"RD, it's not even close. The dialogue is telly, and the characters need a ton of work."

"Come on, bro. We'll keep working on it..."

"You should keep developing it, bro. That's great. But I can't afford another Foot Shooting Party in my career right now."

"Fuck, bro."

"I'm sorry, R." Leo opened his arms. "Give me a hug, bro."

It was a sad embrace. RD sagged in his arms, his eyes blinking rapidly as if fighting away tears.

Everyone left but RD and Artie. I stayed back because RD was my ride.

Artie reached out his hand and I shook it. "Thanks again for reading Jason, dude." There was some pain in his smile.

"I wish it had gone better, Artie, I'm so sorry. I feel like I let you down."

"It's OK, bro. Everyone struggled with the script today for some reason." Artie turned to RD, "It's not all bad news, though. I talked to Stutman, and they're in for twenty-five grand."

"Seriously? Why the fuck would they want to invest in that shit?" RD gestured to the screenplays on the table.

"As long as they come up with the money, who cares?"

"What do you mean, bro?"

"Who cares what they think? If they give us the money, we're good to go. We'll get the script right."

RD shook his head. "No, bro. Leo's not making Last Respects."

"Did he say that? Or are you just assuming?"

"No, he said it."

"Did he say why?"

"Come on, Artie."

"It's got some kinks in it, but it's not a bad screenplay, RD."

"Yeah, well, Leo thinks it's cheesy and forced."

"It'll be fine—we'll work on it and get it right. Let's go grab something to eat and talk about it."

"I got shit to do for my mom. And I gotta take this guy all the way back to fuckin' Koreatown. I'll call you later."

· · ·

THE DRIVE back to the Pagoda was painfully quiet. I broke the silence with an apology.

"Yeah, what the fuck happened?" said RD. "How could you do so well with me and then just fuckin' suck like that?" He was smiling, but he wasn't happy.

"I don't know—my nerves, I guess." I sighed deeply. "I suck at auditions."

"Doesn't matter. Leo hates the script anyways." RD pulled up to the curb at the Pagoda and yanked on the parking brake.

"Maybe I can help. I'm a writer."

"Really?"

"Yeah. I've been writing my whole life. Short stories, poems, lyrics, all kinds of shit. I've been playing with screenwriting lately…"

"Can I read something?"

"I mean, it wasn't something that I necessarily wanted to share with anyone—it's just me kind of messing around, ya know?"

"It's a rough draft, that's cool. I just want to see if you can write."

"Yeah alright. I'll be right back."

I ran upstairs to grab my battered screenplay pages and returned as fast as I could. I handed the screenplay to RD through his window.

"You gotta flip it over," I said. "It's on the back."

He didn't. He opened the script on the right side, glanced at the title page, and looked up at me with a wry grin. "This is No Worries—are you just fucking with me?"

"No, that's a coincidence. Turn it over, it's on the back."

He turned and opened it. "You wrote it by hand?"

"I don't have a computer…"

He flipped through some pages.

"It's a slice-of-life kind of thing," I said. "Based on some people I saw at the Frolic Room."

"Are you serious?"

"I am. Is that bad?"

"No, not at all. I like it."

"It's pretty rough, but it should give you an idea of what I can do."

"Cool. I don't know if anything's even gonna happen anymore, but you never know."

"I'm so sorry, RD. I feel so fucking awful."

"It's cool, bro. It wasn't all your fault. Besides, we've all crashed and burned at some point. Wish it wasn't with my fuckin' screenplay, but it happens. We'll see you around."

———

THE NEXT MORNING, I walked into Hollywood feeling sad and defeated. There must have been something in the air making life difficult because even my telemarketing gig was a wreck. Terry was freaking out on Jim because Jim came in plastered. Apparently if we showed up drunk it was a problem, but getting wasted during our shift was perfectly fine. The confrontation must have rattled Jim's nerves because he got the shakes so bad he could barely get a cigarette to his lips.

A police helicopter flew in low over our building, and the sound of the engine bounced and rumbled between our walls and windows dramatically. It was loud and disturbing, but everyone knew it was just the cops. Everyone except for Jim. His eyes suddenly filled with terror. They had gone somewhere else entirely, where or when I couldn't possibly know, but he wasn't with us suddenly.

He dove for cover under his table, banging his head hard as he went. He yelped from the pain and shouted something incoherent. No one knew what to do, we all just sat there stunned. Jim's ordeal lasted all of two minutes before he returned to reality and began sobbing. He kept apologizing, saying he thought it was an earthquake. He wiped the wet from his face, pushed himself up from under the table, and stumbled towards the door, mumbling the whole time. I followed him outside.

"Hey, wait a second," said Terry. "Where are you going?"

"For a smoke," I said without looking back.

I walked with Jim to the stairwell. We didn't say anything as we descended the steps, but I could sense my presence was welcomed. When we got outside I gave him a twenty-dollar bill I had wadded up in my pocket. I felt like he needed something and it was all I had.

"Thanks, man. I'm gonna head home." He wiped his nose. "Get some beer."

"I'll see you tomorrow, Jim." I patted him on the back and watched him disappear into the morning crowd that swarmed the boulevard every day for t-shirts, hats, keychains, and tiny Oscars with their names engraved on them.

WHEN I GOT BACK to the Pagoda, Bill was getting ready for his shift at Tower Records. His hair was wet from his shower, and it stuck to his face and neck like thin black snakes. He was scurrying around in his boxers and T-shirt rather frantically.

"You're home," he said. "Wow."

"Yeah." I slumped onto the couch. "Shitty day."

"Are you, OK?"

"Yeah, yeah. I'm fine."

"How have you been, Dale? I haven't seen you in a while."

"Yeah, I know. We keep missing each other."

His gaze lingered on me for a moment, "I miss you, man."

"Yeah, sorry, bro. I've been hanging out with those guys quite a bit. RD and them."

He tucked his hair behind his ears. "I wouldn't have pegged them as your type... *Bro.*" He grinned and dashed into his room for a pair of jeans.

"Why?" I said.

"They're so fucking petulant." He pulled his jeans on and buttoned them up. "You're more mature than they are, don't you think?"

"Hmm. I like them. They're funny, and yeah, I guess you could say they're immature, but I think they're just uninhibited."

Bill laughed. "OK, if you say so, man." He sat on the couch and put on his shoes.

"You working eleven to five?"

He shook his head. "Ten to four. It's my last shift. I quit."

"Really? Wow. That's a big deal. Why? What happened?"

"My boss pulled some bullshit and fired a guy because he forgot to bag a couple of videos for Whoopi Goldberg. She dropped like two grand on like eighty videos, and he missed bagging two of them. It was so nothing. But she was pissed because she had to come all the way back to the store to pick them up. She complained, and my boss fired him."

"You witnessed this?"

"I saw the whole thing."

"What a fucking bitch!"

"Why is she the bitch? She's entitled to the things she paid for, and she's entitled to be pissed off if someone fucks up. She didn't ask for anyone to be fired—she didn't even ask for the manager. He just overheard her, and after she left, he fired him."

"What a fucking asshole."

Bill laughed. "Exactly. If it were anyone other than a celebrity, James would have gotten a warning at most. So, I'm not going to wait around for that to happen to me."

"Wow, when did all this go down?"

"Two weeks ago."

"I'm surprised you didn't say something sooner."

Bill laughed. "What do you mean? You're never around, Dale. Between you and Jeremy, I basically live alone now."

"What are you going to do?"

"I got a job at Starbucks."

"Really?"

"I'm so excited! I've always wanted to be a barista."

"Like, since birth, or..." I grinned.

"Very funny."

"That's awesome, congrats."

He glanced at the wall clock. "I'm going to be late, I gotta go.

Oh, and um, RD left a message. I thought it was for me, so I listened to it accidentally. Sorry about that."

"You're good."

"I'll see you..." he shrugged, "Whenever I guess."

"Yeah, I'll see you later, Bill."

We hugged awkwardly and Bill sashayed out the door.

RD's message was encouraging. He wanted to discuss my screenplay but didn't want to get into the details over the phone. He wanted to talk in person, which could only mean one thing, he wanted me to run the breakdowns with him again.

BEFORE I CLICKED MY SEATBELT, RD asked if I was cool with making a few deliveries for his mom.

"Of course, bro."

"Awesome. I love delivering breakdowns for my mom, don't you?" He punched the steering wheel. "It's so much fucking fun!"

After a sharp left-hand turn, we headed west on Beverly Boulevard.

"So, yeah, dude, I read your handwritten script." RD chuckled, "Your handwriting is kind of awful, bro." He darted to another lane, then hammered the gas to narrowly make a yellow light. "It looked like it was written by like three different people." He chuckled again.

I clenched the door grip tightly, bracing for an accident. "I wasn't planning on anyone reading it."

"It's cool. It's a first draft so it's all over the place... but you can definitely turn a story, bro."

"Thanks!"

"I read some to Artie and a few of the guys, and they liked it too."

"Wow, that's unexpected."

"No one went crazy for it or anything," he said, slapping me back down a couple of pegs, "but everyone thought it was good."

"Well, I'm flattered."

RD shifted the car into fourth gear. He was speeding like a

motherfucker. "Yeah, so, if you're down for writing with me and Artie, we're down to work with you."

I didn't respond immediately. I was a little stunned by the news and terrified of RD's driving at the same time.

RD shrugged, "If you don't want to, that's cool."

"No, I do! I absolutely—yes."

RD hit the brakes hard in order to barely make a red light. I had to grip the handle even tighter to being tossed into the windshield.

"There's no money in the budget for anyone, though, not even Leo."

"That's cool."

"It's all going to gear and shit like that, but if everything works out, you'll have a credit in the main titles along with me and Artie and, you know, you'll have a writing credit with an Oscar nominated actor, which is pretty fuckin' cool."

"That's incredible."

He shrugged, "It could be, or it could be nothing. But if we got into something like Sundance or something like that... boom, dude. Do you know what that would do for you?"

"I don't—I've never heard of Sundance."

His eyes popped wide. "Life fucking changing, dude."

I smiled big. "I'm ready for that."

"We gotta make something good, though."

"It's all I've ever wanted to do with my life, RD."

"Let's fucking do this!" He smacked his steering wheel hard, shifted back into first gear, and took off from the green light with chirping tires. "Let's make fuckin' films, bro!"

———

THE THREE OF us wrote together three to five nights a week for months. Most of the time, we worked up at Artie's lovely place off Beachwood Canyon. It was difficult at first. Artie clung to a lot of the writing I thought needed to be reworked or cut, especially the "telly" unrealistic dialogue. Artie had good ideas, but he clung to his bad ones like something in his life depended on them. I'd remind him about Leo's notes, but he'd still dig in. RD was a good mediator. He presided over our differences and faithfully cast tie-breaking votes. I loved every minute of our time together, every argument, every quip, and every tiny triumph. Through it all, we became better writers and closer friends.

Artie scheduled a tour of an abandoned hotel in downtown San Diego called the El Cortez. It was the perfect location for *Last Respects*, thirty stories high and abandoned to decay in the elements for years. There were feral cats and who knows what else lurking in dark corners. The walls were busted, beams were exposed, cracked toilets and sinks littered the bathrooms, the beds were broken and filthy. There were some rooms that looked recently occupied by someone, which only thickened the tension. The air glittered in slices of golden sunlight. I pulled my shirt up over my nose and mouth for a makeshift mask, but I could still taste whatever filth was floating all around us. The El Cortez was creepy, dirty, and dangerous—and I loved every inch of it.

———

LIFE at my telemarketing gig became painfully mundane. Terry chewed me out constantly for missing work and not calling. I apologized and told him I'd try not to let it happen again. Then I'd get on the phone and make us some money, and he'd be happy again. Working for Terry had become challenging, mentally and logistically. I was leading a double life. Broke-ass telemarketer by day, fledgling filmmaker by night, and it was wearing on my sanity.

———

RD and I caught the matinée screening of *Basketball Diaries* on opening day, and then went straight over to Leo's house to shower him in praise.

"What did you think?" Leo's eyes were bouncing from RD's to mine.

"Dude." RD ginned and nodded. "Dude."

"Did you like it or not, RD?"

"Dude."

"Fuck you, RD." Leo led us into his house.

"I'm just fuckin' with you, bro. You're fuckin' amazing."

Leo grinned. "Are you being serious?"

"Yes. You're incredible in Basketball Diaries."

"Did you actually do the drugs?" I said.

We entered Leo's room and Scott Bloom was there, reclined on Leo's bed with his legs crossed.

Leo shook his head. "No. Never."

"What's up, fellas?" said Scott.

I nodded to Scott, and asked Leo another question. "How the fuck did you do that?"

"I spent a lot of time with Jim Carroll."

I nodded. "Very fucking impressive, man."

"Thank you. So how many people were in your theater?"

I hissed. "Three."

"Fuck. Three total, or three plus you guys?"

"Three total."

"Oh, no, that's so terrible."

RD waved it off. "It was the one-forty-five. What do you expect?"

Leo sighed. "No, bro, that's not good."

"The movie is good," I said. "You're fucking great in it. It's gonna do fine."

"I hope you're right, bro."

I was wrong. *Basketball Diaries* totally bombed in the theaters, and Leo's career seemed deeply rutted in low-performing arthouse films.

———

I WAS SPENDING a lot of time at RD's condo in Studio City, so I inadvertently hung out with many of his mother Edie Robb's clients. Edie Robb, in my opinion, was not great at managing careers, but she did have a remarkable eye for talent. I got to know and really like Seth Green, whom Edie had represented since he was a kid. He was around a lot because Edie repped him of course, but also because his sister rented the open room in RD's condo. Seth and I got into some great conversations that made me appreciate him and his points of view.

One afternoon, Seth and I were sitting around the condo talking while RD was at an audition or something, and at one point in our conversation I made the mistake of calling him "bro." His nostrils flared and told me sternly to never, ever, call him that word again. I didn't mean to laugh, but it was silly to me.

"Sorry, I had no idea. What's wrong with 'bro'?"

"It's fucking ridiculous. You guys sound so stupid. You don't hear it? RD got mad at his dishwasher for whatever reason and, after he kicked it, called it bro. Don't call me the same thing you call your busted dishwasher."

"That's funny. It just rubs off, you know?"

"I'm kind of surprised you hang out with those guys."

"Oh, yeah, why is that?"

"You don't seem like their type."

I chuckled. "What type is that?"

He didn't answer, he just grinned and continued, "You should do yourself a favor and cut them loose."

"Who? RD?"

"Leo and Tobey, mainly."

"Why do you say that?"

"I think it's fairly obvious they don't respect much of anything, or anyone."

I couldn't understand why Seth would say such things. I had been all over town with those guys—restaurants, bars, house parties, theaters, and never once did I witness anything I would call disrespectful to people or property. "Thanks for the advice, Seth. I appreciate it. And I'm sorry I called you 'bro,' I'll try not to do it again."

He grinned. "Thanks, Dale, I appreciate that."

INSTEAD OF DISTANCING myself from those guys, I began spending more and more time with them at RD's condo. I'd crash on RD's couch for as many as two or three nights in a row before heading back to Koreatown for a change of clothes. There were nights when it felt uncomfortable staying there, but sometimes we'd go so late that getting back over the hill was impossible.

"Yo," said RD, pulling me out of a light sleep.

"Hey, bro." I cleared my throat as my eyes found their focus on RD descending the stairs. "Good morning."

"It's almost eleven."

I bolted upright. "Oh shit. I missed work again. I'm gonna lose my job. Fuck."

"You should just move in already. You're always here—"

"Yeah, I'm sorry, RD. It was late and you already crashed. I thought it would be cool if I hit the couch—"

"It's totally fine. I'm being serious, you should just live here. Kaela's moving out, you can take her room."

"As embarrassing as it is to say, I probably can't afford it. I don't even know if I still have a job."

"We can work that shit out. Besides, we're making this fuckin' movie and that's gonna take months. This way, I won't have to pick you up and drop you off every day."

"What's the rent?"

"I don't know. Can you afford three hundred a month?"

"Yeah, if I still have a job."

"Cool, bro. Move in at the end of the month."

I HAD MIXED feelings about moving out of the Pagoda. Bill was a good roommate but, truth be told, I don't know that he cared about me all that much. We were good to one another, but we didn't hang out and we didn't have a lot in common. Still, I felt some sadness when we said goodbye. Maybe I knew somehow that I would never see him again.

. . .

MOVING into RD's condo was as easy as walking through the door with my backpack over my shoulder. I trampled up the stairs into my new, fully furnished bedroom, dropped my backpack in the corner for the first of a thousand times, and sat on the bed to take it all in. Life was happening so fast. I had a job, a place to live, and a movie in development, and I had been in town for less than a year.

SINCE EDIE RAN her management company out of the condo the place was nicknamed "The Office." Kevin Connolly first gave it that nickname back when he roomed with RD a couple of years earlier and the condo had become the central hub to their group of friends. The Office was the place to hang out all day, and it was also the starting point of most nights out. Between our friends and Edie's clients, we were never alone in that condo. My place of residence was, in effect, a social club. I met tons of people there, and a few became good friends, like Ethan Suplee. Blake and Ethan were working together on *Boy Meets World* when Blake started bringing Ethan around. Ethan started coming over on his own and before long, barely a day would go by when Ethan wasn't hanging at the condo with us.

———

RD and I had gotten stuck in traffic delivering the breakdowns for his mother, so we were late for the table read of Last Respects.

I knocked on Leo's door. Leo greeted us with a scowl. "Where the fuck have you been?"

"We're a few minutes late," said RD. "Fuckin' relax."

We followed Leo inside his house.

"You're thirty minutes late, and it takes forever to get this shit started. Where's Artie Glackin?"

"I have no idea," said RD. "But we can't start without him, he's got the scripts."

David Stutman, one of the investors from the first table read, cut into the conversation. "I offered to pick up the scripts, but Artie said no."

RD shrugged. "We gotta wait for him anyway. He's the co-director."

Leo sighed. "When he gets here, we need to start right away. No fucking around. I got other shit to do tonight."

Something was off with Leo. He was abnormally tense. "Yo, Dale," he said. "What's this shit I hear about you doing actual heroin to research your character?"

"Who told you that?" I glanced over at Scott Bloom. We had hung out a while back, and he suggested I do a little heroin research. He questioned how I could accurately write a character like Jason (who dies from an overdose) without knowing what it really felt like to be on the drug. He called it willful ignorance. It made sense to me, so one afternoon he and I drove downtown and bought a $20 balloon and got totally fucked up in his house in the hills. Scott was right. Heroin was unlike anything I could have imagined. It was the most beautiful feeling I had ever experienced, and that's what made it the most terrifying drug I had ever used. "Yeah," I said, faking nonchalance. "I did."

"That's a little nutty, don't you think?"

"Stupid, if you ask me," said Tobey.

"I did it responsibly."

Tobey scoffed and Leo laughed. "That's fucking hilarious," said Leo. "Hey, come over tonight and let's shoot up some heroin—responsibly."

"I didn't shoot it up, I smoked it, which *is* more responsible. And you know what, bro? It was so fuckin' amazing and beautiful." I flashed my eyes dramatically at him. "It was the best thing I ever felt in my life."

He shrugged. "Suit yourself, bro. But I wouldn't do that shit for fuckin' Spielberg—know what I'm sayin'?"

"Yeah, well, you don't have to, you're the prodigal actor. The rest of us have to dig a little deeper."

"No film is worth risking your life for, bro. Especially not this one."

"*Especially?* Oh, wow."

"That's not what I meant. You're not even getting paid, so why take huge risks like that?" He sighed, "God, where the fuck is Artie Glackin?!"

And right on cue came a knock at the door and the arrival of Arthur Glackin.

"Bro! Where the fuck have you been, bro?" said Leo.

"Yeah, I know. I'm so sorry." Artie stepped inside the house carrying a small box of scripts. "My car broke down on Los Feliz. I was stranded on the side of the road for like forty-five minutes."

"Where's your car now?" said Kevin.

"Outside. Everything's fine. I got a boost from Triple A. I guess the battery died when I went in to pick up the scripts for tonight." He held up the box of screenplays.

"I'm glad everything is OK with your car," said Leo. "Let's get started, please. Or we'll be here all night."

The cast was scattered throughout the living room, a few on the couch, others on chairs and on the floor with their backs against the wall. There were also a couple of Leo's friends who were there to party with him afterwards.

Artie stood up and thanked everyone for coming and participating. He also thanked Leo and Leo's mom for hosting. Then he took a seat and the reading finally began.

Leo's performance and his attitude went to complete shit inside the first five minutes, and it spread like wildfire through the rest of the cast. Scott Bloom and Kevin Connolly became especially brutal, delivering their lines with utter contempt. What surprised me was their cruelty. They openly mocked and laughed at our work. I could have lived with falling short as a writer, but having our effort treated that way was painful and demeaning.

When the reading ended, Leo didn't waste any time making

his feelings known. "I'm sorry guys, but it's just not there. I can't commit to this film."

"Why the fuck did you have to mock it, though?" I said sharply. "In front of everyone."

"There's no nice way to do this, guys. I'm sorry."

"Whatever, bro." I waved him off. He didn't answer my question and I didn't really care.

"Maybe we were a little harsh," said Kevin. "But the script just isn't there yet. It improved a lot in my opinion, but it's still not ready for prime time, and I think you guys probably know that."

"You guys just have to get better at writing," said Scott. "It's as simple as that."

David Stutman huddled up with RD and whispered something in his ear. Then he approached Leo, and they went into Leo's bedroom and closed the door.

I slumped in my seat next to Artie and sighed.

"Don't let it bother you," he said. "Let's stay focused and get back to work on the script."

"Leo's not going to do this movie, Artie."

"Yes, he will. Don't worry."

"Dude, he just took a giant shit all over it. Come on."

David and Leo emerged from Leo's room. David was nodding and grinning as he approached RD. RD looked surprised to hear whatever it was David was so happy about. RD walked over to Artie and me and told us that David had just pitched Leo a totally different project.

Artie was instantly livid. "What the fuck, RD? Are you serious?"

"Calm down, it's cool, bro."

"No, it's not fucking cool, RD. We already told him no to that."

"Listen, Artie. Calm the fuck down and listen before you react."

Artie pressed his lips closed, but I could see the screaming going on behind his eyes.

"I told him it was cool."

Artie's jaw dropped. "Why would you do that?"

"Because bro, I want to make a film with our friends, and Last Respects ain't it. Leo likes David's idea. Stuts is gonna pitch it to the rest of the guys. Please, just come into Leo's room and listen. Maybe it's cool."

"No, bro. We already turned that crap down months ago."

"Come on, Artie. Don't be stupid."

"Nah, I'm out. You can tell me about it later if you want."

Artie gave me a sullen hug goodbye. "I think you should stay," I said. "See how it plays out."

"Nah."

"Maybe this is hasty, Artie."

He nodded. "Maybe. Will you grab all the scripts? I gotta get outta here."

I shrugged. "Yeah, I guess."

Artie walked away.

RD shook his head. "He's fuckin' crazy."

"I don't blame him," I said. "Is this David's ten-page thing you made me read? Saturday whatever-whatever?"

"Yes."

"Come on, RD. There was nothing there. It was just a bunch of shitty, forced dialogue."

"That's the thing, bro. We get to improvise most of it. And we'll write it. You, me, and Artie..."

I glanced across the room and saw Artie at the front door talking to Scott.

"RD, we just spent months and months writing and every one of them just shit all over it. Why would I put myself through that again?"

"Bro, think about it—improv. Mike Leigh! We get to do the Mike Leigh thing we talked about."

"No screenplay at all?"

"Partially..."

I shook my head. "It's not going to happen, dude. Leo's got Marvin's Room in what? Two, three months? The script needs to be ready to shoot right now, bro. There's no time to write even part of a screenplay."

"I just said we're not going to write another script, bro."

"That's not what you said—" I looked back at Artie as he made his way to us. "You staying?"

Artie nodded. "I'll hang for a few minutes, see what's up."

"Good. I'm glad."

"I'm still not happy about any of this."

The three of us joined the others in Leo's room and listened to David's pitch. The guys were responsive, asking questions and exploring possibilities. They all seemed pretty energized by the new concept. There was an air of restrained excitement between them, as if one was afraid of revealing more enthusiasm than another.

"I hate the name," said Leo. "The Saturday Night Club sounds ridiculous to me."

"Like a Breakfast Club copy," said Scott.

"We can change the name," said David like a salesman.

"So, what are we talkin'? Fifty, twenty-five percent improvised, or what?" Kevin raised his eyebrows. "Or is it all improvised?"

David shrugged. "Not all of it, no. Half, maybe."

I rolled my eyes.

"Well, I, personally, love the idea of doing improv," said Kevin.

Scott nodded. "It could be interesting."

Kevin continued, "I mean let's be real here, it could end up a fucking disaster, but as an actor, bro? This shit sounds like the most fun to me, hands down."

Tobey leaned forward. "So, we're sitting around a diner improvising and then you guys are going to just randomly intercut that footage with real documentary footage?"

"Not random footage, it'll be for a reason" said David, beaming. "Pretty cool, right?"

Tobey grinned. "It could be."

"So, are we talking about social issues, or personal shit?" said Scott. "Like, what are we, as the characters, talking about exactly?"

David fidgeted like a little boy that needed to piss. "Well, right now in the script they talk about AIDS, so you guys would improv about AIDS, obviously. And then we would, you know, insert the documentary footage... but we cover whatever we want; personal stuff, gay stuff, drugs, family issues. We would work all that out."

"Gay stuff," RD clomped his teeth together twice. "Why don't we do this—me, Dale, Artie, and Stuts will hang out and figure out a shooting plan and put together a loose script we can work from. We can meet up in a week or whatever and show you guys what we came up with. If everyone is down after that, we'll make the fucking movie."

Leo clapped his hands together. "Yes, RD, that's perfect! Can I get the fuck out of here now, please? I got people waiting for me outside the Viper Room."

11

THE SATURDAY NIGHT Club seemed like a giant waste of time to me. We weren't going to write a script of any length in a few weeks, not one Leo would approve. David's pages were underdeveloped. There was no discernible dramatic structure or direction. The characters were flat, and the humor was contrived. About the only thing that was interesting to me was the idea of a bunch of friends pulling an all-nighter at a diner. I felt like that had a ton of potential. But it didn't matter because we still didn't have enough time to develop it. RD seemed focused on the opportunity rather than what was realistic. I called him out on Leo being the only reason he wanted to make David's film in the first place and it pissed him off.

"No, bro," he said. "You're totally fucking wrong about that. Of course I want to make a movie with Leo, everyone in Hollywood wants to work with the kid, but I want to work with the rest of the guys just as much. It's about all of us, not just Leo, bro. Leo's a big part of it. Obviously. But he's no bigger than any one of those guys. If we lost Kevin, Scott, or Tobey, the whole thing would fall apart."

"Well, you're going to lose Leo if we have to write a screenplay. He's going to have issues with whatever we come up with. Everyone else will want to give notes, too."

"Especially Tobey."

"Yeah, and the next thing you know we're writing for the next year or longer. Nothing will get made."

"I mean, you make a great point."

"Mike Leigh doesn't work from a script at all, RD."

RD sighed. "What if they don't go for it, though?"

"Then it's dead... We're not going to write a script in time anyway, so it doesn't matter."

He nodded thoughtfully. "Let's run it past Stuts and Artie."

David resisted going full improv at first, but he came around pretty quickly after I explained that the project would likely be sunk by notes and rewrites and never get made. Artie Glackin was still hurt over *Last Respects* and had grown so bitter with David that he was willing to throw the whole opportunity away on principle alone. I agreed that David shouldn't have pitched his idea, but he did, and maybe it wasn't such a bad thing in the end because the guys were excited about it. The only person Artie would be punishing by passing on the movie would be himself. He said he'd rather not make any film at all than make one that started with a betrayal, so Artie Glackin officially removed himself from the project.

Scott Bloom was renting a mid-century modern bungalow up in the Hollywood Hills with his brother, Brian. We all gathered in their backyard to discuss the new project. The news about Artie didn't seem to bother anyone.

"Wait, so explain this some more," said Leo. "We do our improvs or whatever, and then you guys are going to go out and shoot documentary footage, is that right? How is that gonna work?"

"I feel like I'm repeating myself," said David.

Kevin nodded, "It is getting a little repetitive."

Leo shrugged and took a hit of his cigarette. "I'm sorry, I'm just trying to picture this thing in my head—"

"It's fine, you're good," said David. "If we have to shoot some doc stuff, we will... but we can also license footage."

"You'll probably do both, I would imagine." said Kevin.

I interrupted. "It's improv, so we don't really know what's going to happen. We're gonna write arcs for each character that are affected one way or another by each other and by the issues we take on—and how or what documentary footage we use is up in the air. We just don't know yet."

"We don't know if we'll use it at all," said RD.

"Exactly," I said. "That's what makes this so fun."

RD shook his head, "Don't get me wrong, I love the idea of mixing in the documentary stuff. Wheats and I were talking about shooting you guys in black and white—you know how in documentaries, it's usually the archival stuff that's black and white and all the present-day shit is in color? We want to do the opposite. Shoot you guys in black and white and then have the real-life shit in color. What do you think of that?"

"I think that sounds fuckin' dope," said Kevin.

"That does sound pretty cool," said Leo.

"And the soundtrack could be so fucking good," I said.

"Yeah, if you mixed the eras," said Scott, "and blend the genres together. That could be fun."

A big smile broke out on Tobey's face. He looked like he was about to say something.

"What?" RD asked Tobey.

"Nothing. Go ahead, I'm sorry."

Leo waved Tobey off. "Yeah, finish what you're saying."

I continued. "I'm saying, what's so fucking cool about this—about working experimentally like this, is that we get to do whatever the fuck we want. It could end up being Naked meets Koyaanisqatsi, or fuckin' Hoop Dreams meets Fresh." I chuckled. "We don't know..."

"Or it could end up being nothing at all," said Scott.

I shrugged, "I mean, sure. I hope that doesn't happen, but anything is possible."

Tobey's smile grew larger.

"Why are you smiling like that, bro?" said RD, "You're creepin' me out."

"Like what?"

"Like you wanna fucking say something..."

"No, I don't. It's just good to see everyone so passionate about this, that's all."

Scott leaned back in his chair, grinning. "Yeah, it all sounds very intriguing. I gotta admit it."

Leo sat hunched over, his eyes distant in thought.

Kevin said, "I personally love it. I really do. Where would it play?" He flared his eyebrows. "Sundance, maybe?"

"Who knows?" said David. "Maybe."

"I mean, I would love to see it at Sundance," said RD.

Tobey chuckled and shook his head. "You're out of your fuckin minds. You don't even know what you're doing yet."

"No, you're right, Tobey." said RD. "We have no idea what's going to happen. We got a lot of work to do."

"Just maybe reel in your expectations a little bit." Tobey chuckled again. "What about the writing? How's that going to work since it's all improv?"

Leo interrupted, "So, wait, RD, are you directing by yourself?"

RD shrugged, "Yeah, I guess—"

"Nice." Leo teased, "A Film by RD Robb... an RD Robb film."

Kevin chortled, "A RD... is it a or an?"

"It's an a," mused Scott.

"Saturday Night Club, A RD Robb joint."

"Stop it, bro. Please." RD said sheepishly.

"It sounds pretty good actually," said Leo.

"Don't be absurd," muttered RD.

"How are you guys writing this fucking thing?" snapped Tobey.

I sighed. "I just said we'll put together the characters and their arcs, and then we'll get together with you guys and start refining it as a group through rehearsals..."

"Thank you, Dale. That's all I wanted to know. That's the first I heard we were going to be involved."

RD chuckled. "What do you mean, bro? It's your fuckin' character! You're in the movie."

"It's common sense," said Scott.

"I wanted to hear it from you guys. Is that a problem?"

"What about the chicks?" said Kevin. "What are you doing about them?"

"We'll do a breakdown for sure," said RD.

"Can we recommend some people? Or..."

"Yeah, absolutely."

"But don't just hire a bunch of girls you want to bone," said Tobey. "Get real talent in here. Take it seriously."

"Of course, bro," said RD.

Leo perked up. "So, what do you guys want to do? This is all very interesting, I think... So much better than Last Respects."

"I like it," said Scott. "I'm definitely down if everyone else is."

"I think, done right, this could be absolutely genius," said Kevin. "I one-hundred-percent think we should do this movie. Absolutely yes for me." He smiled at Leo. "Are we going to do this thing or not, bro? It's obviously up to you."

Leo nodded slightly, his eyes scanning ours. "It's up to all of us, bro." He turned to Tobey. "What about you? What do you think?"

Tobey shrugged. "I'm down if you are, bro. The experimental aspects are interesting to me."

Leo paused for another moment, his head still nodding. "Yeah, OK, I'm in–I'll make this fuckin' movie with you guys."

I'm pretty sure my heart stopped right there. *Did Leonardo DiCaprio just commit to doing a movie that I'm going to write?*

"You guys gotta promise me you won't fuck it up," said Leo. "Pleasepleasepleaseplease don't fuck this up. My agents will kill me."

"It's gonna be great." I said.

"We're really doin' it this time?" said Kevin. "No bullshit?"

"Yeah, bro," said Leo. "It sounds cool."

Kevin rubbed his hands together. "Holy shit, I can't believe it. We're making The Saturday Night Club!"

"We gotta change the name," said Leo. "I can't be in a film called Saturday Night Club."

"Yeah, yeah, it's terrible. It's gotta go," said RD.

"I like the name," muttered David.

I WANDERED ALONE through the streets of Hollywood with a head full of dreams. I needed to understand the film from my perspective. I was going to be working with a lot of people with strong creative ideas, and so I needed to know what this film meant to me.

I started thinking about the conflict between my dad's generation and mine. My father and his friends were obsessed with degrading us. They called us things like lazy, incompetent, and ignorant all the time. My dad would insult and berate me with bullshit like, "You'd fuck up the Lord's Prayer if it wasn't written down for you." He was right, I would, but it had nothing to do with my memory, I just didn't have any use for it. My dad had an arsenal of these pointless sayings, all meant to label us as a bunch of fuck-ups, while conveniently forgetting his own youth and the stupid shit he did when he didn't know any better.

My dad was a greaser in the 1950s and early '60s. At one point, he even got busted for joyriding, which was just cute slang for auto-theft. These geniuses would steal a car just to go cruising around town, hitting on girls, and doing stupid tricks like burning out tires. I wondered what his dad would have thought about him, had he stuck around long enough to raise him. Would he have called him out for his mistakes, or would he believe that his bad behavior was a symptom of an entire hopeless, doomed generation?

Maybe it was a lofty idea, but I wondered if our film could address some of the generational animosity in people like my father. I wanted to make something that pushed against that tension in a meaningful way.

After a few miles ambling along the boulevard, I found myself outside the Laemmle Sunset 5 cinemas just as the sun dipped below the horizon and turned everything to gold. I called RD from a pay phone and invited him to an 8:30 screening of *Il Postino*.

PART II

12

DAVID STUTMAN GREETED us at the door of his little blue bungalow in Venice Beach, absolutely brimming with excitement. "I got the money!" He blurted before even inviting us inside. RD frowned and left his high-five hanging. "It's real, I swear," said David before dropping his arm back to his side, un-fived.

"Oh yeah? How much?" said RD.

David shrugged and opened the door to let us inside, where we were greeted by a wriggling pit bull. "That's Sara," he said proudly. "She won't bite, she's a sweetheart."

I got down on one knee and gave her a good scratch.

RD repeated his question. "How much money, David?"

"I'm not sure yet, at least twenty-five grand."

Sara nosed my hand up to her crown and I mussed the top between her floppy ears.

"See? You don't have the money," said RD.

"Yes, I do..."

Sara started licking my hand.

"Dale, if you don't stop her now, she'll lick every inch of you."

"You have the money—you don't have the money. Which is it?" said RD.

"I don't have the money, but it's a done deal. Trust me. He just needs to see the contracts."

RD tossed up his arms. "See what I mean, bro? Leo's not going to sign a contract without getting his agents involved—and it's CAA, so they will one-hundred percent become a giant pain in the dick." RD shook his head, "It's not a done deal at all."

"Well, I can't get the money without something in writing. They're not just going to take my word that Leonardo DiCaprio is gonna show up when we say he will. They need proof."

"I'm telling you if we put something in front of him that's all legal and shit, he's going to take it to his agents. He doesn't understand that shit, bro. Neither do I."

"And I doubt his agents will let him do it at all." I said. Sara leaned heavily against my leg. "The first thing they're going to do is ask for the screenplay."

"Exactly," said RD. "Keep CAA out of it, bro. Trust me."

"I need something. It doesn't have to be a big, long contract, just something that says that he agrees to be in it."

"Something like, 'I, Leo DiCaprio, the greatest actor of all time, agree to appear in the film Saturday Night Club?'" said RD.

"Yeah, pretty much. But with the shooting dates."

"I thought you were talking like a real contract. He'll probably sign something like that."

"Then we're good," said David.

"By the way," I said. "I've been thinking we should replace Artie Glackin."

"Why? With who?" RD got flustered. "I'm not going to direct with someone I don't know."

"Not for directing, you're the director. Someone to write with us."

"Who?" said RD. "Why?"

"I think we need a girl. Last Respects was all about dudes, this thing has like three or four chicks in lead roles and I think if we had a chick involved it would be a good thing."

RD shook his head. "Too bad Artie didn't stick around."

"Artie's not a chick," I said.

"No, but he's a fuckin' pussy. What about Bethany Ashton?"

I laughed, "Bethany would be great."

"Who's she?" said David.

"You met her, bro—Hot brunette. Bethany Ashton."

David shook his head. "I have no idea who you're talking about, RD."

RD nodded. "Yeah, you do. Hot brunette, bro."

David giggled. "Still no clue."

"Doesn't matter, she's cool, and she's a good writer. She's shopping a feature around now, and it's getting decent traction."

"I need to meet her first," said David.

"Why?" said RD.

"You guys know her, I don't."

"You're not gonna get to know her in one meeting. Read her script."

"I will, RD, but I want to meet her. What's the problem?"

"How about we ask her to sit in on a writing session?" I suggested. "Audition her, so to speak."

"Yeah, sure," said David. "That works."

———

RD's OFFICE PHONE RANG. He stomped over to the phone and snatched the receiver from the cradle. "Talent Works!... No, mom, I haven't delivered the fuckin' breakdowns yet—because I'm in the middle of a writing session right now... I'll do them when I'm finished... I'll do them when I'm finished. Did you hear me? Mom!" He listened a moment, seething mad. "Mom, stop fucking calling here, or I swear—I don't give a fuck about your shitty clients... Yes, they are shitty—you have like three good clients, the rest are fuckin' hacks... Yeah, well, I don't care. Hire a fucking service then, I can't deliver them until later." He sighed heavily. "Mom, I gotta go, I'm directing a DiCaprio movie, I'm a little busy right now. Goodbye." RD slammed the receiver back in its cradle and rejoined David and me at the table. "Sorry about that. My mom's such a pain in the ass."

"All good, bro," I said. "Let's figure out who's playing who here."

"Should we write this shit down?" RD walked back to the desk and grabbed a legal pad.

"Let me see the script, David."

David picked up the script from the dining room table and his finger left a streak of something white and greasy on the glass.

"That's disgusting, bro." RD darted into the nearby kitchen for a damp rag and rubbed away David's mess.

"I just had lunch—that's probably just mayo."

"Probably?" I said.

RD shuddered. "Gross."

I took a deep, resetting breath. "Let's do this. Which character is the lead?"

David recomposed himself. "It's an ensemble—"

"No, I mean, who is the leader of the group?"

"Der."

"Der?" I smirked.

"Yeah. Yup." David smiled back.

"Why Der? I'm curious."

"He's the leader—I don't know. He just is…"

"No, no, my bad. I mean, why did you name him Der?"

"Oh. I don't know. Because I like the name. What's wrong with it?"

"It's… unusual. A little goofy, maybe."

"Why?"

"I mean…it's Der. Say it again."

"Der."

"See?" I chuckled. "That's funny."

"Whatever, bro," said RD. "Let's move on, we can talk about his stupid name later."

"His name is not stupid." said David.

RD scoffed. "Der is the dumbest name ever, bro. It's not even a real name."

"Yes, it is. I got it from an actor."

"He's an actor, he can make up whatever name he wants. He could have called himself, Shitfuckforbrains O'Brien…"

I chuckled, "OK, OK, Leo is playing Der."

RD spat out some water. I laughed, I tried not to, but I did.

"What is so funny?" said David.

"Nothing. Leo's gonna love it," said RD. "Leonardo DiCaprio is..."

"Der!" I said, my grin brimming with laughter.

"Let's keep going," said David.

I shifted uncomfortably, trying my best not to burst. "Who is Der really? What's his last name?"

David sat up. "I don't know, maybe Der..."

I pounced. "Der Der?"

That was the melon that broke the monkey's back, the drop that overflowed the barrel, it was the last swallow of booze before the black-out. We laughed so hard tears sprung from our eyes.

"That's not what I meant. Stop laughing, or I swear, you guys, I'll fucking leave right now."

"OK, I'm sorry, I couldn't resist." I wiped my eyes and took a deep breath. "Whew!"

RD regained control for a moment before succumbing to a second round of the giggles. That set me off again, and there we were squealing and wheezing again, both of our faces wet with fresh tears.

"Are you guys being fucking serious right now?"

"OK, let's go. Let's keep going," RD wiped his eyes. "I'm ready. I'm sorry, David. It's Dale." He turned to me. "Stop."

"It's you, bro, you gotta stop," I said through small aftershocks.

"Never mind us, Stuts," said RD. "Just keep going."

"I don't have a last name for him or any of the characters."

"OK, fine," I said. "What about his big thing, his big life altering event?"

"We never got that far."

"Let's start there, then."

The doorbell rang.

"That's Bethany." RD jumped up and scooted down the split-level stairs.

Moments later, he and Bethany were back at the table. I stood and welcomed her with a hug.

She looked at me and RD more closely. "Have you guys been crying?"

"No. Yeah. Well, we were, but not from sadness..." RD sat back in his chair and grinned.

"They were laughing at my writing," said David.

Bethany frowned, "Oh no, that's terrible!"

"I'm David, by the way."

"I'm Bethany, nice to meet you."

"We were not making fun of your writing," said RD, before turning his attention back to Bethany. "One of his characters has a funny name, and we laughed at it. Nothing more." He shook his head at David. "Don't be such a pussy."

"Whatever, RD." David asked Bethany if she had a chance to read the script.

"I didn't know there was one." She turned to RD. "I thought you said it was all improv."

"It is. The script is like ten pages, we're not—"

"Twenty," said David.

RD waved David off, "Who cares. We're not using the script at all. We're using the characters and the scenario. We're basically starting from scratch."

"We've got a lot to do," I said. "There are eight characters in the ensemble and a bunch of supporting roles. It's a lot."

"Well, I hope I can help," said Bethany.

"Jump in if you have ideas, or whatever." I grabbed my notepad. "Right now, we're deciding on who's right for what role. We've decided on the first one, Leo is playing a guy called Der."

A grin opened on her face.

"Yeah," I said, acknowledging her reaction.

"Cute name." Her smile widened and it almost sent me overboard.

David perked up in his seat, blissfully unaware Bethany was being facetious.

"Do you know the basic idea behind everything?" I said.

She nodded, "A bunch of friends hang out at a diner, which I'm assuming leads to some deep, heady conversation and maybe a little debauchery..."

I grinned. "That's pretty much it."

"I love it."

"So we're starting with Der. He's the leader of the group, or the center of attention, at least. We're working on what his big life altering moment was—something from his past, obviously."

"Does it have to be dramatic?" said Bethany.

I nodded. "I'm thinking something major... like a death, maybe."

She nodded. "I like a death in the family—it's universally relatable."

RD sat up. "I agree. Maybe a girlfriend, or a parent."

I remembered this after-school special on suicide that really hit me hard as a kid. One of the characters killed himself on screen by running his dad's car in the garage. When his parents found him it was such chaos. I kept staring at the kid's blue lips, terrified and confused. "What about a suicide?"

RD nodded. "Interesting. Like his dad or something? That would fuck with Leo big time."

I shrugged, "Let's see where it goes. Why would his dad do it?

"Depression," said Bethany.

I nodded, "Over what?"

"Nothing," said Bethany. "Just depression itself. What if it was because of his medication? I just read a story about a guy who killed himself after taking... I don't remember which drug, but whatever it was, he was on it for something like three months, and his depression got worse, and he killed himself."

My jaw dropped open. "That is so fucked up!"

RD nodded. "It's interesting. I'm not a hundred percent on it. I feel like it'll become about the drugs or whatever. I want to stay focused on the characters."

David shrugged. "We don't have to focus on the suicide at all..."

"I don't know, man," I shook my head. "I think we have to resolve everything we introduce. Maybe a character in the cast is on the same drug. That could be interesting, but it would take up a lot of the story."

RD waved his hand and hissed, "It's a pain in the ass. I don't want to do that."

"What if he killed himself because he was gay?" said David.

"Oh, I like that," said Bethany. "Especially if one of their friends is gay."

"That's Scott Bloom," I said.

RD chuckled. "Why?"

I shrugged. "It's certainly not Kevin Connolly. I guess it could be Tobey, but..."

David shuddered. "No, not Tobey. Please."

RD laughed. "Why?"

"I can't explain it—just no. Scott's perfect. The character Brad is gay in the script." David sneered at RD. "You'd know that if you read it."

I grinned. "I think we should go full-on Priscilla, Queen of the Desert with Scott too."

RD's eye's popped open wide. "A transvestite!"

"Why not? Think about Scott in a dress in black and white. His eyes will look gray."

RD nodded.

"Have him done up in some dope makeup... I think he would be incredible."

RD shrugged one shoulder. "Yeah, alright. Scott plays a chick named Brad. I fuckin' dig it."

"I think his story should be tragic, too," I said. "Something super heavy."

The session lasted several more hours, with our story and characters evolving and devolving along the way. By the end of the night, we laid some great foundation, and Bethany Ashton officially came on board as a writer on the project.

———

AFTER SEVERAL WRITING SESSIONS, we got together with the guys up in Scott Bloom's backyard to get some feedback. It was a lovely afternoon to be up in the hills, with blooming wildflowers and succulents all around.

Leo took a deep drag of his cigarette and leaned back in his woven deck chair. "I'm not playing someone named Der." He cut through the air with a short karate chop. "Never gonna happen."

David whined, "Why?"

"It's non-negotiable."

"Why, though?"

Leo tucked his chin nearly flush with his neck, pulled his shoulders back, contorted his face, and then chirped repeatedly, "Der, Der, Der... Hello, hi, I'm Der..."

Everyone but David cracked up.

"OK, fine," said David. "What do you want to call him then?"

"I don't care, bro, anything but Der, please."

"Derek?"

Leo nodded. "Derek is perfect. Thank you very much."

David grinned and continued. "Der's—*Derek's* really big thing is that his father committed suicide after he was caught having sex with a man..."

"Who? The father or Derek?" said Kevin.

"Derek is sitting right there, you fucking idiot," scoffed Tobey.

"I'm asking who was having sex with the man, you dumb fuck."

"Yeah, I'm sorry, guys..." Leo winced before he continued. "You guys are gonna probably hate me, but I don't think I like that either."

"Why?" said RD.

"I just... I don't. I'm not feeling it, I guess. I'm fine with all the suicide stuff, but—"

David furrowed his brow. "You don't want him to be gay?"

"Sounds homophobic," muttered Scott.

Leo shook his head. "That's ridiculous."

"I just said it might look that way."

"No, bro, I think they're hitting the issues on the head again,

133

like they did with Last Respects. I don't want to play someone with all these fucking issues."

I rolled my eyes. *Here we go with this shit again.*

Tobey sat up in his chair. "I agree with Leo. It's good, you guys are coming up with good stuff, but..." He held up his hands and pushed an imaginary mass in front of him. "I think you can be a little more subtle. No, no, no, not subtle—more layered. Like more conflict, stuff like that. Know what I'm saying?"

I chuckled. "I have no idea what you're saying."

"He's talking about subtext," said Scott.

"Yeah, that's part of it." Tobey shrugged. "I can't explain it properly, I guess."

"People commit suicide over this issue all the time," said David. "Someone could be doing it as we speak."

"I realize that," said Tobey. "I—that's not what I mean."

"How are we supposed to make that more subtle?" I asked. "It's suicide, Tobey."

"It's just too easy the way you have it now. That's what I'm saying. It needs to be more complex."

"Complex?" I shrugged incredulously. "What the fuck does that mean?"

Tobey's thin lips pulled back into a shitty grin. "I don't know, Dale. I'm not the writer. That's you guys. I'm just giving you my notes."

I looked at Leo. "You got any ideas? Suggestions? Anything?"

Leo shook his head slowly. "I don't know. Let me think about it some more."

"All right, cool," I said. "We'll keep working on it."

"Let's talk about Brad," said RD.

"Yes," said Scott. "Let's talk about Brad. I'm cool with his name. That's fine. But I don't know how I feel about playing a transvestite. I don't know if I'm into it."

Leo piped up. "Why can't my character be a transvestite, bro? I want to play a character like that, not some douche named Der!"

"What I find hilarious is that he..." Kevin nodded toward Scott, "was just calling you out for being a homophobe and here he is fuckin' doin' the exact same thing." Kevin shook his head, "The hypocrisy, bro."

"I have no problem with transvestites," said Scott. "I just don't want to play one. It's improv so I want to play Brad a bit closer to home, I think."

RD sighed. "So, rewrite Brad and Der from scratch. Brutal."

"You don't have to rewrite Brad from scratch. What if he's bisexual?"

I nodded, "Works for me."

"Me too," said RD.

"Me three," said David.

"Let's keep going. Who's next?" RD glanced at Tobey. "Ian. Let's talk about him."

"I like him." Tobey shrugged, "He's pretty cool. You just based him on me, I take it?"

I shook my head. "You just said we made him cool."

"Very funny. I mean I think I would probably prefer he wasn't so much like me, but—"

"What do you mean?" I said. "He's not like you at all."

He shrugged, "I'm a vegetarian, so is Ian."

"There are lots of vegetarians, Tobey. I've been a vegetarian longer than you have."

"Yeah, but I also take loads of supplements, and so does Ian."

"So do I, bro," said RD. "I'm the guy who got you into all that shit in the first place."

"OK, tell me one thing Ian is that I'm not."

"Amenable?"

"Wow, Dale you really are a stand-up comedian."

"I'm just fucking with you. Ian is like the fuckin' the elder of the group. He's the wise one—the moral leader if you will. That's the way I see him anyway, but you can do pretty much whatever you want with him. If you don't like something we came up with, don't do it."

"Yeah, that's pretty cool. Like I said, I do like him. There's work to be done is all—but this is a good start so far."

"That's great. We're gonna tighten all these characters up a lot in rehearsal." I said and turned to Kevin. "What do you think of Jeremy?"

"I'm fine with Jeremy," said Kevin. "For the most part, anyway. I obviously don't know what it's like to be an out-of-work actor, but I got all you guys to help me with that." He chuckled. "No, seriously, though. I mean, obviously I can bring stuff to the table, right? Like during rehearsal or whatever?"

I nodded.

"Yeah, should we bring anything other than ourselves?" said Scott.

"You should, yes," I said. "Thank you for mentioning it. We want you guys to bring something secrete to the set—a secrete even to me and RD. It should be something that you think will get a big reaction from your cast mates."

"The bigger the better," said RD.

"Anything we want?" said Scott. "Guns, wild animals... whatever."

I nodded. "Yes on the wild animals, but a big no on the guns or weapons of any kind."

Kevin chortled, "Bring a fuckin' Uzi and just start gunning down anyone who sucks in the scene."

"Speaking of getting killed," David stood up, holding a file folder in his hand. "I need you guys to sign this for our investors, or they're going to kill me..." he handed out a two-sentence contract to each of the guys. "This just says you intend to show up and shoot the movie in July. It's so I can get the money."

Tobey held his paper up flippantly. "Is this supposed to be my contract?"

David's head bobbed from side to side. "Yeah, sort of. We'll sign something more formal later. This is to show the investors that everyone is going to show up and shoot a movie in July. But as far your deal goes, like your compensation and all of that— everyone is working for SAG plus ten, and the same back end, which RD and I still need to work out."

"I assume it's going to be favored nations?" said Scott.

"Yes," said David, "but everything is deferred until we sell. If we sell."

"What is favored nations anyway?" I asked.

"It means no one gets paid more than me," said Tobey.

"It means all the actors get paid the same." said Scott.

"Same thing," said Tobey. "What about the back end?"

"We haven't figured out the specifics yet," said David. "It's gonna be good though."

Tobey shook his head. "I don't know, bro. How are we supposed to agree to something without knowing what the fuck the deal is?"

RD rolled his eyes. "Come on, Tobey, don't be a pain in the ass. Everyone is getting the same across the board, and it ain't gonna be much."

"How do you know that RD?" said Tobey sharply.

"It's a tiny movie," I said. "It's pretty obvious."

Kevin spoke up. "We all knew none of us were getting paid for this, Tobey. Of course we're all getting the same deal. Of course. Are you suggesting you deserve more than that guy?" Kevin pointed to Leo.

"I didn't say anything like that," said Tobey. "I'm saying we haven't discussed it, and it feels like these guys are making a bunch of assumptions that they just expect us to go along with."

"Yeah, we are," said David. "We have no other choice because every penny is going towards film stock, gear, and crew. Every penny. Every actor is getting the same rate and the same back end. You guys are the leads, so your back end will be more than the supporting cast, but that's about it. If you don't want to be in the movie, say so now before I go through all the trouble of raising the money."

"How much is the budget?" said Tobey.

"Small. Clerks small."

"Twenty-five thousand?"

"Maybe a little more if we're lucky," said David. "I'm still working on it. That's why I need those." He gestured at the piece of paper in Tobey's hand.

Tobey's face relaxed, "That is tiny. Alright, fine. I'm good with whatever you guys say then."

David exhaled audibly. I noticed the sweat beads on his brow before he discreetly wiped them away. "OK, just sign and date it and give it back to me, please." David handed a pen to Leo with a sheepish smile.

Leo pressed the pen to the signature line and paused. He looked each of us in the eye and said, "My agents are going to have to sign off on everything before you guys do anything with this film, you understand that, right?"

"Absolutely," said David.

RD and I nodded and agreed. "Yes, of course."

"Perfect," said Tobey. "Whatever Leo's agent says is cool for him is cool for me too..."

Scott rolled his eyes. "So, favored nations then."

DAVID STUTMAN RODE in the front passenger side of RD's car. I was in the backseat behind him. RD was gliding through the switchbacks of Laurel Canyon Boulevard like a slalom skier.

"I'm not going to lie, RD," said David. "Those guys were making me nervous. Especially Tobey."

"Tobey's just being a pain in the ass," RD waved it off. "Don't worry about him, he'll do whatever Leo says."

"Leo made me nervous too with all that agent talk. Your friends aren't going to screw us, are they?"

RD shook his head. "No way, bro. Leo's an Oscar nominated actor—of course his agents are gonna have a say."

"Just be glad they're getting involved *after* we shoot," I said.

"Exactly."

"I'm just afraid they'll try to get him more money or do something else to fuck everything up," said David.

RD shook his head. "Leo won't let them. Trust me, bro, there's nothing to worry about. He's not doing this for money. Clearly."

"Why is he doing it, then?" said David.

"What do you mean?" RD shifted down as we hit the bottom of the hill, well above the speed limit. "To help out his friends."

13

"DALE," RD whispered from his bedroom.

It was the middle of the night. I was in my usual position, lying on my back, staring up at the ceiling thinking about my life.

"Yeah." I whispered back, even though RD and I were the only ones home.

"I can't sleep, can you?"

I cleared my throat. "No."

RD appeared in my doorway lit by the amber streetlights spilling in through my window. He leaned in the door frame on his shoulder. He was in boxers and an oversized, stained under-shirt, with his greasy hair up in a hairband. "How are we going to pull this shit off, bro?" He grinned uncomfortably.

I chuckled a bit and pushed myself up into a sitting position. "I have no idea."

"I know you don't want to write anything, but I think they need something at least... some kind of line, or maybe even a few lines to get them from one subject to another."

"Yeah, that makes sense. I just didn't want to write anything that Leo had to approve. I was literally thinking a few seconds ago that we should have index cards for everyone, one for each improv, maybe write some shit about their character's points of view or whatever. Lead lines are perfect."

"You know what's so weird, bro?"

"Hm?"

RD pinched and adjusted his balls. "I'm not terrified right now. I thought I would be, but I actually feel pretty relaxed."

"Yet there you are, awake at three a.m., standing in my doorway, playing with your nuts..."

"I just can't stop thinking about this movie, bro."

"I know—I love it so much."

"I have no idea what's going to happen, which would normally terrify me, but for some reason I'm fine with it. I'm borderline OCD for fuck's sake, but I actually like all this chaos right now. Why is that?"

I smiled, "Because you're following your destiny."

He grinned. "Do you really believe that shit?"

I nodded. "I do. I think even if we're the ones making it happen, destiny is playing out, and you either betray it or you fulfill it."

"What if somebody gets murdered?"

"Yeah, it can be taken away, too."

RD's mind drifted for a moment but he came right back. "I guess I'm lying. I am a little terrified about directing. What if I can't communicate what I want them to do, and I just end up looking like a fool?"

"You're gonna be fine."

"What would Tony Robbins tell me right now?"

"To ask better questions."

RD thought for a moment. "Like what?"

"Like... how can I best serve my cast and crew creatively? Or maybe, how can I direct this film successfully while having fun with my friends at the same time?"

RD grinned, his head subtly nodding. "I like your index cards idea. We'll pick some up tomorrow on my mom's Staples card. I'm gonna try and sleep again." He adjusted his balls one last time. "Sweet dreams, fucker." Then he turned, pulled his boxers down to his ankles, and penguin shuffled away, bare-assed. I watched and laughed until he was out of sight.

"Sweet dreams, RD."

RD HEAVED a large cardboard box overflowing with headshots onto his glass octagon table.

Bethany Ashton's dark mascara eyes widened. "Holy shit, that's a lot of headshots."

"They're still coming in, too." RD turned to David, "We gotta get an office, bro."

"Maybe I can help," said Bethany. "What's your budget?"

"We don't have anything in the budget for office space," said David.

"Well, we need one," said RD.

"We don't even have the money yet, RD. And when we finally get it, do you really want to blow it on an office rather than gear or crew?"

"Yes, bro, I do. We can't do this in my house, OK? I'm already running a business out of here."

"We're all busy. I'm doing like three jobs on this film—all you and Dale are doing is creative shit. I gotta deal with everything."

RD shrugged, "You're the fuckin' producer, bro. I don't know what to tell you."

"Sounds like you need a good line producer," said Bethany. "I've got someone who's a super badass. I can connect you guys, if you like."

David shook his head. "I'm talking to someone right now who's awesome. He worked on Swimming with Sharks."

"Let's look at these later," I said as I lugged the box from the table back to the carpet. "God, there must be hundreds."

"Hundreds, bro," said RD.

I walked over to the desk, grabbed a couple of packs of index cards and brought them back to the table. "What do you think about Meadow Sisto for Juliet?"

RD's head bobbed from side to side, as if the idea itself were bouncing around inside. "She could work. Would she audition?"

"I can't imagine why not."

RD shrugged. "Yeah, bro. You want to set it up?"

"Yeah, I'll talk to her."

RD glanced at the index cards and then back at me. "You want to explain this shit?"

"Yeah, sure." I picked up some cards. "We're going to write each of the improvs on index cards for every character." I held one up. "They'll have the topic, some character point-of-view stuff, lead lines like we discussed... so like, transitions and stuff... and maybe things like emotional triggers with some of the other characters. Anything important to the character in that improv. And some of this will change as we go along, as we flesh the characters out."

Bethany smiled and applauded lightly. "This is so great."

I smiled at her. "You wanna start with the girls?"

"I love working on girls." RD rubbed his hands together and pulled his chair up closer to the table. "From a non-sexual standpoint."

Bethany laughed rather generously. "RD, you're so hilarious— you should totally do a role in the movie."

I nodded. "You really should, R—"

"No. Fuckin. Way. I need to concentrate on directing."

"What about you, David?" asked Bethany. "Are you doing a role?"

"Me? Oh god no. That's a terrible idea."

Bethany laughed. "Not even a featured extra?"

"Absolutely not."

Bethany flared her eyebrows at me. "And what about you?"

"I think I am, yeah."

"Yay! What are you playing?"

"A drunk homeless dude, based on a guy I ran into a couple of years ago."

"That's neat," she said.

RD finally took Bethany's bait. "You should do a role, Bethany." He said as if it was his idea.

"You think so?" she said.

He nodded. "Fuck yeah."

"That could be fun. I'll give it some thought." She smiled at RD and then David and me. "Thanks for the offer."

———

RD, David, and I sat around RD's octagon table across from *Swimming with Sharks* line producer, John Schindler. John was a unique and interesting guy, I sensed something benignly strange about him that I could not quite put my finger on, but he seemed to know what he was talking about.

I finished up my crudely drawn diagram of a four-camera set up and pushed it forward for everyone to see. "I think it looks something like this..." I pointed to the camera marked with the number four. "This shot is above the table looking down. Overhead."

John Schindler shook his head. "Yeah. It's cool, but it's not possible to shoot with all these cameras. I doubt they'll fit on the set. We're not on a stage."

I shrugged. "Well, one camera is not enough."

"But it's all you guys can afford," John spoke in a thin, measured tone. "Can I smoke?"

"Go ahead," said RD.

He lit one up.

I turned to RD. "Marisa Ryan is having problems cutting *Sessions* together as we speak because she shot with one camera."

"How do you know that?" said RD

"She said so. But she didn't have to. It was obvious when we were shooting. My performance was all over the place from one take to the next. Like radically different at times. And she only had the one angle each time." I shook my head. "It sounds like a nightmare."

"She can jump cut," said RD.

"Every time?" I shook my head again. "That's not gonna work. And the worst part is that she got really great performances from everyone. I promise you she's leaving some of the best stuff behind because she shot with one camera."

John wet his thin lips and inhaled deeply before continuing his argument. "I get it—you want to do it for continuity, and multi-cam is a good solution for that, but it causes new, much bigger problems. Quite a few."

"What specifically?" I said.

"The budget for one. We don't have the money for a second camera, let alone four." John took a quick drag of his cigarette. "For every camera, you're also adding several crew members, you need an AC and an operator for each. We would need a loader and at least one swing AC. And then there's the film stock—it almost triples the amount of film stock, which would have to be processed and telecined. Telecine is very expensive."

David stiffened up resolutely. "Look, it sucks, but we gotta listen to John. He knows what all this shit costs—"

I pointed to my diagram. "We need a minimum of three cameras, David. We can lose the overhead shot, but we gotta cover eight people around a table. I keep telling you in plain English, if we shoot with anything less than three cameras, this movie will not work. Especially with our cast. They're fast and funny. No two takes will be the same." I shrugged. "This is an easy decision if you want to avoid a nightmare."

"Let's just make it three cameras," said RD.

David shook his head vehemently. "We can't, RD."

"Why not?"

"You just heard the man—we can't afford it."

"Look. bro. I'm bringing all my friends to this thing, including Leonardo-fucking-DiCaprio. We can't afford it? Bullshit. Go raise more money then."

"It's not that easy."

"Yes, it is, David. If we don't have three cameras, we don't make this movie."

"Oh, take the ball and go home," said David. "Nice, RD."

I shook my head in total disbelief. "We're talking about the difference between success and failure right now. This shouldn't be a hard decision. It won't cut together, David. You'd be wasting your investor's money doing it any other way. We'll fail."

"We can cut to the documentary footage."

"Back to the same fucking angle every time?"

"No way," said RD.

"I didn't say that," said David.

"Are you suggesting we just pan around the table and gamble with what we capture?"

"He's right. It's better to be safe," said John. "The extra angles will give you guys a lot more to work with in post."

David's sigh was big and dramatic, like a child's. "How much more do we need for the extra cameras?"

John pulled his chair up closer and opened the folder in front of him. "Things are tight already…"

"Great…"

John scanned a spreadsheet. "I would say at least ten grand, probably closer to fifteen for everything."

David's eyes nearly popped out of his head. "Fifteen K more? Are you fucking serious?!"

John looked up from the document and chuckled. "That's just to get it in the can. We're going to need more money for post, for sure. Telecine, like I said." John took a hit of his cigarette and crushed it out in the drinking glass in front of him. "Making movies is expensive."

RD broke out in a jingle, *"Stuts raises more funds, Stuts raises more funds, we can shoot three cam-er-as cuz Stuts raises more funds."*

———

TERRY STOOD center stage of the karaoke screen, bathed in magenta, yellow, and blue, his face dotted with white disco lights. Both of his hands gripped a microphone tightly. Like most Fridays, Terry had rented a private karaoke room at the hottest club in Koreatown and invited his telemarketing crew. Skip, Kathy, and I were huddled inside a purple vinyl booth with an assortment of Korean finger foods on the table in front of us. Jim sat off to the side with both legs stretched out, holding a bottle of beer with both hands. We were already buzzing and waiting for Terry to perform the first song of the night.

The song began with some light guitar. It wasn't immediately recognizable to me, but it had a familiar 70s pop groove going on. Kathy knew the song right away, and she squealed with delight. Terry giggled.

"You're amazing, Terry!" She looked at me. "It's Streisand!"

Terry Myeong sang "Woman in Love" with less than one percent of Barbra Streisand's talent and thrice her passion. There wasn't a dry eye in the house, but our tears were all from hysterical laughter. Terry didn't give a fuck about us, though. He let every lyric rip as if he wrote it himself.

"Terry, honestly if you want to be rich you need to take that shit on the road." I wiped away my tears. "You should do a whole stand-up show of just you singing karaoke."

Jim howled, "Yeah, but don't do it as Terry—do it as Michael Callahan. That's what you call it, 'An Intimate Evening with Michael Callahan.'"

We all howled.

"Let's hear you sing something, big mouth," slurred Terry. He handed Jim the mic, then stumbled over to the table and grabbed some short ribs with his chubby fingers. He tore some of the flesh from the bone with bared teeth. "Let's go," he said while chewing and wiggling the greasy rib in the air. "What are you going to do, huh?"

Jim gussied himself up, trying the mic in both hands before settling on his right. A cigarette burned between the thumb and finger of his left hand. He took a deep breath and turned to the screen. "Wait and see," he said just as the first crunching chords of AC/DC's, "Dirty Deeds Done Dirt Cheap" blasted from the speakers. It wasn't as funny as Terry's Streisand, but it was pretty damn close. It was like Sylvester Stallone doing Sinatra, after pouring a bunch of beer, whiskey, cigarettes, weed, coke and whatever else found its way down Jim's throat in the last week, and then forcing that voice to grind out a Bon Scott impression. It was divinely horrific, and like Terry, Jim didn't give a single goddamn. He left it all on the stage.

Skip did a boring number from "Sunday in the Park with George", and I absolutely butchered "Walk This Way" by Aerosmith, but it was Kathy who stole the show. She was amazing, like Bette Midler meets Bonnie Raitt. She sang Patsy Cline and Tammy Wynette to perfection, but she brought the house down with her version of "Woman in Love", which she dedicated to "World renowned, award-winning karaoke artist, Michael Callahan."

Jim eventually passed out in the booth. Skip and Kathy split, leaving me and Terry as the last men standing. I took a sip of my beer.

"You're missing too much work," said Terry. "You're lucky there was a phone today."

"Yeah, I'm sorry." I shook my head. "It's this movie, man."

"I understand, but I only have so many phones. You know what I'm saying?"

"As soon as I'm done, I'll be back to normal."

"I filled the phone with someone full-time."

I sighed. "That sucks, Terry."

"You're gone for a week, sometimes more."

"I get it, but it still fuckin' sucks."

"Next time a phone opens, it's yours—but I need sales."

I nodded in Jim's direction. "How does that guy make you money? Honestly."

Terry let out a long, hissing breath. "He doesn't make any money."

"How the fuck does he survive?"

"He gets paid."

"You just pay him out of your pocket for nothing?"

Terry shrugged. "What am I going to do, fire him?"

"No, Terry. Of course not."

———

RD and I were sitting around the condo shooting the shit one evening when the doorbell chimed unexpectedly.

"Who the fuck is that?" RD got up and headed for the door.

Joel Michaely was at the security gate with a backpack slung over his shoulder. "Hey, R."

RD stood in his doorway a few feet from Joel, his finger hovering over a white button that, when pressed, would unlock the security gate.

"I need a place to stay tonight. My parents are freaking out. They've been fighting all fucking night and I can't stand it anymore. I have an audition in the morning for 90210, and it's possibly recurring. Buzz me in."

RD sighed. "You're killing me, Joel. You can't just drop in like this is a motel."

"Come on, RD. I'll save at least a half hour on the drive. I'll sleep on the couch. You won't even know I'm here."

RD pressed the button and Joel pulled open the buzzing gate.

"Dude, I don't want to find any fucking Michaely hairs in my tub, you got that?"

Joel laughed awkwardly as he passed RD in the doorway. "What are you talking about?

"You know exactly what I'm talking about—don't go leaving your gross body hair all over my bathroom."

They ascended the split-level stairs. Joel chuckled again. "I don't..."

"Yes, you do. And if you do it again, you can't stay here anymore."

"OK fine. I'll triple check, I promise." Joel smiled at me. "Hey, Dale."

I nodded at him. "What up, Joel?"

Joel plopped his bag on the carpet and sat next to me on the couch.

"Sorry your parents are tripping," I said.

"They're fighting constantly. They can't stand each other."

"Sucks, bro." RD sat at his desk.

"I just wish they'd divorce and get it over with." Joel noticed the box of headshots. "Are those what I think they are?"

"Yeah," said RD.

The doorbell rang.

"I sent your breakdown to Amber," said Joel. "Are you gonna audition her?"

"Yes!" RD shouted as he ran down the split-level to the door. "I fucking love her."

Joel called out after him. "How come you won't put me in your movie, RD?"

RD shouted back, "Because you're not right for anything."

"What do you mean? I can play anything. Let me be the waiter!"

I shook my head. "That's gonna be a chick. Her name is Flo." I heard Ethan Suplee at the front door.

"It doesn't have to be," said Joel.

"Yes, it does."

RD and Ethan joined us.

"What's up, fellas?" Ethan said with a grin.

I smiled. "Sup, Sups?"

"Hey, Ethan!"

"Joel, what's going on?"

"Nothing. I'm just trying to get RD and Dale to cast me in their movie."

RD bristled. "Joel, there's no role for you right now. That may change in the future, we're writing every day. But right now, that's how it is."

Joel shook his head. "Listen to you, you're such a big-time director all of a sudden."

"I want to do a role too, bro," said Ethan.

RD threw up his hands. "See, bro? Everyone wants a fucking role. Jay wants a role, Johnny wants a role, your mom wants a role... We can't put everybody in the movie."

"It's the first of many," I said.

"Exactly," said RD. "We'll put you guys in the next movie."

"I want to be in this one," whined Joel.

"Yo, guys..." RD shooed us with his hand. "Let Sups sit on the couch."

Ethan shrugged, "Why, RD? I'm fine."

"Nah, here ya go, man." I got up and moved to a bar stool. Joel did the same.

Ethan chuckled, "Well, if you guys insist."

"Sups is on the Sups couch," said RD proudly.

Joel giggled. "That's so funny."

RD sang an impromptu jingle. *"Sups is on the Sups Couch, oh, yeah! Oh yeah. Sups is on his very own couch."*

"I like it," said Ethan as he balanced his cigarettes and lighter on the upholstered arm.

The doorbell rang again.

"Who the fuck is this now?" RD ran down the steps to the door. I could make out Kevin Connolly's distinctive voice and machine gun laugh.

"Who's that?" Ethan craned his neck, trying to see who was at the door. "Connolly?"

RD and Kevin joined us.

"What's up, everyone," said Kevin. "Oh, hey, Joel Michaely. How are you, bro?"

"I'm good, Kev. You?"

"Sweating my fuckin' balls off. Jesus."

"I know, it's so hot."

"Where's Nikki?" said Ethan.

"She's with her mom and brother. She might hook up with us later."

"Is it true you guys are moving in together?" said Joel.

Kevin furrowed his brow. "We're talking about it. How did you hear about that?" He looked my way.

I shrugged. "I didn't say anything."

"You can't take a shit in this town without everyone knowing about it. Jesus Christ."

The phone rang. RD looked up to the heavens and begged, "Please, don't be my fucking mother." He lifted the receiver, "Talent Works." He paused a moment, and then the tension in his face gave way to a grin. "What's up, Blake Sennett? Hang on, hang on, let me put you on speakerphone." RD punched the button. "You there?"

"What's up?" Blake's voice was thin and tinny coming out of the tiny half-watt speaker. "Who's over there right now?"

RD scanned the room. "Fuuuuckin... fuuuuckin... Connolly, Wheatley, Michaely-hairs, and Sups is on the Sups couch."

I smirked. "And Blake is in the box."

"Ethan's there?" said Blake. "Stealin' my friends. RD Robb is stealin' my friends."

Ethan shouted, "What's up, Blake?"

"I'm in the box! What are you guys doin'?"

"We're not really doing anything." Ethan chuckled, "You should come over."

"I don't know, it's pretty nice in this box. The walls are so soft."

"Just come over, bro," said RD.

"OK, maybe. I'm hanging up now."

RD tapped the button to disconnect from the call.

"Yo, what are those?" Kevin gestured to the crate full of headshots.

"Headshots," said RD.

"For Saturday Night Club?" He rubbed his hands together. "Can I take a look?"

"No, bro. I don't want to get them mixed up and all over the fuckin' place."

"Anything good?"

RD shrugged. "Yeah, maybe. We haven't gone through them all, but yeah, there's a couple..."

"Can I just see the ones you guys like?"

The doorbell rang again.

"No, bro." RD glanced at me. "Yo, can you get the door?"

"Sure." I scooted down the stairs and opened the door to Leo standing behind the gate.

"What the fucks goin' on?" he said.

I buzzed him in, and we headed up the stairs.

Not long after Leo, Scott, Blake, and Tobey arrived. "The Office" was packed and buzzing.

"Yo, Leo, check those out." Kevin pointed to the box in the corner.

"What? The box? What is it?"

"Headshots," said Kevin.

"For our movie?"

Kevin flared his eyes. "Yeah, dude."

"Let me see those," said Leo. "Pass that shit over here."

"No, bro... please don't," said RD. "I don't want them all over the place."

"What do you mean, bro?" Leo got up and walked over to the box. "I just want to see a few of them. What's the big fuckin' deal?"

"Relax, RD," said Kevin. "It's just some fuckin' headshots."

"They're mostly garbage..."

"Come on, RD." Scott shook his head. "That's not garbage. Those are human beings with hopes and dreams just like you and me."

Leo ignored RD and started flipping through the photos.

RD's shoulders dropped, "Yeah sure, do whatever you want."

We spent the rest of the night combing through a mountain of headshots. It was fun, but I was surprised how hard these guys were on other actors. They laughed about how they looked, mocked their resumes, made fun of their names. It was shitty, and I said something about it.

"We're not being cannibalistic," argued Scott. "They're being delusional."

"Yeah, bro," said Leo. "Everyone thinks they can act, but not everyone can."

"Yeah, OK," I said. "But we're just looking at headshots at this point."

Scott wagged his finger in the air. "That's not the point I'm making."

"I know, but I'm saying maybe they can act. We don't know yet. How could we?"

Leo grabbed a headshot from the rejection pile, glanced at the front and back. "You really think Vanessa here is going to show up and blow your mind, Dale?" He flicked the headshot in my direction. I nearly fell over catching it.

"I don't know, maybe. She could," I said.

Leo waved me off, "Come on, man."

"Yeah, she might," said RD. "Who knows? But is she right for the role? Read our character descriptions, bro. We asked for hot chicks. Vanessa is the furthest fucking thing from hot. Look at her." He walked over and snatched the headshot from my hand. He held it up for everyone to see. "She's fuckin' ugly, bro."

A couple of the guys chuckled.

"I'm not trying to be funny or mean. I don't know this chick from my ass. I'm just saying that she is nothing like any of the characters we described in our breakdown—"

"So what, I—"

RD held his hand up to stop me. "I'm not finished. If Vanessa thinks she is hot, then maybe she is delusional. It sounds harsh, but, like I'm not going to submit myself for James fuckin' Bond, you know what I mean?"

Leo fanned his hand out, "RD Robb is..."

"Double-O-Seven," Kevin chuckled. "No, you're absolutely right, RD. You gotta know where you are in life. How the fuck can you get anywhere if you don't even know where you're starting from?"

"That's deep, Kevin." Scott smirked. "Did you come up with that yourself?"

Kevin squinted. "It's common sense, bro."

Leo picked up another headshot from the pile. "It's not like I want to talk shit about other actors. This is a unique situation. And you guys are my friends, so I'm going to tell you what I think."

Tobey shrugged. "Which is also common sense."

Our conversation went back and forth as headshots of girls were thrown into three piles for Yes, No, and Maybe.

Eventually, the guys left, and we were surrounded by a mess of headshots that stretched from one end of the room to the other, just as RD predicted. The three of us sat at the table with the pile of headshots of the girls we liked the most.

Joel grabbed one and looked at both sides. "Let me help you with the casting at least."

RD shook his head. "We don't need it."

"Come on, RD. I want to be involved."

"Then find us a cheap office space. Dirt fuckin' cheap."

"Seriously?"

"Yes. Look at all this shit—it's driving me crazy. We live here for fuck's sake."

"I think my dad has space in one of his buildings in Encino. Maybe I can hook you guys up there."

"We have no money, though. We need to put every dime into the movie for gear and shit like that. Is it available now?"

"I think so. I want to be involved, so let's make a deal. I think I can make something happen."

RD clapped his hands together. "Fuck yeah, Joel Michaely."

"If I get you the space for free, how about I get a producer credit?"

RD's eyebrows sprung up. "You're not getting a producing credit for some office space, Joel. That's absurd."

"Co-producer?"

"No way, you're high."

"Associate? Otherwise what's in it for me?"

RD paused a moment. Using his thumb and finger, he pulled at the fleshy part of his upper lip, paused and looked at his fingertips a moment, and then gave them a quick sniff. "Associate Producer, for six months' rent."

"Three. My dad won't give it up for half a year I don't think."

"Yeah, alright. Get us office space for three months, rent-free, and we'll give you an associate producer credit."

Joel stuck out his hand. "Shake on it."

RD shook his hand. "You got a deal, bro."

I stood up and stretched. "Congrats Joel. I'm going to bed—goodnight, fuckers." I trampled upstairs.

I was so tired I think I fell asleep before my head hit the pillow.

. . .

"JOEL MICHAELY, GET YOUR FUCKING MICHAELY-HAIRS OUT OF MY TUB!" RD's thundering voice outside my bedroom door ripped me out of a deep sleep.

"I cleaned all of them up, RD—I swear!" Joel's voice was small and panicked, hurrying up the stairs.

"No, Joel, they're everywhere. What did I tell you?"

"I checked, RD. I made sure I rinsed everything! The tub, the sink..."

I sat up in my bed, laced my fingers behind my head and tuned into the latest episode of The RD Robb Shit Show.

"Come here then, fucker." I heard both sets of feet shuffle from the hallway carpet into RD's bathroom. "What is that? Huh? That is a fucking Michaely-hair! And *that* is a Michaely-hair." Joel chuckled, and that made me chuckle. "And *that* is a Michaely-hair in my sink!"

"I'm sorry, I'll get it—"

"...and there's another fuckin' Michaely-hair... They're every-where. GET THEM ALL OUT RIGHT NOW!"

14

I SNAPPED the legs of a folding table in place on my end, RD did the same on his, and we flipped it over to stand it up. I pushed the table flush against another table to accommodate the cast. RD grabbed a box containing all the character index cards and we started unpacking them.

RD pointed along the table. "Dude, chick, dude, chick, dude, chick, dude, chick, right?"

"Or chick, dude, chick, dude—"

"No, I think it's dude first..."

"Or maybe, dude, chick, chick, dude, chick, dude, chick, dude."

"Let's go with that." RD broke into one of his oddly infectious melodies. *"Dude chick, chick, dude, dude, chick, let's do some improv and shit."*

Joel appeared, flashing his bright smile. "What's up, guys?"

I grinned. "What's up, Associate Producer, Joel Michaely?"

"Do you love it?"

"Love what?"

"What do you mean? The space!"

"I'm kidding—it's fucking perfect."

Joel turned to RD with beaming eyes. "Do you love it, RD?"

"Yes, it's cool. It's a little small, but much better than my place."

Joel chuckled awkwardly. "At least my dad is good for something. I just got back from Clueless by the way."

"How was it?" I said. "How was Sisto?"

"Amazing. Jeremy is great, but Brittany Murphy stole the show. She's incredible. And the theater was packed."

"I don't want to hear about Clueless," said RD. "Fuck that movie, bro."

"Who cares? You're gonna be a big director. Brittany Murphy is gonna be a star."

RD sighed, "That's fuckin' great. I'm happy for her."

John Schindler arrived and set up a video camera to tape the rehearsals.

David Stutman arrived late as usual. He marveled at the space. "This looks really great, guys," he said.

"Glad you like it." RD sneered. "Thanks for your help."

"Hey, I'm working too, RD. I'm getting the money and working with Schindler to finalize the budget. It's not all fun, creative work, you know."

"Do me a favor," I said to David. "Grab some of those fold up chairs and put them around the table where you see index cards."

David grabbed two chairs from the stack up against the wall. "Where's Bethany?"

"She had something else tonight, but she'll be here tomorrow." I scanned Derek's character cards, looking for anything Leo might find objectionable.

RD looked as worried as I felt. "Looks good, right?"

"Yeah, I think. We'll see how it goes, bro." I inhaled deeply and the fear of another rejection hitched my breath.

When the guys finally arrived and settled in, we went over the process, explaining how to use the index cards, the lead lines, and other considerations. The important thing we drove home with them was that we were experimenting. The only thing mandatory in any given exercise was beginning with and returning to the subject of each improv. Everything else was game until we said it wasn't.

"This is gonna be fuckin' awesome," said Kevin. "Yo, what about the chicks?"

"It's just going to be you guys until we start auditioning," said RD. "We're setting up a bunch of girls now, but it'll be a couple of days before we get them in here. We're gonna sit different girls in the rehearsals with you guys until we find who you vibe with the most."

"I like that a lot," said Leo.

"Come on, let's get this shit started," said Kevin.

"Everyone ready?" said RD.

"Wait, wait, what are we doing?" asked Tobey.

"Check your index card, bro. I just went over it. We're going to start with Derek entering the diner—he does the whole lesbian shtick, which leads to the masturbation improv."

Everyone looked at their index cards. Leo furrowed his brow. "I thought I had the lead line for the masturbation improv?

"Nope, it's Kevin," I said.

Kevin picked up the card and gave it a quick glance. "So, after he says all that shit about lesbians and whatever, I tell him to just admit he was beating off, and that's what gets us into the next part? How do I know when to do that?"

"You'll feel it," said RD. "Don't worry about it, it's just rehearsal. Leo, come over here—to where I am." RD pointed to a spot on the carpet. Leo complied. "This is where you'll enter from. Just walk up to the table, the guys will say what's up or whatever, and then start with the shit. Derek's setup is that he couldn't find a chick to bring tonight, but instead of admitting it, he lies and says he was banging a couple of lesbians..."

"And then they call me out on that," said Leo.

RD nodded. "Yeah, of course."

"So, am I combative, or embarrassed? What?"

"Be whatever. See what works."

"It's definitely on the lighter side," I said. "I don't think shame is in Derek's vocabulary, but a little vulnerability couldn't hurt."

"OK, fine." Leo took a deep breath. "I think I know what to do."

"These are your friends," RD added. "You're there to have a

good time. And when we shoot, there'll be three chicks at the table, so think about that."

Leo cleared his throat and lit up a new cigarette. "I'm ready when you guys are."

RD returned to his seat next to mine. "All right, everyone, settle in and... *feel* rehearsal!"

"What?" Scott started laughing just as Leo sauntered up to the table. "I'm sorry, bro."

"For what? I just got here?" said Leo in character.

"No, I'm out of it already." Scott turned to RD. "Can we start over? I'm sorry, your 'feel' thing caught me off guard."

"Yeah, what's that all about?" Kevin snickered. "It was a little weird, I'm not gonna lie."

"Why? What difference does it make what word I use?"

"It sounds pretentious," said Scott. "It took me out."

"That's your problem, Scott," said Tobey. "You gotta stay focused."

"Yeah, I don't know what to tell you," said RD. "It's not an action film, bro. It's about people and emotions."

Scott pressed. "Just say 'action' like everyone else—forget the artsy shit. It's distracting."

"I disagree, Scott." Tobey shook his head and turned to RD. "You're doing Legrant, right?"

"Yeah," said RD.

"Your acting coach?" said Scott.

"The man's a legend, Scott. And RD's one hundred percent right. This movie is emotionally driven. 'Feel' is a far more appropriate word... Maybe just let RD be the director."

"Not for nothing, but he's working with the director right now," said Kevin. "What else is he supposed to do?"

Scott cracked a grin. "This isn't your acting class. We're making a real film here."

Tobey flared up. "If something so trivial is going to knock you out of character, bro, how are you going to hold up when the cameras are rolling for real?"

Scott took a draw of his long brown cigarette. "I'll be fine. I was just distracted for a second. It happens." Scott's eyes switched to RD. "Let's go again."

"All right, Leo, back to one."

Leo returned to his mark and RD called "feel."

Leo sauntered up to the table and began. "What's up, guys?" Leo, playing Derek, sat at the table with the other characters, Ian, Brad, Jeremy, and their invisible dates. "I see you brought some beautiful ladies with you tonight. Nice to meet you girls."

"What about you, bro?" said Kevin, in the character of Jeremy. "Where's your chick tonight?"

"She couldn't come. She had some shit to do—*they* had some shit to do."

"Oh really?" Kevin raised his eyebrows and grinned. "They, huh?"

"Yeah. I was with two chicks earlier. I was going to bring them both, but—"

"Oh wow," said Tobey. "That's a lot of chicks."

"Yeah, bro, two lesbians." Leo grinned. "Good times."

Kevin took his cue. "You are so full of shit, bro."

"No, I'm not. What do you mean?"

"You weren't fuckin' two lesbians earlier tonight, any more than I was suckin' Brad's dick."

Tobey's jaw dropped open.

"What the fuck is that supposed to mean?" snapped Scott, playing Brad. "Why bring my dick into it?"

"No, bro, I'm just saying that he wasn't fucking two lesbians... I'm saying he's bullshitting."

"Why drag my sexuality into it, though? What's that about?"

"Relax, bro, we weren't talking about you. I was making—"

"That's not true. You called me by my name. Are you delusional?" Scott as Brad tapped his cigarette until the ash fell into the ashtray. "Are you OK?"

"Bro, stop already. This is fuckin'... fuckin' ridiculous..." Kevin raised his hands in surrender. "I'm out. I'm sorry. I'm—I'm completely out of it."

Scott tossed his hands up. "What the hell, man?"

"I just feel like you're all over the place, bro."

"Me? No. I was just starting to get into it, what do you mean?"

"Yes, bro. You were way off..." Kevin looked back at us for some support, but he didn't get any.

We both sighed. "It was kind of great, bro," said RD.

"Really?" said Kevin.

"I loved it," I said. "I wish you were still going right now."

"Really? That's... I thought you guys just said to Leo that the scene was supposed to be on the lighter side. Besides, we were way off-topic. We're supposed to be on the..." Kevin looked down at his index card.

"Masturbation," said Tobey.

"Right. We're supposed to be going into the masturbation, but we were all over the place."

"We were not all over the place," said Scott. "You need to relax. Maybe be more adventurous. We would have gotten there eventually."

"We were nowhere near the subject of masturbation, Scott. Not unless..."

"Yes, we were..."

Kevin held up his hand like a traffic cop. "No, we weren't—Let me finish. Thank you. Not unless you just drop it in there like a... What's that called again?"

"A non sequitur," said Scott.

"A non sequitur, exactly."

"That's not true. What if I had said, you wish, you meaning Jeremy, wish you could suck my, meaning Brad's dick? Or what if I said that you're—meaning Jeremy, of course—"

"I know who you mean, bro."

"You're nothing more than a closeted homosexual who probably beats off to the thought of a hard dick in his mouth."

"Jesus Christ, bro..."

I leaned in and whispered to RD, "This what we're after. This is gold."

"Yeah, yeah." RD stood up and walked to the table. "First, all the shit you were doing just now was genius. You need to be saying all that while in character. Like, try to do and say everything in character."

"Never come out," I said.

Kevin still looked highly perplexed. "Can we talk about that last improv more because—is that what you guys had in mind, or did you want something lighter? I'm genuinely confused by the direction because I could have sworn you said it was lighthearted before we started."

I spoke up. "I mean, you were right for the most part—it's not the masturbation improv we were shooting for because it became more about Jeremy defending his homophobia, and Brad dealing with some kind of bigotry or whatever."

"All of that was interesting as fuck, though," said RD.

"It absolutely was," I said. "But—"

"Don't be afraid to go down a road or whatever," said RD. "Just circle back to the topic and look for lead-lines to transition in and out with. Just have normal conversations in your character."

"I guess you guys can take care of it in editing anyway," said Kevin.

I nodded. "But to your point, Kevin, the masturbation improv is about being vulnerable. It's revealing something very personal without being confrontational... at least that's how I see it."

"Absolutely," said RD. "So, let's do it again—leave Brad's sexuality out of it this time."

"My bad guys," said Kevin.

"It's not your bad, bro," said Tobey. "That's improv. You gotta let it flow, baby."

"Where are we picking it up from? I'm so confused right now." Leo laughed at himself. "I have no idea what's happening right now."

"You just arrived, and you're telling us about your fictional lesbians," said RD.

"OK-OK-OK, I remember—fictional lesbians. I'm ready now, let's go."

"Everyone settle... and feeeeel."

I GLANCED at the digital alarm clock on my nightstand. I had been checking the time every few minutes for the past hour. It was just after three in the morning and my insomnia was wearing me down. I got up and crept quietly into the hallway. RD's bedroom door was open about a foot wide, just enough to peek inside. He was curled up under a thin summer quilt. I couldn't see his face, but I knew he was awake.

"Psst."

RD popped his head up like a meerkat, his eyes big and smiling.

I smiled back. "Thought so."

"What's going on?"

"Nothing. Just thinking about all the cool shit we did today."

"Connolly is a fuckin' genius, bro."

"He really is..."

"Where does he come up with the shit he says?"

"I don't know, but this movie is gonna be so good for him."

"It could be..."

My thoughts drifted. "I want even more conflict. I want to watch them tear each other apart."

"I can't wait to get some chicks in there," said RD.

"Really? I'm kind of nervous about it. The guys were so good tonight, I feel like the chicks are going to fuck up the chemistry and flow."

"No, bro. It's going to get even better. Trust me."

———

JOHN SCHINDLER CALLED the first of what would become weekly meetings to update RD, David, and me on his progress. David raised the money we needed to expand to three cameras, but the budget was tighter than ever.

"I'm just telling you now that you're not gonna get more than two takes for each scene," said John.

"Well, I can't fucking work with that. Even if it sucks, we have to move on?"

"We're all making sacrifices, RD. Yours is probably the easiest. Some of the crew is deferring their whole pay so you can have three cameras."

"Nice. Make me feel guilty."

"I'm just telling you what's up. That's my job. We've got three nights, that's it. When the sun comes up on the last day, it's a wrap, and whatever is in the can is what you'll have in post. If you want to do a hundred takes of the same scene, that's your business, but I wouldn't recommend it."

RD shook his head. "Jesus Christ, how the fuck are we going to pull this off?"

"Get it in one take." John chuckled. "We'll be fine, RD. The cast is amazing. Oh, and I think I may have found the perfect location. It's a cool diner with a bar attached to it, so we wouldn't have to move for the entire three days."

"When can we see it?" I said.

"I'll let you know. Soon. The crew is coming together nicely. We attached our gaffer, best boy, and key grip today. They're incredible pros. We're very lucky. I'll bring them to the office so you guys can meet them." John glanced at the index cards, picked one up and skimmed over it, curiously. "So this is the screenplay, huh?"

I smiled and nodded. "Yeah, pretty much."

John chuckled. "That's pretty neat."

15

RD STOOD CONFIDENTLY in front of all four guys and three hopeful women in our first full rehearsal. "It's a hang-out movie. You're at the diner, talkin' shit about whatever the topic is. It's the same kind of shit we do all the time. Just have fun and see where the conversations go." RD looked back at John. "You ready, Schindler?"

John found the record button and pressed it. "We're rolling."

"Awesome." RD returned his attention to the actors. "We're doing three rounds. Prostitution, masturbation, and then a free-for-all. I may or may not cut, but until I do, just keep going, even if it feels like it's falling apart."

RD trotted back to sit next to me on a folding chair.

John held up his hand. "Let's get the girls to give their names and the character they're auditioning for, please."

A brunette with olive skin and dark brown eyes as dead as driftwood spoke first. "I'm Carla Floyd, I'm reading for the role of Amy." She drew out her vowels and finished "Amy" with a valley girl's lilt. I was unaware until that moment that valley girls were an actual thing. I had just assumed the whole bit was the brainchild of some brilliant, unknown comedian. Leo, who was sitting to the right of Carla, chuckled.

To the left of Carla was a blonde girl with ocean blue eyes. "I'm Amy Gates," she said. "And I'm reading for Juliet today."

I already knew the girl sitting between Kevin and Tobey. I first met her when she sang with Blake Sennett at a party a few months back and blew us all away.

"Hello. I'm Jenny Lewis. I'm reading for Sara."

"OK. We're starting with prostitution..." RD waited a moment before making the call. "And everyone, *feel*."

Kevin Connolly adjusted in his seat and then got us started. "Can we talk about hookers for a minute?"

Leo chuckled. "That's so random! Why would you want to do that, I wonder?"

Kevin chuckled, "I don't know. I was just... I was just sitting here and started thinking about hookers."

Leo chuckled again. "Just out of the blue?"

"Yeah, just randomly popped into my head."

"Go ahead. Tell us about hookers, bro."

Within minutes, the actors were all over the place, stepping over each other's dialogue, making the scene unusable.

"This is so bad," whispered RD. "What should we do?"

I whispered back, "Tell them to let each other finish a fucking sentence for starters."

"They just need to find their rhythm," said John. "Give them time."

We gave them a couple more minutes, but it only got worse. RD called cut and approached the table. "You guys are stepping all over each other. Let's start again and try to get into a flow. Let the conversation develop. Let people finish what they're saying. It ain't a talking competition." RD turned to leave, but then suddenly turned back around. "Let's try something different. Let's make this round about a homeless guy. He just came in and asked you guys for some money. The manager had to escort him out, and you guys are talking about it."

"Did we give him in any money?" asked Kevin.

RD shrugged, "I don't know, did you?"

"Give him actual cash-money out of my pocket? No fuckin' way. I would buy him some food or whatever, but supporting a drug and alcohol problem that's clearly destroying the person's life would not be an option. I wouldn't do it."

RD raised his hand. "Whose character gave the homeless dude money?"

Leo and one of the girls raised their hands.

"What's your name again?"

"Carla?"

"Carla. Why did you give the bum money?"

She shrugged. "Because he asked for it."

Tobey and Scott chuckled. "That's a good answer, actually," said Tobey.

RD turned to Leo. "How about you? Why did you give him money?"

"So he would leave."

"Scott?"

"I didn't."

"Why?"

"Because I don't like being put on the spot like that... and I'm not even sure if he actually needed money."

Kevin laughed, "Right, he's a fuckin' brain surgeon by day and a filthy beggar by night."

"No, I'm just sayin' that I don't know what I'm contributing to. It's the same thing you're saying."

"Doesn't matter," I said. "We get to make it all up. There are no wrong answers."

"Alright, fine," said Kevin, "Let's go again, I'm ready for this shit."

RD turned toward the camcorder. "John?"

John pressed the record button and gave RD the thumbs up.

RD turned back toward the cast. "Start whenever you're ready."

After another awkward beginning, they were back to clamoring and stepping all over each other.

John Schindler came over and knelt between us. "Let's put them on a metronome, man. These guys are artists—let's give them a tool to find their rhythm."

"Who the hell has a metronome?" said RD.

"I do, back at the house," said John. "But for today I can keep time on my knee." He tapped his knee a couple of times to demonstrate.

I shrugged. "It's interesting."

"Cut," shouted RD. "We're gonna try something different..."

After explaining the concept to the actors, John pulled up a chair beside them and started tapping a slow, steady rhythm on his knee.

"Give each other some space," said RD. "Let everything breath. This is the free-for-all. Ian can start us off." He nodded at Tobey. "Cool?"

"Let's go, baby."

RD paused a moment, giving John's timing a chance to take hold. "OK. Whenever you're ready."

After a moment, Tobey began. "I have an unhealthy obsession with serial killers."

Carla clapped her hands together. "Oh my god, so do I! Did you know Charles Manson was a member of the Beach Boys?"

"That's not true," said Tobey as Ian.

"Yeah, it is. He was a Beach Boy, but he got kicked out because he threatened to kill someone—a producer, I think. Or maybe it was Brian Wilson... I can't remember exactly right now."

"He knew one of them," said Scott as Brad. "Dennis maybe. But he wasn't in the band."

"Yeah, he was. They recorded together and everything. Although the tapes never got released, or were destroyed or something..."

"Where did you hear this complete and utter nonsense?" said Kevin as Jeremy.

"I read it. It's true."

"Where? The National Enquirer?"

"No. I can't remember exactly, but everything I read is credible."

"Oh really?" Scott squinted his eyes. "Like what?"

"Like, Cosmo is one thing."

"What is that?" said Scott. "A science magazine?"

She straightened up in her seat. "Cosmopolitan Magazine."

Kevin busted out laughing first, and that triggered the rest of the cast.

"It's a credible magazine." Carla crossed her arms. "Have you ever read it?"

"Yeah, Derek was beating off to it earlier tonight, actually," said Kevin as Jeremy. "He reads that shit all the time."

The table roared, everyone except for Carla, of course. I saw her poor hand shaking beneath the table.

Leo as Derek laughed. "I thought for sure you were going to say the Washington Post or the LA Times, or something like that."

"Or Rolling Stone," muttered Scott as Brad.

"I definitely thought she was about to get into some heavy shit about the cosmos..." said Jenny as Sara.

"Charles Manson, forgotten Beach Boy turned cosmic serial killer," joked Tobey.

That was right about when Carla came undone. She began waving her hands in front of her face frantically and muttering something incoherent. She fumbled with the index cards in front of her, looking for something to say.

"Everything all right?" Kevin raised his brow.

"Yeah-yeah. Let's talk about something else. What about summer? Do you guys like the beach? I..." She took a deep breath. "I love the beach so much."

No one responded, so she kept on going.

"We should all go to the beach one day—wouldn't that be fun, Derek?"

"What are you talking about?" Leo chuckled uncomfortably.

"We should go to the beach sometime... maybe later tonight." She flared her eyes at him seductively.

"No, I don't think I want to do that." Leo looked over at RD, his eyes begging for it to stop.

RD rose to his feet. "OK, cut, cut, cut. Let's take a break."

The rest of the guys went for a smoke while RD and I went over our notes. Leo took a seat at our end of the table.

"She's not coming back, I take it?" said Leo.

RD shook his head, "No chance."

"She had a rough day," said Leo. Something was off with Leo and I learned a long time ago to kill the monster when it's little, so I asked him what was up.

He began with a sigh. "I don't know man... I don't know what my character is fuckin' doing most of the time. I like a lot of the shit we're doing, like my father's history and all that, but I just, I'm not sure what to do with him as a whole. He also seems super one-dimensional."

"I mean, I think he's certainly more than that, but yeah, he's mainly a dick."

"Why?"

"Probably a bunch of reasons," I said. "But I think most of his issues stem back to his dad. Can you imagine losing George suddenly? Like tonight? You leave here, and you go home—you go to his house I mean, and he fuckin' killed himself. You discover his body—"

"Bro, that's not necessary."

RD interjected, "That's Derek's story though, bro. He found his dad hanging in the fucking garage... dead."

Leo adjusted in his seat. The garage was a nice touch by RD. We hadn't discussed where or how the suicide took place.

Leo postured up. "So, basically, Derek is fuckin' pissed at the world because of his father's suicide, and he takes it out on the people around him in different ways."

"I mean, yeah," said RD.

"He's not pissed at the world," I said. "He's pissed at women."

Leo winced. "You don't think that's a little, I don't know... a little on the nose maybe?"

"No. That's the fuckin' gold."

He shook his head slowly. "Suicide is so dramatic, bro."

"Yeah, that's the point," I said. "It's a lot to go through."

Leo stared off for a second. "Yeah, OK," he said. "I think I got it.

I'm just gonna play him as the asshole version of myself times ten. Is that cool?"

RD shrugged, "Yeah, fine... but bring something redeeming. We want you to be somewhat likable..."

Leo shrugged, "Why? Who cares if people like me?"

RD shrugged back. "Yeah, you're right. Who cares."

16

SUPS WAS SPRAWLED out on the Sups Couch like a Roman emperor waiting to be fed fat grapes. "Bro, I have to be in your film." he said. "Enough of this nonsense."

RD grinned. "We'll figure something out."

"Let's figure it out right now." He pushed himself up with a grunt. "I don't understand why you don't want me in your movie. I'm in Kevin Smith's new movie, but I'm not good enough for an RD Robb film?"

RD chuckled. "You'll be in it, don't worry."

"I'm not leaving here tonight without a role, RD." Ethan took out a cigarette and lit it. "I got all night."

I laughed. "We'll find you something."

"No, bro. If we don't do it now, it'll never happen. We're figuring it out tonight, right now."

"Why?" RD was laughing now. He loved having something Ethan wanted. I think he enjoyed watching Ethan, or anyone, grovel.

"I just know, RD. Because it's going to get too busy and more people are going to get involved, and then it'll be too late. Come on, bro. I'm not stupid."

"Do you have a character in mind?" I asked.

"No. You guys are the writers."

RD shrugged. "Come up with an idea, and we'll talk about it."

"No, RD. That's just another way I get screwed out of being in this movie."

RD smiled and shook his head, "Nooo..."

"Yes. I'll come up with something—it'll be awesome, but you'll have to run it past your team of writers, who'll decide they don't like it. The whole thing will end up a complete waste of my time, and I still won't get a role in the movie. Or, even worse, you'll put me in some random scene that ends up on the cutting room floor. I'm not stupid, RD."

RD kept giggling. "No, bro, nothing like that is going to happen."

"Let's do a scene together."

"Who?"

"The three of us! It's genius!"

RD shook his head. "No, I'm not acting in the film. You can do a scene with Dale if you want."

Ethan nodded at me. "Are you in it?"

"Yeah. I was gonna play a homeless dude."

"What's that about?"

I shrugged. "I wander into the diner, interact with the table... get some money, or don't, maybe. Then I get kicked out. That's about it. That all leads to an improv around homelessness and addiction and shit like that."

Ethan nodded slowly. "Yeah, that sounds kind of fun."

I chuckled. "Yeah? You wanna be homeless with me?"

"Sure, why not?"

"A bum duo," said RD. "I kinda like it."

I chuckled. "Big bum, little bum."

"What—so we just go in and start begging? That's our thing?"

"I don't know, maybe. Not for food, though."

"That's true." Ethan patted his big belly and flashed a warm, contagious smile. "I obviously get plenty of that."

"Money and booze," I said.

"And cigarettes," said Ethan.

"And cigarettes. And then we just sort of stumble into their web of–"

"Web. Nice." He turned to RD. "Are you listening to this fuckin' writer over here? We stumble into a web…"

I chuckled and continued. "I thought they might try and coerce me, or us, into doing something for money."

"Something humiliating?"

"No, no. Like, ask us to sing or something. Or maybe we could just break into a song on our own, like a couple of happy hobos' kind of thing. Be like those dudes that wash windshields at red lights. We just fuckin' walk up to people and start singing in their face until we get paid." I laughed.

"That's pretty funny," said Ethan. "So, we never actually ask for money directly?" Ethan started giggling. "People are going to wonder how I got so fat, though, because I am not a good singer."

RD guffawed.

"RD Robb, laughing at fat jokes." Ethan chuckled. "But it's improv, right? So, I can do pretty much whatever I want?"

"Yes and no. We don't want to be too…" RD couldn't find the word, so I offered up stringent. "Yeah, whatever" he said. "It's about how you're feeling in the scene at that exact moment. Let the writing point you in a direction, but let your feelings take over from there."

"Yeah, I heard you're all about feelings," said Ethan mockingly.

RD bristled. "Oh yeah? What did you hear?"

Ethan tried to wave it off. "Nothing, never mind."

"No, bro. Don't give me that shit."

"Nothing. Just… I heard you call 'feel' instead of 'action.'"

"Yeah, so what?"

"Whatever, it's a little weird."

"Why?"

"Because people have been calling action for centuries–"

"Decades," I said.

"You know what I'm saying. I think people can get the wrong idea. You know how people are, RD."

"About what? What people?"

"It could be anyone—I'm saying it's possible with anybody."

"Yeah, well, that's absurd. And I don't really give a fuck. I learned that shit from a legend."

"Whatever. I love you like my sister, you know that, bro."

"What a bunch of dicks."

"It was nothing, RD. I promise. Everyone's just excited about the movie. Why do you think I tried so hard to get in it? I'm in the film, right?"

RD shrugged. "If Dale's cool with it. It's his scene."

I nodded. "Yeah, man. Let's do it."

"Awesome! Thank you, Dale. Thanks, R."

"Just stop talkin' shit," said RD.

"I'm not talkin' any shit. I'm telling you, it was nothing. You know I love you, RD. We all love you." Ethan opened his arms and RD snuggled in for a hug. "I just didn't want to be left out of your big debut."

RD's voice sounded sweeter muffled by Ethan's pillow top shoulder. "You were always going to be in the movie."

———

I WAS in Hollywood after picking up the last of my pay from Terry, so I called up Jeremy Sisto to see what he was up to. He was stressing out over an upcoming screen test for Ridley Scott and thought going clothes shopping might help calm his nerves. We met up at one of his favorite spots on Melrose, a vintage shop called Wasteland.

I had no intention of buying anything, but it was fun flipping through the racks and bullshitting with Jeremy. Then I came across a shirt that I am all but certain put a spell on me. It was the strangest fucking thing. As soon as my fingers touched it, I was overcome with a profound need to possess it. It wasn't even all that great. The material was a weird bronze color, almost army green, with short, wide sleeves. The entire shirt was dotted with tiny, golden pineapples. It had an oversized lapel and a massive left breast pocket big enough for more than one pack of cigarettes. I was obsessed with the shirt, but one look at the price tag changed my mind. I couldn't afford $50 for one shirt so, though it pained me, I hung it back on the rack. Moments later, I spotted Jeremy sneak the shirt off the rack on his way to the register.

Jeremy did that sort of shit all the time. He would buy people stuff, even if he was low on cash himself, or he would do some kind of outrageous favor that no one else would do. I've personally witnessed him feed countless homeless people in two different countries, but occasionally, very rarely, his generosity was annoying. I did not want him buying me a $50 shirt just because I admired it, but the only way to stop him was to buy it for myself. So, I paid the cashier the ransom and left Wasteland clutching an unwanted bag.

"Put it on," he said, "Let's see what it looks like."

I did, and it felt a little weird. A bit big, maybe. I couldn't stop thinking about the money as I pulled and adjusted the seams.

"Yeah," he said. "It looks good."

"Really?" I put both my wallet and cigarettes in the breast pocket. "Fits both!"

Jeremy chuckled. "Nice shirt," he said, and I believed him.

RD and I reconnected at the condo to go over cinematographer reels. I expected some kind of reaction to my shirt, it was literally the first piece of new clothing I had acquired since knowing him, but he didn't say a word. His eyes lingered on it for a second or two, but that was it. He had a shitty energy about him, but I just tried to ignore it and stay focused on the task of finding our Director of Photography.

We watched quite a few tapes before one finally stood out to us. Steven Adcock's reel was solid from end to end, but there was one shot from a bar scene with Joey Lauren Adams that got us most excited. Steven had bounced a key light off a white card directly on the table that gave her an almost ethereal beauty with bold features thanks to the contrast of the strong under light. Adcock's composition and camera movement were equally beautiful. Absolutely nothing seemed forced in his work, and that was what we needed most from a cinematographer to pull off the voyeuristic feel we were looking for.

RD wanted to keep watching reels but as far as I was concerned, there was no point. Adcock was our guy. RD was in a shitty mood to start, so we had an intense argument over it, until he finally stomped off to his bedroom to watch the rest of the tapes alone. When he emerged a couple of hours later, he still had a shitty attitude, and Steven Adcock was still our first choice to shoot our movie.

WE ARRIVED at the production office before everyone else and started setting up tables in relative silence. David Stutman arrived, bubbling with energy. He tilted his head curiously at me.

"Is that a new shirt?"

"Yeah," I said. "I snagged it from Wasteland today."

He leaned in closer, squinting. "Are those... pineapples?"

I chuckled. "Yeah."

"That's random."

RD stood abruptly. "Where the fuck is Bethany Ashton, bro?"

"She'll be here," I said. "Chill."

"No, bro, I don't want to chill. I want to get to fuckin' work. We said we're starting at four o'clock, then she should be here at four fuckin' o'clock."

Bethany arrived 15 minutes late, before RD could unravel completely. We brought her up to speed with the casting, and which of the improvs we had rehearsed so far. When she asked how everyone was doing in rehearsals, I used words like amazing, incredible, and brilliant. RD interrupted me before I could finish. He hated hyperbole, even if it was the truth.

"Dale's off his ass for a change. It's fine, the work is good, but the cast is all over the place half the time, and there's no structure... there's no real point to it right now."

"No point?!" I threw up my hands. "What the fuck are you talking about?"

"Meaning them," said RD. "I'm not talking about us."

"Well, I proposed we make Derek's story the center—"

"Don't start with this shit again, bro. Please."

"Not because it's Leo. His storyline is perfect as the set turning points of the movie. It's great structure."

RD smiled at me, but it wasn't a friendly smile. "I already told you we weren't going to do anything like that." He finished his sentence through gritted teeth.

David gestured toward me. "Surprisingly, I agree with Dale on this point."

"We are not making a Leonardo DiCaprio film, David. So get it out of your head."

I jumped right back in. "We're talking about the turning points. Aligning the film as if he were the protagonist even though he is not. It's a fucking compass for the movie, RD." I threw up my hands. "Why is this so difficult to understand?"

RD took a deep breath. "Bro. We're not making a film centered on one fucking actor. I don't care who it is."

"That's fine. All's I'm talking about is structure. I keep repeating myself. Structure RD. If you want it to make sense, then something has to carry it. It's still an ensemble cast. You're the only one calling it a DiCaprio film."

"If it's not about Leo, then why not structure it around Jeremy? Or Ian?"

"I just said, Derek has the most interesting story. And yeah, he's obviously our strongest actor."

RD shrugged. "I don't know about that, bro. Kevin or fuckin' Bloom might run away with it and carry the whole thing. Leo doesn't give two shits about this movie, bro—he's just gonna phone it in, like he did with Last Respects. This is just a pain in the ass for him, trust me."

"Where is all of this coming from? Did he say something to you?"

RD shook his head. "The guy is shooting with Meryl Streep and Robert De Niro next month, genius. He doesn't give a rat's ass about this project."

"That's not true at all. He's involved. He's been fucking amazing in every rehearsal. What's really goin' on?"

"Nothing. We just don't agree."

"OK, then you come up with the turning points."

RD shrugged again, dismissively. "They all fuckin' hang out and talk about shit that's going on in life, and we learn a little bit about each of them as characters and hopefully a little more about life in general. Like we talked about, bro."

"Cool. What are the turning points, though?"

"They fuckin' talk, bro. I don't know yet, it's an improv project."

Bethany interjected. "Do you have something in mind, Dale?"

"I just want to talk about it with you guys. If you just listen, RD, I'd bet fuckin' money—"

"You don't have any money."

"Ouch," said David.

I sighed and tried to smile. "Why are you... Can I continue without you being a dick?"

"I mean, sure...but—" RD paused and sighed, "Never mind, I'll just end up repeating myself again." He waved his hand at me flippantly. "Go ahead, do your thing, bro."

I took a deep breath. "I think the night gets out of control at some point, right? The more tired they get, the easier their emotions fray. Communication breaks down, arguments ensue. The dynamic between the cast starts crumbling as the night wears on. But it's not just them, it's the whole diner... the server, the cook, everyone and everything starts to unravel..."

RD shrugged. "Why?"

"Why? It's just one of those nights when everything is fucking crazy, I don't know. Like a full moon or something. Structure wise, it's what gets us into the third act."

"Do you know what happens?" said Bethany.

"I don't... maybe there's a fight or something."

Bethany raised her eyebrows. "A fist fight?"

"Yeah... You know, shit gets all chaotic, someone storms off, maybe someone else gives chase and more shit goes down."

"Could be a chick that walks off," said RD. I could see the

creative juices flowing behind his eyes. "Or maybe it's one of the guys actually, and, like you said, Wheats, one of the chicks goes after him..."

"Yeah, I love that. It would give us something cool to cut to. Hmm, I wonder what character this storyline fits best with..." I grinned a dickish grin at RD and he rolled his eyes. "It's a great turning point for Derek. He shows up empty-handed but he's the one that ends up with a chick at the end of the night. That's pretty cool."

David raised his hand. "So Derek pisses everyone off and runs away. One of the girls chases after him and they fuck? Is that the idea?"

RD grinned. "Which means someone at the table loses their girl to Derek..."

I nodded excitedly. "And on top of that, everyone else is feeling shitty about what they did to Derek to make him storm off in the first place—"

"It would be cool if we could tie all this into his father's suicide somehow," said Bethany.

"Oh we will, no doubt about it. And we intercut that with him trying to get laid." I smacked RD on the shoulder. "I love it!"

"Who's gonna play that chick?" said RD.

"Meadow Sisto, for sure," I said. "I watched that girl seduce Leo at Jay's one night until he was wrapped around her finger. She'll be amazing."

"Well, she's still gotta audition, but yeah, that would be huge for her."

Bethany leaned back and smiled. "This is so awesome. Have you given any thought to the final image?"

We went quiet a moment.

"I think they all walk off into the rising sun, right?" I grinned. "The night is over. Life goes on."

RD grinned. "What about a B-Story?"

Bethany sat up in her chair again. "I don't know if this is a B-story per se, but I have an idea for Jeremy that I've been tossing around in my head."

"Let's hear it," said RD.

She sat up straighter. "I, um, I came up with this idea because I thought it would be so much fun to play a big-time Hollywood producer—" She giggled nervously, "A Lauren Shuler Donner type, you know what I mean?"

I rubbed my hands together. "I love this already. Have you heard about her hand-picking dudes right out of The Beverly Center and taking them home?"

Bethany grinned, "Not that part necessarily, but..."

David said, "What the hell are you guys talking about?

Bethany and I started to answer at the same time, but she insisted I continue.

"There's a rumor that Lauren Shuler Donner goes to the Beverly Center on a regular basis and hand selects guys that she wants to fuck, and then sends her assistants to proposition them."

"That's kind of hot," said David. "Is it true?"

I shrugged. "I have no idea, but I do hang out at the mall a lot more often." Absolutely nobody laughed at my hilarious joke. I turned to Bethany. "Keep going, I'm sorry."

"Yeah, so, my character—this big shot producer, goes in for a late-night snack, or whatever, and of course Jeremy recognizes her as soon as she walks in—maybe—"

RD interrupted, "It would be funny if he recently tested for her—"

"Yeah and didn't get the part!" I chuckled.

"Yeah," said RD. "That's the point, bro."

Bethany lit up. "I love that idea so much because I thought he would approach me for some reason, and we would talk a little bit, and then I would try to seduce him. That's such a perfect back-story, you guys."

David giggled. "So Jeremy fucks his way to the top?"

"We'll see," I said. "Does she proposition him?"

"Oh, absolutely, yeah." She giggled. "I'll invite him back to my place for a little casting couch action for sure."

RD smacked the tabletop. "I fuckin' love this. This is so good."

"Me too," said David.

"I named her already." Bethany turned a timid smile, her eyes switching from mine, David's, and RD's. "Grace Forrester."

I leaned back in my chair and smiled. "Just... Absolutely wonderful."

THE GUYS WERE the first to arrive for rehearsal. As they greeted me, they each said, "Nice shirt." "Is that a new shirt?" "Where did you get that shirt?" and, "Are those tiny pineapples?"

Once everyone, including the ladies, were in place, John Schindler put his metronome near the cast, set it to 60 beats per minute, then started the video camera.

The guys picked up where they left off. Their dialogue was sharp and witty right out of the gate. Jenny Lewis offered a great a mix of dry humor and poignant introspection. But the rest of the girls were generally awful.

Meadow arrived about midway through the evening, looking relaxed and confident. I was going over my notes when she found me.

"Hey," she said, smiling. Her attention shifted to my shirt. "What is that?"

"This?" I tugged at my lapel.

"Yeah," she squinted, "What? Are those..."

"Pineapples. Little pineapples."

Her eyebrows furrowed as her eyes met mine again. "W —why?"

I sighed, "Is it bad?"

She chuckled, "You went to Wasteland with Jeremy today, huh?"

"Yes..."

"His shirt is even worse."

"This is terrible," I said and she laughed, crushing what little self-esteem I had left. "I feel really fucking stupid right now."

"Oh, no, don't be upset, honey..."

"I don't know why I thought it was a good shirt. Is it really that bad?"

Her eyes filled with sympathy. "It's not good, Dale. Do you have an undershirt you can wear?"

"No. And I left my shirt in your brother's car."

"It's fine for now. It's just a shirt." She shrugged and grinned. "Change it as soon as you can though."

"I spent fifty bucks on this thing."

She hissed.

RD approached and opened his arms to Meadow. "Hey you." They hugged. "Good to see you."

"Good to see you too, RD."

"You ready to do this?"

"Absolutely."

We walked her to the table and gave her some direction for the scene along the way. We sat her between Tobey and a girl named Christine, who was auditioning for the role of Amy. After a couple of rounds, Christine all but disappeared while Meadow got stronger and stronger. At one point, Meadow found herself toe to toe with Leo after he joked that vegetarians, especially vegans, should themselves be killed and eaten.

Meadow's eyes narrowed. "You know what it seems like to me? Like you're insecure about it."

Leo guffawed. "Why would I be insecure about vegetarians?"

She smiled and shrugged. "I don't know. Maybe your subconscious is trying to tell you something about the bad choices you're making..."

Leo shook his head. "I don't think that's it."

"You sure? What if you're not getting the message because you're too self-absorbed to see all the horrible shit that happens as a result of your personal actions."

Leo adjusted in his seat. "What do you know about me, huh?"

"I know from that response alone that you're more concerned about your tender ego than you are about how the things you're doing, like eating flesh, is destroying the environment. It's not all about you, Derek. The sooner you realize that, the better off we'll all be."

"Oh shit..." Scott chuckled.

Kevin sat back in his chair, his head stacked on his neck like it was about to get smacked. "Dude" escaped his lips like a fluttering moth.

Leo looked over at Tobey, his voice slightly wobbled. "What about you—you're a fuckin' vegetarian, what do you think?"

Tobey chuckled. "Yeah, I mean, I agree with Meadow for sure..." He recognized his mistake immediately. "Well, shit, I'm sorry." He looked at Meadow, grinning at himself and shaking his head. "What's your character's name again?"

"Juliet, ya doofus," said Meadow.

"Juliet, that's right." Tobey chuckled, "I'm sorry I fucked it all up. My bad."

RD looked at me with wide, excited eyes and mouthed, 'Holy shit!' He stood up. "Cut! That was fucking awesome!"

Leo looked a little battered and Kevin rubbed it in, "You just got fuckin' smashed, bro."

"Yeah, I know. I know," said Leo. "I didn't know you were a vegetarian, Meadow."

She shrugged. "I'm not."

Leo grinned. "Nice work."

Meadow beamed a smile back at him. "Thank you, Leo. That's nice of you to say."

AFTER REHEARSAL, we sat around with the guys and discussed which of the female performances we liked most. Jenny Lewis and Meadow Sisto dazzled us, so they were going to get offers. There was some debate about who should play Amy. It was between RD's girlfriend, Heather McComb, and Amber Benson. They were opposites in almost every way, and they both did great work. Amber's Amy was dark and a little disturbed, while Heather's was bubbly and virginal. Both characters would be fun to mess with, but there could only be one, and Amber Benson got the votes.

We decided on The Formosa to celebrate finalizing our cast. Everyone went home first to freshen up. RD and I stayed back at the office to pack up the index cards. I grabbed a blank card and wrote down each cast member's name in alphabetical order.

Amber Benson
Scott Bloom
Kevin Connolly
Leonardo DiCaprio
Jenny Lewis
Tobey Maguire
Meadow Sisto

I pushed the index card across the table to RD. "Your cast, sir."

He lifted the card and looked at it for a moment and then smiled. "Let's get the fuck out of here."

WE JUMPED in RD's car and hopped on the 101 freeway headed for Hollywood.

"Yo, can we stop at the house? I gotta change this shirt, bro."

RD shook his head, "No, you're fine. You look good."

"Please, RD... this thing was the worst mistake ever."

RD had a mischievous grin. "What do you mean? It's your nice new shirt! Besides, stopping will add like a half hour."

"It will not take a half hour to grab a fucking t-shirt."

"Yeah, bro. Getting off the freeway. Getting back on the freeway."

"You're boning me so hard right now, RD."

He laughed. "What do you mean? You look good." He glanced in my direction as he passed the last exit for the condo. "I love your new shirt."

I shook my head. "What a fuckin' dick move, bro."

THE FORMOSA WAS PACKED. A large contingent of our clique was already there. Johnny Whitworth, Jay and Lisa, Marisa, Meadow, and Jeremy, Leo, Tobey, Scott, Ethan, Kevin, Nikki Cox, Blake, and there were film and TV stars, some I knew, most I did not, all crowding the tables and grouped along the walls. Most of our group was situated at the front of the bar.

Everybody's favorite server, Cass, approached me with her usual warm smile. Her gaze lingered on my shirt.

"It's dumb," I said. "I know."

"What's that, honey?" She leaned in closer.

I grinned and spoke up. "I said you look amazing."

"Aw, thank you," she said with a beaming smile. "It's good to see you, too, hon. Rolling Rock?"

"Yes, please."

She took the rest of our orders, and, to my surprise, RD ordered a Jack and Coke. I had never seen him drink before, not at dozens of parties, bars, restaurants, or weekend trips.

He shrugged off my reaction and mouthed, "Fuck it."

"Go slow," I said. He rolled his eyes and turned away.

With drinks in hand, Kevin made a brief toast to the cast of *The Saturday Night Club*. I raised my beer in salute and took a good swallow.

Johnny Whitworth came up to me with an inviting smile.

"How you doin' Johnny?"

"I'm good, Mr. Dale. Congrats my friend."

"We'll see what happens. It's exciting."

I loved Johnny Whitworth's look. He had a bad-boy thing going on, always in denim and leather, with his hair combed back with some kind of Brylcreem like Patrick Swayze in *The Outsiders*. He even had a badass scar on his upper lip that hinted at something legendary. I half expected him to whip out a switchblade comb and start grooming and talking to me with a lit cigarette bouncing between his lips. "What are you doing on the film exactly? Acting?"

"I have small role, but writing the movie with RD is my main thing."

"That's fucking incredible. Didn't you just get here? How long have you been in the business?"

"A little while now... a year and change, I guess."

"A year and change." His lips parted into a grin. "That's wild. You see all these people? See RD over there?" He pointed to him. The light glinted off his silver ring and caught my eye.

"I do."

"RD, and most of the people in this bar right now, have worked their asses off to get where you are right now. RD's been in the business since he was an infant."

"I know, that's so crazy."

"But look at you, man! Your very first thing and you're working with one of the hottest actors in the business."

"I got very lucky."

"Yeah, you sure did... Where are you from, Canada?"

"Yeah."

I caught Kevin's eye and he nodded in my direction. "Yo, you need a beer?"

"I do."

I dipped out of my conversation with Johnny and followed Kevin to the bar.

Kevin and the bartender exchanged looks but Kevin was still left waiting. "Are you legally allowed to work here right now?

I was stunned by Kevin's question. No one had ever asked about my immigration status before. "I'm working on it."

"Do you need a permit or visa or whatever?"

"There are a few ways... it's complicated."

"Doesn't matter with this, though, huh? Since you're not being paid?"

"I think being a creator means something, but I don't know. What's with all the questions? You're making me a little nervous."

"No, bro." He chuckled. "No, because once you have your paperwork, I can get you a guest spot on Unhappily Ever After, if you want."

"Oh fuck." I laughed. "Are you serious?"

"What? You thought I was gonna turn you in?"

"No, you just caught me off guard. That's fucking amazing."

"Don't be so paranoid. No, I'm directing a couple of episodes this season, and I can put you in one of them easily. I mean, even if I'm not directing, I can still get you on the show. You won't even have to audition. You'll get your SAG card."

"Dude, that's the nicest thing anyone has ever done for me. Holy shit."

"Of course. We're friends, bro."

Nikki intercepted Kevin before he could get his drink order in, and they disappeared into the crowd.

I found RD chatting with Blake and told him about Kevin's offer. He scoffed. "Are you fucking serious? I've been friends with that fucker for ten years, and he hasn't offered me shit."

Blake spoke between dabbing the gluey strip of a rolling paper with the tip of his tongue. "When you get all that shit sorted out, I can get you a guest spot on Boy Meets Nuts, too."

"You're fucking with me..." I was stunned.

Blake shook his head. "No. I'll get you on the show. I'm in good with Michael Jacobs."

"I just got offered two roles on two different TV shows and I don't even have a fuckin' headshot!"

A darkness came over RD, his face lost expression. "Fuck you, Blake."

"Why fuck me?"

"My mom's your manager, for fuck's sake."

Blake laughed. "You don't want to do Boy Meets World, RD. It's good for Dale, he's just getting started—you're a big-time actor." Blake was being a dick and RD knew it.

"Fuck you, bro."

"Why? You've been on Broadway, you do feature films. You don't need Boy Meets World."

"I just want to act, bro."

"You really want to be on the show?"

"Yes."

"No problem, RD." Blake reached across to gently stroke RD's face but RD pulled away. Blake, much like RD, made a game of showing his affection in weird and provocative ways.

RD took a tiny sip of his cocktail.

"How many of those have you had?" I said.

RD shrugged. "This is still my first."

I chuckled. "You're tipsy. That's funny."

Blake laughed. "I thought you were on your third by now. Look at you, dude, you're drunk after a few sips."

It was true, RD's eyes were bloodshot and glassy.

"I'm not drunk at all."

I laughed. "Holy lightweight."

"I'm not a fucking lightweight, bro."

"You're loaded after a half of a cocktail, RD. That is the definition of a lightweight. You're a tiny guy—it's nothing to be ashamed of."

"Oh, yeah? Well, you're a fuckin' douche, how about that?"

"Jesus Christ, bro. Relax. I'm just talking a little shit."

RD stuck his jaw out and stepped toward me. "You're a fuckin' know-it-all-faggot-piece-of-shit, that's what you are."

"RD. Get out of my face."

I took a step back, and he got right back in my space. "What are you going to do? Huh?"

"RD, stop. Now. This is the last warning."

He stepped even closer. "What are you gonna fuckin' do, huh?"

I pushed him away with just enough force to reclaim my personal space. RD was drunk, though, so he fell backward dramatically. He spilled the contents of his cup all over my shirt, jeans, and chucks.

"Fuck, RD!"

He dropped his cup and lunged toward me. He hooked his fingers into my front pocket and ripped downward, tearing half of it off. My cigarettes and lighter fell to the floor. I pushed him away again, and he crashed into a table, spilling drinks and causing chaos. He regained his balance and lunged for my shirt again, tearing several buttons down to my belly. I reached for his neck, but Cass came from out of nowhere and got between us before I could thoroughly wring it.

"What are you guys doing?!"

"He's a piece of shit, Cass!" RD shouted from behind Cass while barely being held back by a very amused Blake Sennett.

"You can't do this in here. You gotta take it outside!"

"Let's fuckin' go, you little prick," I turned and headed for the door. I heard someone behind me, it sounded like Kevin, shout "FIGHT!" just as I shoved open the doors.

I was followed into the parking lot by a small crowd of drunk, rowdy people. My shirt was stained and torn, my chest and belly exposed. I stunk like RD's Jack and Coke.

RD lunged forward again and tried to grab at what was left of my shirt, but I swung an open hand that caught him on the side of the head. The blow sent him stumbling. He regained his balance, screamed like a banshee, and charged me at full force. He's small and quick, and he knocked me on my ass. My tailbone hit the pavement and sent bolts of pain up my spine. I screamed and got to my feet. The crowd melted into a blur as I took a heavy step toward him with white-knuckle fists. He dodged inside and grabbed another fist full of my shirt and ripped it again. I shot toward him, but the little fucker darted across Formosa Avenue before I could get my hands on him. I caught up to him and gave him another open-handed shot to the side of the head, but not before he grabbed what was left of my shirt and tore it from my body completely. He held up the rags like entrails and shook them in my face. I finally got a hold of him and lifted him straight off the ground and tossed him into a nearby hedge. His grip around the back of my neck was strong enough to pull me in with him. I tried to get after him in the bush, but the branches scraped me all over.

Scott Bloom pulled me out of the bush by my belt. I tried to catch my breath. Ethan helped RD to his feet. RD had leaves and branches all over him and in his hair. His face and arms were scraped up and dotted with tiny crimson beads.

"You're a fuckin' dick, bro," I said.

"So are you," he said.

We stepped toward each other again, but Kevin got between us.

"That's enough," said Kevin. "What the fuck is wrong with you guys? Both of you. You're friends, for fuck's sake."

I pointed at RD. "He fuckin' attacked me—what was I supposed to do?"

RD snapped back. "Because you're fucking prancing around in that ridiculous shirt acting all self-important... meanwhile you're nothing without me, or any of us."

"What the fuck are you talking about?"

Kevin waved his hands between us like white flags. "Never mind all of that. That's fuckin' nonsense."

RD barked, "You think you're so fucking important, but you're not. You're a piece of shit."

I clenched my fist and stepped forward, but Kevin held me back.

"What are you doing?" said Kevin. "He's your friend."

"He's a fuckin' asshole."

"Are you saying he's not your friend?"

"No. He's my friend, but..." Just hearing myself say RD was my friend changed the way I felt. I was instantly less angry and more confused. "I don't know where any of this is coming from. Look what he did."

"Never mind that." Kevin turned to RD and pointed at me. "Is he your friend?"

RD nodded. "Yes."

"Then start acting like it, bro. Both of you. You're grown men, for Christ's sake."

Scott grabbed my shredded fifty-dollar shirt and held it up like a caught fish. He fetched a lighter from his pocket and lit the poor, tattered thing on fire. The flames climbed quickly, and he tossed it to the side of the road, where it burned and bubbled into a charred pile of poly-goo.

RD and I muttered half sincere apologies, but there was still a lot of tension between us. I had to bum a ride back to the valley. I wasn't gonna ride with RD, and I didn't have the fifty bucks for a cab. Blake offered me a ride. He didn't talk much on the drive, other than to warn me that my shower was probably going to sting.

When I arrived at the condo, RD was in his room with the door closed. I kicked off my shoes, got out of my remaining clothes and laid down on my bed and passed out.

THE FOLLOWING MORNING, I awoke to the sounds of RD rattling around in the kitchen downstairs. I jumped in the shower and the dozens of scrapes and scratches burned just like Blake said they would.

When came down the stairs and RD and I finally saw each other, we both broke out into big dumb grins as we did our best to avoid eye contact. I felt so fucking stupid about the whole thing.

I broke the silence. "What the fuck happened to you last night?"

RD shook his head, "Honestly, I don't even know."

"You were shitty the whole day."

"No... was I?"

I chuckled. "Was it my shirt? Did it really enrage you so much?"

"No, bro... I mean, that thing was fucking hideous, I did us all a favor, let's be honest."

I sniggered. "What the fuck was it then? You were crazy."

RD took a deep breath. "Sometimes you're so fucking overbearing, I don't think you realize it, but you just kind of take shit over... which is fine some of the time, you're a smart dude, but it can also be very frustrating. It got to me, I think."

"I don't know what you mean by that. Like, what specifically? When? How?"

"Whenever we're writing, or like now, during the auditions, it's happened once or twice. Or just when we're standing around talking about whatever."

"I do it all the time?"

"Not all the time, no... mostly when we're working or talking about the film."

"Well, I'm excited. I'm passionate. And I get these ideas that I gotta get out of my head, or they're gone forever. What else am I supposed to do?"

"I get it, but..." He sighed, "I don't know..."

"Just say it—say what's goin' on."

"I love your stuff. You know? We work really, really well together. It's just, it's fucking weird sometimes."

"Are you breaking up with me right now?"

He chuckled. "No."

I waited a moment, expecting him to say more, but he just stood there silent with his eyes on the floor.

"Come on, man. I can't change what I don't know."

"I feel like at times you're undermining me in front of the others. You talk over me sometimes, and you also pitch things to the cast that we've never discussed in our writing sessions, and that makes me look bad."

"Why would that make you look bad?"

"Because I'm the director, bro. I should know what's going on."

"I'm the writer. We're collaborating on an improv film. What did you think would happen?"

"I don't know. I thought you would discuss things with me first, I guess."

I held my hands up cautiously. "It's improv, we have to adapt on the spot. And besides R, you and I talk about things as they're happening all the time, and you're the one who brings the notes to the cast whether they're mine, John's, or anyone else's."

"Not all the time."

"Most of the time. I'm not trying to undermine you or anyone, I'm just working on this movie. I thought I was doing a good job."

"You are, but there are these times when you're so—I mean, I already said it. Overbearing."

"OK." I shrugged. "I'll curb my enthusiasm—"

"No, bro, just be mindful of the way you're being, that's all I'm saying..."

"I will. I'll do my best. I guess I don't really understand what my role is in this thing sometimes."

RD shrugged. "You should just be directing with me—you basically are anyway."

"I'm OK with being a writer. You know? I don't want to be creatively marginalized, but—"

"No."

"I don't know what parts of me are offensive and what parts of me are useful. I don't know what to hold back, or what to do, but I don't want you to feel that way."

"Don't hold anything back, bro. That's not the way."

"I think you're awesome, RD. I'm really grateful for this opportunity. I'm sorry if I've overstepped my boundaries... And I'm sorry I threw you in that bush."

He nodded as a grin opened on his face. "I'm sorry for ripping your ugly ass shirt."

I chuckled. "You destroyed my ugly ass shirt."

We laughed at ourselves. RD walked over to the blinking answering machine and hit the play button. There were a bunch of new messages. The first was from Kevin.

"Yo, what's up...are we still making a movie or what? One of you fuckers give me a call and tell me what's going on." *BEEP*

"Hey RD, it's me, Tobias Maguire—just calling to see if Dale murdered you in your sleep. If not, call me back. Bye." *BEEP*

"Yo, guys, it's Leo. Just calling to let Dale know I got an extra shirt here if he needs one. K-bye." *BEEP*

There were messages from Scott, Ethan, Blake, and others, and after each one of them I felt more and more ridiculous.

I slumped in my chair. "We should put our fight in the movie, RD. The whole fucking thing; burning shirt, rolling in bushes. All of it."

RD grabbed a yellow notepad from the desk, brought it back and dropped it in front of me. There were four barely legible notes:

Derek pisses off Brad - tension builds
Tension breaks Brad hits Derek - they fight

195

Derek rips Brad's shirt off
Ian burns shirt in the street

I looked up at RD and smiled. "I have some thoughts."

17

RD and I spent hours re-plotting story lines and turning points. We came up with new sub-plots and even a couple of new characters. We discovered new themes, metaphors, and conflicts. Our stupid fight had become our greatest inspiration.

At the production office, RD and I stepped all over each other trying to explain it all to David and Bethany. David, who looked exhausted by the deluge of our excitement, interrupted our pitch. "Yeah, I don't think I like it. First of all, Derek has to have a confessional."

"No, bro, he has it at the table." RD tapped his notepad. "That's what's so genius. We have all these other fuckers in front of mirrors examining themselves and their friends, trying to figure out why they're all fucked up." RD's smile grew wider, "But Derek knows what his problem is. Women."

Bethany smiled. "It's great. It takes care of everything."

"What's even better," I said, "is that it's not women at all."

RD raised his eyebrows and clomped his teeth. "Subtext." *Clomp, clomp,* "Dale loves subtext."

"How do we learn all of this backstory?" asked David.

"Derek sees a dude get slapped by a woman," I said.

"Oh, that happens at the diner?"

"Yes."

"I thought you meant that was the backstory—"

"No, he sees the shit go down at the next table and it fucks his head up. Jeremy presses him until he confesses that his father committed suicide after he caught his mom cheating, and now he's all fucked up about women. When the guys try to console him, he gets up and walks away. Juliet chases after him. We cut back and forth, from Derek trying to get in Juliet's pants to Jeremy and Ian fighting about Derek. The fight eventually moves outside. Ian rips Jeremy's shirt from his body, and Brad fuckin' burns it."

"Did Brad burn your pineapple shirt?" David smirked.

"Scott Bloom burned my shirt, yes."

He laughed.

"I think it's perfect," said Bethany.

"I think it's a little over the top." David held up his hands up in surrender, "But I'm obviously outnumbered."

Bethany leaned forward. "This is all very interesting for the girls."

"Oh, yeah?" I said. "How so?"

"They're going to be on edge with all that testosterone in the room—well, that or really turned on by it."

RD giggled. "Turned on? Really? Why?"

Bethany nodded, her smile turned a little wicked. "The maleness, with all that aggression pouring out of them—it's either gonna intimidate or stimulate."

WHEN LEO ARRIVED FOR REHEARSAL, RD and I took him aside and pitched the new storyline surrounding Derek's father's suicide.

"I like this, guys. I like it a lot, but one thing..." Leo paused and looked at us both with a sort of mischievous grin.

"What, bro?" said RD.

"I am not going to cry in this movie."

"No!" I threw up my hands. "Come on!"

He laughed, but it was a big deal to me. Everything I imagined about this sequence revolved around Derek having an emotional breakdown. I didn't think it would work without it.

I took a thoughtful breath before I spoke. "The guy's dad killed himself, and this is the first time he tells his closest friends on the planet why it happened... think about George—"

"Ah-ah-ah. No. No more of that shit, Dale. Listen to me because I don't want to discuss this again. I'm not crying in this movie, so we don't have to talk about my dad dying or any bullshit like that."

I looked at RD, he looked at me. I looked back at Leo. "You're a giant pain in my ass, you know that?"

Leo chuckled, "I can tell a story emotionally without crying like a fuckin' baby, bro... I don't know if you've heard, but I'm pretty good at this acting thing."

OUR REHEARSALS WERE RAPIDLY EVOLVING the characters and storylines. RD and I learned to be more mindful with the distribution of our notes, careful not to interrupt the creative flow of a particular moment. This allowed the nights to flow beautifully with an almost seamless creative synergy. Mistakes and inconsistencies were fixed naturally by the process. There was a fine, intangible line between the cast and the material, and it was as if the film itself, in some existential way, was keeping us all from falling too far off course.

———

RD and I drove deep into the valley to check out a potential location for the shoot. The air in mid-July was scorching hot, but I loved riding with the windows down in southern California. It made me feel alive and free.

We arrived at a charming old diner in Van Nuys on Victory Boulevard. I dug the tall, rectangular sign out front, even if the name "Don's Plum" was unremarkable.

John Schindler and David Stutman were already waiting for us in the parking lot behind the restaurant. John wanted us to see the diner first, so we walked around to the front entrance on Victory.

The interior was excellent. There was a single row of Formica tables that ran the length of the restaurant, set beneath large windows that faced the boulevard. Big, deep booths ran down the center of the space, creating aisles on either side.

"The booths couldn't be more perfect," I said.

Directly across from the entrance, chrome swivel stools lined a long counter, all facing an immaculate stainless-steel kitchen. Every inch of Don's Plum epitomized the classic American diner.

To the left of the entrance, behind the center row of booths, was a swinging door that led to a dimly lit bar, an ideal spot for the scene between Jeremy and Grace Forrester.

RD pointed to a long, tufted vinyl bench that ran the length of the bar. "This would work for Derek when he ditches the others—after the slap."

I imagined the scene playing out in my mind.

"Check out the jukebox!" said David. "This place is incredible, John."

"How the fuck did you find it?" said RD.

"Just driving around, man." John said, grinning. "That's how I find most of my locations."

"It's fuckin' perfect," I said.

"Well it's ours if we want it."

"We should just call the movie Don's Plum." Everyone laughed but I was serious.

"That's a terrible name for a movie," said David.

———

LEO HAD some business out of town, so we took a little break from rehearsals. Scott Bloom got his hands on some killer LSD that he and I gobbled up early one evening while we lounged around in his backyard. It was a wonderful trip, every moment was glowing and omniscient.

Once the sun went down, we took to the hills like feral creatures, ducking contact with humans and non-humans as we darted from one shadow to the next. The sky was clear and dark, but there were no stars. Los Angeles was so bright it made the whole universe disappear.

We finally made our way down the hill, into Hollywood. It was very late. Or very early. The streets were barren and unusually quiet. We wandered further south until we arrived at Hollywood Boulevard, where one of the busiest tourist attractions on the planet had been completely shut down. Access was blocked to all traffic in both directions, and the street surface had been invaded by giant, banana-yellow machines with claws bigger than a dinosaur's. I watched with horror and reverence as a giant claw smashed down onto the surface of the street with a magnificent crack, exploding Hollywood Boulevard into hunks of black rock. At one point, the tractor raised its steel claw so high that it came to within biting distance of the T. rex sculpture installed on the roof of Ripley's Believe It or Not Museum, as if threatening to mortally strike the prehistoric beast.

While I stood transfixed by the booming sounds, the beeps and whistles and shouts, the growling engines, and bright lights, and the battle between dinosaur and machine, Scott had learned that Hollywood Boulevard was having an actual subway installed beneath it. Incomprehensible!

After tripping out on the boulevard, we wandered back up the hill, all the way to the top of Mulholland Drive, and watched the sun rise. As we so often did, Scott and I ended up in a philosophical discussion about art and society and aristocracy. We talked about money and its relation, or conflict, with artistry, and what it might take for either of us to sell out for comfort and stability. I didn't see the need for comfort or stability as an artist. If I had to tough it out for a movie, or any other art form, than that's what was needed. Money was not a priority.

Scott said that's not how Hollywood worked. He said everything is about money and no one, not even Jack Nicholson, could avoid it. As we sat on the cliff side of Mulholland with our feet dangling above the sagebrush and deerweed, looking over the estates of the rich and powerful, my disgust for greed began to boil. All the fancy people below us, lounging in their fancy mansions, with their freshly leased luxury vehicles parked in long driveways, all got rich by choking the beauty out of film for nothing more than money and social status.

"Why?" I said blankly. "They already have everything. Look at all this shit." I pointed to the billions of dollars of real estate, the luxury cars, swimming pools, and tennis courts, and then dismissed it all with flick of my wrist.

Scott shrugged. "It's not enough." He sniggered. "They have everything, and it's still not enough."

"America's motto," I said as I struggled to my feet. "The Land of Not Enough."

I reached deep into my front pocket where I kept my money and I pulled it all out. I shouted something profane and unoriginal like "fuck the rich," or "eat the rich," and then I threw my cash and coin at them like it was a fist full of feces. Scott bellowed with laughter and got to his feet too. He poured his water out like he was dumping it on their heads and said something about fucking the rich and, for whatever reason, I felt like we were different from all the people below us. Like we were cut from a different cloth. We saw the creative world in ways the rich couldn't because they were in it for all the wrong reasons. We loved film for the sake of film itself, and we valued stories more than success, and in some way that made us guardians of it.

As the acid wore off, I left Scott's and began the long thirsty walk over the hill from Scott's house to my bed in Studio City. With every step, my regret for tossing my bus fare at the rich people of Hollywood grew deeper.

———

WE INVITED some of the crew to the final night of rehearsals, so our relatively small office space was suddenly packed with a dozen extra people all buzzing with anticipation. When RD began speaking to the cast, the room went silent.

"You guys ready?" said RD.

"Let's go, baby," said Leo.

"Let's talk about something we haven't done yet... what about my balls? You wanna talk about my balls?"

A few people laughed.

RD looked back at me. "What should we talk about, Wheatley?"

I shrugged. "What about music?"

"Yeah, why not?" RD turned to the cast. "You guys cool with music?"

"Including hip hop?" said Scott.

Leo butted in, "Of course, bro."

"What kind of question is that?" said Kevin.

Scott shrugged. "A lot of people still don't believe hip hop is real music."

Kevin shook his head. "That's such fuckin' nonsense, bro—"

Scott continued, "Some people think it's more like collage art or something. It's like the Andy Warhol thing. Art imitating art."

"Are you going to sit there and tell me that hip-hop artists aren't musicians?" said Kevin.

"I'm not telling you anything," Scott replied indifferently. "You're free to believe whatever you like."

RD returned and sat next to me. There was a pause in the action at the table. RD nudged them. "Just keep goin' guys. This is great."

Jenny joined in the conversation. "I don't know—I mean, of course hip-hop artists are writing songs, their lyrics are amazing. I guess there's maybe a difference between arranging music compared to composing something note by note, maybe."

"Right, Snoop Dogg didn't sit down and write Gin and Juice." Kevin's hackles were all the way up.

"Well, he used samples," said Jenny. "I'm not taking anything away from him, I'm talking about the music only. And let me just say for the record that I love me some rap, OK? Baby Got Back is my fuckin' jam."

Leo hooted and high-fived Jenny, but she kept talking to Kevin. "You seem a little worked up. Did I make you mad or something?"

"No," said Kevin, "I would just think that you of all people would recognize songwriting for what it is, regardless of the genre."

"I do... I think I do." She giggled.

"How crazy is it that we witnessed the birth of an entirely new genre of music?" said Meadow.

"Did we really though?" said Amber Benson, "Will rap still be around in twenty-five years?"

"Are you serious?" said Kevin. "It's already been around for... maybe not twenty-five years, but pretty close."

"But it didn't get popular until something like the mid-eighties," replied Amber. "So, in reality it's more like ten years old."

Leo's eyes narrowed. "No, in reality it's more like twenty years old..."

"I'm talking about popular culture," sneered Amber. "Not your hipster bullshit."

Leo's eyes flashed. "My hipster bullshit? What the fuck are you talking about?"

Amber quickly retreated. "Never mind."

"Rap music is here to stay," said Kevin. "End of conversation."

The improvisations flowed into the night, seamlessly transitioning from one topic to another. Humor and tension twisted up and resolved itself, and then got all twisted up again. When it was all over, the crew gave the cast a huge round of applause. Something special was taking shape, and all we could do was hope it would still be there when the cameras started rolling.

After the crew had gone, RD and I hung around with the cast. There was that familiar feeling of not wanting the night to end. Someone suggested we play an acting game. I recommended the one we used to break the ice with Jeff Goldblum back in Vancouver. It wasn't a game really, but it created some cool stories. We would simply go around the table and say something significant or even secret about ourselves, and then do the same for our character in Don's Plum.

Tobey started us off with a bomb, "My dad robbed a bank and went to jail. That kinda fucks with my head."

"I would guess so," said Meadow.

"I'm sorry that happened," said Amber.

Tobey nodded. "He's not a bad guy, he didn't even use a weapon. He made a bad decision. Sucks for him. Do I just go right into Ian now?"

I nodded. "Yeah, dude."

"I, Ian, have an anxiety disorder or something where I become easily claustrophobic and get panic attacks."

Scott grinned. "That's interesting..."

"So, my turn?" said Kevin. "I won five-hundred-thousand dollars in a Las Vegas casino as a minor and had it all stolen from me. True story."

"What?!" said everyone all at once.

"Tell us everything!" said Meadow.

"I gave my fuckin' cunt roommate a ten-dollar bill, I pointed to the machine I wanted her to play. Told her if we win, we'll split it. She agreed, and she fuckin' walked over—"

"You picked the actual machine?" I said.

"I one hundred percent picked the machine, bro. And it was my fuckin' ten bucks. She put my money in and on her third pull —triple diamond, triple diamond, triple diamond. Half a million bucks. Just like that."

"And she just kept it?" said Meadow. "Who is this person?"

Kevin crossed his arms. "I'll never say her fuckin' name again as long as I live."

Meadow laughed. "How did she steal it, though? I still don't understand."

"She wanted to take it all in one lump sum, and I didn't want to do that because you lose a huge amount..."

"Like half, right?" I said.

"A third, I think. Doesn't matter, I lost it all. She fuckin' gave me my half of the first payment—twelve Gs, or something like that. When the next payment was due—well, I didn't hear from her at all, so I was immediately suspicious she was up to something. After calling her house and her work a hundred fuckin' times, I finally got a hold of her and she said she decided to take it in one lump sum and, you know, said I wasn't entitled to any of it because

I was a minor at the time. It was all in her name, there was nothing I could do about it, and she knew it."

"That is an unbelievable story," said Jenny. "I'm sick over it."

"I fuckin' never hated a person in my life until that shit happened, bro."

"I don't blame you," said Meadow. "I hate her, and she didn't do anything to me."

"Enough about that bitch. I wish I never brought her up. Now I do Jeremy?" He adjusted in his seat. "OK. I don't trust anyone when it comes to money."

A couple of us laughed.

"I don't care if it's my brother, if it's fuckin' Derek, Brad... doesn't matter. I don't care if you want to borrow twenty bucks, I want something in writing."

"Very funny," said RD. He nodded in Amber's direction.

She shrugged and smiled. "I don't know... I still live with my mom."

Everyone chuckled.

"There's not a lot to say about it, though. Rent is expensive and she's cool. I love her."

We all sat silently waiting for Amy's confession.

"Oh, right! Sorry." She took a breath and looked up to the ceiling. "I'm afraid to tell my dad I'm homeless. He thinks I'm traveling with a new job right now, but in reality, I'm jobless, and I have nowhere to live."

"That's fucking awesome," said Meadow.

"Yeah, very cool," said RD. "Scott, your turn."

"I'm envious of my brother a little bit. Michael. He's an amazing musician and I think I wish my talent was musical rather than acting, like his. Sometimes."

"You don't want to be an actor?" said Meadow.

"I do. But if I could choose between the two, I think I would choose music. I think. I love acting." He slid down in his seat slightly. "As for Brad... I'm at a crossroads, and I've got to choose between a life of creative writing, which is my passion, or the life of a tax-paying, procreating, proletariat."

"Why can't you do it all?" asked Meadow. "That's what most people do."

"I can't—the daily grind kills my creative vibe."

"Sounds like you need to make a deal with the devil," I said.

"I'd love to," said Scott. "Is that you? Are you the devil, Dale?"

I chuckled. "Meet me at the crossroads and find out."

"I just want to say that I think RD and Dale should have to participate in this too," said Meadow.

"We don't have characters," I said.

"You do," said Meadow. "And this was your idea so you're definitely playing. RD, you're next. Just skip the character part."

RD thought a moment. "OK, this is pretty crazy. I accidentally punched my mom and broke her jaw."

"You punched your mom in the face?!" Amber said, totally horrified.

"How do you accidentally punch somebody in the face?" I said.

"I didn't mean to hit her. I was just swinging my fists, punching the air sort of thing..."

"Why?" said Leo.

RD's face turned pink. "I don't know, bro. I was like ten years old having a fuckin' tantrum... and it just happened."

"Oh!" chuckled Leo. "I thought this was recent."

"No, bro. I was a kid. It torments me to this day, though. Go fucker, it's your turn."

Leo took a deep breath before he began. "Sometimes I'm a little embarrassed by how good my life is—how much good luck I have."

"Are you seriously about to gloat right now?" Kevin laughed.

"No, I'm not. What I mean is that nothing bad ever happens to me. My parents split up, but I was a baby. And they're both happy people. They don't fight or hate each other. I love them both, and we all get along. If anything, the divorce was good for us. So even the bad shit that happens to me isn't all that bad."

"Do you feel guilty about it?" said Meadow.

"Guilty? No, absolutely not."

"He just said it embarrasses him," said Kevin.

Meadow shrugged at Leo. "I thought maybe because you see all your friends struggling you might, I don't know, care, maybe."

"Are you worried it's going to just all go away one day?" said Jenny.

Leo nodded. "I'm worried about that a little bit. I don't think about it a lot, but anything can happen in this business."

"What about Derek?" I said.

"Derek. Right. I fuckin' don't believe in love. I don't believe in family. I have friends I care about, but I don't expect anyone, not even them, to be there in the end when it all counts."

When it was my turn, I told them about how I had helped save a rain forest on Vancouver Island. The British Columbia government had an 8% stake in the logging company that had clearing rights to Clayoquot Sound, the largest intact, self-sustaining watershed in North America. The controversy made headlines around the world and hundreds of activists from all over traveled to Canada to protest. There were thousands of people blocking the logging roads and picketing at the Parliament building. We established Peace Camp where as many as 2500 tents were up at one time. At one-point, the loggers spread truckloads of salmon all over the camp and hundreds of activists were trapped in their tents as dozens of grizzly bears fed on the fish. But they didn't discourage anyone.

The protest hit a breaking point and violence broke out at the Parliament building. They made all kinds of arrests, but we proved too much for the government. They halted all logging and granted a 100-year stay on any logging in the sound. Within a couple of years, scientists had already discovered dozens of new species thriving at the tops of the giant trees.

I caught a few subtle eye rolls, but I didn't care. Being a part of saving that forest remains the thing I'm most proud of in my life. I was just a tiny part of it, I didn't even get arrested, but I was there blocking the roads, I was there picketing outside of Parliament, I was there marching with Midnight Oil and The Tragically Hip when they staged their rally at a farmer's field at the edge of the forest. I told everyone who would listen about what was happening and why we had to stop the government. I told them where to call and write. And because of what we did together, we won. We beat the corporations and we beat the fucking government. I'll be long dead and forgotten, and that rain forest will still be there, thriving and healing the planet.

Leo hissed and shook his head.

I shrugged. "What?"

"A little self-serving, don't ya think?"

I shrugged. "No."

"Why do you think it is, Leo?" said Meadow.

"He's taking credit for saving an entire rain forest—"

"But he didn't say that," said Meadow.

"You know what, let's start a new game," I said. "We'll call it the 'Fuck You Game.' You have to start everything you say with the phrase, 'fuck you for... whatever-whatever.'"

Everyone giggled.

"Did you just make this up?" said Meadow.

I nodded. "That includes responses. I'll go first. Fuck you, Leonardo DiCaprio, for trying to make me feel bad for saving a rain forest."

"I didn't. That's not what I—"

"Ah, ah. No, bro..." I wagged my finger at him. "It's the 'Fuck You Game.' Respond with 'fuck you, Dale—"

"Fuck you, Dale, for making up this stupid game..."

18

JOHN SCHINDLER CALLED a meeting with RD and me the day after the final rehearsal. He told us David Stutman had become a nightmare to work with, and he warned us that if we didn't get some help, we could be in some serious trouble. John's hands were full finding gear and crew, and there were things David needed to be doing that he was not.

I believed John. David had difficulty separating the opportunity from the reality of the work involved. He was absent for most of the writing sessions, despite taking a writing credit. He and his writing partner deserved "story by" credits for coming up with the idea, but neither of them deserved writing credits. David was also absent for most of the logistical planning and didn't contribute to the casting or recruiting the crew other than attaching John Schindler. And all that would have been fine had David been content with finding the money and contributing the underlying material, but instead he positioned himself as the producer and as a writer. The problem was that he wasn't doing either job very well at all.

To solve the problem, we hired Gary Lowe, a bona fide indie producer recommended by Bethany Ashton. Gary was a smooth, stoic professional who knew what he was talking about. We brought him on to work closely with David and clean up the production. He diagnosed many issues and came up with solutions for all of them. Wherever John Schindler struggled to find crew, Gary had excellent alternatives. He was the final piece we needed to pull the movie off.

The second thing on John's agenda was addressing a growing concern among crew members about RD being a first-time director. The danger, John said, was that we could lose some important folks who are deferring their pay and end up with a false start on our hands. We would not survive a false start, and John knew that better than anyone. Leo was available for two days only, July 28th and 29th, 1995. He would otherwise be busy for the rest of his life.

"So, what do we do about it?" I asked, even though I suspected what John's eventual answer would be. RD was silent and rigid. Maybe he knew what was coming as well.

John continued with his charade. "Well, if someone experienced was co-directing, someone who can communicate the technical aspects of what you guys are thinking to the crew, I think that would help."

"Mm-hmm. Are you suggesting that you be that technical co-director, then?"

John shook his head. "No... It doesn't matter who it is as long as they can do the job."

I nodded slowly. "Do you have someone in mind then?"

"Not off the top of my head. I wanted talk to you guys first. Obviously I'm capable of doing the job. I know the crew, and they already trust me."

And there it is.

"So, if you were named the co-director, that would take care of their concerns you think? We'd be OK, then?"

"I'm sure it would help. Is that something you would be comfortable with, RD?"

I interrupted RD before he opened his mouth. I wasn't going to let John corner him into giving up something as huge as a co-director credit without talking about it in private first.

. . .

RD JAMMED the gear stick into third with a little more force than was necessary.

"It's a fucking shakedown, RD."

"He can have the fucking credit. I don't give a fuck."

"I just don't want you to believe a word of that bullshit. You're as capable as anyone, R. And you know these guys better than anybody else so you are the best person for this fuckin' project. He's so full of shit, bro, *everybody* wants to work with Leo—no one is quitting this movie. We need to call his bluff."

"It's not worth the risk. We'd lose everything. We're not doing that."

RD was right, but it was infuriating. "It's fucking extortion."

RD sighed deeply, and shifted down as we approached a stop sign. "Let's just make a good movie."

WE ARRIVED home to messages on the answering machine. RD hit the speakerphone and dialed into his voice mail. Leo's voice was the first to ring out.

"What's up, guys? Give me a call, I have some concerns I want to talk to you about. Call me. Bye."

RD pressed the number to save the message and hung up the phone. "Jesus Christ," he said. "Is this whole thing about to fall apart?"

"No. Don't fucking do that."

"Bro, you heard his voice."

"Don't make shit up. Call him."

"What do you think it's about?"

"I have no idea. Call him."

"I'm terrified. What if he changed his mind?"

"RD—"

"Maybe his agents, or fucking Rick or some shit, found out and—"

"RD, stop. That's not... Let's just call the fuckin' guy and find out what's going on. He's not gonna kill the movie."

"You don't know that. What if he is?"

"Then we'll deal with it. What other choice would we have? Do it now."

RD smacked the button on the phone and a fresh dial tone hummed. He punched in some numbers and moments later Leo answered.

"Yo, Nards," said RD. "What's up, bro?"

"What's up, RD?"

"Wheatley's with me."

"What's up, Dale?"

"Hey, what's goin' on? You OK?"

"Yeah, I'm fine. I just want to talk about Amber Benson."

"What about her?" said RD.

"I've been thinking... I don't think she's strong enough for this film, bro."

RD rolled his eyes. "Dude, please don't do this. We're shooting in like a fuckin' week."

"I know, RD. I know. I'm not sure what it is, but on the last day of rehearsal, she was kind of weak and all over the place. She didn't have any actual point of view going on... She was breaking up conversations with random, irrelevant shit, interrupting everyone's flow—I mean, you were there, you saw it."

"I thought she did a really nice job." I said. "She surprised me, actually."

"Really?"

"I'm not saying she was perfect, no one was, but she got mixed up in some interesting tension for sure."

"Doesn't matter, we already voted on it," said RD.

Leo exhaled audibly. "I know. I just went along with everybody. I should have said something when we voted. I can't change that, so I'm telling you how I feel about it now. She needs to go."

RD shook his head. "We're not doing that, Leo. We told her she got the fucking role. We've been rehearsing with her for weeks."

"Just tell her you went in another direction... She'll understand."

"No, bro. Who the fuck are we going to replace her with?"

"Heather McComb. I like her. She's got a cool vibe."

RD sighed forcibly. "What if we say no?"

"R, don't. Please." Leo's tone was dead serious.

"What are you gonna do?" said RD. "Bail on the film a week before shooting?"

"RD." Leo paused. We all paused. "Just replace her. OK?"

"I'm fuckin' shocked."

Leo sighed, "Don't be so dramatic, RD."

There was another moment of awkward silence. We could hear Leo's breathing on the other end. "It's for the best."

"Let us talk about it," I said. "We can't just fire her. It's more complicated than that. She's written into the whole movie. We don't know what Heather is going to do with any of the material. This sucks."

"I know. I just want us to make the best movie possible."

"OK, bro," said RD. "Thanks for dropping a massive bomb on us fuckin' days before shooting."

"I'm sorry, I just felt like I had to say something."

"It's all good. Say hi to your mom for me, bro."

Leo chuckled and called out to his mom. "RD, says hi, mom." Irmelin said something that made him giggle. "My mom says hello back, RD. Talk to you guys later."

RD hit the speakerphone button. "What the fuck are we going to do?"

I knew before Leo hung up. "Check it out... OK. Connolly picks up Amy as usual—who is still played by Amber Benson—"

"Bro. Leo, bro."

I held up my hand. "Amy agrees to hang out with Jeremy at the diner, and he agrees to give her a ride somewhere very far, like San Bernardino or Anaheim."

"Vegas." RD stretched the first vowel, so it sounded like Vey-gas.

I laughed. "That's hilarious."

"I'm serious."

"Yeah, sure. It doesn't matter where she's going—well, actually you're right, Vegas is perfect because then there's much more at stake—"

"Exactly—"

"Because, RD, what I'm trying to say is that she ends up getting into a confrontation with Derek, who berates her until she freaks out and leaves. I'm saying that if Leo wants her out of the film, let's make him take her out on camera."

RD paused, mulling it over. "Vegas is genius…"

"Stop! You're obsessed."

"No, bro, this is so good. Connolly is so fuckin' desperate to bring a chick to Don's Plum that he fuckin' agrees to drive a hitch-hiker the five hours to Las Vegas as long as she'll hang out with him at a diner for a few hours with his friends."

I chuckled. "That's very funny."

"And that makes Amy's breakdown an even bigger deal because how the fuck is she going to get to Vegas after losing however many hours hanging out with a bunch of fuckin' losers?"

"It's a better role than Amber started out with, even though she's only working one night now." I clapped my hands together. "Get that motherfucker on the phone."

"I get to completely fucking obliterate her on camera?" said Leo.

RD and I were both leaning over the speakerphone.

"If that's what you want to do," said RD.

"The answer is yes, Leo. You are welcome to blow her into itty-bitty fuckin' pieces."

Leo laughed. "I can do whatever I want? Anything at all?"

"Anything," said RD. "It's gotta be legal."

"I'm not gonna fuckin' hurt anyone, RD."

There was a long pause. RD and I stared at the speakerphone, holding our breath.

"Fuck yeah, bro, I'll do that shit. One hundred percent."

I grinned and exhaled.

"Has she already agreed to this?"

"Not yet," said RD. "We called you first, obviously."

"OK. If she's down, I'm down. I love it."

"So, which night would I be working?" Amber's voice came through the speakerphone in an even tone.

"The first night," said RD. "Friday."

"Actually, we might need you Friday and again on Sunday for Amy's confessional."

RD nodded. "That's right, it's two days. You're only losing one day."

"And Leo is going to—what was the word you used, Dale?"

"Obliterate." I tried my best not to smile when I said it. "It was Leo's word, actually."

Amber sighed. Her breath sounded like whiskers against the mouthpiece. "Obliterate. Right."

"We're not sure how specifically it will go down," I said. "We'll figure it out once everyone is on board, but the way we see it now is you and Leo end up in an argument that gets so out of control you gotta get out of there. You guys have a big fight at the table, and you run off."

RD and I stared at the speakerphone, waiting and barely breathing.

"Yeah. It sounds super fun—I'd love to do that."

HEATHER MCCOMB SAT NEXT to me on the Sups Couch. She had a big grin on her face. "Wait a minute, wait a minute. Back up. Leonardo DiCaprio suggested you guys hire me? Are you sure?"

"Yes," said RD.

"Me? Heather McComb? Why?" She laughed at herself.

RD laughed. "What do you mean? Because of your audition."

"I didn't think I did a very good job, but hells yeah I'll play Amy."

I shook my head. "Not Amy."

Her face crunched up. "But... Didn't you just say—"

RD and I told her about the new scenes, and that she had to come up with a character as soon as possible.

The doorbell rang and RD scampered down the split-level stairs to buzz Ethan Suplee in.

Ethan sauntered in like he was Biggie Smalls. "What's up, kids?"

"Ethan!" squealed Heather as she ran in for a big bear hug. "Did you hear? I'm in Don's Plum!"

"I heard," he said. "Congrats!" He gave her another big-brother squeeze. "We should go out and celebrate!"

LEO WAS unavailable to rehearse with Heather because he was in Vegas shooting a car commercial for Honda. I asked him why he, an Academy Award nominated actor, would agree to be in a car commercial. Actors of Leo's caliber didn't normally do endorsement deals in the 1990s. Attaching your likeness to a brand could turn off some filmmakers and cost you the next great part.

"They're giving me three million dollars and two cars." Leo shrugged. "And it only airs in Japan, so I don't really give a fuck."

So, while Leo was out of town shooting car commercials for a million dollars a day, the rest of us rehearsed with Heather McComb. Heather did a great job and whipped up a fun character she affectionately named Constance. I particularly loved the inner conflict between her character's innocence and apparent desire for social acceptance. RD and I worked Constance into the scenes leading up to and following Amy's dramatic departure and they all fit seamlessly.

———

WE FINISHED up casting the supporting roles. Bethany recommended Byron Thames and Stephanie Friedman and we fell in love with them for the roles of Don and Flo.

Flo was originally a tip of the hat to the TV show "Alice" and my favorite character on the show, Flo, played by the immortal Polly Holliday. But Stephanie took our ideas and turned them on their head when she presented Flo as a caricature of her character's true self. It was a strange and complex choice, and I was a little apprehensive about it at first, but she came up with something funny and poignant, and she pulled it off brilliantly.

Byron went almost serial killer with his take on Don, the proprietor of Don's Plum. Again, I was also taken aback by his choices at first, but it didn't take long to fall in love with the darkness he brought to the character. I had seen Don as a simple, sleazy business owner who used what little power he had to indulge his desires and exploit his workers. For me, Don represented the business side of Hollywood, a perfect character to hover over our cast, but Byron added this whole Ted Bundy dimension to the character that we didn't see coming and I loved it.

WHEN I WASN'T WRITING or rehearsing, I was getting a crash course in producing from Gary Lowe. He took me under his wing and taught me about running a production from an oversight perspective, and I soaked it all up like a sponge. Gary was a fast thinker. When problems arose, most of the time he had a fix within seconds. More complex issues might have taken him minutes. His decisions were always based on what benefited the production most. He was a common-sense leader, my favorite to learn from. What I found most admirable was how diligently he protected the movie itself. He recognized when the creative process was in any kind of jeopardy, and he found ways to eliminate or mitigate disruptions before they got out of hand. He didn't mince words, and rarely had to repeat himself. When he asked for something, the person understood what he wanted, and they were almost always able to deliver it. He worked every department flawlessly, moving through each, solving problems and putting out fires without ever distracting the filmmakers or the talent from the delicate process we were in. I could not have asked for a better mentor for my first production. I felt ready for whatever might come our way.

19

JULY 29, 1995 - DAY 1 OF SHOOTING

I MANAGED to sleep for a few hours before our overnight shoot. RD and I were unusually quiet through our breakfast of cereal with rice milk.

The freeway was jammed, so we took side streets to the office. LA looked hazy and beautiful in the late sun. The air was hot and dry, but there was something sweet in it.

When we arrived, the production office was in full swing. Questions and information flew at us from all directions as department heads got their last-minute items in order. It was like we were speed dating crew members. After all that madness, we jumped back into RD's Acura and headed to the location.

"I feel like I've been tricking myself, bro." RD's eyes were fixed on the road.

"What do you mean?"

"I'm fuckin' terrified right now."

I chuckled.

"It's not funny. I feel like I'm about to have a panic attack."

"What terrifies you, RD?"

"I'm afraid that people aren't going to respect me. That fuckin'

Schindler is going to step all over me and make me look like a fool."

"That's not going to happen."

"How do you know that?"

"Because if I or Gary Lowe see anything like that, we'll put a stop to it."

"What if people just generally don't respect me?"

"What do you expect to get from a question like that?"

"I don't know."

"That's fuckin' reckless, dude. Ask a better question."

"Like what?"

"Like, how can I unite and empower my cast and crew emotionally and creatively so we can produce the best movie possible?"

RD grinned. "Tony Robbins."

"If you unite people by making everyone on our set your equal, they'll feel like they're truly contributing to the creation of the film and not just showing up for a hundred and fifty bucks. Make your film their film and they'll give you their souls."

He laughed.

"It's true," I said. "We're all here to create something objectively beautiful. We're in Hollywood because we have the fucking audacity to believe we can create something bigger than ourselves. Doesn't matter whether it's crew, talent, or whatever, no one wants to be at the bottom."

"Some will be, though."

I shook my head. "Doesn't have to be that way, RD. We're all more-or-less driven by the same big dream, right?"

He nodded.

"So, if we have a culture where people are living that big dream, regardless of where they are in the chain, they'll give us their souls. I will. I am. I live, eat, and breathe this movie, it's all I can think about, and I'm making how much?"

"Nothing."

"Not a fucking penny, RD. Take my soul, just give me this life."

RD laughed. "You're absolutely right, bro."

"So, let's fuckin' do it! Let's commit right now to making our little set a creator's utopia where no one is competing for anything, and everyone is contributing to and evolving a collective vision. If you pull that off, RD, leading comes naturally. People know where they're at in life. A PA isn't going to show up on any set and start directing the film. They know they're PAs, extras know they're extras, but if you can empower them and everyone else on your set so that they feel as though whatever it is they are doing is an integral part of making this thing work, which is true, then I don't think you can fail, bro."

RD saw something that dropped his jaw wide open. "Holy fuck."

I turned, and the sight sent my heart into my throat. An entire restaurant transformed into a full-blown movie production. Our production. There were three huge trucks lined up along the adjacent residential street with several other smaller vans. Don's Plum's exterior was buzzing with dozens of people, most of whom I had never seen before. It was magnificent. I pointed out the windshield. "There's Schindler!"

John spotted us as we finished the turn onto Valjean Avenue. He waved us into the parking lot where there was a space reserved for us. The rest of the parking lot was crammed with trucks and trailers.

RD took a deep breath and looked around. "OK, bro. Let's do this."

We exited the car as John approached.

"Hey, guys," John opened his arms like a cult leader welcoming fresh minions. "Welcome to the set of Don's Plum."

"This is amazing, John," said RD.

"I'm so blown away," I said. "These people are fuckin' hustling."

John chuckled. "We got a great crew. Let's go see Eric Davies. Follow me."

We swept through the bar and into the main diner where crew and gear were flying in from all directions. Steven Adcock, our Director of Photography, and his gaffer, Frederick W. Marx III were directing a man, who I later learned was our key grip and *the* Cool Breeze from Tom Wolf's *The Electric Kool-Aid Acid Test*, to set up the lights.

We found Eric Davis, our first assistant director, in a corner of the diner holding a clipboard in one hand and a walkie-talkie in the other. He nodded in our direction. "Good to see you guys. We're gonna be up soon. Remember, we don't have a lot of time. No more than two takes, RD."

RD sighed. "I don't know if we can pull that off."

John smiled. "You'll be fine. You guys killed it in rehearsals."

Paul Faaland, our second assistant director, materialized out of nowhere, with eyes on RD. "Kevin Connolly is here."

"Awesome! Where?"

"Hair and makeup. I can walk you guys over."

I LOVED WALKING around the set. I could barely get my head around the reality that so many people were doing so much work just so we could play make-believe.

Paul knocked on the door of the wardrobe truck. The door opened, revealing Kevin Connolly sitting in a swivel chair, yukking it up with our makeup artist, Lydia.

"RD Robb! Dale Wheatley! Holy shit!" He looked back at Lydia. "Is it all right if I jump out really quick? I need to talk to the writer and director." He snuck us a smile. I loved that he loved calling us by our titles.

"Of course," she replied.

Kevin rolled out of the truck. "What's up, guys? Holy fuckin' shit! What is all of this? This is so fuckin' legit!"

"I know, dude," said RD. "It's nutty."

"You guys really did it. How the fuck can you afford all this gear?"

I laughed and shrugged. "I have no idea."

RD's eyes locked on a necklace and pendant around Kevin's neck. "What's this?" He lifted the pendant to get a better look. "Is this from wardrobe?"

"No, this is Leo's. He lent it to me a long time ago and I never gave it back to him... you guys said to bring something to surprise the other guys, so let's see what happens." Kevin chuckled.

"Don't put it on now," said RD. "Wait till you're on set. He'll see it."

Kevin hid the necklace under his shirt.

John Schindler popped up out of nowhere. "Hey guys. Oh, hey Kevin, what's up? This is pretty cool, huh?" He gestured to the hustle all around us.

"Dude. This is crazy. This is your crew from Swimming with Sharks, huh?"

"Yeah, some of these guys were on that film, some are from the music video world."

"I'm impressed."

"Thanks man." John turned to us. "Sorry to interrupt, but are you guys busy right now?"

"Go do your thing," said Kevin. "I gotta go over my lines anyway, you know what I mean?"

We laughed because there were no lines in our movie.

JOHN USHERED us back to the set where our DP, Steven Adcock, was messing with some gear.

"Hey Steven, I found RD for ya."

"Oh, hey, guys," said Steven. "Video village will be up soon so you guys can look at what we're doin' here. I'm overexposing by a stop and a half on the table, that'll give us the blow-out look you guys wanted—you'll have plenty of room to play with how hot you want it in post."

"Awesome," said RD.

"Once we're done with these lights we can shoot Derek's entrance. I thought we would set the camera up right there." He pointed to the aisle between the tables and large pane windows. "Derek enters, and we just track him all the way to the table."

"A wide shot?" said RD.

"We'll start out wide, yeah. We're all on zooms, so we'll get the prettiest picture we can find. We could even throw down a little track for some movement if you want."

RD nodded.

"We're shooting a second angle over there with camera B."

RD's eyes were busy. Something was clicking around in his head. "What about this? What if we shoot him entering the diner through the fish tank?" He moved closer to the tank that stood near the entrance, made a little 16:9 crop with his fingers and framed up his idea.

Steven nodded. "That's interesting."

"Frame it up so the tank takes up most of the shot, and have Leo come up and look inside at the fish or whatever, and then carry on to the table. I don't know, I think it could be cool."

"I like it..." Steven turned to Eric. "I need, like, fifteen to light the tank, and we'll be good to go."

Eric checked his watch, then looked at the schedule. "Yeah, OK. Fifteen minutes."

John reappeared. "Hey guys, I need to borrow you again. There's a problem with Leo."

"He's here?" said RD.

John nodded. "Something's up with his wardrobe."

RD's shoulders dropped dramatically. "What's the problem?"

John shrugged. "I'm not exactly sure."

We whipped through the maze of people and gear until we arrived at the wardrobe trailer. Leo was outside the trailer chatting with our wardrobe girl, Christina, who had a few shirts draped over her arm. After some small talk, I asked what the problem was with Leo's wardrobe.

"I want to wear this shirt," said Leo. "But I only have one of them."

"Can I see it?" said RD.

"I'm wearing it."

I shrugged, "It looks fine. What's the problem?"

"He's only got one of them," said Christina. "If he gets any stains on it, or ashes, or burns, or anything like that, you guys will be in trouble."

"I'll be fine, I'll be careful," said Leo. "It's two nights."

"Don't eat in it," I said.

"I won't."

Christina grinned. "He's going to be smoking, eating, and drinking in it while he's at the table, isn't he?"

"Yeah, on both nights," said RD. "This is a disaster waiting to happen. Let me see some other shirts."

"I don't like any of them." Leo turned to Christina apologetically. "No offense."

"None taken, sweetheart." She held up her arm of folded shirts. "Here are some alternatives if you want to see them."

RD took one of the shirts from Christina's arm and held it up over Leo.

Leo whined like a child. "No..."

"Just try it on—"

Leo shook his head. "I already did. It ain't happening."

RD sighed. "You're killing me."

"I'll be careful. Don't worry, bro. This isn't a big deal."

"I guess we can just get him in and out of it whenever he's not shooting," said Christina.

"We'll be fine," said Leo as he ran his fingers through his hair. "Where's everyone else at? Where's Kevin Connolly?"

"I think everyone is in the bar," I said.

"You guys are busy. Go do your thing. I'm gonna catch up with the guys." Leo left for the bar entrance.

"You guys doing all right?" John jump-scared RD.

"Where the fuck did you just come from?"

John chuckled. "The diner."

"You're all over the place. Speaking of, where the fuck is David Stutman?"

John grinned. "Last time I saw him he was setting up craft services."

"The producer of Don's Plum is doing crafty? I gotta see this shit." RD tapped me on my chest with the back of his hand. "Wanna grab some crafty, Wheats?"

John led us to a folding table where there was an array of

candies, raisins, granola bars, red vines, bananas, apples, oranges, packs of seeds, soda, water, juice, coffee, and tea. David Stutman appeared, proud as a peacock, carrying a box of single serving potato chips.

"What's up guys?" David grinned. "How do you like my crafty?"

"Yeah, bro, it's great." RD scanned the goods. "It's a little weird that one of the producers of the film is doing craft services, though."

"Well, we saved almost a thousand dollars because I'm doing it," said David. "Besides, you guys have shut me out of pretty much everything else."

RD stopped him right there. "That's total bullshit, David. You were too busy with whatever else to come to the rehearsals, and the writing sessions before that. Me and Wheatley worked every day. Bethany was there three or four nights a week, while you were nowhere to be found. So don't start your shit now when we're about to shoot a movie that we've been working on every day for months. Years if you include Last Respects."

"Jesus, RD," said David. "Where did that come from?"

"Nowhere, bro. I'm not even pissed. But don't make shit up that isn't true. We were in the office every day and you were not. And I honestly don't care—but don't make shit up."

I glared at David. "Why are we doing this right now? We're about to shoot our first fucking scene."

David pushed his glasses higher up the bridge of his nose. "Whatever," he said contritely. "I don't want to argue, RD. I got you a shit ton of red vines."

RD smiled. "Thanks, bro, I fuckin' love red vines." He grabbed a few from the container and wrangled one into his mouth.

Paul Faaland showed up at the table just as we turned to walk away. "Hey, guys. Tobey is here, he was asking for you, RD."

"Cool," said RD. "Where's he at?"

"The bar."

"Let's go, Wheats."

We walked quickly to the bar, only to learn that Tobey had

been sent to hair and makeup, so we doubled our pace to the makeup trailer.

"So far, I feel like all we do is speed-walk all over the place."

RD responded to me by picking up the pace.

Tobey spotted us as we approached the trailer and hopped out of the makeup chair without a word to Lydia.

I apologized for the interruption, but she said it was cool.

"Yo, I just wanted to say what's up," said Tobey. "And, you know, find out what we're doing first—maybe get a little direction before we roll the cameras."

"I'm pretty sure they're setting up for Leo's entrance first." RD turned to me. "Am I right?"

"You are right," I said.

"You're not in that shot, obviously. Then we're gonna flip the world and shoot Leo's arrival at the table, which you are in."

Tobey nodded. "That's when Leo shows up without a girl, correct?

"Yes," said RD.

Christina exited the wardrobe trailer holding a Polaroid camera. A ring with dozens of developed Polaroids swung on her belt loop. "Hey Tobey, I need to get a photo of you, sweetheart." She returned to chewing her gum.

"Yeah, of course." Tobey pointed to the ground. "Right here?"

"Here is fine."

Tobey turned to RD and me and asked casually, "Cock in or out?"

RD thought about it for a moment. "Out," he said with an equal amount of nonchalance.

Tobey looked at me and I shrugged like I didn't care. Then he unzipped his fly and pulled out his giant, foreskinned dick.

Christina snickered and snapped the photo with a pop and a flash. She pulled the film from the camera and started waving it rapidly in the air.

"OK, wait, back up, back up. Back up to when Leo comes in." Tobey stuffed his dick back in his pants. "Does he say all that shit about the lesbians because he's afraid of being chastised, or... or, does he actually think we'll believe him?"

"You wanna see it?" Christina asked with raised eyebrows.

Tobey leaned in for a look. "Yeah, not bad."

Christina held the Polaroid up for RD and me, and it was indeed a very clear picture of Tobey Maguire holding his exposed penis in the workplace for no apparent reason. Christina punched a hole in the bottom corner of the film and added it to her ring, and then sauntered away.

Tobey was wasting our time, so I tried to shake him loose. "I think it's pretty much how we've rehearsed it, Tobey." I watched his eyes fade out, but I kept going anyway. "Nothing's changed. Leo's insecure about being the only one without a chick, and so he makes up a ridiculous story that you guys fuckin' destroy."

Tobey held his absurd glare on me for another moment, then spoke to me as if I were a child. "Dale, do you mind if I talk to the director, please? Is that OK with you? I know you guys are close, but I would like to discuss my character and my scene with the actual director of the film, if that's alright with you."

I tried my best to smile. "Yeah, sure."

"Thank you."

"I'll be in the diner," I said. "I'll see you there." I turned and walked away.

JOHN SCHINDLER WAS CHATTING with a tall blonde woman when I approached.

"Oh hey, Dale. This is Blair Gawthrop, she's our script supervisor."

I told her my name and we shook hands. She was elegant, almost to the point of looking out of place.

John continued. "Dale is one of the writers of the movie."

She smiled warmly. "Well, Dale, thanks for having me on the show."

"This is my first movie," I said. "So I'm just leaning on this guy pretty much." I pointed at John with my thumb, and he grinned. "I don't really know what a script supervisor does, I'm afraid..."

"Well, normally we would make specific notes about each take for the director and the editor in the actual script, tracking the circle takes and recording specific notes from the director. That's going to be a little different on this project though because there is no script, but it'll still be similar."

I grinned, "You're improvising too."

"Yeah, we really are. What else? We make detailed performance notes, so editors can quickly find alternative takes and angles to the circle take. We're also responsible for continuity, which is important. Do you know what that is?"

"Not really."

"We make sure everything stays the same from one take to the next. Like cigarettes."

"We were just talking about how everyone will be smoking," said John. "It could create a continuity nightmare."

"That sounds bad."

"No, don't worry," said Blair. "We've got it figured out. But we're going to need a lot of cigarettes."

Blair's plan was to have a couple of production assistants collect the cigarettes from every actor at the end of each take, taking note of the length of the cigarette and ash at that exact point in the scene. Then they would cut a fresh cigarette to the correct length, light it up and burn it down to the right amount of ash, and then place it on the actor just before the cameras roll. It was brilliant.

"You want to help out?" she said.

"Yes!"

"Nothing too heavy, just be another set of eyes. If something doesn't look right, tell me, and we'll hold the roll and get it fixed. Cool?"

"Fuck yeah, Blair!"

She smiled and high-fived me.

RD tracked me down, and we huddled up with Eric Davies for a run-through of the first scene.

"Steven, you ready to rehearse camera?"

"Yeah, yeah, sounds good." Adcock gave RD a little nudge. "Love the shot."

RD grinned. "Awesome."

Steven asked if we had a stand in. Eric held up his finger and jumped on his walkie. "Paul, you copy?"

I raised my hand. "I can do it."

"No bro, you're behind the camera with me," said RD.

Paul's response was garbled and unintelligible, but Eric understood him fine. "Can you grab an extra to stand in for Leonardo, please?"

Paul's "copy that" sounded more like "coffee fat" through the tiny walkie-talkie speaker.

Within a minute, a lanky dude was standing on a mark outside the restaurant. RD walked him through the simple blocking and then huddled up with the rest of us at video village.

"All set?" asked Eric. We nodded. Eric's voice was loud and commanding. "Quiet for rehearsal, please."

"Quiet for rehearsal, please," shouted someone else from out of sight. That led to yet another person, even further away, repeating the phrase even louder. The entire production stopped in their tracks. The stillness was sudden and beautiful.

Eric turned to RD. "Action when you're ready, sir."

RD nodded. "Action."

"Action on rehearsal!" Eric's command was once again echoed by the others.

The extra entered through the door lazily and sauntered past the fish tank. Steven Adcock panned the camera smoothly, tracking him in a lovely frame.

RD sat there a moment, considering the shot. "Yeah, not bad," he said. "I wonder if—"

"Cut, RD?"

"Sorry, Eric. Cut."

"Cut on rehearsal!" Eric boomed.

"That's a cut!"

"That's a cut!"

"Can we do it again? I want to see you—" RD pointed at the extra. "What's your name?"

He gestured to himself, "Randy."

"I'm RD, good to meet you, bro. Do me a favor and take a beat at the tank. Take a look at the fish for two or three seconds, and then continue off camera like you just did."

"Just lean down or..."

"Yeah, bend down and watch them swim around for a second. Say what's up or something."

Randy chuckled.

"Are we ready?" said Eric.

"Yes, sir," said RD.

"Back to one for rehearsal, please," said Eric.

Everyone settled in.

"When you're ready, RD."

"Action," said RD.

"ACTION ON REHEARSAL."

Randy entered. Adcock tracked him inside and up to the fish tank where he bent down, looked through the glass, smiled at one of the fish, and then continued into the restaurant.

"Cut," said RD.

"CUT ON REHEARSAL."

"That was good for me," said Steven.

"Yeah, that looked great. Beautiful shot," said RD. He looked at me.

"Yeah, lovely," I said.

"Steven, you ready for talent?" said Eric.

Steven glanced at his AC who flashed him five fingers, then he said, "Camera's up in five."

"Camera's up in five people. Where's my second?" Eric's eyes darted around rapidly.

"I'm right here," said Paul Faaland, appearing out of thin air.

"We need Leonardo, please."

"Copy that."

Leo was on set inside a minute and we got the shot in one take. His performance was flawless, of course. It was such a simple and unceremonious moment for something so monumental. The shot marked the start of my career as a writer and a producer, but really it felt like much more than that. It was the start of a new and unbelievably exciting life. It was the realization of my dreams manifested in a single moment. It was so much all at once, I could barely keep up. And what a fucking huge debut for RD Robb. The first time he called action was to Leonardo DiCaprio. And I felt it, I felt the significance and importance of the moment. I think everyone did. Kevin, Tobey, Ethan, and Scott were all there watching what was otherwise a mundane establishing shot, yet they all had similar smiles on their faces, like the ones you see on parents watching their kids at their first recital. It truly felt like the beginning of something special for all of us.

As soon as we cut the final take of Derek's entry into Don's Plum, the crew jumped into action, tearing down the lights, winding cables and shifting the entire setup in a new direction.

A short time later, three cameras were assembled in what would be our primary setup for most of the shoot. Once Adcock and his guys were finished lighting the scene, the cast was brought in.

RD approached the cast and clapped his hands together. "What's up, everyone?"

"What's up, RD Robb?" said Leo with a big brother smile.

"Hey, RD," said Jenny Lewis.

"What's up, Mr. Director Man," said Kevin.

"You guys ready?"

"I'm ready," said Scott.

"Let's go," said Tobey.

"OK, it's the same shit we did in rehearsal. We're starting from the beginning with the masturbation improv. Jeremy outs Leo for showing up empty-handed."

"I think you mean 'Derek', RD." Leo flashed a playful grin at RD.

"Derek, sorry, bro—"

Leo winked, "I'm just messin' with ya. Call me whatever you want."

"Try not to step on each other. We're burning film so we won't get a lot of takes."

RD returned to video village and huddled up behind the monitor beside me.

Eric boomed, "Settle in, please." The set went dead silent. "Roll cameras."

Stephen Adcock: "A speed."

Brian Bellamy: "B speed."

Peter Blue Rieveschl: "C Speed."

"Roll sound."

Brian Tracy: "Sound speed."

An AC moved in with a clapboard and slated each of the cameras. Eric looked to RD for the signal.

RD nodded at Eric and called action.

"ACTION!"

And the first improvisation began.

It was absolute crap. And so were the two takes that followed. RD gave some great direction but nothing worked. The only thing we could do was continue to grind until their nerves settled.

Eric bellowed, "Back to one."

The cast did a nice job on the fourth take. There were even a few laughs from the crew, but in my opinion, we still didn't have a complete scene. "We gotta go again, R."

"You think?"

Eric shook his head. "Come on, guys, that was good. We need to move on."

"I think we need one take that's solid from beginning to end," I said. "We need a transition... it's a mistake to move on without getting it."

"I agree," said RD. "We're going again."

Eric didn't like it. He didn't like doing the sixth take either. When we asked for a seventh, he warned us that we could lose the day if we didn't move on and snapped at him.

"Maybe instead of wasting time arguing about it every time, we should just shoot the next take?" I regretted my tone. Eric was only looking out for us, but I heard him the first time.

"We have to go again," said RD.

"RD—"

Gary Lowe, who had been listening nearby, interrupted sternly. "Eric."

Eric looked at Gary.

"Just do what the director is asking for, please." Gary's words were calm, but non-negotiable.

Eric threw up his quitting hands. "Back to one, people. We are going again."

We stood our ground and got a seventh take, and it turned out to be the magical one we were hoping for. Maybe it was all in my head, but it felt as if we had won over both the cast and crew by fighting for their best work. Whatever it was, the cast started crushing scenes in one or two takes. RD and I found our rhythm and, to Eric's delight, we started ripping through the schedule with relative ease.

IN BETWEEN SHOTS, RD and I took Amber aside to discuss her impending conflict with Leo.

"You're doing amazing," said RD.

"Really?" said Amber. "I don't really feel like I'm doing much of anything most of the time."

"You're gonna love it," said RD.

She giggled. "If you say so."

"How do you feel about Derek?"

"I feel like he's a dick."

RD snickered. "Yeah."

"Oh my god!" she said. "This is it! This is the obliteration of Amy!"

RD chuckled. "It's coming up, yeah. It happens after the obesity improv..." RD turned to me suddenly. "Bro, where's our four-hundred-pound fat dude?"

"Oh fuck—I'll be right back. You guys go on without me."

I hunted down Paul Faaland and after a call to the extras casting agency, we learned that our obese extra was a no-show and they didn't have a replacement. The scene was scheduled to be up within a couple of hours, tops. We were in big trouble.

"Send a PA to look for someone," said Gary.

"Like, someone off the street?" I said.

Gary shrugged. "Why not? What do we have to lose?"

Gary grabbed the nearest PA and told him to hit the streets and find us a fat person, ideally a man, willing to be berated on camera for $400 in cash.

The PA looked at us like we were crazy. "You're serious?"

Gary nodded, poker-faced. "Yes. For the third time, go and get us the fattest person you can find. I don't care where you find them."

"I don't know where to even start looking."

"It's America, just drive around. You'll find someone who wants to make four hundred dollars."

The PA sighed dreadfully. "How important is this?"

I grinned. "We're in big trouble without this character."

The PA shook his head. "This truly sucks."

"Why? You get to save a movie today—how many times are you going to get that opportunity?!"

THE CAST and crew continued ripping through the schedule. It was a beautiful thing, but we needed more time to replace our obese extra. Eric bought us a little more by calling for an early lunch.

RD and I grabbed a seat at a folding table alongside most of the principal cast including Leo, Scott, Tobey, Kevin, Meadow, and Jenny. I plopped my plate of food down in front of me and took a bite out of my veggie burrito.

Kevin grinned at RD and me. "It's going good, huh?"

"Un-fucking real," I said with a cheek full of burrito.

David Stutman joined our side of the table.

RD nodded. "It's going well."

"It's going incredible, RD," said David.

Tobey chuckled. "I don't even know what it is we're doing."

"Me neither," said Leo.

Scott shrugged. "That's not necessarily a bad thing."

"It's a movie about a bunch of friends hanging out and talking shit about life," said RD. "What's not to get?"

"Yo, what's up with our back end?" said Tobey.

"Yeah, can you explain that for us?" said Meadow.

David nodded. "Everyone in the principal cast is getting a point each."

"Meaning one percent?" said Tobey.

"Yes."

Tobey huffed.

"I don't want mine," said Leo. "You can give it to one of these guys."

David shook his head. "I can't. I have to give it to you, but you can do whatever you want with it after that."

Leo frowned, "Why?"

"Because everyone has to get their pay. I don't know."

"Well, I want to negotiate what I get," said Tobey. "Why do you just get to decide?"

"Everyone in the cast is getting the same," said David. "Nothing has changed from our first discussion at Scott's place."

"That's not true. I just found out we're getting one measly point. What are you getting?" Tobey's eyes jumped from David to RD to me.

I shrugged. "I have no idea."

"That's because we don't know yet," said David. "Everyone in the movie is getting back end—and I mean every single person except extras and PAs. The entire crew, all the actors..." He gestured to RD and me. "We'll split whatever is left."

Tobey shrugged. "What if I don't want to accept your offer?"

David chuckled.

"I'm dead serious."

Leo interrupted. "I can give mine away, correct?"

David nodded. "You can do whatever you want with it. It's your property."

"OK, cool. I'm giving my point to him." He pointed at Scott.

"Me?" Scott put his hand on his heart.

"Yeah, happy birthday, bro."

"It's your birthday, that's right," said Kevin.

Jenny and Meadow chimed in with birthday wishes.

Leo reached into his pocket and pulled out his wallet and retrieved a one-hundred-dollar bill. "Here, take this too." He handed it to Scott, who took it instinctively.

"What's this for?" Scott held the money over the table indecisively.

"Happy birthday," said Leo.

"Are you serious?" said Scott.

"Yeah." Leo chuckled. "What?"

Scott laughed. "Why?"

"I mean, if you don't want it..." Leo reached for the bill, but Scott pulled it away.

"No, no. I didn't say that. It's just such a... I don't know..." Scott folded the bill up and put it in his pocket.

"An uncle gift," said Meadow and we all laughed.

"Bro, fuck the hundred bucks," said Kevin. "He gave you his back end in Don's Plum, that could be worth, fuckin'—"

"Tens of dollars," I said, and got a pretty good laugh.

Kevin reached across the table and clasped hands with Scott. "Happy birthday, bro."

"Thank you."

"Twenty-two?"

"That's right."

"Bro, you look way older than just two years older than me," said Leo. "Maybe try some face creams or something."

Paul Faaland approached me, and I liked the smile on his face. "He found someone?!"

Paul nodded. "He did."

"Is he here?"

"She. She's in makeup."

We excused ourselves and headed for the makeup trailer.

"I really wish she was a dude," I said.

Paul smiled. "I think you're gonna love her."

· · ·

"HELLO, Dale and Artie, it's nice to meet you. I'm Phyllis." Phyllis reached out her hand and we shook it.

Phyllis was an attractive black woman. She was big, but far from the 400-pound spectacle we had originally cast. I asked her if Paul told her about the scene.

She nodded. "He said I was gonna be teased about my weight."

"You're OK with that?"

"Oh, I don't care. Let me ask you something. Who is the big-time actor I'm doing my thing with tonight?"

I chuckled. "Leonardo DiCaprio."

"Leonardo what now? I never heard of him."

"He's a good actor," said RD. "He's been nominated for an Oscar!"

"Oh, wow. That is a big deal. Do you think he'll take a picture with me?"

RD nodded. "I'm sure of it."

"That's very exciting."

"You're so sweet," I said. "I feel terrible they're going to make fun of you."

"Don't be. I can't handle it."

"They can be brutal," warned RD.

She frowned. "What do you mean brutal?"

"Just saying awful things—things people shouldn't say to other people."

"Oh, well, if it's just about my weight, then I don't care. I'm just so excited to be in the movies!"

Phyllis was wonderful. It must have been romantic being plucked off the streets of Los Angeles in the middle of the night and put in a movie with a big up-and-comer like Leonardo DiCaprio, but the sudden change of casting made me nervous. We were supposed to be outing fat white men for their gluttony and greed, not picking on an overweight black woman. We decided to ditch the obese improv altogether and instead focused on Derek saying something insulting and derogatory about Phyllis' weight as she passed them by triggering Amy into a confrontation about the way he treats people.

Leo sat in the booth across from Amber Benson while Lydia touched up their makeup. "You good?" asked Leo. Amber said she was, but he wasn't convinced. "I'm just checking because I'm about to be fuckin' awful."

Amber eyed him for a moment before her lips formed into a mischievous grin. "Bring it on, man."

Paul Faaland arrived with Phyllis on his arm. RD introduced her to the cast and told them the story of how we found her, which delighted everyone. Leo apologized to Phyllis in advance of his insults, but Phyllis just waved it off.

"Don't worry," she said. "They're paying me good."

RD and I stationed up in video village inside the bar, right behind the swinging door that separated the two rooms. We watched everything unfold on the monitors alongside Blair Gawthrop, John Schindler, and Gary Lowe.

Eric called for everyone to settle in their places and walked Phyllis to her mark. "Pictures up."

Someone out of sight yelled, "Picture's up," and the cameras rolled.

"A speed."

"B speed."

"C speed."

"Sound speed."

Eric slipped into video village, steadying the door behind him.

An AC darted in and out to slate all three cameras, and we called action.

Phyllis walked past the table. Derek covered his mouth, trying to conceal his laughter. "Bro, you need to send her back to sea, bro —that chick is fat!"

Amy curled her lip, offended. "You think that's funny? You think it's funny to degrade other people?"

Derek retaliated viciously. "How about I take my shoe and shove it in your mouth? How about that?"

"You just want to fuck me, that's what it is," said Amy.

Derek guffawed. "Ah... yeah! You squatty-piece-of-shit-hippy-cunt!"

"Yo, man, why don't you chill out a little bit." Juliet's half-assed attempt at defending Amy failed as soon it left her lips.

Back at video village, I was so captivated by the scene I almost forgot to breathe. We were also looking for the right moment to introduce Constance, played by Heather McComb, who was standing nearby waiting for her signal.

"She was fat, it was funny," said Sara.

I nudged RD. "Now."

"Yeah, fuck it." He turned to Heather. "Action Constance."

Constance entered the diner.

Derek stared Amy down. "Stop looking at me like that—I'll fuckin' throw a bottle in your face, you goddam whore."

Sara spotted her hold flame Constance as she walked by and asked her to join them in the booth.

"Everyone, this is my friend Constance," said Sara.

Derek kept slinging his contempt for Amy while Constance slipped her arm around Sara's shoulder, then slid her hand down Sara's blouse.

"Hi, Constance, I'm Derek." Derek gestured to Amy. "This is a whore."

"This is past ridiculous," said Jeremy.

Derek was about to come completely apart. "Go! I can't look at your face anymore. I'm going to throw something at you, I swear."

"Stop, bro, you're being an asshole," said Ian.

Amy shrieked, "You guys are such fucking assholes!" She pushed and kicked her way out of the booth and hurried off toward the bar.

Jeremy hollered, "Hitchhike to nowhere. Stupid bitch!"

Amber barreled through the door, into video village, where she was met by nearly every one of us hushing her with hand gestures. The cameras were still rolling.

Amber huddled up next to me and RD.

I mouthed, "You were fucking amazing."

Amber was all smiles. She looked down at her bare feet, giggled, and whispered, "I left my sandals."

"Where?" said RD.

"Under the table."

"Go back and get them," said RD.

"Are you serious?"

"Yes!"

Film was burning.

"Go now, Amber," I said.

Amber stood up, instantly transformed back into Amy, and rushed out the door.

"Oh, no! She's coming back!" Derek squawked.

Jeremy recoiled from Amy as she reached under the table and snatched up her sandals. She turned and immediately headed back toward the barroom door.

Derek picked up where he left off, "Get out of here, you slut. Bitch. Whore."

Amy snapped and turned around and screamed at the top of her lungs. "YOU ARE SUCH A FUCKING ASSHOLE!" Then she hurled one of her Birkenstocks straight at Derek, narrowly missing his head. The cast screamed.

Leo grabbed an empty water glass in front of him and lobbed it over his shoulder like a Molotov cocktail. The glass smashed on the linoleum just as Amber slipped through the door into the safety of video village.

I was shocked. RD was shocked. We were all fucking shocked. Leo just threw an actual glass at an actor. Amber was fine, she fucking loved the whole thing, but it was very dangerous.

I expected RD to cut, but he didn't. I gave him the universal sign, slicing away at my neck with my fingers, but he waved me off. Instead, he twirled his index finger in the air to indicate we were to keep rolling.

That was the first and only time I saw Leo totally out of character while the cameras were rolling. He knew throwing a glass at a barefooted actor was a stupid, dangerous thing to do. He could have sliced open her feet and shut down the production. Derek tried to hush the table, as if that somehow might conceal what had just happened. His eyes darted all over the place, looking for any sign of Don, Flo, or anyone else. "OK, OK, be quiet. We're going to get kicked out of here..."

Sara laughed, "How funny is it that she threw a Birkenstock at your head?"

Derek laughed, "I know..."

"Cut," said RD.

"AND THAT'S A CUT." Announced Eric.

The crew burst into applause. They applauded Leo and the rest of the cast in the diner and back in video village, a dozen or more of us applauded Amber.

"R, we gotta send in Don," I said. "Derek would get kicked out of the restaurant for that."

RD nodded. "Yeah, you're right. How fucking awesome was that scene, bro!"

I turned to Eric. "Man, I hate to do this to you, but we gotta add a new scene because of all of that."

Eric was visibly discouraged at first, but then a smile suddenly broke open on his face, and all the tension he'd been carrying since the start of the shoot fell away. It was as if he had just realized what I had known from the start—that Don's Plum was making itself and our job was to simply guide it wherever it wanted to go.

At the end of the day, Blaire Gawthrop gave us a breakdown of the day's spoils. We had shot just over seventeen minutes of actual runtime in one night. That's the equivalent of shooting seventeen pages of scripted material. In other words, we kicked serious ass.

SLEEPING THAT MORNING WAS IMPOSSIBLE. I just laid in my bed with my eyes fixed on the ceiling, soaking in something between ecstasy and utter disbelief. I knew RD was doing the same.

"RD. You awake?"

He didn't respond. Instead, he just appeared in my doorway in his boxers and a wife-beater, his hair up in a band. "That was the greatest night of my life," he said, pinching and twisting his balls through his shorts.

I chuckled. "Yeah man. Me too. You were brilliant tonight."

"Oh yeah, why's that? I mean, I know, but..." he chuckled. "Why do you think so?"

"I would have cut a bunch of times, and we would have missed out on some of the best stuff we got tonight. That was huge."

"You gotta let shit play out, bro."

"What a fucking night, RD. I cannot believe it."

"Yeah, and tomorrow's gonna be even better."

JULY 30, 1995 - DAY 2 OF SHOOTING

I WOKE up at around three in the afternoon in a state of euphoria. I hadn't slept for more than a few hours, but it didn't matter. I was in my bliss. RD and I spent the afternoon reworking and rewriting the parts of day two affected by the performances of day one.

"What will they surprise us with today?" I muttered rhetorically.

RD shook his head. "No idea, bro. I was thinking that we should change it up and have Sara follow Derek into the bar instead of Juliet. Juliet's not gonna go running after Derek at this point."

"No, she hates him. Jenny and Leo are burning it up. Kinda sucks for Meadow."

RD shrugged. "I don't think she'll care. She's fucking killing it."

"She is bro. They all are."

WE WERE quiet again on the drive to Don's Plum. We arrived to a set buzzing with crew members. We huddled up with Davies, Schindler, Lowe, Adcock, and Blair Gawthrop to go through the day's schedule while the rest of the crew unloaded the gear.

By the time the cast had arrived, we were up and ready to go, and everyone picked up right where we left off on night one. We started smashing through improvs, one after another. The material was dark, funny, and even a little sad at times. The performances were beautiful to behold.

It wasn't all peachy-creamy, though. Tensions rose out of nowhere between Leo and one of our crew members. It shouldn't have been a surprise with such a frenetic pace happening all around us, but their argument caught me off guard. Leo and our boom op, Dave Haddar, barked and snapped at one another—I didn't catch what it was about, but it made Leo angry enough to flick his lit cigarette right at Dave's face. Thankfully, he missed, but the cigarette exploded like a tiny firework off Dave's shoulder, sparking chaos on the set. By the time RD and I got to the table, Schindler, Davies, Lowe, and the sound mixer, Brian Tracy, had already intervened. Everything settled down as quickly as it boiled up, but the incident left a lingering unpleasantness in the air.

When I got Leo alone, I asked him about what happened. I chose my words and tone carefully, we couldn't afford to have him walk off the set, but we also couldn't afford to get shut down because of some bullshit from one of the cast members.

"It's over. Forget about it," he said.

"You realize that guy would have sued you for everything you have if that hit him in the eye?"

"Don't be so fucking dramatic, Dale."

I sighed. "You're the one who told me not to do crazy shit for small movies, bro. All it takes is one bad decision."

Leo nodded. "Yeah. Well, nothing bad happened, so there's nothing to worry about."

JOHN SCHINDLER APPROACHED RD and me to pitch a shot inspired by Scorsese's *Goodfellas*. It was a dolly shot, of course, with track circling the perimeter of the booth. The camera would drift around while the cast riffed on the topic of the moment. It was a cool shot for something scripted, but for an improv film it wouldn't amount to more than an aesthetic shot for a transition, or as part of a montage. RD liked the shot.

"I like it too, but why would we do it?" I asked. "Scorsese had a purpose. He didn't just throw it in the middle of his movie because it looked cool."

John shrugged, "How do you know that?"

"I don't, John, but don't you think it's safe to assume?"

He shrugged again. "Sometimes you just need to spice up the cut."

"Why? Is it really worth ripping all this down and putting the crew through a whole new set up with track and whatever else?"

"Just having these three shots through the whole movie is repetitive," said John. "Trust me, I know what I'm talking about."

"They're on zooms, it's not just three shots. Have you seen My Dinner with Andre?"

"Yeah, and it was a little boring at times."

I waved my hand at him. "Come on!"

John shrugged. "It liked it, but the cinematography was boring, you gotta admit."

"This isn't Goodfellas. Don's Plum is a dialogue movie. It's what they're saying that matters." I looked to RD for support but didn't get any. "R?"

"I think it could be interesting."

"Can we get any other angles? Because if we can't, there's no fucking point to this shot." My tone was sharper than it probably should have been. John pulled Steven Adcock into the conversation, and he confirmed we could only shoot one of the cameras. We also didn't have enough track to surround the table, so the best he could pull off was a horseshoe pattern. I hated it.

"You think it's worth it?" said RD.

Steven shrugged. "You're the boss. It could be a cool shot. We'll make it look good."

Eric tapped his watch. "We gotta decide now, RD."

RD asked Steve if you could add one more camera angel. Steven nodded, "Yeah, but it won't always be clean."

"That's fine, we just need something to cut away from."

"Yeah, we can throw a b-cam on sticks."

RD thought another second. "Fuck it, let's do it then."

Steven called over to Cool Breeze. "Let's get the track in here. All of it."

"You got it, Daddy-O." Cool Breeze headed for the door.

RD rested his hand on my shoulder. "I just feel like the cut needs it."

"I'm cool, R. I'm sure it'll look good. I'm just greedy for that improv. Since this is kind of a throwaway, maybe we should just do a free-for-all and save the scripted topics for the three-camera set up?"

"Yeah, cool."

Despite Cool Breeze and the rest of the crew busting their asses, John Schindler's shot still managed to take the better part of two hours to set up and at least another thirty minutes to shoot. Watching the time tick away while they worked through an almost endless series of squeaks, knocks, bumps, and micro jitters to get one measly shot was beyond frustrating.

Fortunately, it didn't seem to bother the cast and crew all that much. Their energy might have lagged a little at first, but after a couple of takes, everyone got right back to crushing their performances. For me, it was like standing by and watching fine aged wine leak from a faulty cork. The free-for-all improvisations were incredible, it was heartbreaking knowing we wouldn't be able to use any of them. After far too many takes, someone declared the shot a success and we were finally able to move on.

Paul Faaland tracked me down and told me to get into makeup. My face dropped.

RD sang, *"We're doin' the Wheats scene, everybody scream, we're rollin' on the Wheats scene, with Ethan Suplee. O-yeah, O-yeah, we're shootin' the Wheats scene..."*

Fear overtook me instantly. "I'm not ready, RD. Let's shoot something else first. I need to get my head around it."

"I don't think we can move it, Dale," said Paul. "I can ask, but..."

RD shook his head. "No, bro, this is the schedule. We can't afford to fuck around. Especially after all that shit."

I double-timed it to the makeup trailer. Lydia smudged my face and bare torso with several shades of brown makeup, messed up my hair, and soiled my jeans. It didn't take much to transform me into a believable bum.

Lydia stood behind me and contemplated my reflection in the mirror. "What else can we do?" Then she flared her eyebrows playfully, "You want a nasty cold sore?"

I flashed my eyes back at her. "I thought you'd never ask."

ETHAN SUPLEE and I took our marks outside Don's Plum and waited for Eric Davies to call action. We agreed to stick to the script. We'd enter the diner, approach the table and ask for money. They'd say no, and I would break into a random, drunken song. Ethan would do his best to sing along but, ultimately, he'd fail. We'd eventually pull on enough heart strings to get some money and cigarettes before stumbling away. Simple.

I couldn't get my nerves under control. As soon as Eric called action, I started freezing up, and we hadn't even made it to the table. I chose to play my character as extremely intoxicated, and Leo's reaction to my stumbling into the scene knocked me right out of character. I immediately regretted the choice, but it was too late, the cameras were already rolling.

"Oh," said Derek as we staggered to the table. "That's a big bum."

"Good evening, sir." Ethan massaged Derek's shoulder and kindly addressed the rest of the table. "Ladies and gentlemen..."

I scrambled to find my way back to my character. I blurted, "I wanna get drunk!" The words spilled out of my mouth like loose Jell-O. The whole cast chirped at me clearly reacting to my over-the-top performance. I was sure I looked and sounded ridiculous and it shook my confidence to the bone. Everything I had prepared disappeared from my memory. I had no character, no song, nothing. I was crashing and burning, just seconds into the scene. I tried to focus on the cast. Derek teased me about my pubes showing, Sara offered cigarettes, and one of them gave us a little cash. Just as I was starting to feel my character again, Don, played by Byron Thames, entered the scene unexpectedly.

"Gentlemen, gentlemen... how you doin' tonight?" said Don.

"We're great," said Ethan. "We're about to be better, though." Ethan stuck his thumb in Don's mouth. That escalated everything. The cast started yipping like we were in an after-school fight.

I swayed on my feet and managed to stay in character. The world whipped around me in a blur.

Don gripped Ethan by the shoulder. "Let me get you to follow me... right this way." Don tried to herd us to the exit, but Ethan resisted. Don ducked his shoulder underneath Ethan's arm and pushed with the full force of his legs, pushing Ethan back.

Derek rose to his feet and took out his wallet amidst all the shoving and arguing. I stumbled and grabbed for Ethan just as he tried to resist Don.

Ethan growled, "Wait a second, sir..." Don pushed him harder, and Ethan exploded. "Don't lay your fucking hands on me!"

There was a big push and I went tumbling down to the cold, linoleum floor. I hit the ground so hard it nearly knocked the wind out of me. I couldn't see anything but shuffling shoes. I heard shouting, the sounds of dishes and cutlery falling from the table, and quick, heavy feet.

Suddenly, Derek was hovering above me. I looked up and met his sad, judgmental gaze. He grabbed a hold of my arm, but I pulled away—fully in character. Others came to help and I was finally pulled to my feet against my will. I yanked away from them violently, and the momentum sent me crashing into the door. The door flew open, busting the hydraulics with a loud snap. I staggered out past the sidewalk into the empty street. Ethan came running for me and gathered me up in one arm. We stumbled away from the diner out of view of the cameras.

I gave Ethan a shove. "What the fuck?"

"What?"

"Why did you start a fuckin' fight?"

"I didn't, Byron did."

"You stuck your thumb in his mouth."

He laughed. "Why was he even there?"

"You fucking stole my scene, bro. I can't believe you would do that..."

"That's not what happened."

"That is exactly what happened."

"It's an improv—I improvised!"

"Why are you laughing?"

"Because you're my friend." He patted my shoulder. "I would never do that to you."

"But you did."

"I didn't mean to. Don't be mad. We'll do it your way next."

RD finally called cut and the two of us returned to the set. There was no time for a second take, thanks to John's dolly shot putting us behind schedule.

I was so disappointed in the situation and in myself that I slipped into an untimely emotional funk. I retreated to the corner of the diner, away from everyone else, and ruminated over every mistake I made.

Leo came over and sat with me. "Yo, you weren't that bad," he said. I let out a strangled laugh and he quickly apologized for his choice of words. "I mean, you weren't as bad as you think. You adjusted nicely. I think you're going to be happy with it in the end."

I feigned a smile. "You pulled me out with that 'pubes' line, you fucker."

"I know, I saw that. I couldn't help it, they were right in my face!" We both laughed. "You did a good job though, you'll see." He smacked my knee and stood up. "We need you out here, bro. Come on, let's get back to work."

We started walking back to the set.

"You might want to put on a shirt." Leo fanned the air beneath his nose. "You're fuckin' ripe, bro."

"Give us a hug," I tried to get my arms around him, but he ducked out and scooted away.

"Don't! I will not wear this shirt if you make it stink with your BO."

. . .

AFTER FRESHENING UP and getting back into my clothes, I rejoined RD in the bar of Don's Plum.

Cool Breeze was rigging the last of a few tube lights along a wall. Camera and sound folks were busy building their gear.

RD pointed to the monitor. "Dude, look at that shot."

Peter had climbed on top of the jukebox with a camera and framed up a sweet top angle of Leo's stand-in selecting a song.

Adcock approached us as we fawned over the shot. "Cool, huh?"

"I love it," said RD.

"All right. We're ready when you are."

RD put Leo on his mark and a moment later called action.

Derek approached the jukebox and browsed the song list dejectedly. Sara entered quietly, just behind him. She reached up and touched the back of his neck. Then her fingertips wandered to his earlobe and he turned away. He walked over to the nearby booth and sat slouched. Sara followed and sat next to him in silence.

They killed every fucking moment.

"Cut."

"THAT'S A CUT."

While the crew set up all three cameras for the next scene, RD went off and prepared Leo while I worked with Jenny in a private corner.

"What's happening here?" said Jenny.

"Well, this scene precedes your confessional..."

"Oh, right. That's important."

"He knows you care at some level—you came looking for him. You've also been flirting all night..."

"Yeah, we have."

"So he probably thinks you guys are gonna bone at some point."

Jenny nodded and giggled. "We're not, though." She took a deep breath. "I didn't believe his story about the suicide at first, did you? I'm not talking about Leo's acting—he was incredible. I thought the whole thing was just an act by Derek to get some ass. But after he split and left us there, I changed my mind."

"Why would he lie about it in the first place?"

"For sympathy. Some men think sympathy leads to pussy."

"Does it?"

She chuckled. "Sometimes."

"What changed your mind?"

"His friends. One of them would have given up a tell if he was bullshitting about something that enormous."

"Could you change your mind again and think he's lying?"

"Yes, of course."

"You don't trust him, huh?"

"Not at all." She laughed. "Do you?"

I laughed. "Derek is not a good fella."

She giggled. "He is intriguing though..." She sat up a little. "There's something there that's compelling... something redeemable, I think."

"Is that what you're looking for? Something redeemable in him?"

"No. That's just what happened after he started talking." She giggled again. "I just want to help him feel better."

RD and I took our place in video village, and for the next hour we were treated to two remarkable actors sparring back and forth flawlessly. Their performance was so special I thought it could go down as one of Leo's finest, and he owed it all to Jenny. She found the heart of the scene and set the tone and pace. Leo worked with it masterfully. His "strawberry shortcake" line was pure poetry in black and white. Everything about their performance was inspiring. When RD called cut, the entire room exploded into applause. It was perfection.

Eric Davies swept in, his clipboard flailing in one arm like a broken wing. "We gotta get outside now. We've got two hours to get the fight scene and the sunrise shot. We gotta move now. That took far too long!"

"Did you see it though?!" I pointed behind me. Eric didn't hear a word I said. He had already rushed through the door on his way to the next shot.

A STUNT COORDINATOR worked with Tobey, Kevin, and Leo on their patio fight scene. It was a short, relatively safe skirmish, but he still went into detail, choreographing every move from the sweeping round house kick by Kevin to Leo getting in the middle of it all to break them up. When we shot it, Tobey was borderline out of control. I wondered if he was trying to settle a real beef with Kevin or just using the moment to get something dark out of his system.

Leo got in between them and delivered his closing line, one of the few written lines in the film. "I want you fuckers to hug, alright," he put his hands on Tobey and Kevin's shoulders. "Because in ten years, none of this shit will fuckin' matter."

I wrote the line because I believed it. I believed that none of the shit we did on those nights out would matter in the grand scope of our lives. They would not define who we were, but they might help us become the people we wanted to be. Those nights exposed our doubts and fears, our struggles with compassion and empathy, greed, and envy. I thought about growing old with all those fuckers, watching the film again and seeing that it had all come true—that none of it really mattered, and that we made it out of the avalanche of our youth more or less unscathed.

Kevin and Leo surprised us all with an elaborate handshake they had choreographed on their own before the shoot. We had written a handshake into the shooting script, but only Kevin and Leo knew just how cool and special the moment would become.

"It took us hours," said Kevin. "We worked hard on it."

"How did it look?" Leo's expression was goofy, like a smiling dog looking for a treat.

"It was fucking amazing," I said. "I can't believe you guys did that."

RD hugged each of them. "That shit is on film forever. How great is that?"

"I can't wait to see it cut together." Kevin's smile was the biggest I had ever seen.

We were all grinning. We had just gone through something extraordinary. We all witnessed amazing performances by the entire cast, and we watched as our crew performed one miracle after another.

We had one last shot to get before calling the day and it was an easy one. It was the moment all the characters run off toward the rising sun, blissfully unaware of the crumbling world ahead of them. We sent all three cameras out handheld, and the actors did their thing, jumping on fences, shaking signposts, running and shouting along the sleepy San Fernando Valley street like nothing mattered and they were the only people on earth.

RD called cut and announced that Leo was a wrap. Everyone, cast and crew, extras and PAs, all broke into applause. Some whistled, others cheered. We had all witnessed and played our part in a stunning performance by Leonardo DiCaprio. The work he did in only two nights in Don's Plum was the stuff of legend. I don't know how he did it. And I don't know if anyone else could.

Leo rushed up to RD and me in a panic. "Guys, we gotta do Jerry's scene! Where is he?" Leo spotted his buddy, Jerry Swindall, and called him over.

RD's face sank. "We can't, dude. We gotta wrap. The diner opens for breakfast in less than two hours."

"We can do it real quick, RD."

Swindall arrived. "Sup, dudes?"

"Sup," I said

"Sup," said RD.

"Sup." Jerry nodded. We all giggled. All Jerry Swindall had to do to make most people laugh was open his mouth and speak.

"Come on, you guys—we gotta do a scene together," said Leo.

"Well, I don't care if we do a scene or not," said Jerry. "So don't do it for me, dudes."

"No, no, that's not true." Leo pawed at him. "Don't listen to him. Please, you guys."

Jerry shrugged. "What would we even do?"

RD looked my way.

I shrugged too. "I have no fuckin' clue."

"Maybe, Derek's on his mobile phone trying to find a chick," said RD. "Jerry comes in and tries to get him blow off Don's Plum and hang out with him." He grinned and shrugged. "I don't know, it's something."

"Nah," said Jerry. "That sounds shitty. No offense." He paused. "Wait. I got it—I got a perfect story for you, dudes. It's about this time I got into a bar with some friends and my friend threw his bottle and hit this other dude right in the dick." We laughed.

"See?!" Leo's eyes were big and bright. "We gotta put this kid on film."

"Combine the ideas," I said. "Jerry's on the phone talking to one of his friends, maybe you're telling that story you just mentioned... Derek enters and uses Jerry's phone to try and find a chick while Jerry tells him this story of getting hit on the dick—"

Leo chuckled. "Like, I just take the phone from him and hang up on whoever he's talking to?"

I laughed. "Yeah, do that—that's fucking hilarious."

We went back into the bar where the crew was packing up everything and pitched the scene to Lowe, Adcock, Schindler, and Eric Davies.

"We're already flirting with overtime, guys," said Eric.

Leo begged some more.

"How hard can it be?" said Gary Lowe. "It's one camera, right?"

Adcock pointed to the tiny hallway that led to the bathrooms. "We could just drop a camera right there," he said. "It wouldn't be a big deal—only take a few minutes to light. Most of the gear's still out. Now's the time if we're gonna do it."

John Schindler got Brian Tracy on board, and within twenty minutes, RD called action on one of the funniest scenes between two actors I had ever seen in an independent movie.

I don't know what possessed Jerry Swindall to keep right on

254

telling his story while Derek propositioned chicks on his mobile phone, but it took all of my restraint to not bust into heaving, hysterical laughter and ruin the whole thing. When RD called cut, we all fucking exploded.

Eric wrapped Leo for a second time. He went around and thanked each of the crew members individually. He and Dave, our boom operator, had a nice little moment of reconciliation. I admired Leo's grace and humility. He was truly wonderful to work with.

A BLACK SUV with tinted windows rolled into Don's Plum's parking lot. I felt a sudden rush of sadness. I didn't want Leo to leave. "I wish you could shoot the last day."

"Wish I could too, but I'm rehearsing with Bobby De Niro first thing tomorrow morning."

"Fuck Robert De Niro," joked RD. "Stay here with your friends."

"I really wish I could, bro. This was such a blast but I gotta go." Leo hugged us and got in the car. His window lowered immediately. "Make me look good, boys," he said.

And just like that, Leonardo DiCaprio was off to New York to continue a life unimaginable.

I thought about what was next for me. I was going back to telemarketing. Back to that awful sales room filled with smoke, cockroaches, and broken dreams, grinding the phones for $50 a day just to eat. It's crazy how different our lives were yet, somehow, through a series of unlikely events, we came together, became friends, and made a movie. I remembered the conversation I had with my brother when I told him I had a feeling Leo and I would work together. I still don't know why I felt so strongly it was going to happen, I'm not a psychic. But when Leo and I met that day at Jay Ferguson's house, I knew my life had changed. A little more than a year later, I had transformed as a man and had an entirely unexpected and exciting future ahead of me.

As soon as RD and I returned to the set, Blair dropped an

absolute bombshell on us. According to her script notes we had shot over one-hundred runtime minutes in two days of filming.

"Noooo," I said while chewing on a red vine. "That can't be right."

"Are you saying I don't know what I'm doing here, pal?" She flashed her supermodel smile.

"Wow, you're serious?" I said.

She nodded. "Even if you guys cut half of it in post, you'd still be at fifty or sixty minutes with another day left to shoot. It's incredible, Dale."

I looked over at RD to see if his head was spinning like mine. "Dude, we may not need any documentary footage."

RD nodded, his eyes wide with surprise. "Did we just shoot a feature film in two fuckin' days?"

BACK AT THE CONDO, we were both too wired to sleep, so we started rewriting day three instead. We created a handful of new scenes, including one with Jerry Swindall who returns to Don's Plum looking for Derek, only to learn that he's in the bar with a girl.

"Leon could show up with Nikki Cox," said RD. "Make Kevin happy."

I EVENTUALLY MADE it to bed for another sleepless day. After the first two nights, everything in the movie had changed a dozen times, but with the main body of the improvs in the can, I could finally see the shape of things like never before. Derek's secret pain turned into lust and cruelty. Ian's passive aggressiveness and holier than thou persona was called out and dealt with emotionally and physically. Jeremy's desperation and insecurity was cleverly hidden behind his razor-sharp wit. And, like lava beneath the earth's crust, Brad's doom added tension and pressure all around them, but never amounted to much. Not yet.

And like puzzle pieces, the girls and all their layers fit perfectly to complete a portrait of generational struggle. They were the balance and reason that quelled the guys' struggle for dominance. They used their fear, uncertainty, and courage, and conquered the men so thoroughly and so perfectly the men didn't even know it had happened.

I felt so lucky to be a part of it.

JULY 31, 1995 - DAY 3 OF SHOOTING

NEWS that we might have shot enough footage for a feature film spread quickly. David said Tobey Maguire fell to his knees and begged him for more profit points while Scott Bloom laughed at the spectacle.

"Did you give him any?" I asked, amused by it all.

David hissed. "Fuck no. I told him, yet again, everybody is getting the same thing."

The cast was giddy that our first two days had gone so well. Why wouldn't they be? They were kicking ass in a movie co-starring Leonardo DiCaprio and, if it worked, it could mean festivals and even a theatrical release. Doors would fly open for them all over town. It was huge news for everyone.

Tobey devised a plan to fuck with David Stutman and he recruited me and Ethan to go along with it. His idea was for the three of us to tell David that we were holding out from signing our contracts until we get a better deal. He said he wasn't serious, that he just wanted to mess with David's head.

"Why?" I said.

"Because fuck that guy, that's why." Tobey laughed, but he was serious. David wasn't well liked among our friends. They often called him things like shady, sleazy, and untrustworthy. I didn't argue because I had similar issues with David. I did my best to work with him affably, but we often clashed because of trust issues. So I agreed to play along with Tobey's little game.

. . .

WHILE STEVEN ADCOCK and a few others set up cameras and mics in the bathroom for the confessionals, we hit the streets with a couple of cameras to get a few crucial exterior shots and some b-roll.

I loved stealing shots all over Los Angeles, especially the rushes of adrenaline I got from avoiding the police. If they had caught us, we would have been fined and shut down. It was probably stupid to take such risks, but the danger was fun. It reminded me of sneaking out of the house at night when I was a kid and getting into all kinds of trouble.

We separated into two units, one focused on Hollywood b-roll without talent, while the other, my unit, got shots of Brad and Sara outside the New Beverly Cinema, Brad lit in the entryway of a downtown building smoking a cigarette, Jeremy picking up Amy, and so on.

When we finished up with the talent, we shot in tunnels, on bridges and overpasses, and in dark alleyways, dodging police here and there along the way. I was having the time of my life and didn't realize just how hard we were running the crew until I noticed the sweat soaked through Brian Bellamy's shirt. I nodded at the rig on his shoulder. "How heavy is that thing?"

"I don't know." Brian shrugged. "Fifty pounds, maybe."

"Holy shit!"

He chuckled. "Yeah, you work up an appetite. When's lunch, boss?"

Lunch was John's department, and he decided the production would treat everyone to Philippe's for our 11:00 p.m. meal break. Philippe's is a historic sandwich shop in downtown LA, famous for inventing The French Dip sandwich sometime in the late 1920s or '30s. It was a very popular place among carnivores, so most of the crew was excited about it.

Brian Tracy, our sound mixer, didn't want to break until we had finished the coverage. He wanted us to have lunch back at Don's Plum with the rest of the crew. His gear was heavy, but he wouldn't let anyone touch it, and he was sick of loading and unloading it at every location, so he tried to force our hand by refusing to pack up for lunch.

Gary Lowe shook his head. "We're not gonna make thirteen people wait for hours to eat because of one person. If he doesn't want to load up his gear, then leave him here. We can pick him up when we're done. Ask him what kind of sandwich he wants."

I thought for sure Brian Tracy would cave, but he called Gary's bluff and lost. He and his boom-op, Dave, were left alone in the dark of night, in downtown Los Angeles, with $50,000 worth of exposed gear, while the rest of us headed toward an air-conditioned restaurant and a hot meal.

By the time we arrived at Philippe's, Brian Tracy had already called ahead, and Cool Breeze was dispatched to retrieve the men and their gear. My concern shifted to the menu, where there was next to nothing for vegetarians.

A middle-aged man in an apron splattered in au jus asked what I wanted, and I ordered fries, coleslaw, and a bottle of water.

We all got our food and RD, David, and I sat with the cast. The meat eaters moaned and groaned and smacked their lips with every bite. Tobey and I exchanged perturbed glances, chewing our fries and coleslaw like mules put to pasture.

Tobey sat up and pushed his half-eaten plate forward. "Thanks for the french fry lunch, Stutman." He shook his head. "Un-fuck-ing-believable."

Kevin and Scott chuckled because they knew David was about to get a tongue-lashing.

"They have PB and Js," said David. "Did you see that?"

"Yeah, so what? A hot meal is too much to ask for on a David Stutman production? I'm working for free, for fuck's sake."

"This wasn't my decision." David held up his hands in surrender. "This was all Schindler."

John overheard his name and came over with a big, ignorant grin. "What's going on, guys?"

"Tobey's giving me a hard time because he's a vegetarian and we're having lunch at a beef sandwich place."

"First of all," said John. "This is not just some beef sandwich place. It's *Philippe's!* They invented the French Dip."

"Yeah, well, I still can't eat it, you know what I'm sayin'?" said Tobey.

"Yeah, I'm sorry about that," said John. "I can send someone out to get you something else—let's do that."

"No, I'm fine, I'm fine. It's too late for that. I like french fries." He smirked. "I eat them all the time."

"Me too," I said with a mouthful of my own.

John smacked himself in the forehead. "Shit! You're a vegetarian, too—I'm sorry, Dale. Maybe I didn't think this all the way through."

"Oh, so it was acceptable when it was only me who had nothing to fucking eat," said Tobey. "OK, I see how it is, John."

"No, no, that's not what I meant. I care about you, I do. I messed this up, I'm sorry." John's entire face was furrowed, yet he was still somehow able to smile. "Please let me get you both something. We can send somebody out for some Subway, how about that?"

I told John I was fine with fries and coleslaw. I wanted to get back to the diner and shoot the confessionals.

Tobey chuckled, "I'm fine, too, John. I'm just being dramatic."

John bowed out respectfully and went back to his seat.

"David, I gotta get my contract back from you," said Tobey.

David rolled his eyes. "Why? What's the problem?"

"Uh-oh." Kevin chortled. "You should've fed him, dude. You're pretty much fucked now."

"Nah," Tobey waved his hand at Kevin. "I don't care about that. I just need to show it to my agent."

"It won't make any difference." David shook his head. "Everyone is getting the same goddamn thing, Tobey. How many times to have to tell you?"

Tobey threw up his hand. "Leo didn't sign a deal."

"But he agreed to everything."

"Dale didn't sign his contract."

"Yes, he did." David glanced my way.

I shook my head. "I never got one."

"OK, well, I'll give it to you when we're back at Don's Plum. Remind me."

I shrugged. "I'll take a look at it, but I don't know if I'm gonna sign it…"

David shrugged back at me. "No problem, we'll just cut you out of the movie. You weren't happy with your scene anyways."

That shut me up quick.

"Seriously, David," said Tobey "This shouldn't be a big deal. I just need to show it to Leslie. I promised her I wouldn't ever sign anything without her looking at it first—I shouldn't have done it."

David shook his head. "I can't Tobey, I'm sorry. I'll make you a copy, and you can show her that."

"What's the big fuckin' deal, David? Is there something in there you don't want her to see? Because I find your reluctance unsettling."

David chuckled nervously. "I just said I'll make you a copy."

"I don't want a copy. I want the fuckin' contract?"

"You already signed it. I need them for the investors."

"You don't have Leo's. And you don't have it because his agents and manager are going to be involved in his deal, and I want the same thing. What the fuck, David?"

David threw up his arms. "OK fine, Tobey. But I'm telling you you're getting the same deal as everyone else."

"I heard you the first time."

"Do you promise to give it back after you show her?"

"Yes."

"Swear it."

"Just give it back to me, David. I want my fucking agent to see it."

"OK, but please don't screw us over."

"Thank you, David." Tobey grinned. "Don't be so paranoid."

"Anyone else?" David's gaze shifted from one cast member to the other.

"I'm good, bro," said Kevin.

"I'm fine," said Scott.

I nodded to David. "I'll sign it. I was just messin' around."

THE CONFESSIONALS ENDED up being more difficult to shoot than first anticipated. We couldn't get a boom in the bathroom, so they had to rig a mic up above the sink and it gave us fits.

Jenny approached me while the crew tweaked the setup for her confessional.

"Hey, can I talk to you for a minute? About my scene?"

"Yeah, of course."

She sat next to me. "I still don't know what I'm doing here—I don't know... I can't figure out what any of this is all about, Dale, if I'm being honest. I love what we're doing, but I don't think any of us actors actually know what it's all for. I don't know what this confession thing is about."

"Are you talking about the film or the scene?"

"Both. I don't know what we're trying to say, you know? So I don't know what Sara's confessing. Is she confessing something?"

"I think it's a different for everyone... I'm afraid to give you my personal reasons because I—"

"No, please, do. I can come up with my own eventually. I just need some overall perspective, I think."

"OK, sure. Um..." I took a breath before beginning. "I used to believe I was a bad kid, you know? I used to believe that everyone my age was because my parents and aunts and uncles, teachers, fucking everybody older than me, said so. They called us lazy and ungrateful and stupid. And I don't know if I started believing them or if I was just rebelling, but I started doing a lot of stupid shit like fighting with teachers and getting kicked out of class. Shoplifting. And I got worse as time went on. I got into alcohol, weed, acid, and eventually, thanks mostly to the acid, I started figuring out the universe a little bit. Those people who were telling me that my entire generation was doomed to fail were the same people who physically beat me in my own home. They were the neighbors who sexually abused me when I showed up to collect for my paper route, and the adults who were supposed to protect us were too busy judging us for things that weren't even in our control."

Jenny's eyes had saddened. "I'm sorry all that happened to you."

"Thank you, but I'm OK. I made it out of all that shit better than ever. What I'm trying to say is this movie, and really this moment you're about to have, is, for me, about healing and about realizing that we will one day inherit this whole thing—all the money, all the jobs, the whole world, and we'll be ready for it. We're capable. And who knows? Maybe we'll even make things right." I paused before I apologized for unloading my past on her.

"No, don't apologize, this is helpful."

"They'll shake their heads at this movie, Jenny, but we're better than they are because we know the truth and we're not afraid of it. We're not going to turn our heads like they did." I gestured to the bathroom. "Do whatever you want in front of that mirror, Jenny, it's your moment. But for me at least, that mirror isn't just reflecting Sara, it's reflecting all of us—it's holding up a mirror to everyone willing to look at it. Mirrors are scary things because they don't lie... all we can do is turn away from them when we don't like what we see."

"Or we can change it."

I nodded. "I'm a big fan of asking meaningful questions and a good one for Sara might be: what does she want to show us about ourselves?"

"This is great."

"We do need one specific thing from you, also—we're getting everyone to do it—when it's all over and you've said your piece, look in the mirror, right into your own eyes, and tell yourself with conviction that everything is gonna be alright. Please remember this, it's very important for the ending."

"OK. I will."

"Let us know when you're ready, OK?"

I joined RD in video village. Jenny took her mark outside the bathroom. Eric got everyone rolling and RD called action.

Jenny strolled into the bathroom. She made eye contact with

her reflection, grinned, and let out a little laugh. "You did it again," her face slipped into something like sadness, "I can't believe... you ruined... a potentially good fuck." She reached for her back pocket and pulled out some neatly folded tin foil. I knew immediately what was going to happen.

I turned to RD and whispered, "You gotta cut."

"Why?" He was confused.

"She's gonna do H, bro."

RD shook his head, "No, dude..."

"Yes. We can't let her do that—this is a mistake."

RD looked at me sharply, his lips and eyes tight. "We are not cutting."

I wanted to fucking scream at him. What about Jenny's career? What about the law? Were we committing a crime? I thought about calling cut myself, but the consequences would be harsh. By the time I realized I wasn't going to do anything, Jenny had already put a dab of black-tar heroin on the top of the foil and applied the fire. The drug bubbled and burped toxic smoke and she inhaled it all through a dollar bill straw. Her eyelids closed, her face lost all its tension. It was done. And it was on film. All I could do was surrender to it.

My shoulders fell slack and I watched Jenny bare her soul for our little movie. She crossed the line between courage and foolishness and made something beautiful out of it, but I couldn't shake the feeling that we had failed her by not cutting when the drugs came out. It would have ruined the shot and probably her entire confessional scene, but it would have been the right thing to do.

When RD called cut, Jenny exited the bathroom to thundering applause. She gave Don's Plum so much through the entire shoot and her confessional really felt like the pinnacle of her performance.

MY FAVORITE SCENE of the day was Grace Forester's seduction of Jeremy at the bar. It was another tricky three-camera set up lit to perfection by Adcock, Marx, and Breeze. The moment got the best of Bethany, unfortunately. She seemed to struggle with improvisation, succumbing to her nerves on just about every take. I could relate of course. She felt bad about it, and I gave her a hug and told her everything was going to work out great, even if I wasn't so sure it would.

Kevin crushed his performance. He had the best timing of any actor in the film, in my opinion. I believed we captured a career-defining performance for him. His hilarious confessional was the day's martini shot, and when Eric called a wrap on Kevin, he got a roar of cheers, whistles, and applause. The crew loved him.

Then Eric called a wrap on production and the place broke into a cacophony of clapping, banging, whistling, and cheering. We weren't celebrating the end of the production, I don't think any of us wanted it to end, we were celebrating what we had accomplished together. If Blair's notes were accurate, we shot over 120 pages worth of content in three nights.

"That might be some kind of record," said Gary Lowe.

"I've never seen anything like it," said Blair.

I was hit by a tsunami of emotions. All it took was three days to connect all these lives together forever. It was so small but the magnitude of it was incomprehensibly massive and beautiful.

I went looking for Cool Breeze. I felt such a close connection to him from the first moment we met. I found him loading the grip truck with light stands. We gripped hands and I pulled him in for a hug. "How's that jaw?" I asked.

Cool Breeze laughed and rubbed his cheek. "Hurts a little, but I could take another one if you needed me to."

On day two of shooting, we needed a man willing to eat a vicious slap from a woman on camera and Cool Breeze volunteered. The violence was the catalyst to Derek's confession about his father's suicide. RD and I were happy with the first take, but Cool Breeze was sure the slap needed more heat to be believable so he told our gracious slapper, Marissa Borsetto, not to hold back on the second take, and she did not.

"I won't ever forget it," I said.

"No problem, boss." said Cool Breeze. "I hope we can do it again sooner rather than later."

I smiled, "I hope you're on every film I ever make, my friend."

THERE WERE SO many others I wanted to work with again—Marissa Borsetto, Blair Gawthrop, Gary Lowe, John Schindler, Bethany Ashton, Paul Faaland, Steven Adcock, Brian Bellamy, Brain Tracy, John Haydon, Peter Rieveschl, Dave, Lance, Fred, Doug, Caroline, Andie, Jimmy, Mike, the entire fucking cast. We developed that precious familial love that grows between people who experience something extraordinary together. It changed everybody and everything. They weren't John Schindler's crew anymore, or the *Swimming with Sharks* crew, they were the Don's Plum crew now, and this was only the beginning of what we could do together.

RD shuffled up to me, looking happy and exhausted. We had barely slept for three straight days—our minds and bodies wound up and vibrating the entire time. We could finally just breathe, and even that was a little overwhelming at first.

RD's smile was tired and sweet. "Did we get it, bro?"

I nodded and giggled. "Yeah, we got it, RD."

We pulled each other in for a hug. RD grabbed a fist full of the back of my shirt and squeezed tightly. "We really fucking did it."

"Yes, we did." I laughed through the lump in my throat.

PART III

20

A RANDOM PARTY broke out at the condo a few days after we wrapped. It started out with me, RD, and Kevin hanging out as usual, and then after a few phone calls and a couple of hours, the place was packed with people. It seemed like everyone I ever met in Hollywood wanted to be at RD's condo that night, and they all wanted to talk about Don's Plum and how the hell we pulled off a feature film in three days.

Ethan Suplee invited half the cast of *Mallrats* over. I got along with everyone, but I hit it off most with Jay Mewes. He and I drank deep into the night, long after everyone else had either quit or passed out. We laughed most of the time, but there were some turns in the conversation when we talked about some of our struggles. I couldn't help but imagine him acting in a dramatic film, something tied to him personally and emotionally. I even played some scene sketches in my head as we sat across from each other. I think I discovered in that moment what I wanted most for my career coming out of Don's Plum. I wanted to prioritize talent over property. The idea of learning what the role of a lifetime might be for someone like Jay Mewes and being in a position to make it happen excited me more than anything else in filmmaking.

. . .

THE NEXT DAY RD and I got an urgent voice mail from Leo that made us both nervous. RD dialed him up on speakerphone.

"RD?"

"Yeah. I'm on speaker with Dale."

I leaned in closer. "What's up, Leo?"

Leo sighed. "What's up, guys?"

"How's the shoot going?" I hoped I didn't sound as nervous as I felt.

"It's fine, I guess." He sighed. "I don't know how I feel about this film, bro."

"Don's Plum or Marvin's Room?" said RD.

"Both, actually. What's this shit I hear about you guys turning Don's Plum into a feature film?"

"Who told you that?" I said.

"Doesn't matter."

"Well, it's not accurate."

"Oh really? Neither of you said that to anyone at your little party yesterday?"

"No, we didn't."

RD cut in. "No, bro, our script supervisor said we shot a fuck-ton of footage... she said that according to her notes we have a possible runtime of over 100 minutes—"

"We're not turning anything into anything," I said. "We're gonna work with what you guys gave us. And yeah, you guys gave us a lot."

"I don't like it."

"You don't like what?" I snapped.

RD held up his hand. "People are rushing to conclusions. We don't even know what we got yet. It could be garbage."

Leo sighed audibly again. "Well, I want to be clear about this now before you do all that work. This was supposed to be for Showtime or whatever... an hour-long thing, or a festival short. Something for all your reels. Not a feature film."

I felt a pang of panic rush through me. "Leo, all we're gonna do is cut together what we shot. That's it. It'll be however long it'll be. What else are we supposed to do?"

"Yeah, bro, we just wanna make a good film—who gives a shit how long it is?"

"I do," said Leo. "And it's not gonna be a feature film, guys, I'm sorry."

"Leo. This is fucking ridiculous. We're gonna cut the movie together. Are you saying we shouldn't?" I looked at RD, totally baffled. "You're not saying that, right?"

"You don't make feature films in one day, Dale. Trust me."

"We shot for three days."

"Three days." Leo exhaled hard. "Same fuckin' thing."

I continued. "Leo. You haven't even seen anything yet. We haven't either, not a single reel. This is horribly premature."

"I don't need to see anything to know it's not going to be a feature film."

"But you don't even know what you're talking about. What if it's brilliant?"

"It won't—I know exactly what I'm talking about. I did this movie to help you guys out, not as some big thing, so get this feature shit out of your heads."

RD cut in. "I thought the goal was always to make the best movie possible."

"It still is—"

"Well, then I don't understand, bro. That's what we're trying to do, besides—"

I interrupted, "What happens if the best possible movie we can make is a hundred minutes? Are we supposed to ruin that so it's short enough for you?"

RD held up his hand again to shut me up. "Look, bro, if you're worried we're gonna put out some piece of shit, let me assure you right now that that ain't happening."

"If you were going to pull this shit, why not let us make Last Respects then?"

"Because I didn't like Last Respects."

I shook my head. "No, you thought the script was bad, but you liked the idea. If the script was good, you would have made it, right?"

"What are trying to say, bro?"

"I'm saying you wanted to make something good. No one was talking about features or shorts. All we talked about was making a kick ass movie together. You made Don's Plum because you thought it could be good."

"Yeah, bro," said RD. "We haven't seen anything yet, but you were there, you guys killed it down to the last minute."

"I just don't—I don't see how you guys can pull it off. I make feature films. They take months, not days."

"Why is that the only way?" I said. "That's so narrow—"

"We're way ahead of ourselves anyway," said RD. "Let us cut it together and see what it is. Maybe you're right and it's total fucking crap."

"I didn't say it was crap."

"No, that's cool, bro, maybe it sucks—let us cut it together and find out. If it does suck, Leo, no one will see it. I promise you that."

"We all want the same thing," I said. "I don't know why you think we'd be OK with putting out a piece of shit just because you're in it. It's insulting."

"I didn't say anything like that."

"What you said was that you wanted to make this movie to help your friends. And now, after it's in the can, you're calling us up and telling us not to finish it because it might be too long. That makes no sense." We all went quiet. There was no way RD and I were going to talk first.

"I don't need this shit right now, I really don't. When do you start editing?"

"No idea," I said. "We haven't even seen the dailies yet—"

RD interrupted, "But when we do we want to be able to cut them together, even if it makes it a feature."

I shrugged. "What the hell else are we supposed to do, Leo?"

Another agonizing moment of silence. I couldn't even swallow.

"OK, fine," he said. "Cut your little movie together. But my agents have to see it and sign off on it before you guys do anything at all. No Showtime, no fuckin' festivals—nothing until my agent and Rick sign off. Agreed?"

"Absolutely," I said. "Of course."

RD shook his head, "You fuckin' stress me out, bro."

"I just don't want you guys to be disappointed, that's all, bro."

"Maybe we pull it off," I said. "How about that?"

"You never know, I guess. Do your thing, guys."

"We all good?" said RD.

"Yeah, we're good. I'll see you fuckers when I'm back in LA"

———

BEFORE JOHN SCHINDLER would press play on the VCR/TV combo and show us the first developed images of Don's Plum, he told us about all our problems. The production was flat broke and needed a lot of cash before we could begin post-production. John's estimate was $70,000 to $100,000. It was an impossible number. None of us had access to that kind of money. David said his investors were tapped. He suggested asking Leo, but RD and I shut that down quickly.

"If anything, he'd be happy we're screwed," said RD.

"Why?" said David.

"Leo's not gonna fund Don's Plum," I said. "Get it out of your head."

"Well, until we come up with the money, we're pretty much at a standstill," said John.

"Why is it so much now?" said David. "I thought you said post would be like ten or fifteen grand tops."

"We burned through three-hundred thousand feet of film, David. I told you shooting three cameras was expensive. This one reel," he gestured to the TV/VCR, "cost almost five-hundred dollars to develop and telecine. Multiply that by three-hundred."

David grabbed his crown. "A hundred and fifty thousand dollars!"

"I can get it cheaper than that, but we're gonna need a lot of money, David."

"That's depressing," said RD. "Can we just watch this shit, bro? I don't want to talk about this anymore."

John pressed the play button and within seconds the first images of Don's Plum flickered to life on the 17-inch TV screen.

I was stunned at first. The overexposed black & white stock turned Don's Plum into something timeless and beautiful. When Leo entered the diner, it took my breath away. He looked so amazing—so much better than I had imagined. The enormity of it hit me like a ton of bricks. I think it hit all of us at once. It was only an image of Leo standing there on his mark waiting for RD to call action. It seemed mundane, and it was on its face, but we all knew what it meant. We knew we were looking at the greatest opportunity of our lives.

21

I'm NOT sure what I was doing when Meadow called and told me Jerry Garcia had died, but I was gutted by the terrible news. I immediately made my way over to Detroit Street to grieve with her.

She had draped a Grateful Dead flag over her window that faced the street. Her eyes were a little puffy and her face looked drained and sad.

"No Vegas this year," she said and sniffled.

"No," I said.

We smoked weed and listened to bootlegs while people came and went. I felt so lucky that I got to experience The Grateful Dead's work in such a profoundly moving way, and with someone as wonderful as Meadow. It was heartbreaking knowing it would never happen again.

22

DON'S PLUM remained financially stalled. John Schindler said things were progressing slowly. He was trying to set up a meeting with an executive from Paramount Studios who could be a huge help, but prospects for finding the finishing money were bleak.

My heart ached like a bad break-up. A hundred grand would likely take months to raise—if we could raise it all. It was depressing to think about, but at least my friends were always there to distract me.

———

BLAKE WAS SITTING on The Sups Couch next to Ethan. I was in the office chair across from them. RD was meandering from one spot to another, restless as usual. I saw something move out of the corner of my eye, like a big bug or something, and it pulled my attention directly to Blake's crotch. It was no bug. Blake had somehow managed to pull out his shaved balls through his fly without anyone noticing. His penis was still tucked away in his pants, but his testicles casually hung from his fly like a smooth bag of coins. I looked up at him and my eyes were met with a loaded grin.

"What's going on, man?" he said. "You good?"

I glanced down again, and he made his balls bob the way we men can, and I lost it completely. I started laughing like a lunatic.

"What's so funny?" said Ethan, dumbfounded.

"You guys see Kids yet?" Blake asked with indifference.

My eyes kept snapping back to his balls. RD caught on and he started cracking up.

"What the fuck is so fuckin' funny?" Ethan was clueless and growing irritated.

"You guys definitely need to see Kids, bro." Blake said while his balls rolled around, accentuating every gesture, emphasizing every word. "You're going to *love* it!"

Ethan finally noticed Blake's balls and he leapt to his feet with surprising agility. "What the fuck, Blake. What are you doing?!"

"What?" said Blake with wide, innocent eyes. He looked down at his balls, then back at Ethan. "I'm just hangin' brain, bro. What's your problem?"

It was true! His bald sack looked just like a goddamn brain! I had never in my life seen something so funny. I wasn't laughing anymore, I was heaving and whining like a mule, my eyes squirting sticky tears. RD was in the same shape, struggling to breathe. He wiped his eyes and nose.

"Why do that shit next to me?" shouted Ethan. "What the fuck is wrong with you, bro?"

At first, I couldn't tell if Ethan was genuinely upset or if he was just milking it, but then the corner of his lip curled up in a hint of a smile.

My eyes went right back to Blake's scrotum. All I could see now was a brain where there were once balls. I can't explain why it was the funniest thing I had ever seen, but it was. I wiped my eyes again and tried to contain my giggles. "You guys want to go see Kids or what?" I asked. "I gotta see that movie."

Blake said, "I've already seen it. Me and Johnny and Jay and Sisto and pretty much everyone who wasn't in your movie went last weekend while you were shooting—it's fuckin' genius, bro. You should go see it for sure."

"You don't want to see it again?" I said.

"No. Never. I'll come with you guys, though and see something else." Blake tucked his balls away.

I wiped my eyes one last time, smacked the speakerphone button and dialed 777-FILM.

"Hello, and welcome to Moviefone. If you know the name of the movie you'd like to see, press one now."

———

JOHN SCHINDLER CALLED with uplifting news. He met with the Paramount executive and showed him the dailies, and the guy really liked what he saw. John set up a meeting for us to meet him and talk about next steps. John also mentioned that he had rented Chuck Berry's Hollywood mansion to post the film. He said it so casually, like it was a normal everyday thing to rent a rock legend's house. He also found an editor who was just breaking into features from music videos, but John saw no point in introducing him until we had a budget and could make him an offer.

———

ONE SUNNY AFTERNOON, Blake invited me over to his apartment to snort some heroin and listen to Tom Waits CDs. It was the most intensely beautiful high I've ever experienced. The raw, soulful music and the kaleidoscope show beneath my eyelids delivered nothing but joy and transcendence.

While fiddling around on his electric guitar in between Waits albums, Blake told me he and Jenny were officially forming a band together, but still hadn't named it. I said I was happy for them. I liked the other girls he played with, but Jenny's talent was truly special. Then Blake played a song that he and Jenny had just written and it was so beautiful I nearly cried.

When the morning came, Blake asked me if I wanted to go out and get another balloon. I told him I was going to pass while I still could and that he should do the same. He didn't. Instead, he dropped me off on 6th and Western on his way downtown for more dope. He developed a heroin habit, and I did not. I worried terribly for him and for Jenny. At the same time, I wondered if the heroin had somehow turned them both into geniuses.

A COUPLE OF WEEKS LATER, Scott and I were hopping from one shitty party to the next until we finally ended up at some low-key gathering up in the hills that killed our night for good. The place was sweet, with a million-dollar view of the city lights all the way to downtown, but there was a super dark vibe in the air. The music was moody and psychedelic, and no one was talking, laughing, or even really moving all that much. They were all out of their minds on H. They were almost all recognizable faces, TV stars, up and comers, artists who worked with amazing directors like Ridley Scott and Francis Ford Coppola, all nodding in and out of consciousness. Jenny was there and it made me sad. Hollywood was so sick. I decided right there I would never touch the stuff ever again, and I never did.

———

RD and I were delivering breakdowns on an impossibly hot afternoon. I don't know whether it was something in the stars or the heat itself, but I was agitated. It was one of those days when I didn't want to talk about anything, and RD didn't want to shut up.

"Yo," he said. "Are you going to the party tonight?"

"Probably. You?"

"I don't think so. Heather and I are gonna go see To Wong Foo, you wanna come?"

"I'll pass. I'm gonna check out the party I guess. I'll catch a ride with Bloom or something."

"John's moving into Chuck Berry's this weekend."

"He rented it. Wow."

"Yeah, bro. We're going to cut Don's Plum in Chuck Berry's mansion, how weird is that?"

"If we ever get the money."

"John's Paramount guy is going to happen, bro."

"Really? John heard from him?"

RD nodded, "We're meeting with him Monday at the mansion."

"Why didn't you tell me? What time? I'm helping Sisto on Monday."

"That's cool, bro. Me, Stuts, and Schindler will go—"

"No, no, I wanna be there. I'll cancel Sisto."

"I think David wanted to just have me, him, and Schindler for this first meeting so we don't overwhelm the guy."

"Are you serious?"

"Yeah."

"The man works at a movie studio. We are not going to overwhelm him."

"It's cool. Just hang out with Sisto and I'll tell you how it went."

"I should be in that meeting, RD."

"You will—not this one specifically, but if it goes any further, you're obviously going to be involved."

"You should be sticking up for me."

"What do you mean? I did. I said you should be in the meeting, but Stuts and Schindler—"

"I thought you said it was Stutman?"

"It was—John agreed with him."

"Fuck all you guys..."

RD laughed, as he so often did in uncomfortable conversations.

————

I WOKE UP SUDDENLY, but I didn't want to open my eyes. I could already feel the headache bubbling like hot tar beneath my scalp, but I couldn't tell how bad it was yet. *What the fuck happened?* We were at a party up in the hills somewhere. I started the night with most of the guys, Scott, Kevin, Tobey, and others... I think we were at Neil Patrick Harris' house... Or maybe it was Chris Young's—I got way too drunk.

I opened my eyes a crack and recognized the couch I was sleeping on—it was Tobey's. I must have gotten a ride with him, but why? When did I lose Scott and Ali? Did we get kicked out of a party for stealing cigarettes? *Who the fuck was stealing cigarettes?* I remember some of us left and ended up at Jerry's Deli at one point—that's when Tobey must have offered me his couch. I had an argument with David Spade about something. *Was it the cigarettes?*

"Good morning," said Tobey, startling me.

I was still wrapped up in a thin bedsheet with my face buried in the cushion. I turned over and massaged my eyes to release some of the pressure. I sat up and grabbed for my cigarettes that were sitting on the table next to some mail addressed to Patricia Arquette.

"Did you sleep OK?" Tobey's voice cracked like a teenager's. I cranked my head around to get a look at him. He was standing with his back to me making coffee, completely naked. No socks, no shorts, no clothing at all.

"Jesus, Tobey."

"What? Does my naked body make you uncomfortable, Dale?"

"Well—I wasn't expecting it, you know?"

He grabbed an apron from a hook on the wall and slipped the neck strap over his head and tied the back with dexterity. "Do you want some coffee?" He chuckled. "You look like you could use some coffee."

"Desperately," I said.

"Hangovers suck, huh?"

"Never had a good one."

"I'm so glad those days are behind me, bro."

"Me too!" said Tobey's roommate, Aaron, as he emerged from his bedroom with spectacular bed head. Tobey met Aaron in AA a few months prior, and they became best buds. Aaron said what's up to us both and headed for the refrigerator.

He wasn't phased in the least by Tobey's bare ass, which was bent over searching for something in a Lazy Susan. Aaron took out some almond milk and poured it in a mug that looked like something someone's mother made in ceramics class. He came into the living area and grabbed a seat at the end of the couch.

"You guys want a tofu scramble?" said Tobey from the kitchen.

"I would love a tofu scramble," said Aaron.

"Yeah, sounds good," I said.

Aaron took a sip from his milk and smacked his lips lightly, tasting it more closely. He grunted. "Something's not right with my milk. I don't know what it is... Something's missing I think?"

Tobey stopped chopping and turned toward the sound of Aaron's voice. "Really?" He put down the knife and strolled over to Aaron's side of the sofa.

Aaron extended his mug towards him. "What do you think it is?"

Tobey looked down at the mug of milk and frowned a little while considering the possibilities. "You want me to fix it?"

Aaron nodded. "If you can."

Tobey casually lifted his apron, revealing his large foreskinned penis. It was darker than the rest of him, gray, brown, and a little red, like a giant nightcrawler. He took hold of it. It was heavy, so he used his entire hand, palm and all, and he kind of flopped it over the rim of Aaron's mug, dipping the head into the nut milk. He gave it a couple of slow, bulky stirs one way and then the other. Aaron sat there, completely still, eyes locked on his milk and the swollen penis stirring it, totally unfazed.

I was fucking stunned.

Tobey removed his penis from the milk. White drops rolled off the tip of the foreskin and back into the cup. *drip, drip.* My upper lip curled. I didn't want to look, but I couldn't look away.

Aaron put the cup to his pursed lips and drew a small sip from it. My hand found its way over my mouth. Aaron repeated the lip-smacking, tongue darting gustatory analysis, his eyes blinking rapidly like two machines processing data. "That was it," he said assuredly. "It's perfect now. Thank you!"

"I got you, bro," said Tobey as his apron dropped back over his junk.

I didn't know whether to laugh or scream. Tobey sauntered back to the kitchen and resumed cooking our breakfast.

"Do not put your dick in that scramble, Tobey."

Tobey and Aaron laughed.

I did not.

———

RD, David, and John met with the Paramount executive at John's new Hollywood mansion. When RD got home, he ran up to my room and sat on the corner of my bed to tell me all about it.

"I loved the guy. He's only seen the same reels we have, but he already gets the film."

I sat up straighter. "Like how? What's his name?"

"Jerry—I don't know how, bro. He just talked about what he saw and thinks it could be special, like a generational piece kind-of-thing. He mentioned Dazed and Confused, and fuckin' Kids. Can you believe that?"

"He didn't see Kids as a bad thing?"

"Not at all. He thinks it's great for us."

"That's great. When can I meet him?"

"Soon, obviously. I don't know exactly when... the next meeting, I would guess."

"How was Chuck Berry's mansion?"

"Surprisingly beat. The place is rough, bro—yo, did you ever hear the rumor that Chuck Berry likes to piss on hookers?"

"What? No!"

RD nodded. "Yeah, bro. So there's this grand staircase as soon you first walk through the front doors, and right at the bottom there's this huge stain, like a water stain on the hardwood floor—"

"Oh, god."

"Yeah, bro. Apparently, he would hire a hooker and stand at the top of the staircase and fuckin' piss all over her."

I shuddered. "That is so fucking dark."

"Schindler needs to get a rug or something or I'll never stop thinking about it."

KEVIN CONNOLLY and Nikki Cox were on a moderately successful show on the WB network called *Unhappily Ever After.* It was a knockoff of *Married with Children,* only their show had a talking sock puppet voiced by Bobcat Goldthwaite, so it was better. The network threw a giant "family and friends" fall season kickoff party at Disneyland for all of their shows, and Kevin and Nikki invited a bunch of us for the full VIP experience. RD didn't want to go, so I rode with Ethan and Tobey to Kevin's place, and we drove to Anaheim in a three-car caravan from there.

We didn't have to pay for a thing at the park, and we didn't wait in any lines. I felt guilty seeing all the children's confused little faces as we cut in front of them, but it didn't stop me from having the time of my life. In fact, my cheeks started to cramp from the sustained and overwhelming happiness I experienced throughout the day.

After the network's party was all over, we met back at Kevin and Nikki's new place in the valley. I was taking a look at the Splash Mountain photograph of all of us screaming our fucking heads off as we dove at a hundred miles per hour to our watery doom. Tobey and I were paired in a coaster car. His arms were raised high over his head, every muscle in his face was flexed. I had a death grip on the railing in front of me, my face almost identical to Tobey's, mouth wide open, clearly screaming my lungs out, my hair whipping behind me.

"That's two powerful people right there," said Tobey from over my shoulder. "Look at us."

"Yeah," I chuckled, "if you say so."

"You don't?"

"No, dude."

"Look at our intensity." Tobey tapped on the photo. "Look at your face, bro. You're a powerful person, Dale. Why does that make you uncomfortable?"

"It doesn't." I laughed and tapped the picture, "but this is a photo of me shitting my pants."

. . .

WHEN I GOT HOME, wrung out by happiness, I found RD sitting up in his bed watching reruns in the dark, buried beneath his blankets.

"Yo," he said. "How was Disney?"

"The most fun I've ever had in my life."

"Happiest place on earth." RD said it like the saddest guy on earth.

"You should have come."

"Couldn't."

"Why?"

"Then you couldn't have gone. They only had so many tickets, bro."

"For real? Who decided that?"

RD waved his hand in the air dismissively. "I've been a hundred times. Did you guys get to cut in line?"

"Yeah. I felt so bad for the kids."

"Fuck them. They're at Disneyland, they're fine. Yo, me, Schindler, and Stuts are meeting with Jerry again, by the way."

"The Paramount guy?"

"Yes."

"When?"

"Tomorrow."

"Am I invited?"

"No. We're still working out his deal, and David thinks it will be distracting to introduce you now. He wants to wait until we have a deal before you guys meet."

"That's ridiculous, RD. You're hiding me. Why?"

"No!" He couldn't help but laugh at the absurdity. "But I think David's right. Why confuse the situation at this point?"

"Confuse the—man, you guys suck."

I turned and walked into my room and shut the door behind me, ignoring RD's calls to come back and watch TV.

———

LEO WAS BACK from *Marvin's Room*. We were all meeting up at his house before heading to the clubs. I was still pissed at RD for keeping me out of the meeting, so I bussed to Los Feliz from the valley and arrived at Leo's long before anyone else. I was lying on his bed, flipping through a magazine that had David Thewlis on the cover promoting *Total Eclipse*.

"This Boy's Life is my favorite film of yours, I think. Gilbert Grape is wonderful, but—"

"It's mine too," said Leo. He was sitting on the edge of his bed playing Twisted Metal on the PlayStation.

We never really discussed his career, so I felt a little awkward mentioning it. "I thought for sure it would have been Gilbert Grape."

"They were both amazing, but This Boy's Life changed everything for me, from one day to the next."

"I read the interview you did in one of the papers in Vancouver. The Sun, I think—you were on the set, if I recall correctly."

Leo nodded, "I think I remember—"

"You talked about how you weren't intimidated by De Niro—how you just went for it, going off script and all of that. I was so inspired by that article, bro."

He laughed, "Why?"

"Because you took a chance and it paid off. And I think that for most people, maybe all people, if they want to make it, they gotta take chances—and that shit is scary."

He nodded. "I got very lucky."

"Yeah, well, you were ready for it."

I started reading the article on Thewlis and *Total Eclipse*. It was surreal reading about Leo in a major magazine while hanging out with him at his house. I thought about the magazine I picked up at SeaTac airport with Leo on the cover and a year and a half later, by fate or luck, I found myself sitting in his bedroom reading about his next movie in a new magazine while he crashed pixelated trick cars on his 27-inch color TV.

"Thewlis is blowing you so hard in this article."

Leo chuckled, "I know."

"I still can't believe you got to work with him. I can't wait to see it."

He sighed, "I don't think you're gonna like it."

"Why?"

"Because it's terrible."

"What's wrong with it?"

"Everything. It's flat. I suck... David's good, though."

"Oh no."

"I'm bummed about it."

"I still can't wait to see it. You're probably just being overly critical."

Leo sighed. "I wish—I need one of these goddamn movies to work. It's stressing me the fuck out."

"It'll happen. Don't worry."

"What if it doesn't?"

"It will." I chuckled.

"Nothing is guaranteed in this business."

"Dude, you're twenty-one years old, rich, good looking, Oscar nominated. You'll be fine. For a little perspective, I'm twenty-five, I have nothing on my resume except Don's Plum, if it ever gets finished. I have no job, no money. I'm not even legally allowed to work here right now. Wow, I just bummed myself out."

He laughed and it caused a spectacular in-game car crash. "You'll be fine too, bro. You're just getting started." He started pounding the X button while steering with his entire, stiffened body. There was an even bigger, more spectacular explosion. "Dammit!" He stood up and ran his fingers through his hair. "Who are we waiting for again?"

"Sups and Connolly."

"Is RD coming?"

"No idea. He's being a dick right now."

Leo chuckled. "You fuckers are always fighting. I'm thirsty for something besides water. You want anything?"

"Nah, I'm good."

The others arrived and we argued about where to go first. I think there were four or five of us that piled into Leo's car. He cranked Wu-Tang on his stereo, and we headed west for the strip.

It was a fast Friday night and, before I knew it, I was half-loaded on shots and beers and we hadn't even gotten to the second bar yet. Leo needed smokes, so he pulled into a gas station.

Most of us hit the munchies aisle while Leo got carded for cigarettes. The only other people in the shop were a girl about our age, and a guy, presumably her boyfriend, who also looked to be in his early twenties. The girl had a nice ass, and I think she sensed the multiple sets of eyes checking it out. She turned and spotted Leo walking from the register and froze. Her jaw dropped open at the sight of him.

Leo froze too, only he looked terrified.

She grabbed her friend's arm, getting mostly jacket, and squeezed it hard. Disturbingly hard. After he shook her off, all hell broke loose. She squealed and hyperventilated, "Oh my God! Oh my God, it's him! Itshimitshimitshim..."

Leo was petrified. The girl lunged forward and he held his arms up helplessly.

"Protect me, guys, she's coming!" Leo waved us closer. "Hurry, hurry!" We rushed around him and joined arms, trapping him in the middle.

The girl's friend rushed up and took her by the arm, but she yanked it away hard and lunged forward. "OH MY GOD, I LOVE YOU, LEO!!" There were tears in her eyes.

We started speed shuffling Leo through the door into the parking lot. She followed so I yelled at her dude to get her under control. He grabbed her arm again, which bought us enough time to pile into Leo's Jeep and get away.

When I looked back, she had already given up on whatever it was she thought she was pursuing. The two of them argued beneath the hard florescent lights. The dude gestured toward us furiously while he jawed at her. She stood there with slumped shoulders, taking it.

I said, "How coincidental is it we run into the one fuckin' person who saw Basketball Diaries?" Everyone laughed, even Leo.

JOHN THREW a housewarming party at his new Chuck Berry mansion. We invited everyone we knew. Tobey, Kevin, Ethan, RD, and I met up at the condo and headed over the hill in a two-car convoy. I was excited to see the mansion, but I was most excited about finally meeting the mysterious executive from Paramount Studios that everyone had been so intent on keeping from me.

John greeted us at the front door. My eyes went right to the giant pee stain. It looked like it could only be a pee stain. There wasn't any water damage above it, and there weren't any random water pipes running up the grand staircase. The liquid had to have come from somewhere, and there was a lot of it.

Kevin cleared his throat, "John, is that Chuck Berry's piss stain, or what?"

John laughed. "It could be, I don't know. Don't worry about it, though. We scrubbed these floors for hours."

Tobey chuckled. "I was going to ask if it was safe to walk on."

I stepped around it anyway. John led us into the main room. It was impressive, even in neglect. It had a twenty-foot-high mahogany beam ceiling, and huge pane windows with sunlight pouring through them. The floors were trashed, but John had a couple of rugs down that helped soften the sight.

"It's pretty beat up, I know," said John to no one in particular. "But maybe after Don's Plum is a big hit, I can buy it and really fix it up."

"I like it a lot," said Tobey. "You want a pool table in here?"

John smiled. "That would be great."

"I'm gonna be in New York for a while shooting—"

"Oh yeah, I almost forgot to say congratulations on Ice Storm. We've got two big stars in Don's Plum now."

"Thank you, John. I'm going to be gone a long time and need a place to store my pool table."

"Yeah, for sure, man. We'll take good care of it. You're welcome to come over anytime when you want to play."

John led us outside to a large, peeling swimming pool enclosed by a concrete deck that spanned the entire exterior of the house. Beyond the pool was a regulation tennis court surrounded by twenty-foot-high fencing with weeds as tall as children woven up the sides. It was all very post-apocalyptic and I kind of loved it.

We spent the next few hours lounging around and exploring the property. The Paramount executive called and cancelled due to something unexpected and I started wondering if the universe itself was conspiring to keep us from meeting.

"He probably had to take a last-minute meeting with Tom Cruise or Sherry Lansing," said John. "He's very busy."

"Let me ask you something, John. Is this guy bringing money so we can finish the film? If not, what is he gonna do for us?"

"He can attract money. He's well connected, and he knows how to put a movie together."

"He sounds really fucking interesting. I'd love to meet him sometime."

"You haven't met Jerry Meadors?" John squinted at RD and then back at me. "Are you sure?"

"I was told you guys all wanted to wait until he was on board before introducing me."

"Really? Doesn't matter, I'll set it up. You'll like him a lot."

———

IT WAS A SATURDAY NIGHT. A bunch of us had gathered at the condo. Leo, Tobey, Kevin, and Scott were there. Sups was on the Sups Couch. Blake might have been over as well. We were drinking beers and trying to figure out what to do. It was one of those nights when everything sounded like a fucking drag, but we refused to give up on a Saturday night.

I grabbed a beer from the fridge and couldn't find the opener so I did a trick with my lighter I learned back in Winnipeg. It's fun because it makes a very loud and satisfying pop. I gripped my bottle high on the neck so that my index finger was tightly wedged under the cap. Then I leveraged the lighter against my knuckle, pressing the bottom edge hard against the cap rim, and then in a fast, jacking motion, popped the cap off. I got a killer pop too, like the kind you make with your finger and your cheek, and it was punctuated by the cap snapping sharply off the ceiling.

Within seconds everyone had an unopened beer and a lighter and were trying the trick. Ethan failed miserably and managed to injure himself. His lighter hand slipped, and his finger was gouged by the cap. It was gnarly looking, with blood and bits of skin hanging off.

Everyone started shouting at him to clean it and get some peroxide on it right away. RD ran upstairs to retrieve a bottle while Ethan rinsed the wound in running water.

RD returned and poured a cap of peroxide on Ethan's torn finger. Ethan yelped and hissed, being overly dramatic for our entertainment.

RD readied the cap. "One more time."

Ethan yanked his hand back. "No way, RD. I'm done. It's fine. I'm cured."

"Don't be a baby. You want to get an infection and die?"

"You put it on already. I'll be fine."

"No, bro, it's still bubbling. You have to do it until it stops."

"That's not true," said Ethan.

Scott interjected. "RD's right, you have to keep peroxide on until all the bubbling stops. If there's bubbling, there's still potential for an infection."

"Nope, not true," said Tobey.

"Yes, it is," replied Scott. "It's a scientific fact."

"Then why, when you put peroxide on your asshole, does it always sizzle?"

Scott smirked. "That's impossible."

"Well, it's true. Maybe you don't know everything."

Scott shook his head. "The asshole would have to be infected."

I shuddered.

"I mean, you can say that as many times as you want, Scott, but I know for a fact you're wrong."

"How? said Scott. "Have you tried it?"

"Yeah, I have."

Scott smiled suspiciously. "You poured peroxide on your own asshole?"

Leo laughed. "How the fuck did you do that?"

Tobey grinned. "I used a mirror. I put a little on there to see what happens... it bubbled." He almost laughed as he said it. "And there was no infection."

"Do it right now," said Scott.

Leo laughed. "I gotta see this."

Tobey shook his head. "I already did it. I don't care if you don't believe me. You're wrong."

"You're full of shit," said Scott.

"Calling me a liar?"

"Yeah, I guess you could say I am."

"You can try it just as easily as me."

Scott smirked, "Nice try."

Leo stood up. "I'll fuckin' do it."

Everyone stirred.

Tobey grinned, "Really?"

"Yeah, sure. What do I do?"

"Drop your fucking pants, buddy." Tobey turned to RD. "Gimme that peroxide."

And just like that, Leo dropped his pants and underwear down to his ankles. He got down on his back, and threw his legs up over his shoulders, presenting his asshole and all the rest of his parts for everyone to see. We exploded into laughter.

"Hand me the fuckin' peroxide, dude." Tobey snatched the bottle from RD, who was too weak from laughter to hold it up.

Tobey poured a little liquid into the white cap and then leaned over Leo's exposed butthole and, with the steadiness of a surgeon, poured a tiny amount of the liquid onto the dark spot. We all stopped.

"There!" said Tobey, pointing. "It's bubbling."

Scott cautiously peeked over. "I don't see anything—"

"What are you talking about, bro? It's bubbling right there." Tobey pointed again. "Look, bro."

"I can feel it working," said Leo in a high, compressed voice from below. "Pour a little more on there."

Tobey leaned in and poured a some more from the cap.

"It's bubbling," said Leo. "Look closer, Scott."

Scott leaned in and shook his head. "No, it's not—"

Leo farted. He ripped a huge one and the ass-pool of peroxide sprayed right up into Scott's face. Scott rushed to the kitchen, screeching and clawing at his eyes and mouth while the rest of us erupted.

Leo sprung to his feet and started jumping around like an ape, laughing hysterically as the rest of us practically fell over each other gasping for air.

AFTER EVERYONE HAD GONE, RD and I talked and laughed about the whole thing some more.

"Did you see Bloom's face?" said RD.

I nodded. "If I was him, I would be so fuckin' pissed-off at them right now."

"He got Leo's ass on his lips, bro." RD shuddered.

I shrieked. "In his eyes!"

"It was kind of genius, you gotta admit."

"I think I might have hit somebody. Like a knee-jerk reaction."

"Yeah, but that would never happen to you because you're not stupid enough to put your face that close to Leo's loaded butthole in the first place." RD shook his head. "What was Scott thinking?"

"It's not his fault," I said. "He trusted his friends."

23

I SAT at RD's glass dining table, massaging my forehead with one hand and smoking a cigarette with the other. Jerry Meadors and I were supposed to finally meet at the condo, but Jerry called RD last minute and changed our plans. He asked to meet at some fancy restaurant in Beverly Hills and RD agreed on my behalf without asking me first.

"I can't afford that shit, RD. Are you gonna pay for it?"

"He will."

"You can't just fucking speak for me, bro. I would have said no."

"He'll pay for it. He's the richest."

"How do you know? Did he say?"

"No."

"Then I'm not going. I'm not gonna show up with empty pockets and order an iced tea, never mind any food."

"Just go."

"No, RD."

"You have to, bro. He's going to be there."

"Call him and ask him to meet me here like we originally planned, or at John's mansion if he doesn't want to drive to the valley. Let's do that."

"It's not that. He's a fuckin' lunch guy. And a dinner guy. I'm guessing we'll probably have breakfast somewhere at some point."

"He can come here after lunch. Why Beverly fucking Hills, RD? What's wrong with Astro Burger?"

RD laughed. "Let's go deliver the breakdowns. I'll drop you off after."

"I'm not going. I'm serious."

"If he shows up and you're not there, that won't be good for the film or for you, bro. You wanted to meet the guy!"

"Not like this."

"If you're so worried about it, just tell him you're broke. I'm sure he'll understand."

I laughed, but it sounded like I was being strangled.

RD DROPPED me right in front of Le Petit Four a good twenty minutes early, which sucked because it was a scorching hot day. He told me to look for a tall guy who looked almost exactly like Benjamin Franklin.

I scanned all the tables in the restaurant from the sidewalk, but there was no sign of Ben Franklin anywhere. I thought about asking the host, but I was afraid he'd offer to seat me while I waited.

I loitered around the entrance for a few minutes until it started feeling uncomfortable, then I meandered around the shop windows, wondering who in the fuck could afford all the shit inside of them. I saw a clock on a wall that said Jerry should be at the restaurant already, so I strolled back to Le Petit Four, but there was still no Benjamin Franklin to be found. I lit up a smoke and continued passing time window-judging people I'll never know. I checked back at the restaurant every five minutes or so, then switched to every ten minutes. At the half hour mark, I had to assume Jerry Meadors had stood me up. I looked for a phone booth to call RD, but I couldn't see any. It would take hours to get back to the valley by bus. I was better off waiting on the outside chance he showed.

It was a good call. Twenty minutes later, a man who looked just like a modern version of Ben Franklin found me on the sidewalk, thirsty and a little disoriented. Jerry was "terribly sorry," but didn't dwell on it except to say that lunch was his treat and that I should order anything I wanted, even the lobster. Then he laughed and said they didn't serve lobster.

We were seated at a table for two with a nice view of the street I had just spent the last hour pacing up and down.

"It's so good to finally meet the enigma, Dale Wheatley." Jerry unfolded his napkin onto his lap. "They've been keeping you quite a secret."

I laughed. "I was starting to think you were made up."

"That's very funny." Jerry paused and locked his eyes onto mine intensely. Normally, I would have found that odd, even intimidating, but not with him. Jerry's gaze was warm and bit mesmerizing. He smiled and said, "Why do you think they were keeping you from me, Dale?"

I shrugged. "I have no idea. Maybe they think I'm unpresentable."

"No, I don't think that's it. How charming, though. RD called you his creative partner."

I nodded, "We work well together."

"I liked RD very much. And I'm very excited about your project, Dale. Don's Plum."

The waiter arrived with waters and artisan bread with extra virgin olive oil. Jerry seasoned the oil, dipped a wedge of bread in it and then took a bite.

I drank water like a stray. "Me too," I said while catching my breath. "I can't wait to start cutting it together. And thanks to you, that's about to happen."

"They told you I've arranged for the developing and telecine transfer of the sixteen-millimeter negative?"

"They did. Thank you so much. I didn't realize how big of a deal it was."

"It's a big favor for sure. A one-time thing, I should think. But I showed your clips at the lab, and they were excited to help."

"What would something like that normally cost?"

"Well, I'm not sure how much it would cost off the top of my head, but tens of thousands of dollars for sure."

"Wow. We're extremely lucky to have you on board. Thank you so much."

"I loved the footage, Dale. It looks absolutely stunning."

I couldn't place Jerry's accent. It sounded almost British, but not quite. "Where are you from, Jerry?"

"I'm from the south. A small town called Danville, in the wonderful state of Virginia. Tobacco country. Ever been?"

"I have not, no."

"I hope you get to see it someday. It's beautiful."

"Virginia. Huh. I couldn't place your accent—I guess I haven't met anyone from Virginia before."

"Well, I wouldn't describe my accent as entirely Virginian... What about you? Where are you from?"

"Canada. Most recently Vancouver."

"Ah, a friendly Canuck, how wonderful. You said, 'most recently.' Where are you from originally?"

"Winnipeg."

"Mm-hmm. A vagabond Canadian, how intriguing. Perhaps I should say a pioneering Canadian? Is there anyone in Hollywood working the way you and your partner RD work?"

"Well, I don't know about Hollywood, but Mike Leigh works with improv—we're following in his footsteps for sure."

"He works strictly with improvisation?"

I nodded. "No screenplay at all."

"Remarkable." Jerry stared into my eyes for a moment. "What sign are you, Dale Wheatley?"

"Capricorn."

He sat up straighter. "Really? So am I!" He was suddenly beaming. "It's great to lunch with a fellow sea goat. Were you born in December or January?"

"January."

"What day?"

"Sixteenth."

His jaw dropped.

"What?" I giggled.

"You're putting me on."

"Why would I do that?"

"Who told you about my birthday? John Schindler?"

"No."

"January sixteenth is my birthday, Dale."

I held my breath. "Now you're the one fucking with me."

Jerry howled and smacked the table. "Well, that's a first for me, Dale Wheatley!"

I loved that he pronounced my name in the same windy way as what, where, and why. I wanted this guy to like me, and I had just become irresistible. "I have to confess," I said. "You're my third."

"Really?"

I nodded, "There was the girl I thought I was going to spend the rest of my life with—she's gone now."

"I'm so sorry."

"Long gone but thank you. And before her was Chief Petty Officer Grant from sea cadets. He was a little prick, that guy. And now there's you, a big-time movie producer. How about that?"

Jerry laughed, eyes wild with disbelief. "Well, I'm honored to be in the company of Chief Petty Officer Grant, the little prick."

We spent the next couple of hours forming what would eventually become a cherished and lifelong friendship. Jerry was a fascinating man. He loved art and film like no one I had ever met. He'd seen everything on the big screen, and the best of it at least twice. We discussed directors from all over the world, old and new, and Jerry knew them all by name. It was the most I had ever learned about Hollywood and movies, and it all happened over the course of a late afternoon lunch in Beverly Hills.

We talked about Don's Plum, of course. He loved that we were a group of close-knit friends being "elevated" by a rising star.

"The world will adore him for it. And I should know, I got him his Oscar nomination."

"Really? That's wild."

Jerry nodded. "Gilbert Grape was a Paramount production. I

convinced my boss and mentor, Nancy Gallagher, to launch a 'for your consideration campaign.' I put it all together."

"That's incredible, Jerry."

Jerry nodded and sunk his spoon into the crust of his dessert. "I don't think Don's Plum is the kind of film that finds its way into Academy consideration, but I would think the Spirit Awards are on the table. Are you sure you don't want some of this crème brûlée? It's absolutely divine."

"I'm OK, thanks." I loved how big Jerry made Don's Plum. He could envision the film in the marketplace as both art and commodity, separately. None of us thought about any of that shit. But Jerry did. He thought about how the film would play in America and throughout the world. He went on and on, dropping names of executives and companies where Don's Plum could land. He went over his initial pros and cons, always mindful not to get too far ahead of himself. He had a vision for the film before it was even finished.

"What if it doesn't work?" I said. It sounded like a stupid question, but I wanted to know if he had given it any thought.

"Hmm. If Don's Plum is shit, you mean?" he nodded. "If it's shit, then we all lose, right? Doesn't matter who's in your film if it's unwatchable nobody's going to buy it. When was the last time you went out to see a movie you knew was awful?"

"Probably never."

"But there's something about this movie, something almost mystical about how it all came together. I could feel the creative forces around the project as John and RD were speaking about everything, and now, after meeting you, I'm even more convinced you guys are onto something special. I only hope I can help get the film into theaters."

I grinned. "Well, for the record, I think the film is going to work. I was just curious if you had thought about it."

"Of course. I haven't seen the footage but for the one reel John showed to me. It could be rubbish. Is Don's Plum rubbish, Dale?"

"No, I don't think so."

"Good. But if it is, then all I've lost is some time and a big favor.

However, if we're right and the movie works, then we'll have a significant head start over most of the competition. It's very competitive out there, Dale. Especially after Clerks and now with the success of Kids... Putting a film out takes a lot of time and resources."

"It seems impossible."

Jerry smiled. "That's what I'm here for. You keep creating."

"The guys said you might be able to sell Don's Plum to Paramount?"

"That'd be a long shot, for sure. But I did say it was possible when John asked about it. There are better fits than Paramount, though. Tri-Mark did a phenomenal job with Kids. Did you see it?"

"I loved it."

"Me too. I also love what Robbie Little is doing at First Look, don't you?"

"Honestly, I know nothing about these people. I know about Miramax."

"Miramax, of course. Have a look at these other companies, Dale. One of them could become a big part of your future."

My thoughts drifted into the future Jerry spoke of. It was a wild thing, being reminded that I was living my dream and that I somehow found myself with a future as an independent filmmaker.

"Who knows, maybe we even get a bidding war started," said Jerry. "But we should be careful what we wish for—what we want is a home for Don's Plum and your future projects. I presume you and RD would like to keep making motion pictures?"

"We would."

Jerry smiled. "Me too."

———

"WHEN DO YOU START EDITING?" Sups asked from the Sups couch.

RD shrugged. "Soon, I guess. They gotta get it all in the Avid."

"What's an Avid?"

"Editing shit—I don't know."

"Can I watch you guys edit? I won't say a word."

"Nope." said RD. "Can't."

"Why not? I won't say anything while you're working, I promise."

"No one can see anything until we're ready. Jerry Meadors' rule."

"Well, it's bullshit."

RD shrugged. "Hey dude, if it was up to me, I'd be fine letting all you guys in."

"Can I meet Jerry? I want to talk to him about this."

"No bro," I said. "Don't start harassing people..."

"Does he know this is a friend's project and not one of his big studio films?"

"No," I said, "he thinks it's the next Forest-fucking-Gump."

Ethan scoffed, "I want to talk to him."

RD chuckled. "Why?"

"Because I want to ask him questions."

"Like what?" said RD.

"Like, why the fuck can't the people who actually made the film see a few dailies—"

"You know why, bro."

"No, I don't."

"Has Kevin Smith let you in the editing room for Mallrats?"

"That's different, RD."

"No... why?"

"Because we're not friends—we are now, but he hired me off an audition. He'd let Jay Mewes in, probably."

"And if it was my decision, I'd let you in, but Jerry's in charge now."

"Why is he in charge? He's a fucking communist."

RD and I laughed. Anyone Ethan disagreed with was either a communist or a terrorist.

"I'm going to meet him eventually. You can't hide him forever."

RD was still laughing. "We're not hiding him."

"And when I do finally meet him, RD, I'm going to tell him exactly what I think."

"No, bro, don't!"

"I don't care if he's Harvey Weinstein. It's the principle of the thing. This is a friend's film."

RD sobered up. "Bro, please don't start shit with him. I'm being serious."

"You know what it sounds like to me and probably to others as well? I'm not saying you guys are being this way, but it sounds shady and secretive. To me it does."

"Why? What do you mean?"

"No one can see any footage, RD. Why? Because some random guy, who none of us even knows, says we can't. That's fucked up. How would you feel if the shoe were on the other foot?"

RD threw up his hands. "What do you want me to do?"

"Tell him who's in charge, RD. Be a man."

RD laughed. "But I'm not in charge, bro. Jerry Meadors is in charge now."

"What about Leo? Can Leo see some of the footage?"

RD laughed again. "No, no one can."

"Yeah, OK. We'll see how that works out for you guys."

"Dude, don't start getting everybody all worked up with this bullshit," I said. "Especially Leo."

"I'm not. I just want to be there when you guys try and tell him he can't see any footage, that's all."

"He's not gonna give a shit," said RD. "Don't kid yourself."

24

JOHN PUT TOGETHER an incredible editing team led by a notable music video editor, Nabil Mehchi. Nabil smoked joints like cigarettes and had the remarkable talent of looking profoundly sad and happy all at once. He had a strong Lebanese accent, but his English was as good as anyone's. The editing bay was set up in a small room just off the kitchen with blacked out windows so we could work during the day.

Nabil's assistants, Paul Heiman and Jeffrey Graham, were locked away in the editing room to sync and organize over 40 hours of raw, digitized footage in preparation for the edit.

The mansion quickly became the new center of our universe. John Schindler hooked me, Jerry, and RD up with a couple of hundred square feet of space on the western end of the mansion to use as our offices. Jerry Meadors furnished the whole thing on his dime, buying desks, chairs, tables, and a beautiful antique rug. The mansion was starting to feel like our home away from home.

———

IT TOOK the guys more than two weeks to organize the project. We rented stacks of giant hard drives to store all the media and once it was all loaded in, Nabil, RD, and I looked through every frame, taking notes and discussing thoughts and ideas as we went along.

I was awed by the cinematography. The shots were breathtaking at times, but what I found most impressive was how dialed into the performances each of the camera operators were. They hit pans and pushes in perfect stride with the actor's emotions and dialogue, as if they were shooting off a well-rehearsed screenplay. It was like they knew what was coming before the actors even did. I don't know how they pulled it off, but after watching every take it was clear that Steven Adcock, Brian Bellamy, and Peter Blue Rieveschl were the real heroes of Don's Plum.

"Wait until you see this stuff edited together on the big screen," said Nabil as he pointed to a closeup of Leo filling up the seventeen-inch computer monitor. "His head will be as big as a friggin' house!"

———

Jerry and I became inseparable, hanging out before and after almost every editing session. He was always at the mansion and in the editing bay, monitoring our progress. I don't know if it had to do with sharing the same birthday, but our conversations were easy and interesting. Even the silence between us felt right. He also smoked the dankest, stickiest bud in southern California, and he was always happy to share. We'd drive around LA in his truck, puffing on joints, talking about the business and dreaming about Don's Plum. I noticed early that he preferred making right turns over left and appeared to even go out of his way to avoid the latter.

"I know it's early," said Jerry as he completed a right turn on the way to a late lunch. "But the cut looks incredible. Nabil is a bloody genius."

"I love him. I'm so excited, Jerry."

"We're going to Sundance, Dale."

"You really think so?"

"Unless you guys can't finish in time..."

"Oh, we'll finish."

"I think we'll be a contender for the audience award. Do you have any idea how big that would be for the film and our careers? And I mean for everyone involved. If Leo doesn't hurry up and make a hit, Don's Plum may become his biggest success."

"You really believe all this will happen?"

"Your life is about to change, Wheatley. I hope you're ready for it."

———

TOBEY'S POOL table was set up in the main room of the mansion where most of the socializing took place. Our friends came around daily and stayed well into the night partying with John Schindler, his wife, and all of John's new roommates. RD, Nabil, and I would cut Don's Plum all day and then join the party that had already formed outside our editing bay at night. Ethan finally got to meet Jerry and they became fast friends. Jerry explained to Ethan and the rest of the guys why no one was allowed in the editing bay until we had a director's cut. He said it was to protect me and RD from becoming confused by too much input too early in the creative process.

When Jerry wasn't around, they all talked about him and how he was smart, experienced, and gay.

Ethan stepped forward into his pool stance. He balanced the cue on his hand bridge and aimed down the cue ball with one eye closed. "Are you saying you wanna bone Jerry Meadors?" Ethan missed his shot.

Kevin crouched into his stance and took aim. "Don't be ridiculous." He sunk his shot.

Ethan chuckled. "He might be down, bro. You never know."

"Bro, I said that if I was gay—no, I didn't even say that. See how you put words in my fuckin' mouth?"

Ethan laughed. "I didn't say anything!"

"I said I find his personality type more attractive—more relatable than a gay guy who's over the top with all of that."

"You like the guy," I said. "What's the problem?"

305

Kevin chuckled. "I do. He seems like a good dude. I feel good about him being involved with Don's Plum. I think we're all lucky to have him. Even fuckin' Leo."

I smiled. "I agree completely."

———

JERRY CAREFULLY PASSED me a smoldering reefer, threw on his right blinker, and cranked on his steering wheel for the easy turn.

"Well, I love your friends too, Dale. I'm so glad they approve of me. At least so far."

"How long does it take before we'll actually see some money? Like from the time we have a deal."

"Depends. If we get a minimum guarantee, and it's more than we owe, then the shareholders would get whatever their participation states in their contract. If we're collecting the money on our own, it can take a minute. And again, it depends on what your deal says."

"What if I don't have a deal yet."

"Are you serious?"

I nodded.

"Why not?"

I shrugged. "I don't know. I have my acting contract, but I didn't get anything for the writing or producing from David."

"You're not under contract?"

"No."

"What the hell is Stutman doing?"

"I have no idea—"

"Are you all getting a small salary at least? You're working twelve hours a day."

"I'm not getting any money. I get fed by the production, and RD is letting me stay at his house for free basically. I'm OK. I'm cool."

"How do you eat when you're not working on the production?"

I chuckled, not because it was funny, but because it was embarrassing. "I don't know—there's always something around."

"You scavenge?!"

I laughed. "No, I'm fine." He wasn't far off, though. There had been consecutive days when I drank water for food.

"Look at you, you're too thin."

"I've always been like this. I'm vegetarian."

"You should be paid for your work. Are you getting a deferment at least?"

"No."

"Well, I'm uncomfortable with this situation. I'm going to speak with Stutman and RD about it."

"I don't think that's necessary. I'm getting back end, we just haven't worked it out yet."

"No offense, Dale, but I'm not asking for your permission. All the contracts have to be finished before we sell the picture. Do you want a deal or not?"

"I do, yes."

"Let's get it done then."

Jerry pulled into RD's condo guest parking off Moorpark Street and put the truck into park. He reached into his pocket, pulled out a small roll of cash and peeled off a couple of twenties.

"Take this—don't say anything." He pressed the money into my hand and squeezed it closed. "It's not a loan, I don't want it back. It's just some dignity money."

"Jerry—"

"You deserve more than that paltry sum... you deserve to be a millionaire, Dale. And you will be one day, but for now, you'll have to get by with forty bucks."

I laughed. "Thank you, Jerry."

I HEARD RD up in his room watching TV as I scampered up the stairs.

"What's happening?" I said from his doorway. I leaned in and got a glance at his TV. "What are you watching?"

"Boy Meets Balls," he said with a sidelong glance in my direction. "How's Meadors?"

I shrugged. "He's good. He fuckin' loves Don's Plum."

"Yo, did you know everyone thinks you and him are boning?" He said it so carelessly.

"Me and Jerry? Having sex?"

RD nodded, "I tell them you're not, but I don't think they believe me."

"He's got a boyfriend. They all know him."

"I know."

"Who says this?"

"You know," he shrugged. "Everyone."

"Who the fuck is everyone, RD?"

"What do you mean, bro? You know who everyone is."

"Jeremy Sisto thinks I'm sleeping with Jerry Meadors?"

"No, not Sisto."

"Oh, for fuck's sake." I turned and walked out of the bedroom.

He called out to me. "Yo, don't go, bro. Ethan and Blake are in this episode. Come back!"

25

Leo's 21st birthday was on a Saturday night. Leo rented out Bar Marmont on Sunset Boulevard in its entirety, including an open bar, and warned us to get there early or risk waiting in line to get in.

Scott and I contemplated dropping acid for Leo's birthday party from Scott's backyard in the hills. Scott held a brown tincture bottle up to the sun and jiggled it. "Where'd Meadors get it?"

I shrugged. "I have no clue."

He unscrewed the lid and drew some liquid LSD into the dropper. "This could be bad," he said just as a drop of acid slid from the dropper onto his tongue.

He passed me the bottle and I wiggled a fat drop onto my tongue and chased it with water. "What's all this shit about me blowing, Jerry?"

He laughed like you do when you've been caught doing something shitty. "What?"

"You know what I'm talking about."

"I mean, people say shit all the time. But not... not... it's just people joking about Jerry, mostly."

"What's funny about that?"

"Nothing. It's just... you guys spend a lot of time together and he's gay, so..."

"You realize how stupid that sounds, right?"

"Why?"

"Come on, it's homophobic, Scott. What the fuck?"

"Why? It's not about being gay—no one cares. People just joke around, man. Why are you so offended?"

"Maybe because you find it funny."

"I don't."

"You're laughing!"

"Because you're so worried about it. Chill out, Dale."

"I just think it's fuckin' pointless."

WALKING into Bar Marmont while tripping on acid felt like walking into an ancient golden sarcophagus with state-of-the-art air conditioning. Everything glittered in faux antiquity. The shiny mahogany bar top reflected glints of gold, red, blue, and green. Tall matching stools with shiny leather upholstered backs lined the length of the bar, all facing shelves made of mirrors that held hundreds of multicolored bottles of spirits. Overhead, bright golden lights burned beneath velvet lamp shades with long braided tassels that hung like jellyfish tentacles. Walking on the soft bloodwood floors felt luxurious to me.

"What's up guys?!" George DiCaprio waved to us from across the room. I waved back but I wanted absolutely nothing to do with Leo's dad while tripping on LSD. "Leo isn't here yet, but grab a drink," he said, gesturing to the bar. "It's all open."

Scott and I headed for the bar. "Are you guys saying that stuff because of my money situation?"

"What? What are you talking about?"

"Are you saying that I'm fucking Jerry Meadors for money because I'm broke or something?"

"No. Why? No, man."

"Then why would I fuck him?"

"Because you're attracted to him."

"That's all?"

"Yeah."

"Oh. OK. I was just—it's so weird, you know? Being talked about like that. I'm trying to figure out why?"

"You're tripping out, man."

"I am tripping. That drop was thick."

Scott's face opened into a giant diabolical grin and he gripped me by my shoulders. "You're alive, Dale Wheatley! You're feeling your life stirring around inside the container you know as your body. It's beautiful, man. It's a fucking miracle!" He adjusted his pants at the button. "I gotta take a leak. If I don't see you again, don't come looking for me. Just enjoy your beautiful life."

"Why?"

"It's the only one you have. It's your life. Don't worry, we'll see each other again." Scott disappeared into the thickening crowd.

I cruised over to the bar and ordered a beer. The whole room twisted and rippled like I was underwater. I saw myself in the mirror shelving and the cuts of glass sliced through the right side of my face cutting it in two.

I felt a tap on my shoulder and spun around to find a beautiful girl looking up at me.

"Dale, right?"

Her lips looked as soft as pillows. She smiled revealing perfect teeth. "Yeah," I said.

"Amanda." She rested her hand on her chest, just below her elegant clavicle. "We met at Lindsey's party a couple weeks ago."

"Oh no!"

"No-no-no, it's cool," she laughed. "I wanted to tell you that I totally understood what you were saying and I think you're right for the most part. The conversation stuck with me for a couple of days, to be honest."

Amanda was referring to a party that Scott and I attended. I got pretty trashed and went on a rant inspired by one of my comedy idols, Lenny Bruce, about how we, as a society, embolden racism by empowering racial slurs. The premise was that we can choose, as a collective, to disarm racial slurs by simply not reacting to them or by changing what and how we associate to them altogether, finding them funny instead of offensive for example.

Lenny's idea didn't age well, but at the time his message felt progressive and I embraced it.

I managed a cordial smile. "Cool, yeah—I remember you. Racism is a difficult problem but maybe we can just... I don't know—"

"Disempower the words that hurt people."

"Totally."

An awkward silence formed between us.

"It's a place to start at least, right?" she said.

I nodded at her. "Yeah, sure." I was far too high for a conversation about the racial divide in America.

"Anyway, I noticed you standing here and—yeah, I just wanted to tell you that."

"I appreciate it, Amanda. I didn't want to make anyone feel bad—"

"Not at all," she said. "It's nice to see you again."

"Yeah, you too." We tapped bottles and sipped our beers. The awkward silence returned.

"I'm gonna go find the ladies room," she said.

"Oh, it's over there." I pointed in the direction of the restrooms and was shocked by the number people that had arrived. The place was suddenly packed. Amanda disappeared into the crowd. I spotted RD and zipped over to him. "Where is everybody, RD?"

RD locked his eyes onto mine and then grinned. "You're tripping, huh?" He jutted his chin in and out in like an exotic bird trying to scare me away and followed it up with the most annoying Truckin' parody of all time, "*Trippin'... fry your brain on drugs. Keep trippin on the Hollywood hugs...*"

Most days I found RD to be highly entertaining, but hanging out with him while on acid was a fucking horror show. When he finished with his bizarre song and dance, he told me that Bar Marmont was at capacity and that most of our friends were stuck outside in a line. It didn't matter that they were on Leo's list. No one was getting in until some people left the party.

I went to see for myself. As soon as I poked my head out the door, half the line outside started calling my name and begging me to get them in. It was upsetting to see our friends out there while the bar was filled with so many strangers.

"Please go get Leo," begged Ethan. "Please, bro." He looked so sad, and I wanted to help him, I loved him.

I pushed back in through the crowd and started hunting for Leo. I looked all over but couldn't find him. I asked others, even his dad, who must have known I was tripping, but he didn't know where Leo was.

"Dude!" I felt someone's hand grip my arm. It was Brandon Morgan. Brandon played the Buddy Holly mechanic in Don's Plum. It surprised me to see him at the party. Aside from the couple of days of shooting, Brandon didn't know Leo. "Come with me, I want to introduce you to someone." He led me through the horde by my arm.

"Have you seen Leo?" I asked.

"I haven't, no."

"I can't find him at his own fucking party."

We arrived at a booth and my eyes immediately landed on Kevin Spacey sitting in between two people. I glanced at the others, but I smiled at Kevin Spacey, and he smiled back.

Brandon introduced us over the noise of the crowded bar. "This is the guy I told you about," he said to Kevin Spacey. "He was the writer for the movie I did with Leo." Kevin Spacey offered me his hand and I shook it.

"Please, join us for a drink." Kevin Spacey offered me a seat with an elegant hand gesture.

I squeezed in one side of the booth and Brandon slid in the other. Kevin Spacey asked about Don's Plum and our process. It was an unbelievable thing to have an actor of Kevin Spacey's caliber ask me about my "process," and I wanted to give him a deep and meaningful answer, but we didn't really have a "process" so I just told him about John's metronome.

"That's very clever. Was it your idea?"

"No, it was our line-producer, John Schindler's... he line-produced Swimming with Sharks!"

"No. No, I believe that was Louis Nader."

"Really? Are you sure?"

"I worked on the movie. I think so."

"Of course, I'm sorry."

Kevin giggled. "Well, I look forward to seeing your movie, what is it called?"

"Don's Plum."

RD appeared at the table. "Yo!" he said to me. He noticed Kevin Spacey and grinned. "What's up, Kevin Spacey? I'm RD Robb." They exchanged pleasantries and then RD's attention returned to me. "Did you find Leo?"

"No, I didn't. I don't think he's here, RD."

"Everyone's still stuck in line. Tom fuckin' Cruise got in, though."

"Are you serious?" I said. "Where? Why is he even here?" I stood up so abruptly it shook the table. "That's such bullshit," I said as drinks rattled and sloshed. "Where is he?"

"Who?" said Brandon.

"Tom Cruise!"

RD pointed to the bar in the distance. "He's there somewhere. At the main bar."

I couldn't see his face, but there was a shorter guy with his hair cut like Tom Cruise, and that was good enough for me. I shouted and pumped my fist, "YO, FUCK TOM CRUISE!"

Everyone at our table froze. RD grabbed my arm, but I pulled away. "No, RD, he's not even friends with Leo. TOM CRUISE HAS TO GO!"

RD pointed out that I was very, very high and should probably refrain from shouting profanities at movie stars, especially at Leo's birthday party. And he had a good point.

I saw Kevin Spacey discretely wave Brandon and another dude out of one side of the booth. He b-lined into the crowd, and I decided I needed to follow him and apologize for my rude behavior. I caught up with him and placed my hand on his shoulder, and when he turned around, he was not happy to see me.

"Kevin, I'm just... I'm so sorry about all that. We have friends—

Leo's friends who can't get inside, and I got worked up because why the fuck does Tom Cruise need—"

Kevin Spacey held up his hand and I stopped talking.

"I understand," he said curtly, and then he smiled. But it wasn't a genuine smile. It was something he'd probably rehearsed in front of a mirror for moments just like this, when he needed to escape from some crazy person at a Hollywood party. "I'm going to the restroom—alone. And then I have another engagement this evening. It was—a pleasure to meet you."

Just as Kevin Spacey made his break from me, I spotted Leo and rushed toward him.

"Dale! What's happening, man?" Leo had a big birthday-boy smile.

"Where the fuck have you been? I thought you left."

"It's my party."

"I know, that's what I'm saying. Happy birthday, by the way."

"Thank you." He laughed a little. "Are you really high right now?"

"I am, yeah—did you see the line outside? Ethan, Jay, Johnny, everyone is waiting in line right now."

"I know, I know. I told you guys to get here early."

"You can't get them in? Really?"

He shook his head. "I'm trying! I don't know what else to do—they won't let anyone in until some people leave."

"They let Tom Cruise in."

"Tom Cruise is here?" Leo craned his neck to see over the crowd.

"Yeah, he's at the bar. Meanwhile, our friends—your friends are stuck outside, but that fucker just gets to walk right in for some reason. Why is that?"

"He's Tom Cruise."

"So? Kick him out and let Ethan in."

"What?!" He guffawed. "You want me to kick Tom Cruise out of my party?"

"Yeah, why not? You don't know him, what do you care?"

"I'm not gonna kick Tom Cruise out of my birthday party, OK?"

The absurdity hit us both and we laughed together. "There's nothing I can do about the line," he said. "Everyone will get in, eventually."

Leo was right. Most of the celebrities didn't stay long. They made their appearance, schmoozed with all the important people on their list, and then moved on to the next event. It took a while, but eventually all our friends made it inside and the party felt right.

George DiCaprio quieted the crowd and gave a speech about his love and pride for Leo. He made a joke or two about Leo growing up and we laughed. It wasn't all that funny, but his sentimentality felt nice in the room. I envied their relationship. To have a father so proud, and to be a son so openly loving to his father was heartwarming to see. And then George unveiled, from beneath a large black cloth, his gift to Leo. He had commissioned a bronze statue from a renowned artist whose name I couldn't remember the second after he spoke it. I sincerely hoped George got Leo something else as well because most 21-year-olds I knew wanted PlayStation games and bottles of booze, not fucking statues.

The party simmered down to our core group, and we had another round or two while we talked about the night and the crowd. RD told everyone about how I scared Keyser Söze away by screaming at Tom Cruise from across the bar. We all laughed about it, but I felt like a fool.

26

"I'm telling you, Leo said to me, he doesn't care if Don's Plum is the next Raging Bull. It will never be a feature film."

I didn't like the look on Kevin's face. There was something smug and shitty about it—something accusatory. I shrugged, "I don't know what to tell you, bro. That's not what he said to us."

"He said he doesn't care if you guys want to waste your time cutting the movie for months and months—it will never, ever be a feature film. And this was yesterday."

RD threw up his hands. "We just started cutting the fucking thing—this is so ridiculous."

I shook my head. "I don't fuckin' get it."

"You guys said Leo was cool with a feature, and he's definitely not. Not even close."

"Well, I'm going by the conversation I had with Leo, not yours," I said.

"The one where you say he agreed to a feature?" said Kevin.

RD jumped in, "Yeah dude. He did. We're not gonna fuckin' lie about something like that."

"Believe me, RD, I want Don's Plum to come out. It would be huge for me, but he fuckin' said it's not happening, not even if it's the next Raging Bull."

"Well—" an involuntary laugh escaped me. "That's just so stupid. How do we respond to that?"

"I wish you guys would just leave things alone," said RD. "You keep fuckin' poking and poking..."

"We can talk about the movie, RD."

RD shook his head. "Yeah, but why talk shit?"

"No one is talking shit. You guys are the ones raising money and attaching big executives when Leo has no intention of letting the movie see the light of day. It just seems a little shady to me and to everybody else."

"Shady?" I sighed. "What the fuck, Kevin? We're finishing the movie we shot."

"And we were raising money and attaching producers for Last Respects, so that's all bullshit." said RD. "Leo gets to approve the film before we can sell it, that's in writing in Meadors' contract so there's nothing to worry about."

"I think you can safely tell Jerry Meadors right now that Leo does not and will not agree to Don's Plum as a feature film."

———

JERRY FINISHED a right turn with a joint burning between his fingers.

"That wasn't my agreement with Stutman and RD at all," said Jerry. "I was told that Leo would have to approve the film, but no one said it had to be better than Raging Bull before he would. That's ridiculous."

"It is ridiculous. He doesn't mean it."

"What does he mean then, Dale?"

"Leo's positive we're making a terrible movie, that's all this is about. We just have to make a good film and we'll be fine. If we don't, we're fucked. But that's the same for everybody, right?"

"He hasn't told you or RD that it had to be better than an actual fucking masterpiece before he'll consider giving it his blessing?" He took a hit of the joint.

"No. But even if he did, I wouldn't believe it, he's just being dramatic. It's the same as me saying I'm gonna kill you if you don't pass me that joint soon."

Jerry chuckled and passed the reefer. "Does he lack common sense?"

I took a hit and spoke while holding in the smoke at the same time. "No. Why would you ask that?"

"He's a little out of control, don't you think? I have a friend who's in tight with the gay writers in town, and apparently Leo said some really homophobic shit about his sex scenes with David Thewlis. He doesn't want to get on the bad side of the gay press, Dale. They are ruthless against their enemies. Someone should warn him about it, frankly."

"I'm not saying shit to him. I just want to finish Don's Plum."

"Do you think there's more to it?

"What do you mean?"

"Is it really because he lacks faith in you and RD, or is it something more?"

"No, that's it. And he's paranoid that none of his movies have made any money, so he's worried that a bad indie could hurt him right now. He needs a hit."

"Well, that's true, he does need a hit. What does your gut tell you about all this madness, Wheatley? Give me back that reefer."

I passed the joint. "My gut says that after Leo sees Don's Plum, everything will be fine."

Jerry exhaled a thick plume. "Mm-hmm. Mine says, let's get some dinner. My treat." He made a right onto Sunset and headed west toward the Plaza.

27

THE ENTERTAINMENT BUSINESS shuts down for a few weeks over the Christmas holiday. There are pods of people working all over town but, by and large, Hollywood disappears from mid-December until after the new year. Both Nabil and Paul travelled home for the holidays, so RD and I suddenly had a lot of time on our hands.

I was up in RD's room folding my laundry on his bed. I flipped around a few channels on his TV, looking for something interesting to watch. Most of it was complete shit. Daytime television was lame in the 1990s, especially on the weekends. I lucked out though and caught *A Christmas Story* right at the beginning.

A Christmas Story was my favorite Christmas movie of all time. It epitomized much of my family's Christmas experience and captured the magic of being a kid on a mission to get the perfect gift. I also had no idea my dad was such a stereotype until I saw Old Man Parker do his Christmas thing. So I stood there in RD's room, mesmerized by the opening titles sequence, with all the perfect snow and warm Christmas lights glowing behind the main titles, delighted by all of it. Then, to my complete and utter disbelief, a title card with three names appeared on the screen, one of which was RD Robb, punctuated incorrectly as R. D. Robb. I paused, sure I was mistaken. I had been close with RD for nearly two years. I knew his whole family. We talked about the *Christmas Story* poster hanging downstairs, he wouldn't have kept that he starred in my favorite movie from me. The name was only up there for a couple of seconds. I must have been confused.

I couldn't let it go so I shouted downstairs for RD, but he didn't respond. I could hear him putzing around, so I called again, louder. "RD!"

"What?" he hollered back

"Are you in A Christmas Story?"

There was a long pause. The character narration began as the opening scene played out in front of me.

"RD!"

"What, bro?"

"Are you in the movie A Christmas Story?"

"Yes."

I froze. All this time I had been living with a character from *A Christmas Story* and didn't know it.

RD scampered up the stairs into his room. "Why?"

I pointed to the TV, and he recognized the movie immediately. A big smile opened on his face. "Yes! Residuals, baby!"

"I can't believe you didn't tell me you were in A Christmas Story."

"There's a fuckin' poster on my wall."

"I thought you loved the movie..."

"I'm a Jew, bro."

I paused and let my stupidity sink in.

"Of course I fuckin' love that movie. That thing literally pays my bills."

Naturally, I started asking him about everything else on his walls. The *Oliver* poster, the *Les Misérables* poster, all of it. He got his signed photo of Gene Kelly in *Singing in The Rain* when he, RD Robb, was on Broadway performing in *Oliver*. Gene Kelly caught a performance and went backstage to meet the cast. Gene Kelly. That was the craziest shit I ever heard. RD was a Broadway kid. He opened *Les Misérables*—and I mean he played the role of Gavroche on opening night, making him a part of the original cast of one of the most influential and important Broadway musicals of all time. He worked with legends like Patti LuPone and Lionel Bart. I had no idea he had such a crazy history—nobody ever talked about it.

I never really thought much of RD as an actor. In fact, I assumed he was probably not very good at it. He was a character actor, and from what I could tell, he didn't have a lot of range. But there he was, an accomplished Broadway performer with impressive film and television credits, even if they were understudies and supporting characters. RD started in show business after landing a diaper commercial in 1975. By twenty-one, he had amassed nineteen years of experience in show business, more than anyone in our group by a lot. I could barely get my head around it.

I wanted to know everything about his past. I started with his name. What did RD stand for? Nothing, apparently. RD is his full first name. I learned that Jews are forbidden by their faith to name a child after someone living. So they named him RD Robb, son of Rodney Robb. RD's name was the result of a religious loophole so he could be named after his father.

Edie Robb, RD's mom, wanted to be on Broadway since she was a child, but couldn't sing. She'd developed a strangely deep, almost masculine voice that made her unmarketable as a performer. So when both RD and his sister were born, they were thrust headfirst into show business. RD's sister got out of it relatively early, but RD booked a lot of work and became a cash cow for the family, out-earning his parents by the time he was ten years old. He made hundreds of thousands of dollars as a child, all of which his mother, Edie, controlled and used to finance her business as an independent talent manager. On the surface, it looked a lot like a mother exploiting her child, but RD truly loved the business, and I think he loved the life she made for both of them. And while his acting days might have been slowing or even coming to an end by the time I came into his life, his career behind the camera was only just beginning, and I couldn't wait to see what he could do with it.

RD returned to his putzing around downstairs, and I resumed

my laundry and watching my favorite Christmas movie, co-starring my roommate, RD Robb as the triple-dog-daring Schwartz.

———

TOBEY CALLED and invited me to see *The City of Lost Children* at Laemmle Sunset 5, his treat. He picked me up in his red compact pickup and we headed south on Laurel Canyon toward West Hollywood.

"How's Don's Plum coming along?"

"Good, man. Everything is good."

"Come on, Dale."

"What?"

"Don't hold back, bro."

"I'm not holding back—we just started editing."

"Yeah, but you're in there doing shit. You know how things are going, how everything looks—"

"Yeah, everything looks good."

"You're just giving me canned answers. It's what you guys do all the time now. I'm your friend, for fuck's sake. We made this movie together."

"Yes, we did—"

"Then include me in the process."

"You are—I am. What more can I do?"

"You can be honest with me when I ask you what's going on."

I sneered at him, I couldn't help it. "You think I'm being dishonest?"

"I don't know, you could be. I just want you to tell me how the cut is looking. No bullshit about how 'it's coming along,' or passive comments like, 'it's looking good.' Why the secrecy?"

"There's no secrecy, Tobey. I'm so sick of hearing that bullshit —the cut looks fucking amazing so far, OK? It's blowing my mind every day, but I'm not supposed to tell you that because we're scared shitless of Leo and over-hyping it. And Jerry says no one sees the cut until it's ready. And truthfully, that makes sense—it's a delicate process we're in. But the answer to your question is the film looks fucking amazing so far. And you guys are amazing in it. I love the black and white so much."

Tobey grinned, "There you go, Dale. Take pride in your work."

"Hey, if it were up to me, I would shout it from the top of the Hollywood sign. But everyone wants to keep it hush-hush until we're ready to screen it for you."

"Do I have anything to worry about? Be honest."

"Would you stop telling me to be honest? What is that about?"

"I don't want you to sugarcoat anything."

"I think you should be very excited."

"Really?"

"I would love to say that you're one of the strongest performances, but the truth is every one of you nailed it. I don't know how it's going to end up, but everything I have seen so far has blown me away."

"What's your favorite thing you've seen?"

"Of yours?"

"Yeah, or any scene."

"You have one of the most beautiful and honest moments in the movie so far."

"Really?" His eyes brightened.

"Yeah. I think you should probably see it in context, though. I can't do it justice—it's the scene as a whole that makes it work, but you're amazing in it."

"You can't do that. You gotta tell me what you're talkin' about. Come on, Dale, be reasonable."

I laughed. "It's during the masturbation improv, everyone's talking about beating off and whatnot, and you talk about putting your finger up your ass, but—"

He shifted uncomfortably. "I don't actually do that, bro."

I just continued, "And you're so fucking timid, and, I don't know, it's just a great moment of vulnerability around a topic that everyone is too afraid or too embarrassed to talk about—which is really what the movie is about, you know? You did it so gracefully, with just the right amount of humor... it's such a great moment for you. You and Leo feed off each other so well." I smiled at him. "I can't wait until you see it."

"That's cool," he said with a new tension in his voice. "I don't actually do that, you know?"

"What?"

"You know, you know." He jabbed the air with his finger.

"Stick your finger up your ass?" I laughed.

He laughed nervously. "I was just trying to be funny. I knew I would get that reaction from Leo—"

"Yeah, bro. He cringes and screeches—it's fucking hilarious. There's also a hint of curiosity in his eyes if you ask me, but that's neither here nor there."

"I just don't want people to think that I actually do that—"

"Tobey—you walk around naked all the time. You poured peroxide on your own asshole and told everybody—"

"I didn't do that either."

"You are such a fuckin' dick, bro!"

He laughed as he navigated into a parking spot on the street. I was glad to get to the theater and shut him off for a couple of hours.

The City of Lost Children was wonderful, bizarre, and timelessly beautiful. I got completely lost in its brilliantly drawn world. I could have talked about that movie all night, but on the drive back over the hill all Tobey was focused on was Don's Plum.

"It sounds like you guys are pulling it off."

"We still got a long way to go."

"Well, I'm excited for you and RD."

"It's great for everyone."

"If Leo lets it go."

I nodded. I didn't want to talk about that subject with him or anyone.

"Based on what you've seen so far, do you think he's gonna be cool with it?"

I shrugged. "I hope so. We'll see how the whole thing cuts together."

Tobey smirked. "I meant what I said earlier, I'm pulling for you guys."

I laughed. "I was kinda hoping you would be. I'm pulling for you too."

Tobey perked up, suddenly excited, "Bro, how much would you make if Don's Plum made, like, twenty-million dollars?"

"That's the most ridiculous thing I ever heard."

"Why? It might. Look at Clerks... And Kids."

"Yeah, Clerks was massive and it only made a few million in the box office—five tops."

"Clerks didn't have Leo in it."

"That's true, but Leo's films aren't making any money in the box office. Most people don't even know who he is."

"Damn, listen to you dissing on Leo."

"I'm not dissing him. He's fucking amazing in every way. But this movie won't make money just because he's in it. That's what Jerry says, anyway. I don't know shit about anything. Jerry also says that because Don's Plum is black and white it's not worth as much. People generally don't see black and white movies in movie theaters."

"OK, whatever, just for shits and giggles then, if Don's Plum, by some crazy miracle, made twenty million, what would you get?"

"Stop, Tobey."

"Why won't you tell me?"

I sighed. "I haven't even signed my deal yet. I don't know for sure."

"You know what you're getting—why won't you say it?"

"Because it's a stupid, ridiculous, hypothetical situation that's never going to happen."

"I mean, it feels to me like you're trying to hide how much you're gonna make on this movie."

I sighed. "I'm not hiding anything. If I make any money from Don's Plum, it's because I earned it."

"You're like a politician, talking around my question..."

"And you're like a fucking cop."

"All right then. If you feel like you need to keep shit from us, there's not much I can do about it. I'm disappointed, I'm not gonna lie. Don't complain when we question what you guys are up to—you're giving us every reason to."

I was exhausted. "Fine, Tobey. If the film made twenty million, how much would I make? I would make one-point-four million dollars in that absolutely ridiculous—"

"Holy shit! Wow!" He was gobsmacked.

"You're reacting to nothing."

"That's a lot of money, Dale. Wow, I wasn't expecting that at all. How much would I make?"

"You get a point, right? Do the math."

"Two-hundred grand." He said automatically. He had already done the math. Then, to my complete surprise, he actually sneered at the thought of a $200,000 payday for three days work on a $40,000 film. "What's up with that?" he exclaimed like a spoiled brat.

I shrugged, "What's up with what?"

His judging eyes said everything.

"What the fuck, Tobey? I'm working every day for nothing. I get paid in beer and fuckin' cigarettes and cold take-out pad thai." I laughed. "I'm working hundreds and hundreds of hours. When it's all done, I'll have worked full-time for probably an entire year compared to your three days—and I know you want to live in some fantasy world where our tiny movie makes twenty million dollars, but that's not ever going to happen."

"You don't know that."

"If we're really fucking lucky, and I mean so goddamn lucky, we'll see a million dollars, one-point-five tops—which would be an OK payday for me. Seventy-thousand or something like that. I think that's fair."

"Yeah, except the cast is why anyone will even see this movie."

"If you're referring to Leo, and you must be, then he gave his point to Bloom. He doesn't care about the money, or Don's Plum. Not at all."

"I'm on your side, Dale, so easy with the fucking tone, OK?"

"It's just that I keep hearing this stupid shit about us being secretive—that I'm fucking blowing Jerry Meadors, and all this other pointless shit, and it's fucking exhausting, Tobey. I'm sorry for raising my voice, but enough with this shit already."

"Everyone's excited in their own way, I guess."

"Excited? What are you going to be like when we pull it off?"

"I hope you get what you deserve. Is there something wrong with me wanting to get what I'm entitled to for my work?"

"No, but take that shit up with David Stutman. I have absolutely nothing to do with the business side of Don's Plum. I voice my opinions, but ultimately, it's RD and Stutman calling the shots. And Meadors now too."

"How many points does Stutman have?"

I shrugged. "No clue."

"Bullshit."

"You won't stop. Stutman and I hate each other. He doesn't tell me anything."

We came to a stop behind a fuel tanker, and the brake lights flooded our interior with glowing red light.

"Yeah, well, by the time I'm done with him, I'll own every fucking point he has." A devilish grin stretched across his face.

"Tobey, please don't fuck with the movie."

"You don't have to worry about me at all. I'm doing whatever Leo does."

The light turned green, and Tobey's attention returned to the road in front of him. I took a deep breath and looked out the passenger window. The Hollywood hills streamed by in a blur. I couldn't wait for the holidays to end.

———

I WOKE up on Christmas morning, 1995, feeling blue. I was almost out of smokes, so I walked over to Dale's Liquor for a pack and some kind of salty snack for later. It was cool and cloudy, which was about as wintry a Christmas morning as I could hope for in the San Fernando Valley. I kept thinking about the bitter cold of Winnipeg, picturing the hard snow piled up higher than the stop signs. I looked down at my feet just as my mind morphed my Chuck Taylors into the old winter boots I wore as a kid. I heard the pleasant sound of the packed snow crunching beneath my soles. Even the pristine smell of freshly fallen snow filled my nostrils, and for a split second, I was pulled all the way back to Manitoba on a beautiful, cold Christmas morning, walking up the gravel road to my childhood home.

LA was quiet. The streets were barren, which made the city feel bigger somehow, and lonelier. When I got back to the condo, RD was awake and mixing a drink of earthy powders meant to improve his health.

"Merry Christmas, fucker." He was standing in his boxers and undershirt, stirring the muddy concoction in his cup vigorously.

"Thanks bro, Merry Christmas to you."

"When are you going to get it through your head, bro? I'm a Jew."

"Happy Hanukkah. Is it still Hanukkah?"

"There you go. Happy Jew Days to you too." He chugged the mud down and his whole body shuddered. "Oh god that's bad." He winced and shook it off. "You want some? It's good for you."

"I don't want that shit anywhere near me."

I WAITED until late afternoon to call my family back in Winnipeg. My mom cried a little. It was the second Christmas in a row that I didn't make it home.

"Will I ever see you again?" she asked through tears.

I told her it was all temporary. I said the sacrifices I was making were going to pay off in the long run. I asked her to trust me.

"Anything happening with the family?" I asked.

"No. Your Auntie Eileen is fighting with everyone again, I don't know what she's so mad at... Oh, I told your Auntie Betty that you're making a movie in Hollywood, and she says, oh yeah? What kind of movie? And I told her I didn't know, you know? I mean, you told me something about it, but I didn't really understand you. So, your Auntie Betty says, I bet you I know what kind of movie he's making, eh? And she's talking in that, you know, accusing way that gets me so irritated. But you know she was right. I didn't know what I was talking about. I didn't realize what she was getting at —" She giggled.

"I don't know what either of you are gettin' at."

"You don't?"

"Not in the slightest."

"She thinks you're making a porno, Dale!" My mother cackled wildly.

"What?!" I laughed with her. "That's ridiculous! Did you tell her I was working with someone who's Oscar nominated?"

"I tried to remember his name but couldn't. I told her all that, yeah. I guess she thinks you're lying."

"Tell her I'm not making porn, ma."

"I think I'll let her keep believing it for a while." The thought of it made her laugh so hard, it triggered a smoker's-cough attack. "Just for a little while, anyways," she said in between coughs and wheezes. "It's so funny, I can't stop laughing."

After all the coughing and laughing, she told me without crying how much she loved and missed me and wished I was there with them. She passed the phone to my brother for a quick chat, and he passed me to my father.

My dad and I have rarely talked for more than two or three minutes at a time, and Christmas was no exception. He said he wished I were home, asked a couple of questions that I doubt he cared much about, and then he told me he had to go baste the ham and check the turkey. "Merry Christmas, son. I guess we'll see you next year."

"See you next year, Dad."

And that was Christmas Day, 1995, with the family. Ten shitty minutes on a collect call.

I had hoped speaking to my family would cheer me up, but it did the opposite. I missed them even more. I told myself it would be the last Christmas I would miss. It was a tough choice to not travel home but, if I left the country, I might not get back in and I couldn't take that risk. I needed to put my head down and work. My freedom would come soon enough.

A few of us Christmas orphans put the word out to meet up at Jerry's Deli and within a couple of hours our crowd grew so large we had to move everyone to the condo. It was unexpectedly festive. Scott passed around a flask of rum. We had some great music playing. Leo was especially gregarious, which was always entertaining.

The party had gone well into the night and, at one point, I was smoking on the deck when someone came rushing out to tell me that Emily Foster was in my bed with her pants off and Leo was getting her off.

"They're fucking?" I said.

"No. Just come on."

We headed up the stairs where a few people were clogging the hall between my and RD's bedroom trying to see something happening in my room. I squeezed in between a couple of them to get a look at what was going on.

I couldn't make sense of what I was seeing at first. Emily Foster, The Emily Foster, was lying on my bed just beneath my top sheet. Her legs were open wide and she was moaning and undulating her hips. She appeared to be masturbating. Leo was on his knees next to her, whispering in her ear loud enough so we could all hear him.

"Can you feel that, baby?" he whispered. "Can you feel me inside you?"

"Yes..." She moaned as her hand worked beneath the top sheet. The dirtier Leo whispered to her, the more vigorously she pleasured herself.

Ethan Suplee was crouched on one knee in the corner of my room, recording the whole thing on a handheld camcorder. I looked around at the others, and they were all stunned like me, their mouths open and their eyes wide and glued to the spectacle.

I wanted to stop it, it was wrong on so many levels, but I felt like if I said or did anything, Leo would've seen me as a threat, and that would've been terrible for me and for Don's Plum. I'm not proud of the choice, but I kept my mouth shut because I was afraid of what I might lose if I didn't. Within a minute or two Emily climaxed in front of us all.

I went back downstairs to smoke a cigarette and process what I had just seen.

Ethan joined me. He was sweating profusely and had a terrible grin. He lit up a smoke. "Yo, did you see that shit, Wheats?"

"Yeah," I said indifferently. "I saw it."

"How nutty was that?"

"Why the fuck were they on my bed?"

He cleared his throat. "She wanted to make out with Leo, that's where he took her."

"Fuckin gross."

"Just change the sheets. What's the big deal?"

"Why were you recording it?"

He shrugged, "I don't know."

"That was probably a bad idea."

"No one will ever see it."

"Then why... Never mind." I gestured to the camera in his hand. "You should delete it then."

"What? This?" He brought the camera close to his chest. "No way."

Emily came downstairs. I tried to make eye contact with her to see if she was OK, but she avoided me and pretty much everyone else. She and her friends hung around for a few minutes, but it was palpably awkward. I felt so bad for her. And on Christmas of all goddamn days.

After she left, the energy was still off. Poisoned. There was a lot of talk about what Emily had done, but no one talked about Leo's role and how manipulative it was. They only talked about slutty, desperate Emily Foster.

I didn't want to be around any of them, but I didn't want to sleep in my bed either. I faked my way through the rest of the night, avoiding conversations about the incident. I caught Leo eyeing me a couple of times, and I didn't like the look on his face at all. I grinned at him, and he grinned back, and it was like we made a secret pact in that moment. My grin said I wouldn't tell anyone what I had just witnessed, and his said, "Attaboy."

After everyone was gone, I took out some of my aggravation on RD. It probably wasn't fair to unload on him, but I did. He threw his hands up defensively.

"What did you expect me to do, bro?"

"Stop them!"

"You didn't! You were standing right there like the rest of us."

"By the time I got there, she was already coming all over my fuckin' sheets."

"She took part in it. No one forced her to do anything."

"That is so fucking weak, bro."

"It's true."

"Dude, she worships Leo. She wants him more than life itself."

"So?"

"So what's he doing then? He's not attracted to her. Was that for us?"

"I don't know—"

"Was it to show his power? It wasn't to get himself off."

"No."

"One minute he's fuckin' shooting peroxide out of his ass into Scott's face—"

RD couldn't help but laugh.

"I'm fuckin' serious, RD."

"I know." He tried to hide his grin. "I don't know what's going on."

"Now this bullshit. I feel so bad for her. I know everyone thinks she's a little—"

"I love Emily. She's a friend."

"—obsessed or... Exactly. She's a close friend, RD. None of us will ever forget this."

"That may be true, but she seemed totally OK with it and, like it or not, that matters."

"Did you ever think she would do something like that?"

"No."

333

"No. Me either. What do you think about her now that she has?"

"I think she's a little nutty. And a little sad."

"What about Leo?"

"Look, bro, it was fucked up, can we shut up about it please?"

"I have one set of goddamn sheets, RD." I slumped in my seat. "Worst Christmas ever."

"Not my best Hanukkah either. And they're my sheets—from a technical standpoint."

28

I SAT at the table across from RD eating cereal.

"Can I pitch you an idea I've been working on?"

"Sure."

"Remember that other idea I had, The Legend of Anne Succubus? It's similar—the entire story takes place at a party. A girl visits the US from Ireland, maybe she's here as an exchange student at first, something like that... She falls in love with America and stays past her visa. Then the INS gets a tip and raids her apartment, but she gets away."

"How?"

"I don't know. She fuckin' runs, bro."

"A foot chase scene would be awesome to shoot."

"Yeah, totally. So she gets away somehow and her best friend throws a big party to find her a man to marry so she can stay in the country."

"Is that it?" said RD.

"Yeah, that's pretty much it. I got the beginning, mid-point, and the end worked out, and I'm playing with the turning points now."

"Yeah, it sounds cool, but what's it really about?"

"What do you mean?"

"You know, Meadors says we gotta know what a film is really

about before we take it on... not just what's on the page. Like how Don's Plum is really about the hypocrisy of our parents."

"Oh, yeah. This is about people who compromise their values to get what they want out of life. We'll dig in much deeper with the cast, but that's the starting point. I think it's also about taking chances with love... It could be at least, depending on who we cast."

"Interesting..."

"Actually, I forgot the best part. As the night progresses, we learn it was this dude, her friend, who was secretly in love with her, who called the tip line. He did it so that he could come to her rescue and marry her."

"That is so fucked up."

I flashed my brows. "Dark, right?"

"I like it. All improv?"

"Yes. Always."

"What's it called?"

"Deportation Party."

"Yeah, bro—I like this idea a lot."

JERRY'S THINNING blonde hair whipped around the cabin of his F150 as we cruised west along Wilshire Blvd. with the windows rolled all the way down. It was sunny and above 70 degrees the entire week, perfect weather to bring in the new year. We were on our way to Kate Mantilini's in Beverly Hills for a quick lunch and, as always, we shared a joint along the way.

"Yeah, yeah! I love it!" Jerry shouted through the street noise and the wind smashing around in the cab. "This is great! Does she get deported in the end?"

"I don't know yet. Maybe. I'm thinking she might die, actually."

"Die? Why?"

"I'm not sure—I just keep seeing her going back to Ireland in a box."

"You can be so morbid, Wheatley. Get writing it, I can't wait to read it."

"No, no screenplay. We're gonna do it all improv again. We'll probably bring on another writer, maybe even Bethany. And we'll work through a lot in rehearsals until it's ready to shoot."

"How do you expect to get the financing without a screenplay?"

"Well, you said yourself that if Don's Plum works, we'll get to make more, right?"

"Yes, but they're going to want to see a screenplay, Dale. It's fine if you improvise off it, but it always starts with a screenplay."

"Why? What if this is the way we work?"

"I don't think they're gonna care. I'm sorry if that sounds harsh. Investors and studios decide which movies they're going to produce by reading screenplays. The town is filled with writers and overflowing with screenplays. There's no shortage of projects to make or develop, even if most of them are shit. You're going to need a screenplay to get the funding to make your film. That's just how it works."

"Even if Don's Plum is successful?"

"Yes. I suppose you could get lucky and find someone who will just throw money at you, but I wouldn't count on it." He took a deep hit of the joint and passed it to me.

I pinched it between my finger and my thumb and gave it a good pull. "That makes no sense," I said through a cloudy cough.

"Sorry to be the bearer of bad news, Dale, but if you want to make it in this business as a writer, then you're going to have to write screenplays. Kinda goes without saying." He paused and thought for a moment. "We could pitch your idea to Mark Amin. He might get it. You're right, Dale, Don's Plum is unique, and the process looks like it works. Who knows, maybe we get lucky. Let's just get the picture done and make it shine." Jerry completed a right turn and then looked me in the eye. "All the doors we need will open wide if we make Don's Plum shine, Wheatley."

"You were so pissed, bro," Ethan chuckled. He was stretched out on the couch that bore his name. We hadn't seen each other since the Emily Foster incident, and he apparently had not gotten over it.

"Yeah, it was great Christmas," I said. "I got to sleep on the couch and everything."

He laughed.

"Did Leo know you were taping them?"

"Yeah."

"Did he watch it?"

"Yeah... some of it."

RD trampled down the stairs. "You guys ready?"

"Aren't we meeting here?" I said.

"We're meeting at Leo's," said Ethan.

"I wanna grab some matzo ball soup from Jerry's before we party." RD rubbed his tummy. "I need to put something in my stomach."

"You guys go ahead," said Ethan. "I have some family shit I have to do first."

"No, bro," whined RD.

"What?"

"You're driving tonight, bro. I want to drink, and Wheatley doesn't have a license."

"I'm drinking tonight, too," said Ethan. "Did you call Kevin?"

"Yes!" RD dashed for the phone and dialed up Kevin on the speakerphone. Kevin picked up after the first ring. "Yo," said RD. "I'm with Sups and Wheatley. You're in the box."

"I'm in the box—you're out of the box. What are you guys doin'? Are you ready to party tonight, RD?"

"I want to party tonight, bro. Can me and Wheatley ride with you?"

Kevin chuckled. "For real, RD? You're drinking?"

"If I don't have to drive."

"I gotta see this. Yeah, I'll pick you up, bro. I'm a fuckin' taxi tonight. I'm picking up Bijou as well."

"Phillips?"

"How many other Bijous do you know, RD? Nikki offered her a ride."

"Cool," said RD. "Come now, we'll grab some Jerry's."

"Yeah, all right. Be ready when I get there. I don't want to stand around and watch you play with your fuckin' balls all night."

I WISHED we could have stayed at Jerry's Deli for the entire night rather than go to an over-hyped, over-priced New Year's party. I wouldn't have bothered if Leo hadn't gotten us in for free.

The club was dreadfully packed, and it wasn't even 10 o'clock. I pretty much stayed in the same spot for the entire night to avoid being swallowed by the mob. I didn't even bother trying to take a piss because the lines were so long.

RD got drunk quickly but maintained it well. It was nice to see him so loose and happy. We had been through a lot over the past year, but we were winning in the editing room where it mattered. I enjoyed watching RD dance and hug everyone around him.

The countdown to 1996 began, and the whole place shouted down the last few seconds of what had been the most important and exciting year of my life. I couldn't believe how much we had accomplished in just one year. I've never hugged so many people in one night. Blake, RD, Scott, Ethan, Leo, Jay, Kevin, Lisa, Emily, Tobey. And of course, there was Meadow, Marisa, and Jeremy, who were like family. No one had ever believed in me like Jeremy Sisto did. He took a risk and changed my life, and I wanted to make him proud more than anyone.

I shook off the nostalgia and started really enjoying the party. I did some dancing, a little more drinking, and lots of laughing with friends. New Year's Eve 1995 was truly monumental.

I was waiting at the bar for some water when my attention drifted over to Leo. He was across the room chatting with Bijou Phillips. He had a drink in one hand and a cigarette in the other. He leaned in closer and said something in Bijou's ear. She laughed. Her eyes searched the party, looking for something or someone. Leo whispered something more in her ear. His hand lingered on her hip where her skin showed between her jeans and t-shirt, and then with a playful little push, she was off.

I tracked her as she walked across the club until she reached RD on the dance floor. RD was twisting and dancing obliviously. Bijou turned RD by his shoulders so they were facing each other. RD's face lit up, bright and smiling, elated to see her. He started moving to the beat again, starting at his hips, trying to draw Bijou in, but she didn't reciprocate. She just stood there with her hands resting on his shoulders seductively. A wicked smile appeared on her face, and then, in a split second and completely out of nowhere, she spat directly in his face.

RD shoved Bijou away and then just stood there in shock. Bijou staggered away laughing, her arms flailing. I looked over to Leo. He looked totally stunned but he was also laughing.

RD wiped at the spit and rushed toward the bathroom. I chased after him.

The line was forever, but RD cut in to use the sink. Kevin Connolly caught up with me outside the bathroom.

"Did you see that shit?" I shouted over the pumping music.

"Did Bijou just spit in RD's face?"

I nodded.

"Why?"

"Fuck if I know."

Kevin was as shocked as me.

RD came out of the bathroom with his face scrubbed pink. He asked Kevin for a ride home.

"What the fuck happened?" said Kevin.

"I don't fucking know. She walked up to me—I thought she wanted to dance or whatever, so I started dancing and then—she fuckin' spit right in my face."

"Jesus Christ. Why don't you and Dale take a cab home?" said Kevin. "I can't just leave Bijou here."

"No bro, that's a fortune. As long as she doesn't spit in my face again, I don't really give a fuck—"

"If she so much as spits out the window, I'm throwing her out of my car," said Kevin. "Let me go get her and we'll get out of here."

KEVIN'S CAR was parked a couple blocks away. He and Bijou walked ahead of RD and me.

"Yo, Kev," I shouted ahead. "You should put that piece of shit in the front seat with you because if she's in the back with me, I can't be held responsible..."

Bijou tilted her head toward Kevin, "Did he just threaten me?" He didn't answer, he just shook his head.

We piled into Kevin's car with Bijou taking the front. I sat behind Kevin. RD got in behind Bijou. RD stared out his window somberly as we pulled away from the curb.

I couldn't contain my disgust. "You wanna know what you are, Bijou?" I said. "You're an actual fucking cunt."

"Whoa, Wheatley. Come on," said Kevin.

"What, Kevin? She spit in the man's face, she's a cunt. Is there a better word? Or maybe I'm wrong, maybe she had a *good* reason to spit in someone's face on New Year's Eve. Bijou? Care to enlighten us?"

She said nothing. Her eyes remained locked on the road in front of her.

"There must have been some reason." I said. "Tell us why." I wanted to know what Leo said to her, but I couldn't ask in front of RD. "Nothing? Were you just having some fun, or am I right and it's just because you're a horrible fucking cunt of a human being?"

"That's enough, Dale," said Kevin. "I don't want to hear any more of that shit in my car."

"Hey, bro, if you want to kick me out, that's your business, but that bitch next to you just spit in my friend's face, and she won't give us a reason. I personally think it's because she's a cockroach, Kevin. A filthy, useless cockroach."

Kevin shook his head. "You're only making things worse."

"That's hilarious. I just want to know why she did it. Tell us why, Bijou, and I'll leave you alone."

She chose to remain silent.

"Yeah, that's what I thought." I leaned forward so I could be sure she heard every word I had to say. "I wish nothing but the worst for you, Bijou. You're the worst kind of human being there is."

I have never been so brutal to another person but I wanted her to feel worse than she made RD feel. And I wanted her to regret it for the rest of her life.

After Kevin dropped her off, we argued about whether I had gone too far. I think it was Bijou who went too far. They told me it wasn't the first time Bijou had pulled crazy shit like that. There was an alleged incident with a cigar cutter and some poor dude's finger that sounded like something out of a Cronenberg movie.

I decided not to tell RD that I had seen Leo whisper in Bijou's ear. For all I knew, he told her to give RD a kiss and Bijou chose to spit in his face instead. Either way, Bijou got what she deserved from me and nothing less.

———

JERRY WAS in the left lane, waiting for an opening to make a rare left turn off Wilshire. He looked like he wanted to smoke the joint he was holding but he needed both hands to make the turn when the opportunity presented itself. The joint seemed to only complicate matters.

"You want me to hold that for you?" I gestured to the joint.

"No, Dale. If I wanted you to hold it for me, I would have asked." He laughed and took a couple of good rips before completing his left turn. "Do you think Leo asked Bijou to spit in RD's face?" He passed me the joint through a cloud of smoke.

"All I know is that I watched him whisper something in her ear, and then she walked over and did it."

"Why would he ask her to do something so wicked? They're friends, are they not?"

"Maybe he said something else."

"Mmm. It sounds too deliberate to be a coincidence. Unless you're embellishing."

"Not in the slightest. He's been acting weird..." I decided to tell Jerry about Emily Foster, but swore him to secrecy first. He was blindsided.

"On Christmas Day?" Jerry reached for the rosary beads hanging from his rearview mirror and gave them a prayerful squeeze. He stopped the truck at a red light and turned to me. "Dale, what is going on with your friends?"

"Honestly, I think they're just wildly immature. This is the kind of shit you do when you're a kid."

"Emily Foster is a household name. If that got out, it would destroy her career."

"Ethan filmed it too," I added. "It's bizarre."

Jerry's eyes widened. The light turned green and Jerry hit the gas. "Why would Leo allow that? Is he trying to throw away both of their careers at the same time?"

"Ethan won't show it to anyone."

"Well, what if someone else gets their hands on it? What then? What about the Scientologists? Believe me, they would love to get their hands on some Leonardo DiCaprio kompromat."

"I don't know. I don't think Ethan would do anything like that."

"You think he loves Leo more than his religion?"

"Yes."

"Sounds naive to me, Dale." He fell silent for a moment. "Leo's making me nervous. We put his approval clause in my contract to protect him from David Stutman, but who is going to protect us from Leo? I'm starting to doubt he's capable of making this decision. What have we done?"

"He's not making the decision alone. CAA and Rick Yorn will be involved."

"If it even gets that far. What if he just decides he doesn't want it out without even seeing it first?"

"He won't. He'll involve his people."

"I can't believe these stories, Dale. It's so reckless. Gimme back that reefer."

I took another pull and passed him the joint.

"Happy New Year, Dale Wheatley." He took a giant hit.

"Happy New Year, Jerry."

29

Leo invited a bunch of us over to his house a couple of days before he was to leave for Mexico to shoot *Romeo + Juliet*. He was expected to be gone for a while and there was a bit of a somber feeling in the air. Ethan, Scott, Kevin, Tobey, Blake, RD, and Leo's stand-in, Justin, and I were all crammed in Leo's bedroom. Leo was excited to work with Baz Luhrmann. *Strictly Ballroom* was beautiful and wildly inventive, so there was every reason to believe *Romeo + Juliet* would be equally breathtaking. The script was all-the-rage in Hollywood. I read it and really didn't see the point. We already had *West Side Story* for a modern-day setting of the story, and it was beloved.

RD asked if Justin was going down to Mexico with Leo.

Justin nodded. "Yeah, dude. And I'm stayin' too. I'm doin' this movie with Leo, and then I'm there for good."

Some of us were stunned by his announcement.

"Why?" said Scott.

"I just need a change of scenery. I'm giving all my shit to Goodwill—you guys want dibs? There's some good stuff, let me grab it and show you." Justin left and returned moments later lugging two heavy garbage bags full of his belongings.

"Ho, ho, ho," said Tobey. "Merry Christmas."

Justin took a seat on the end of Leo's bed and opened the first bag. He grabbed the PlayStation that was sitting on the top and held it up. "Who wants it?"

"I'll take the PlayStation," Ethan spoke faster than a stock trader on the trading floor.

"Congrats," said Justin. He handed the machine to Ethan along with the controllers and a tangle of cables. "I already gave the games to Leo, though—"

"It's all good." Ethan's face broke out in red patches. "Are you sure about this? This is awesome, but I'll gladly pay you something for it."

Justin waved his hand. "Not necessary."

"Wow." Ethan shook his head appreciatively. "Thank you."

I was suddenly annoyed with myself that Ethan got the PlayStation uncontested.

Justin took out a very nice sweater and held it up with one hand. "Not going to need this one in Mexico. Everything is washed by the way." Someone yelped, Scott I think, and Justin tossed him the sweater.

RD nudged me and said under his breath, "You should get in on some of those clothes, bro."

"I'm good, R."

"What are you talking about?" he whispered. "You barely have anything—you wear the same shit every day."

"No thanks to you, fucker."

"Yo, Dale should get in on some of those clothes, guys."

"Stop, RD. Please." I felt my cheeks flush red hot.

"Don't force him," said Tobey. "He's clearly uncomfortable with it."

"He basically has no clothes—he needs this shit more than anybody here."

Leo nudged my shoulder. "That's why I told you to make sure you're here, bro. Dale gets first dibs on the clothes, guys."

Everyone agreed and I instantly felt small. Leo shot me a grin. His intentions were good, but I hated being outed as the poor guy.

All these guys were stable and making money. They had bank accounts and credit cards. Scott had his holding deal at Universal, Kevin was on a series, Blake and Ethan were recurring on *Boy Meets World*, RD had his mom and residuals from *A Christmas Story* and a few other commercials and bit-parts. Tobey was still living on his *Great Scott* money and was on a fucking rocket ship to stardom. Keeping up with these guys over the last year and a half without any money was hard, but I thought I was pulling it off. I didn't realize my situation was so obvious, or that it even mattered to anyone.

I hoped they didn't see me as a loser. I chose to take huge risks and chase greatness, just like all of them. I wasn't lazy, irresponsible, or unfortunate. In fact, I would say I was the opposite of all of that. I just believed in myself enough to risk everything.

Justin reached into the bag and pulled out another nice sweater. "You gotta get this. This shit is dope." He handed me the sweater.

RD nudged me. "How awesome is that sweater?"

"Thank you," I said drenched in shame. "Thank you so much, Justin."

"I'm just gonna give it to Goodwill, you know what I mean? Take everything you want."

A half hour later, I was sitting on Leo's bed with a whole new wardrobe of shirts, jackets, jeans, sweaters, all draped over my lap in a heavy mound. After doling out all his belongings, Justin bowed out to warm goodbyes from us all.

The rest of us hit the town, starting at Formosa, then on to bar hopping along the strip. Leo invited his new, magician friend, David Blaine. Blaine was the center of attention wherever we went, surrounded by women that were awed by his wild card tricks and, in particular, his ability to levitate. I had never been more amazed by a person in my life. When David Blaine bit my quarter in half and spit it back together inside my beer bottle, I questioned whether or not he was human.

We ended the night at IHOP on Sunset Blvd. There were probably six or seven of us piled into a booth. Leo put on a hilarious lisp and ordered the Rooty Tooty Fresh 'N Fruity pancakes to the server's delight. We all howled, loud and drunk, not caring about whether we were making a scene, and I couldn't help but wonder how much longer Leo would be able to do this with the rest of us, to just exist out in the wild anonymously.

30

"WE MIGHT REALLY HAVE SOMETHING, WHEATLEY," said Jerry. He was slouched forward with one hand on the steering wheel and the other holding an extinguished joint. He scanned the city intently. "Don't you agree?"

"I do."

"I suppose we could be tricking ourselves, but I don't think so. That scene with Jerry Swindall is the funniest thing I've ever seen!" He cracked up just mentioning it.

"How will we know for sure?" I asked.

"If it's truly good? We'll test it. When the film is ready, I'll arrange it. I'll take it to one of the colleges. The tests won't lie. We'll know exactly what we've got after that."

A bolt of fear ripped through me.

"Don't look so scared, Wheatley. They're going to love it." He took a hit of the extinguished joint and frowned. "Do you have any idea where we are right now?"

I chuckled. "I don't."

Jerry guffawed. "I got us lost. I hope we're still in California." He read one of the street signs aloud. "Grab the Thomas Guide under the seat and look that up, would you?"

I reached beneath the seat and grabbed the thick book of maps and opened it on my lap.

"Have you dined yet this evening, Dale?"

"No."

"Do you like bolognese?"

"I don't think so."

"Oh, that's right, you're a vegetarian. What am I thinking? I don't know why I keep forgetting that. Let's dine at Kate Mantilini, my treat. I know you have no money."

"I sure don't," I said and turned to look out my window.

"Not for long, Wheatley." He laughed jovially.

I chuckled. Just the thought of becoming independent again made me giddy.

Jerry made a random right-hand turn. "Where are we, Dale? I guess I'll just start guessing our way back to Beverly Hills since you're no help with that thing." He gestured to the Thomas Guide on my lap.

"Oh! Sorry." I fumbled with the book.

"No, never mind. I recognize where we are now. How the fuck did we end up in Inglewood?" He glanced at the joint between his fingers and frowned. "Is this out?" He took a couple of smokeless pulls and then handed it to me. "Light that, would you?"

WE WERE SEATED in one of the private booths with a window facing Wilshire. Jerry ordered the bolognese and I got the vegetable plate. The waiter left us with a carafe of water and loaf of warm bread.

"We should start thinking about what we're going to do with all of your friends after Don's Plum is out and successful. I assume you're going to work with them again?"

"They'll be in everything we do," I said. "Not the same cast every time but... you know, like Hal Hartley and what's his face."

"Martin Donovan. I know exactly what you mean. What about your Deportation movie, do you have a role for Kevin Connolly?"

"I think everyone will be in it except Leo and Tobey because they're so huge. There's a massive party scene."

Jerry paused in thought. "Kevin Connolly is incredible in Don's Plum."

"Yes, he is."

"Have you told him?"

"No. I told him he's gonna be happy with it, but you guys keep telling me to keep my mouth shut, so I do."

"I've never a said such a thing in my life. I said no one should see the cut until it's ready, but you can say anything you want to your friends. America is a free country, Dale."

"RD gets crazy about it."

"Well, I don't get it. I don't think we should tell people it's the greatest movie ever made, but telling your friends they're good in it? I don't see anything wrong with that at all. I've told Kevin he's marvelous." Jerry leaned forward and lowered his voice. "I'm telling you, Dale, when Don's Plum succeeds, we need to be ready with projects in development for each of them... And Scott Bloom —women will be crazy for him. He'll be this sexy, enigmatic thing."

"Like Clooney, but in the movies."

"And better looking if you ask me. And Ethan Suplee—" Jerry gasped. "My God. He could be so huge." He leaned forward again and whispered even lower. "How haven't I thought of this before?!"

I couldn't possibly know what he was talking about. Jerry Meadors loved a cold open. "What's that?"

"Fatty-fucking-Arbuckle, Dale. Ethan would be brilliant!" When he said brilliant, his eyes flashed for dramatic effect.

"Hmm," I said. "Very interesting."

"Why hasn't his manager thought of this?"

"Maybe he has."

"If he hasn't, he should be fired."

I laughed.

"I'm not kidding. Do you know what happened to Fatty Arbuckle?"

"I've seen a couple of his films at the silent theater."

"Did you know they tried him for murder?"

"I did not know that."

"Twice, Dale. It's so scandalous. This town can be so terrible at times. Hollywood is heaven until you get on the wrong side of it." He leaned forward to whisper again—I wasn't sure who he thought could be listening to us, but it certainly added to the drama. "Fatty Arbuckle, at his peak, was a bigger star than Charlie Chaplin."

"Are you sure?"

"It's true. He was the biggest star on the planet. And when he wanted to sign with a different studio, Mack Sennett, who owned his contract, went fucking crazy. He hired a young actress, who may or may not have been a prostitute, no one is quite sure, but he hired her to get Fatty drunk and naked and get some compromised pictures of him that Sennett could use to blackmail Fatty into staying with his studio, Mack Sennett Studios. Her name was Virginia Rappe," Jerry rolled the r, "—and she eventually seduced Fatty Arbuckle at a house party. They were both reportedly drunk and dancing and Fatty kicked up his heels and accidentally struck Ms. Rappe—" he rolled the r again, "—in the stomach. Not long after the incident, a day or two, Virginia fell ill and died."

"Jesus Christ."

"Mm-hmm. Internal bleeding."

"That's so unbelievable."

"It really is. Evidence eventually surfaced that she had just gotten an illegal and apparently crude abortion days before meeting Fatty Arbuckle, so when he kicked her, it ruptured something in her abdomen and she bled. I won't get into the details now, we'd be here all night, but Arbuckle was framed and ultimately tried twice for the crime. He was acquitted the second time around, but by then his career was in total ruin. It's an incredible story, Wheatley, and Ethan couldn't be more perfect for the role."

"I wonder if Ethan can handle the physical stuff."

"Fatty was a physical actor, for sure. I think we can get Ethan there, don't you? I would hope so. It's the role of a lifetime."

"It really is."

"It would be very good for his health as well. He wouldn't have to lose weight necessarily, but he would need to be in excellent shape."

"He can do it. I think he worries about whether he would get work if he got thin. He's the adorable fat guy right now, you know?"

"Mm," Jerry nodded. "It's such a cruel town, isn't it?"

I wasn't sure that it was, but I agreed anyway.

"Ethan is beautiful and so charming just as he is," said Jerry. "I couldn't imagine him any other way. But I do worry about his health."

"We all do, Jerry."

———

I walked out through the Spanish double doors of the mansion onto the patio and took a seat under one of the umbrella tables closest to the pool. White sunlight danced on the water's surface—a warm breeze swirled up around me. I put my cigarettes and lighter on the mesh metal table and took the copy of *Variety* out from under my arm and began perusing the headlines. John Schindler came out from the kitchen and sat across from me. He also had a pack of cigarettes and an ice-cold bottle of Miller Lite.

John tilted his beer at me. "There's a bunch in the fridge."

I chuckled. "Is it even noon yet?"

He giggled, "It is somewhere."

"Maybe in a couple of hours."

John took a nervous sip. He always looked so nervous to me. "Cut is looking good, man."

"Yeah, I love it."

"Nabil thinks you'll have a rough-cut fairly soon."

"We're getting there—but, dude!"

John nodded and sipped his beer again. "System crashes?"

"That's why I'm sitting here right now. Thank god for Eric Zimmerman."

"I'm trying to get new drives, but we don't have the money."

"I don't understand. I thought Stutman raised more money?"

"Yeah... I don't know what's happening with him. He said he had forty k and I budgeted everything around that number. Then all of a sudden, it's down to thirty with no explanation. Then two days later, I overhear him talking about a fucking liposuction appointment."

"A what?"

John took a big sip and shrugged. "That's what I heard him say."

"That better not be true."

"Who knows. It's always a different story with him. He's got one guy with money over here. Then it's another totally different guy overseas. He brought one guy, a young guy, over here the other day. I never know what's really going on."

"He better not be getting liposuction with Don's Plum money. I'm working for free."

"All I know is, as of right now, we don't have the money for drives and David has promised to come up with more money." He lit up a cigarette. "Where's RD?"

"Snoozing on the couch while Eric re-whatevers the RAID."

"Oh by the way, have you met, José?"

"No."

John raised his voice, "José, come here for a second. I want you to meet someone."

John guzzled his beer as an older, scruffy Latino dude with graying hair stepped onto the patio.

"Come here. Meet Dale." The beer stung John's eyes.

"Si," said José meekly.

"This is Dale. Dale this is José."

I stood up and offered him my hand. "Hello."

"Hello," he replied in a soothing, raspy voice and thick Spanish accent.

"José's helping with the property. He's staying in the guest room in the back here." John nodded toward the northern wing of the house.

"That's amazing," I said. "Good to meet you, José."

He nodded. "Yes." José's face was aged and hardened, but the deepest creases appeared when he smiled.

"José," John squinted up at José and held out his empty bottle. "Could you grab me another beer, please? Get one for yourself as well."

"OK," José turned back toward the sliding doors that lead to the kitchen.

"He doesn't speak much English, but we still communicate great."

"Where'd you meet him?"

"Home Depot. I hired him over the weekend to clean the pool and do a couple of other things around the property."

"And you decided to keep him. How sweet!"

"That's very funny. No, I asked to drive him home, and he said he didn't have one. He pointed to the street. I couldn't do it. I had this free room in the back. Besides, he's really handy."

I was touched. José returned cheerfully with two ice-cold bottles of beer. He sat down and took a deep and satisfying swig.

"You know what," I said, "I think I will join you fine men after all."

Before I could get up, José was already on his way to the kitchen. "No pro-lem."

"See what I mean?" said John. "He understands."

When José returned, we clinked the tops of our bottles and drank. The lager stung the back of my throat and flowed coolly down. José sat in the sun, squinting and smiling at the day.

———

RD and I each carried a metal chair into the editing bay and set them next to the others, facing the Avid monitors. Jeffrey was preparing the cut to be screened, checking sync and making sure all the media was linked.

"Did I bring too many chairs?" said RD.

I pointed and counted by name. "Meadors, Schindler, Stutman... Yeah, you got one extra."

"Doesn't matter. I'll go let everyone know we're ready." RD Charlie Chaplin'd out of the room. He walked like film sped up.

I turned to Jeffrey. "We all set?"

He turned around. "Yeah, I think we're good to go. Everything looks really good."

Jeffrey had just watched the entire cut to make sure there weren't any glaring issues.

"Cool," I said. "I'm so fucking nervous right now."

"Don't be, everything is tight."

"Yeah? Alright."

"I have to say, I really like it, man."

"Really?"

"Yeah. I think I might even love it." He laughed adorably. "I started out... I don't know... How should I put this?"

"Hating it? You can say it."

"No, not hate, not at all" He giggled, "It's just not a movie I would normally be into, but Don's Plum grew on me quickly. The cut is beautiful. It's powerfully acted—it's really well done."

"That's so cool. Thank you, I feel better about it."

"Did I hear you say you came to LA from Canada?"

"Yeah. I was one of those guys who visited and never left."

"How long have you been here?"

"Almost two years."

"And you made this film already? That's incredible. You're living the storybook version of the American dream, do you realize that?"

"I hadn't really thought about it."

He let out a little incredulous laugh. "Dale, this movie is going to change your life."

"What's up guys?" David Stutman stepped through the doorway ahead of John Schindler, RD Robb, and Jerry Meadors.

"Which chair is mine?" said Jerry.

"Any one you want," I said.

"Why are there four? Is there someone coming I don't know about?"

"No," I said. "We brought too many."

"Well, let's not have an empty seat on the very first screening of Don's Plum, Schindler, why don't you see if José would like to join us?"

"I don't think he'll be able to keep up with the fast English," said John.

"Speaking English is not a requirement for enjoying motion pictures, John. Ask him if he'd like to join, would you?

"Yeah, sure. Be right back."

Jerry turned back to me. "And I'd like a more comfortable chair. Would you help me carry mine from our office, Wheatley? Perhaps we could partake in a bit of reefer while we're at it."

We walked over to our office, took a couple of hits off a joint, and then I carried Jerry's very comfortable armchair to the editing bay. It looked like a throne next to the others. John returned with José, who seemed delighted to be invited. Once everyone had settled in, Jeffrey hit the play button and our first-ever screening of Don's Plum began.

I paced outside the editing room like an expectant father. Before long, the laughing started, and it didn't stop until the film's dramatic turn into the third act. I didn't stop pacing until the credits rolled.

Jerry rushed over to RD and me. "It's fucking brilliant! Don's Plum is absolutely brilliant. What more can I say?"

Jerry was suddenly all business. We discussed reshoots and I told him we were re-writing some of the opening scenes that got messed up on the first shoot. "We need to register a screenplay at the WGA," said Jerry. "You should transcribe the script, Dale, and include your new scenes and we'll take care of the copyright. I'll arrange for another round of telecine. How exciting, gentlemen. Don's Plum is a success!"

JERRY and I jumped in his truck and headed to Beverly Hills to grab a burger.

"I'm not sure what I was expecting," said Jerry as he made a right turn onto Franklin Avenue. "I had high hopes, but it's... it really is brilliant, Dale. I realize I can be entirely too verbose at times, but that's not the case here." Jerry puffed the joint. "I have no idea where I'm going right now. Do you?"

"Hamburger Hamlet."

"That's right! I'm famished!"

"Jerry, does the Leo situation make you even more nervous now that you've seen it and you know there's something to lose?"

"It really doesn't, Dale. Surely Leo knows art when he sees it. I don't think anyone on the planet that sees the film I saw today would argue that Don's Plum isn't art. I don't care if you love it or hate it with all your guts, and some people will hate it, but Don's Plum is the epitome of arthouse cinema. Don't you think so?"

I nodded. "I do, yes."

"Leo will do what's right," said Jerry. "He's an artist."

"I hope so. I can't help but play out the worst possible scenarios in my head..."

"Like what? No, never mind. Don't say it. Don't let those negative thoughts go any further into the Universe than they already have. If you're going to obsess about something, obsess about winning Sundance."

31

WE CAME HOME after a long day of editing Don's Plum to a message from Leo. He was back in LA, on hiatus from *Romeo + Juliet,* and he wanted to hang out. He invited us to see a band playing The Union, which was a cool little bar on the strip we frequented.

RD and I invited Jerry and he offered to be our designated driver. Everyone was there, Kevin, Tobey, Ethan, Leo, Scott. We got to the club early, which was good because the place filled before the show started.

The performer, who only Leo had seen before, was an acid jazz artist called Toledo Diamond. His music was smokey and sultry and alluring. He had choreographed a sizzling hot burlesque performance with three sexy dancers clad in lingerie and garters. It was the hottest thing I had ever seen. That night remains the one and only time I went home with a girl from a bar. Her name was Kate and she drove a white Chevette.

Kate had an early call-time for job on a TV show, so she dropped me off at the mansion a little after five in the morning. I was unshowered, in the same clothes, and still a little drunk. I passed out on the porch and was woken first by a screaming cat, and then a second time after the sun had risen, by José, who stood over me with a curious smile.

"Buenos días."

"Morning, José."

"Quieres café?"

"Yes, please." I sat up and rubbed the sleep from my eyes. "More than air."

John was the first to greet me as I stumbled into the kitchen. He was standing at the island counter with a cheek full of donut and sipping something hot from a wide-mouthed mug. "You're here early."

"Yeah."

John giggled. "Rough night?"

"Yeah. I passed out on the fuckin' porch."

John chuckled. "Did you see the cat out front?"

"I heard a cat. A very upset cat."

John took another bite of his donut. "It was torn to pieces a few feet from you."

"What?!"

He swallowed and nodded. "By coyotes. Took the head off and everything."

"Are you fucking serious? How can you eat a donut and tell me this story at the same time?"

John giggled. "You're lucky they didn't eat you."

Two cups of coffee and a couple of donuts later, I finally started feeling normal again. Jerry and RD arrived and we met in our office briefly before we began editing for the day.

Jerry scanned me up and down with a bemused scowl. "Dale, why are you in the same clothes?"

"I didn't make it home."

Jerry's eyes flared. "I see," he said. "Did you get a name?"

I nodded. "Kate. From Kent."

"Kent, England?"

I nodded again. "I love her accent."

"Well, once we're finished here, maybe you should get a shower. Let's talk about our project, shall we? I've been thinking a lot about the cut lately, and I think I'd like to send it to my friend Florence Daman. She's in Paris, so it will take some time to get her response, but I'm curious to hear her thoughts. I won't bore you with her credentials, but she knows film better than anyone I know."

"I think that's great," I said. "What's bugging you about the cut, though?"

"I don't know that anything is bugging me. You guys did an incredible job. Nabil is masterful. I just want to see if Florence will have any thoughts. She's brilliant and I think Don's Plum has a French New Wave vibe, don't you?" He didn't wait for an answer. "I'm not exactly sure what to expect, but I think she'll get it and if she has any ideas, they'll be, more than likely, very helpful. Besides, Dale, that'll give you some time to roll between the sheets with your new girlfriend, the heifer from Kent."

RD laughed so suddenly he spit water up through his mouth and nostrils, all over himself.

TOLEDO DIAMOND's shows became a regular Monday night thing for us. We became super-fans, packing The Union nearly every week with as many friends as we could gather. I secretly hoped Kate would show up again, but she never did. After a couple of weeks, RD and I got up the nerve to ask Toledo if he'd like to be in Don's Plum and he agreed on the spot.

———

JERRY HOOKED RD and me up with passes to an early press screening of *Primal Fear* on the Paramount lot. It was a new film starring Richard Gere and a relatively unknown actor, Edward Norton and it was one of the best movies I had seen all year. Edward Norton's performance was transcendent. RD couldn't wait to get to the Formosa to tell the guys all about it.

Leo and a few others had a table already, so RD and I squeezed in with a couple of chairs.

RD tapped the tabletop. "Dude, Wheatley and I just saw a fucking amazing movie."

"Which one?" said Leo.

"Primal Fear."

Leo's eyes narrowed. "It's not out yet..." Then he figured it out. "A press screening?"

RD nodded. "Un-fucking-real."

"How did you guys get into a press screening?" said Ethan. "Meadors?"

I nodded.

"Of course," sniggered Ethan.

"How was Edward Norton?" said Leo.

"He's gonna win an Oscar," said RD.

"Goddammit. Are you serious?" Leo shook his head.

"Yeah, bro," said RD. "He was incredible."

Leo tossed up his hands. "Unbelievable!"

"What?" I chuckled.

"I fuckin' handed that shit to Edward Norton, bro. On a silver platter."

"What are you talking about?"

"I passed on that role."

RD's eyes popped opened wide. "Are you fucking high? Did you read the script?"

"Yes. I loved it."

"I'm so confused," I said

"I know, I know. I came that close to taking it, bro." He held up his finger and thumb and showed us the tiny space between them.

"Why would you turn a role like *that* down?" asked RD.

"I didn't want to work with Richard Gere."

I couldn't believe my ears. "Why? Days of Heaven, fuckin' Officer and a Gentleman. Are you crazy?"

He shrugged. "He creeps me out."

"Are you talking about the stupid rumors?" I said sardonically. "Seriously?"

Leo screeched. "I can't, dude."

"That's so stupid," said Scott. "Come on, man, you don't believe that."

"Yeah bro, what were you thinking?" said Kevin.

"What are you talking about?" Leo squawked at Kevin. "You said yourself it was possible."

"First of all, I didn't know you were asking me because you were thinking about turning down a huge movie—"

"What difference does it make?"

"Bro, it's a rumor. All I said is that it could be real... rumors come from somewhere."

"It was probably an experiment by some shady publicist or something," said Tobey.

"It cost you a huge role." Scott smirked. "That's so crazy."

Leo shook his head. "I can't believe I just handed that kid a fuckin' career."

RD stuck the knife all the way in. "You handed him an Oscar."

"Enough of that. What about Don's Plum?" Leo took a cigarette out from the pack on the table in front of him. "How's that coming along?"

"Good," RD and I said, milliseconds apart.

Leo lit his smoke and took a deep drag. "Don't bullshit me, guys."

"There's still a lot of work to do, but it's going well, I think." I turned to RD. "Right?"

"Yeah, dude. You'll see it soon enough." said RD.

"How's my scene with Jenny Lewis?"

"In the bar? Dude. I think it could end up a classic scene one day."

Leo giggled, "Seriously?!"

I felt RD's hot eyes on me. I stammered, "Not like Brando and Vivian Leigh or anything. Indie classic, obviously."

"Stop," said RD. "You sound ridiculous."

"Why? They're amazing in that scene."

RD glared at me. We had talked about this scene a hundred times, and we both felt the same—it's incredible. "You gotta stop hyping shit, bro."

363

Leo seemed amused.

"What am I supposed to do, lie to him?" I gestured to him. "He asked a question."

"Are you saying it's not a good scene, RD?" said Leo.

"No, it's a very good scene. I'm saying Johnny-fuckin-hyperbole over here is off his ass with this 'classic' nonsense. It's a good scene —you and Jenny are great in it. I think you'll like it."

"Cool," said Leo. "I'm looking forward to seeing it."

RD and I argued on the ride home over my so-called hyperbole.

"Why is telling them they're great, bad?!" I shrugged. "I don't fuckin' get it? Jerry thinks it's stupid, too."

"I don't give a fuck what Jerry thinks. If they don't agree with you, bro, we lose all credibility. Even if they think it's good, you still said it was fucking legendary, so now if they don't agree, you look bad. Don't hype. It creates a disadvantage."

I laughed. "Why are you people like this?! You're all crazy."

32

"I HEARD BACK from Florence in Paris and she absolutely loves the cut," said Jerry. "I can't tell you what it means to have her support. She will be a force for Don's Plum in Europe and beyond."

"That's great," said RD.

"She did have one piece of advice. She said to cut the bathroom confessional scenes non-linearly. She thinks if we do that, the film will be brilliant." Brilliant is a better word when spoken by Jerry Meadors. It's the way he rolls the r just enough, with a touch of sustain on the i, as if infusing the word with brilliance itself.

"What does that mean, non-linearly?" I said.

"It means cutting the sequence out of order."

"Just fuckin' random cuts all over the place?" said RD, bewildered.

"That's her advice, RD. Take it or leave it."

"WHAT DOES THAT MEAN?" asked Nabil with droopy marijuana eyes.

"Like, you know, cut things out of order," I said.

"No," Nabil laughed a little. "I know what non-linear means— did she say how to do it in the cut? Did she have specific ideas?

Because I'm telling you guys, everything is so balanced right now, you can throw everything off very easily. And quickly too. It could be a nightmare."

"All Jerry said she said was to cut it non-linear," said RD.

"We've got a backup, right?" I asked.

Nabil nodded, "Yes, of course, but we're still talking about hours and hours of work."

"Let's play around and see what happens. R?"

"Yeah, bro. Let's do it."

Nabil spun his chair around and hit the space bar on his keyboard. "OK," he said. "Let's see what this lady in France is talking about."

The cut started playing and we watched very closely without knowing what we were even looking for. Fifteen or twenty minutes into the cut, I spotted something. "Stop it here. After Leo says his bit about the fat lady—"

"At the 'send her back to sea' line?'" asked Nabil.

"Yeah. Or maybe a little before, I said. "Yeah. Right there, perfect. So, what if we throw Juliet's line in there about how assholes are everywhere?"

"We breed them like flies," said RD, doing his best impression of Meadow.

"OK, let's check it out," said Nabil.

Dozens of clicks later, Nabil roughed the insert cut into the timeline and played it back. Giant smiles stretched over our faces.

"Play it one more time, please," said RD.

"Let me tweak it, give me a minute." Nabil worked on the clip on both ends of the cut, trimming and finessing it a little more with each pass. When he finished, he moved the playhead about a half minute before the new cut, tapped the space bar and leaned back in his chair to watch.

It worked perfectly. Florence was right.

Nabil nodded and chuckled. "This changes everything, guys. Everything."

RD sat there stunned. "Wow."

The whole movie changed. I loved the cut before Florence's

note. It was funny, compelling, emotional, energetic—I thought it was almost perfect, but there was something missing, and I think all of us knew it. I thought it was because the film was incomplete, and that the new scenes would fill everything out nicely, but I was wrong. Jerry knew, either by intuition, skill, or a combination of the two, that there was something more to be realized with the cut, and he just happened to have had the perfect person in his life to uncover what that something was. It was flawless film producing.

We spent more than a week re-cutting the confessionals and, as expected, the new cuts added incredible depth and dimension to the characters in ways none of us had imagined. We used the cuts to foreshadow emotional turns and dialogue. We used them to add accents to subtext and the more abstract, internally driven concepts in the film. The experiment evolved into a call-and-response style of editing that was thought-provoking and poetic. It was magic.

———

"CAN I see the film before I leave for New York?" Tobey glanced at me, then back at the road.

I shook my head. "You know we can't do that."

"Why not? Why do they get to see the movie before me? That's not fair."

"Maybe you'll be able to make it. It's a long way away still."

"I know my own schedule, Dale. I'm shooting until the fall, end of August at the earliest. I'll be in New York the whole time. I just don't think it's fair that everyone gets to see the movie except me. It's upsetting. How would you feel if you were the one being left out?"

"Just fly back for the screening."

"Who's paying for that?"

"Put it in your Ice Storm deal. You're a big star now."

"My deal's done, bro." He turned his Toyota pickup into a mini-mall parking lot somewhere deep in West Hollywood and parked his truck. "Dude, I'm a little terrified right now."

"Are you getting all four out?"

"Yes."

I waved it off like it was nothing. "It's fine. You're gonna be fine."

"You got yours out already?"

"No fuckin' way."

He sighed. "You sure you don't want to come up? Hang out in the lobby."

"As fun as that sounds, I'll pass. I'm gonna stay here and read."

"What are you reading?"

"East of Eden." I showed him the cover.

"Good?"

"Best book I ever read."

"Can I borrow it?"

"It's not mine. Are you gonna go get your teeth pulled out or what?"

Tobey chuckled. "I'm stalling, huh?"

"Go do it, bro. I'll be here."

Hours later, when Tobey finally emerged, his cheeks looked painfully swollen. He asked me to drive, his speech muffled and slurpy through the blood-soaked cotton balls.

"OK, Don Corleone," I joked.

Tobey chuckled a bit and then held up his hand. "Shhtop," he said. "I can'tch laugh—I chan'tch looschen sthah clotchs."

"Oh, sorry, sorry," I said as I slipped the truck into drive. "I'll talk to R and Jerry about letting you see the cut before you leave. If they're cool, we'll set it up."

"Sshlanks, Dale. I appresscshi..."

"Don't talk. Your mouth is broken."

———

"WHAT ARE YOU DOIN'?" Ethan stood behind me with his hand resting on my shoulder.

I was at my desk at the mansion, writing the screenplay for

368

Don's Plum on my new-to-me but otherwise used Macintosh Powerbook 5300c that the production purchased for the task.

"I'm transcribing the cut into a screenplay and drafting a few new scenes."

"Sweet." He read a little bit over my shoulder. "Oh, this is Don's Plum!"

I chuckled. "That's what I just said."

"That's weird. What are you gonna do with it?"

"Jerry wants us to register the script. Copyright shit."

"But you didn't write the dialogue—I don't understand. It's their dialogue, right?"

"I'm just doing what Jerry asked, I'm sure he has good reasons. It's helping me write the new scenes, which is great."

"That doesn't seem right to me."

I sighed. "What doesn't seem right, Ethan?"

He removed his hand from my shoulder. "You didn't write the dialogue. They did. Will they be listed as writers too?"

"That's not how it works. Everyone's going to know they improvised. We're proud of their work, but RD, Bethany, and I wrote the film. We created these characters... well, Stutman came up with the idea initially, but we took it from there. We wrote all their histories and story arcs, and RD and I wove it all together into Don's Plum. It's not so different from what Mike Leigh does, and he's the only writer credited on his films. So I don't know why you're being weird about this, but everything is cool. I promise."

"Why would you want to take credit, though?"

"Because I wrote the movie. What's up with you?"

"I'm just lookin' out for my friends."

"Are we not friends?"

"Yeah, we are. And if I saw someone doing something shady—"

"I'm sorry, shady? What is that? I'm not doing anything shady. I'm sitting at my desk out in the open. You were just reading over my shoulder."

"I think the actors should get the credit they deserve."

"They will. Actors improvise, it's a part of the craft. You didn't

369

come up with the Big Bum Little Bum scene or those characters, I did."

"Yeah, but I'm the one who pushed Don until he snapped—I'm the one who caused all that chaos."

"So what? RD is the one who sent Don into the scene to break it all up. You improvised a character that I created in a scenario I also created. If you don't understand what I am saying, then I'm sorry, I can't help you. Can I get back to work?"

RD entered through the Spanish double doors, cheery and oblivious. "What the fuck is goin' on, boys?"

I sighed. "I'm just trying to write, bro."

RD patted Ethan's shoulder. "Yeah, bro, let's leave him alone. He's writing new scenes!"

————

BLAKE INVITED me to tag along with him while he shopped for a new guitar. We went to this dope mom & pop shop on Sunset and immediately got locked inside the store with Seal as he tried out a few guitars in a short but marvelous performance. His acoustic voice was pure magic, it was a beautiful few minutes to witness. After Seal left the store Blake and I had a ball passing guitars back and forth testing them out. Blake eventually settled on a beautiful hollow-body guitar that was worth more money than I had since I landed in LA. He put the guitar in the backseat and asked if I wanted to grab some In-N-Out.

"Yeah, let's go."

"Do you have any money?"

I shook my head. "No. I'm good though."

He grinned. "Why did you say yes then?"

"Because you wanted to go."

"Did you expect me to buy you something to eat?"

I sighed. "No, Blake."

"I will if you need me to."

"No, I wasn't expecting anything."

"It just seems weird that you would say yes without, you know —having money."

"I honestly wasn't expecting you to do anything, dude. I'm not even that hungry. I'm just following your lead."

"When's the last time you ate?"

"I'm not going to answer that."

"Why? Today?"

"Dude, why do you get off making people feel uncomfortable?"

He laughed. "I don't. I'm sorry. Let me buy us In-N-Out."

"Na, I'm good. That was too weird."

"I'm sorry. I didn't mean to upset you. Sometimes I say the wrong shit. I worry about you, Dale."

"I don't need you to worry about me. I'm fine." I laughed. "I eat all the time."

"I'm taking us to In-N-Out."

BLAKE REACHED into the bag and pulled out a grilled cheese animal style and handed it to me. Saliva flooded my mouth like a dam broke.

"I was lying when I said I wasn't hungry. I almost drooled all over myself."

"That's so fuckin' gross."

"I said almost." I giggled and took bite of my sandwich.

"People spit and cough and leak out of their eyes and noses constantly. It's everywhere."

"It's true, bro," I said with a cheek full of bun, melted cheese, grilled onions, and a heavenly sauce. "The person who made this probably sweated all over it..." I licked my fingers.

Blake was also licking his fingers and chewing at the same time. "And we just accept it... we accept people leaking all over our burgers and we eat them."

"They're so good, though."

He giggled. "I know—fucking legendary."

"Have you ever seen Tobey blow his nose directly into his shirt?"

Blake almost knocked over the tray of fries on his lap. "Yes!"

"It's the most disgusting thing I have ever seen a human being do in my life. Then he'll walk up to someone and hug 'em."

Blake laughed. "That's fucking nasty. I never want another person in my apartment again."

"Does it bother you I'm in your car right now?"

"Kinda."

"Do you want me to leave?" I reached for the handle with my greasy fingers.

"No, don't go, Dale. I love you, man."

I took another bite of my grilled cheese and said with a full mouth, "I love you too, Blake."

———

"Bro, I really love this scene!" RD held up my screenplay of Don's Plum. He was reading it again for the third time while we waited for the others to join the production meeting being held in our office at the mansion.

"Which one?"

"I love how you wrote the scene between Scott and Jenny."

"Did you catch all the references to the first shoot?"

"Yeah, yeah, of course—"

"That Sara doesn't want Brad to mention anything about their night to his friends—she doesn't want anyone knowing they fucked."

"Oh..."

"In the cut now, when Tobey and Meadow first slide in the booth, Scott says, 'We had a wonderful night'..."

"Right, right, right! Jenny's reaction!" RD smacked the table. "Amazing!"

My eyes narrowed. "She's fuckin' pissed, right?"

"I always wondered why."

"Now we know."

"Why though?"

"Why doesn't she want anyone to know? She's about to go meet

372

his best friends, and she's a self-described slut. You saw the movie, bro."

"She's already thinking she might fuck one of Brad's friends?"

I laughed. "She wants to keep her options open."

"No, you're right, bro. She lets two different people play with her tits at the table, and then a few hours later she almost bangs Leo in the bar. And now she starts the night by boning Brad."

I nodded, "And now we're laying the foundation for her confessional from her very first scene."

"It's so good."

I chuckled. "I love working this way, RD. It's the greatest feeling on earth."

"You think we'll always be able to do this?"

"I hope so."

John Schindler walked in holding up my script. "Great job, Dale."

"Thanks, John."

"Where's Jerry?" said RD.

As if cued by RD, Jerry Meadors sashayed through the Spanish double doors, his Ben Franklin mane of blonde hair fanning behind him. "I'm sorry I'm late, gentlemen. I had to drive Peter to a job interview. Is Stutman joining?"

"He said he's cool with the script," said RD. "Just give him a budget and he'll raise the money."

"I'll believe it when I see it." Jerry turned to me with a lovely expression. "I've read your script, Wheatley—it reads almost as good as it plays on the Avid."

I grinned. "Fun little read, right?"

"It really is. Are we here to discuss the new scenes?"

"Yes," said John. "There's only one major issue I see, a budget issue."

"The destruction of a perfectly good Jeep?" said Jerry.

John chuckled. "Yup."

"Can't we just buy a shitty one?" said RD. "I really want to smash a Jeep, bro."

"Grab one from a junkyard," I said. "It doesn't even have to run."

"I doubt we would find one that matches from the first shoot," said John. "Sorry, but we can't buy a car for you to destroy with a baseball bat."

"We have to figure this out." I said. "This is how Amy's story ends."

"Why does she have to destroy a whole Jeep?" said Jerry. "What if she just slashed the tires? Tires aren't so expensive."

"Great idea," said John.

"What's going to be more fun to watch?" I said. "And where'd she get the knife? She doesn't carry one, she's a hippy."

Jerry scoffed. "What do you know about hippies? Half the ones I knew carried knives. Hippies love whittling, Wheatley."

"Dale's right," said RD. "Amy's out of control. Tire slashing seems more premeditated to me."

"What about the windshield?" said John. "We can replace that for a few hundred bucks. Shoot it in slo-mo. Then we can just use Louis' Jeep again."

"He's not going to let us take a bat to his Jeep," I said. "Will he?"

"We're not, we'll be smashing our own windscreen. He doesn't even have to know about it."

"He'll find out when he sees the movie."

John laughed. "He'll be a good sport about it. He's a good guy."

"We have a solution then?" said Jerry.

"Works for me—I just want to see something get smashed," said RD.

———

JOHN SCHINDLER PUT a budget together and David Stutman came up with the $40,000 surprisingly fast. We wrangled up the cast and the crew and booked them for three days in March. Almost every one of our original crew was able to return. We lost Steven Adcock, he was booked on another project, so RD and I decided to offer the job to our B-camera operator, Brian Bellamy. We drove over to his house in south LA to tell him and he was over the moon.

"Many blessings, you guys. It's an honor." He lit a freshly rolled blunt with a zippo.

"It was an easy decision," said RD. "I can't wait until you see the work you did. It's incredible."

Brian passed me the blunt. I hit it too hard and spiraled into a coughing fit. Brian, on the other hand, inhaled massive pulls like they were fresh air.

"This is a big deal," he said holding in the smoke. "There aren't a lot of us."

"What do you mean?" I asked.

"Black DPs." He exhaled a storm cloud. "Very few of us get this opportunity. I won't let you guys down."

We gripped hands and pulled it in for an embrace. I told him he was giving credit where none was due. We made our decision based on what was best for the film. We loved Brian personally and professionally, but he got the job because he was a badass cinematographer. But Brian's reaction made me realize that we were making Don's Plum in a really rare and fortunate environment, completely free from Hollywood interference. We didn't have to deal with agents, studio execs, or meddling producers trying to force their selfish mark on our movie by dictating who we could or couldn't work with. I felt bad for Brian because he was a brilliant talent and he was forced to deal with people who were willfully, maybe even maliciously, denying him promotions and opportunities to fulfill his dreams just because he's black. I felt a little ashamed too because, until then, it hadn't occurred to me that his life was any different than mine.

THE CAST RESPONDED WELL to the new material. David Stutman did get a bizarre request from Jenny Lewis, though. She wanted $2500 in cash for one night of work, and she wanted the cash delivered in a brown paper bag. I was positive David was bull-shitting.

"It's real, Dale. She wants the money in a lunch bag."

"She's fucking around." RD chuckled. "I'll talk to her."

"It's favored nations anyway," said David. "I can't give her the money."

"What are we going to do about Tobey?" I said.

"What about him?" said RD.

"He wants to see the cut before he leaves for New York because he's not going to be back before fall. I think we should just let him see the fucking thing. He feels like he's getting left out, and I don't want to deal with him crying about it."

Jerry postured up a little. "I've already said how I feel. I don't think anyone should see the film until it's ready."

"I don't understand why he can't just fly in for the screening," said RD. "He's got money."

"It's not about the money," I said. "He's not coming back to LA until the movie is done. I get it."

"I think we should let him see it," said David. "Will he like it?"

I shrugged. "He loved Kids."

"Yeah, he did," said RD. "But it's not the same when you're watching yourself."

"Do you think Tobey is bad in the movie, RD?" said Jerry.

RD held up his hands. "I'm just following your policy, Jerry."

"That's great, RD, but it's not because I'm worried about what anyone will think of the film. The film is unfinished, and film-makers don't screen their unfinished work for people outside of post-production."

"What if he doesn't like it?" said RD.

"I'm not worried about that," said Jerry. "I've gotten to know Tobey—Don's Plum is right up his alley. He's staking his ground in the independent scene with Ang Lee, which is a brilliant strategy —he's no leading man. Don's Plum can only help him, and I think he'll recognize that pretty quickly. Will he be alone?"

I shrugged. "He didn't say."

"He's going to want his manager there for sure," said RD.

"RD, if you think Tobey will hate the movie," said Jerry. "Then we shouldn't screen it for him."

"I didn't say he would hate it. I don't know how he'll feel. It's risky with him is what I'm saying."

"Well, how upset will he be if we don't allow him to see it before he leaves for New York? Will he speak poorly of us to Leo and the others? Seed discontent?"

RD shrugged. "Yeah, he might."

"Damned if you do, damned if you don't," said John.

Jerry nodded at John. "What about you, Schindler? You haven't chimed in much. What should we do?"

"I think we're fine if Tobey sees the film," said John. "I say go for it."

"Me too," I said. "I vote yea."

"Yea," said Jerry and David.

RD shook his head. "Yeah, OK then. You want me to tell him?"

"Let me handle it," said Jerry. "I'll set it up at Paramount. If he's bringing his manager, let's roll out the red carpet for them. I have one last item before we adjourn, David. Dale Wheatley's contract."

David shrugged. "What about it? We just need to sign it."

"What's he getting? What's his credit and compensation? He didn't seem to know, and there's nothing in the contract book."

David looked at me puzzled. "We talked about it..."

I cleared my throat. "You mentioned some things, but I don't know what my deal is. I haven't seen anything."

"Well, we talked about you getting a writing credit on a shared card with the rest of us," said David, "and an associate producer credit on a shared card with Joel Michaely and Bethany Ashton. And some back end, seven points I think we said..."

Jerry leaned back and crossed his legs. "David, Dale Wheatley is not an associate producer on Don's Plum. I've never worked with an associate producer that I can recall, but I have worked with many producers, and Dale Wheatley is very much in their company."

David shrugged. "Yeah, I mean, he's done a lot. I'm open to co-producer."

"David, look me in the eye and tell me that Dale Wheatley doesn't deserve to be a credited producer on this movie. He works as hard as anyone, if not harder. He's earned it."

David was squinting so tightly I could barely see his eyes. "Pro-ducer-Producer?"

"Yes."

David shook his head vehemently. "No way. You guys wanted another producer and forced me into bringing on Gary Lowe. I'm not adding another producer. No way."

RD spoke up. "Dale has done a lot more for this film than you, David."

"Fuck you, RD. This film couldn't exist without me."

RD shrugged, "Or without me, or Dale, or John..."

David wouldn't budge. He couldn't look me in the eye either. I chose to stay out of the conversation. I thought having Jerry, RD, and John fight to get me the producer credit I deserved said more about my contributions to Don's Plum than I ever could. David fought for a while, but he eventually caved, and I was given a formal deal as producer along with the lead writing credit in the main titles.

RD SHIFTED down into second gear. I gripped my grab handle as he rounded a tight bend on Laurel Canyon Boulevard.

"How crazy is it that we have two stars in Don's Plum all of a sudden?"

RD nodded. "Yeah, it's fuckin' crazy. I talked to Jenny by the way."

"Everything good?"

"Yeah, she's cool, but David's right. She wants twenty-five hundred in cash." RD laughed. He took a hard turn into a switchback, I grabbed the grip-bar to keep from tumbling onto his lap.

"What are we going to do?" I said as we hit the straightaway.

RD shifted into third gear. "We have to give it to her," he said. "What other choice do we have?"

"How the hell are we going to do that?"

RD shrugged, shifted the car into fourth, and hit the gas hard enough to make it through a yellow light. "In a fuckin' paper bag, bro."

33

SEEING Don's Plum's parking lot teeming with our crew again filled me with blissful nostalgia. Not only had we created something unique and special together, but working with all of them had utterly changed me. It revealed my creative reason for being. There was no more confusion about what I was supposed to do with my life. I found my purpose and I could almost feel the universe making the path forward. RD wasn't the same wide-eyed, first-time director we saw eight months prior either. He had control and confidence. He knew exactly what he wanted and, even more importantly, what he didn't want for the film. We had both come so far in such a short period of time, and we had our crew, above and below the line, to thank for it.

RD and I huddled up with Eric Davies, Brian Bellamy, and the rest of the crew to go over the scene. Our first shot of the day was the bashing of the Jeep in the parking lot behind the diner. Amber arrived on time, accompanied by her mother, and was ushered into wardrobe and makeup by our second AD. Louis Trabbie loaned us his Jeep again, presumably unaware of our violent intentions.

Amber came out of makeup and joined RD. He began by reminding her where we'd left off. "You just fuckin' threw your Birkenstock at Derek—"

"I'm so fucking pissed!" said Amber.

"Oh yeah, you're fuckin' pissed, all right. Not only is Jeremy not getting you to Vegas like he promised but he fucking humiliated you—"

"He called me a bitch."

"He called you a stupid bitch." RD gestured to the vehicle like a game show model. "And now you're gonna fuck up his Jeep with a baseball bat."

"Yes!" Amber feigned a couple of jabs and a right hook.

"You remember the bat you saw in the back of Jeremy's Jeep, right behind the back seat."

"OK."

"Walk around, grab it, and then walk back around to the front and start just fuckin' smashing."

"Just hit it anywhere?"

"No, sorry." RD chuckled, "I wish. Just smash the windshield. Then walk around to the back and take out the taillights."

"Yay! This is so fun."

John brought the bat over. "Let's get you to do a couple of practice swings, Amber. Get warmed up a bit."

John put the bat in Amber's hands, and it was immediately obvious that she had no idea how to swing it. John worked with her for a few minutes until Eric called the picture up. RD put Amber on her mark, and we started rolling.

"A-speed."

"B-speed."

"Roll sound, please."

"Sound speed."

"When you're ready, RD," said Eric.

"Action," said RD.

"ACTION!" announced Eric.

Amber almost skipped into the scene, grabbed the bat from the back of the Jeep and gripped it firmly. She took aim and swung it, but instead of smashing the glass the bat just bounced off and thudded down onto the hood of the car.

"Cut," said RD.

"THAT'S A CUT!"

John inspected the hood of the car for damage. Thankfully, there was none. "Hey, Amber," John said as he approached her. "How's the weight? Is it too heavy?"

"No," she said. "I think I just wasn't expecting it at first. I can handle it. I won't let it slip."

"Listen to me," RD said to Amber. "You gotta get fuckin' mad, Amber. They humiliated you in a restaurant full of people. Derek called you a cunt and Jeremy just laughed."

Amber began swaying on the balls of her feet—something was starting to simmer.

"Don't let them get away with that shit," said RD. "When I call action, get your revenge! Got it?"

"Yes!"

"Let's fuckin' do this!" RD stalked back to the monitors.

"Back to one!" called Davies.

"Remember what I said, Amber." RD growled, "REVENGE!"

Amber's blood was in a boil. Her breathing was fast and high on her chest, her cheeks flushed red from anger.

RD shouted, "ACTION!"

She ran up to the Jeep and took a big swing. But once again the bat just bounced off the glass without leaving so much as a mark.

RD sighed. "That's OK. Do it again."

She missed several more times. RD lost it for second. "DO IT AGAIN! STOP FUCKING AROUND, AMBER!"

I looked at Amber's mother. She was tense and concerned, with her hand over her throat.

RD stopped himself before going too far. It was all just theatrics anyway. "Smash the damn glass, Amber."

Amber swung the bat again, and once again nothing happened.

"Cut," said RD.

"THAT'S A CUT," called Eric.

RD sat for a moment, leaving Amber standing aimlessly with a heavy bat in her hand. When he saw Amber's mom move in to comfort her, he marched over to Amber. "Leo didn't want you in this film. You know that, right?"

"What?"

"He thought you sucked. He thought you were weak. That's what he said."

"He's entitled to his opinion."

RD grinned. "He wanted us to fire you but we refused. Ask Dale if you don't believe me."

Amber crossed her arms and glanced in my direction, but I looked away.

RD pressed. "He told everyone in the cast too. He told them you suck."

She shifted uncomfortably.

"He said you were all over the place and you didn't know what you were talking about half the time."

"I really don't care what any of them think."

"No?"

"No."

"Why? Because they're right?"

"No, because—"

"Because you fuckin' suck. You can't even swing a bat convincingly." RD turned away from her.

"NO, I DON'T SUCK, RD."

Amber's mother stepped forward, but I held her up with a hand gesture.

RD turned and shouted, "YOU GET ONE MORE FUCKING CHANCE TO BREAK THAT GLASS—I DON'T WANT ANY MORE BULLSHIT! SWING THAT FUCKING BAT AND BREAK THAT WINDSHIELD, OR GET THE FUCK OFF THIS SET AND I'LL DO IT MYSELF."

Amber started crying.

"Let's go!" growled RD. "BACK TO ONE!"

"Roll sound."

"Sound speed."

The cameras rolled and RD shouted, "SMASH THE GLASS, AMBER."

Amber marched up to the Jeep, with tears streaming down her face, and she swung the bat with a wild scream heard over the damn mountain. And at that moment, the glass snapped and the head of the bat sank deep into a sudden glassy web.

"AGAIN!" screamed RD.

She swung the bat even harder, and there was another thwack. Glass sprayed out from the impact.

"One more, Amber. The hardest one you've got in you!"

She cracked it again beautifully.

"Now get the taillights."

"Don't hit the Jeep," said John.

She marched around to the back of the car and broke each tail-light with one swing of the bat.

"Perfect," said RD. "Cut."

"CUT!" shouted Eric.

Amber turned and collapsed into the rushing arms of her mom, crying.

RD walked over to them.

"That was unnecessary," muttered Amber's mother.

"I'm sorry," he said. "You OK, Amber?"

"Yeah. You really got me going there." Amber chuckled and wiped away the tears. "I broke the damn glass."

"Yeah, you did."

They hugged. "Thank you, RD."

"Leo was wrong," said RD. "You're fucking brilliant in this movie. And everyone's gonna see it."

Amber giggled and wiped her cheeks again.

Eric turned to me. "We're good, right?"

I nodded, "Yes, sir."

"WE ARE MOVING ON, PEOPLE!

———

Day two of our second shoot was focused on Brad and Sara's opening scene which, in the movie's timeline, takes place right before they head over to Don's Plum. We chose John's master bedroom as the location for the scene. Jenny was late, which gave David fits since he delivered the paper bag full of money a week prior, but we used the extra time to get the gear set up in the cramped bedroom. It was tough getting three cameras in such a tight space, but our crew made it work.

Jenny Lewis arrived and she looked wonderful. She refused to do any nudity for the scene, not even underwear, so we re-imagined Sara in a sort of fully clothed, post-coital contempt for Brad. Her motivation was the same—get Brad out of her bed and her apartment as quickly and painlessly as possible. In stark contrast, Brad was beyond comfortable lying around naked in Sara's bed, smoking cigarettes and chatting about the nuances of life and love.

We opened the scene with a shot of Brad's ass in the right third of the frame. Sara was reclined on the bed, fully clothed and above the covers. Brad delivered the lead line, "So Sara, what did you really think of the movie?" and slid into the bed. Everything went perfect. Cut, print, next setup.

The crux of the scene was simple. Brad wanted Sara to join him and his friends at Don's Plum, and Sara wanted Brad to leave her apartment and probably never call her again. But from the very first take, it was apparent that we were going to have some difficult challenges, and most likely my writing was the obstacle.

One of the differences from the first shoot was that I had written the new scenes from beginning to end, with arching dialogue and action, but we still wanted the actors to fully improvise just as they had done in the first shoot. Not only was their improvised dialogue better than anything I could write, but it was also a necessary part of the continuity of their characters and the flow of the overall movie. Introducing written dialogue at that stage in the production only confused them. It was fascinating to me because improvising off fully written scenes was the standard in film. Woody Allen, for example, would write his screenplays with all his clever dialogue, but he would often encourage his cast to say whatever came to mind during filming, to use his writing as a compass. In the first shoot, we had introduced a somewhat novel approach to improvisation, and then foolishly reverted to the old way of doing things for the second shoot, and it broke our process. The only solution was to work through it, but it was a frustrating lesson.

We worked with Jenny and Scott together and separately. We took breaks. We kicked people out of the room to try and balance the energy, but nothing worked. To make matters worse, one of John's neighbors figured out we were shooting without permits and blasted their music loud enough to shut down our production and extort us for money. John had to pay them a few hundred bucks to shut them up.

Our troubles with the scene lasted throughout the night, but we kept working, and in the 11th hour something clicked between Jenny and Scott, and the two of them delivered phenomenal performances in what would become one of my favorite scenes in the movie.

DAY three of the second shoot was the most fun and creatively interesting of the three, even though it was probably my worst writing. Shooting Toledo Diamond and his dancers was a visual feast. Brian Bellamy nearly broke his back getting some of the sweetest shots in the entire movie.

We hired José to play Juliet's barback and even wrote him a couple of lines so he'd get residuals for life if Don's Plum got distribution. The supporting cast was great. Marisa Ryan stole the day when she whipped out a surprise apple in the middle of the highly provocative jazz burlesque show and took a big crunching bite out of it.

Tobey couldn't resist being a dick. He refused to sign his agreement again, causing a bunch of drama we didn't need. He apparently also threatened to take all of David Stutman's profit points away. How he planned to pull that off was a mystery he kept to himself. RD and I just wrote it off as Tobey being Tobey.

. . .

THE SECOND SHOOT was a blast and I think our growth was on display, but there was something missing that I couldn't quite put my finger on. The experience wasn't nearly as intoxicating as the first shoot, and I wondered if that feeling was something that only ever happens once, when a filmmaker makes their debut, or if it's something magical that we chase after from one movie to the next.

34

JERRY SET up a screening of our rough-cut for Tobey and his manager, Eric Kranzler, on the Paramount lot on the day after we wrapped the second shoot.

Paramount Studios is like a little town with streets, cul-de-sacs, even a few tall office buildings, so it's very easy to get lost on the lot. Our screening room was tucked away pretty good, so Jerry asked if I would wait for Tobey at the visitor's parking area just beyond the main gate, to make sure they found their way to the theater. I agreed and went straight over to the parking lot.

Generally, I care very little about my physical appearance. As the late, great Gord Downie wrote, I "got the real bum's eye for clothes." I don't wear accessories of any kind, not even a watch. I don't comb my hair with anything other than my fingers. I'm always showered, but I dress like a bum. I'm also an incessant pacer. It's how I think through most of my problems and deal with anxiety, which is why I was pacing in the parking lot that day.

I regretted the decision to let Tobey see the cut and I was ruminating about him potentially hating Don's Plum. I started arguing with him out loud, as if he were right there with me. I got a little too into it and managed to attract the attention of an armed security guard in a golf cart. He rolled up right in front of me, hard-faced and all business. He said I had to leave immediately. Apparently he had gotten a call from someone in the offices behind me reporting that a vagrant had gotten on the lot and was wandering around ranting to himself. I explained everything as best I could and, after making a couple calls on his walkie-talkie to verify my claims, he went from wanting to escort me off the lot to calling me Mr. Wheatley. We had a pretty good laugh about it.

Tobey and Eric arrived and, even though we laughed about my mistaken identity, the whole vibe seemed a bit off to me. I should have been excited to screen Don's Plum for one of my best friends, but instead I felt dread. We got to the theater and took our seats. Within moments the lights went down and Don's Plum illuminated the screen in black and white.

I go through periods when I feel nothing but contempt for my work. Sometimes it's so bad I can't discern the good from the bad because to me it's all fucking garbage. That's how I felt about Don's Plum in that screening for Tobey. I hated nearly every minute of it. Self-deprecating thoughts bounced around my head like bats chasing mosquitoes. *He hates it. He's gonna tell everyone it's trash. They're gonna think RD and I are a joke.*

When the lights came back on, we all sat there in silence for what felt like an eternity. I think we all expected Tobey to speak first, since the screening was for him. But he just sat there staring at the blank screen for a couple of minutes. When he finally spoke, he called Don's Plum "incredible."

"Really?" said RD, who looked more surprised than he should have been.

"Yeah, bro. I didn't know what to expect today, but I definitely did not expect that. Wow."

I grinned at Tobey's manager. He grinned and nodded back. I took a deep, easy breath.

"It feels so real," said Tobey. "It's much darker than I thought it would be." He turned to Eric. "What did you think?"

"I thought it was good. Very real, like you said, Tobey. We'll talk some more, but very interesting film, guys. Excited to see how it turns out."

"Well," said Tobey as he stood up. "I'm so happy that I got to see it. I'm really surprised—shocked is probably the better word. Thank you so much."

Jerry shook Eric's hand. "Will you be joining us for the wrap party tonight at the H.M.S. Bounty?"

"I can't. I have other obligations, but thanks for the invite."

"What a shame. Tobey, what about you?"

"Yeah, I'll be there for sure."

THE H.M.S. BOUNTY was a small nautical-themed pub located at the historic Gaylord apartment building on Wilshire and Normandie near downtown. We packed the place with friends, cast, and crew.

I grabbed Jerry by the arm. "Dude! The lady from Poltergeist is here!"

"Mm-hmm. Her name is Zelda Rubinstein. She's a friend."

"You're friends with the lady from Poltergeist?!"

"Yes, but her name is not 'the lady from Poltergeist', Dale. It's Zelda Rubinstein."

RD appeared out of nowhere. He leaned in and whispered in my ear. "We got a serious problem, bro."

"What's up?"

"Come on," he gestured to the exit.

I excused myself from Jerry and followed RD outside. Scott Bloom was there waiting, leaning against the wall like James Dean, puffing on a chocolate brown Nat Sherman. He acknowledged me with a nod.

"Eric Kranzler hated our film, bro," said RD.

"What do you mean?" I said.

"Exactly what I just said, bro."

"But..." I held out my hands hopelessly. "That's not what he said two fucking hours ago."

"I know, bro," said RD.

"They both said they loved it, right?"

"Tobey definitely did." RD's eyes shifted to Scott. "Apparently,

390

Eric told Tobey that they have to do whatever it takes to stop the film."

"No way, that's ridiculous." I looked over at Scott. "Is that true?"

Scott nodded affirmatively. "Yeah, that's what Tobey told me."

"Really?" I turned and walked back through the door. I heard RD call for me, but I kept walking.

I spotted Tobey in a corner booth sitting with some people, and I walked straight over to him. "What's going on with you and Kranzler?"

Tobey smiled. "Oh hey, Dale. Good to see you."

"Yeah, man. What's this I hear you didn't like Don's Plum?"

"I didn't say that."

"No? I also just heard Eric wants to stop it by any means necessary. Is that true?"

"No, bro, that's not true. Who told you that?"

"The only thing that matters is whether or not it's true."

"It's not. Eric and I talked about it some more, and, you know, it's fucking raw and gritty. All Eric said is that he's worried it might be too real, you know? He thought it was fine for the cast of Kids but, yeah, it's his job to think about these things. It's a compliment, Dale."

"Compliment? Threatening to stop Don's Plum is a compliment?"

"He didn't say anything like that."

"What did he say then?"

"That you guys made something really believable, and that it affected him. It affected us both. Congrats, that's a very hard thing to pull off in this business."

"Why are we hearing shit like this, bro? I fucking begged those guys to let you see the movie before everybody else."

"And I appreciate it."

"Everyone said it was gonna be trouble and I said it wouldn't because it's you, Tobey... I trusted you."

"I liked the movie—I can't wait to see it finished. Eric too. We support you guys one hundred percent. I have always said that I will do whatever Leo decides. That hasn't changed and it's not going to.

"I'm so fucking confused, dude."

"There's nothing to be confused about. Everything is good. Whoever told you all that, Scott or Ethan I assume, misunderstood me. Enjoy the night, Dale. You guys did great!"

Tobey got out of the booth and we hugged. "You have nothing to worry about, OK?"

I sighed. "OK, bro. If you say so."

Jerry Meadors introduced me to Zelda Rubinstein and the two of us hit it off famously. I sat with her for most of the night, talking about movies and directors and asking her about what it was like to be directed by Steven Spielberg. Zelda was a treasure.

By the time the bar closed and our wrap party disbanded, I had forgotten all about Tobey's trouble and was instead overwhelmed by the love and gratitude I felt for everyone at the party who made Don's Plum a reality. I realized that what I loved most about our process was the deep and fearless collaboration it took to make the movie work, and I felt so fucking lucky I got to experience that for the first time with some of my closest friends.

JOHN SCHINDLER ASKED RD and me to pick up checks from David Stutman, so we had to drive all the way out to Venice to meet him. Normally, David would have made the trip to Hollywood, but he was unable to because he was recovering from liposuction surgery.

We knocked and David took a long time to answer. We could hear him shuffling with heavy feet before he opened the door painfully.

"What's up, Lipo-boy?" I said.

David rolled his eyes. "You're hilarious."

RD shook his head, "You look like hell."

"I'm on a ton of codeine and it's not helping at all."

David's pit bull, Sara, came wiggling into the living room to greet us. I scratched around her neck and head.

David gripped his shirt. "You wanna see?"

I blocked my eyes. "No. God."

"Fuck yeah," said RD.

I couldn't help but look while David lifted his shirt to reveal his red, swollen torso wrapped in blood and puss-stained gauze. The acrid smell of medicinal ointments cut into my sinuses like razors. David managed to grin. "We partying at Formosa tonight?" he asked with a cocked grin.

"That looks so painful," said RD.

"It hurts to breathe."

"How can you afford this shit, bro?" RD said.

"I sold a couple of my points in Don's Plum."

RD hissed. "That's so fucked up."

"What?"

"We're all working for free, busting our asses, and you're fucking selling off pieces of the film to get cosmetic surgery. You don't even look any different!"

"I'm just swollen, it'll look different when I heal. And they're my points, RD, I can do whatever I want with them."

"We can barely afford to post the film, bro. You used money from Don's Plum to get liposuction." RD shook his head. "I don't know what's worse, that you did it, or that you don't get that it's fucked up."

"They're my points, RD."

"Yeah, I heard you the first time. Where's the checks? We gotta get to work. The movie's not finished yet, David."

———

THE NEW SCENES were digitized within a week and we were back in the editing bay with Nabil to lay them into the cut. The film had entered a new and unfamiliar phase where everything became about the business of Don's Plum. We were creative in the editing bay, but the feelings of adventure and freedom had been replaced by deliberation and urgency. It seemed like every conversation we had was about how to position the film for festivals, distributors, and agents. They were important subjects, but the shift in the energy from purely creative to something almost mechanistic didn't sit well with me. I felt the dynamic around our friendships changing as well. It was hard to put my finger on what specifically it was, but the more the film came into existence, the more uneasy I felt.

———

ONE AFTERNOON IN EARLY APRIL, RD and I had lunch with Kevin Connolly and Ethan Suplee at a pub style restaurant called Dalt's in Burbank.

"He was all covered in blood and puss."

"Jesus Christ, RD! We're fucking eating." Kevin shook his head. "Why the fuck would David Stutman get liposuction? He's not even that fat?"

RD shrugged, "No clue, bro."

Ethan chuckled, "How the fuck can he afford it? That's shit ain't cheap."

RD raised his eyebrows. "The fucker sold his points in Don's Plum."

"Are you serious?" said Kevin. "Does the person who bought them know Leo has approval rights?"

"I don't fuckin' know, bro," said RD. "I don't care. I just want to finish this film and never work with him again."

"That is some shady-ass shit right there," said Kevin.

"Enough about Stutman," I said. "You're ruining my lunch."

Kevin chomped on a curly fry and chuckled. "You guys wanna go see *Flirting with Disaster* after this? I think it's playing down the street."

RD shook his head. "I can't. I gotta go do this notary bullshit for Stutman because he can't do his fuckin' job correctly."

"What is that?" said Kevin.

RD shrugged and took a bite of his sandwich. "Nothing."

Kevin focused on RD's envelope. "Is that like an official document for the film?"

RD was chewing and couldn't answer. He held up his finger to both of us indicating he wanted us to wait for him.

"RD?" said Kevin.

RD repeated the gesture with his finger.

"What the fuck are you saying, RD?"

"He's chewing," I said. "He wants you to wait."

"What?"

"He chews his food fifty times now. He's counting."

"He's counting his chews?" Ethan chuckled.

I nodded, "It can take him a while too. You can fuck him up by just counting out loud, though. I do it all the time."

RD began waiving his hand in protest.

Kevin shook his head at RD. "You can't make us wait through fifty chews, RD. How many are you at right now, fifteen?"

RD shook his head.

"Twenty?"

RD indicated something lower with his thumb.

Kevin shook his head, "No, way bro. One, two, six, seventy-two, eight, twenty-one..."

Ethan and I joined in, "Thirty-one, twenty-two, seven, forty-three, forty-four—"

RD stopped chewing and his face dropped. He had lost count.

"Swallow your food and finish our fuckin' conversation," said Kevin.

RD swallowed in a pout. "Don't do that shit. Tim Ray said I have to chew fifty times for my gut health. You should be chewing fifty times too, bro."

"Can we talk about this thing you're doing with Stutman? What is it?"

"We're just doin' Meadors' shit, ya know? It's nothing."

"No, RD, I don't know. That's why I'm asking."

"It's just producer bullshit. Stuff for the production book."

"I want to learn all this stuff too."

RD chuckled. "There's nothing to learn. It's nonsense."

"OK, I want to learn the nonsense. I want to learn everything you guys are learning. I want to produce and direct films someday too, bro."

"It's for the contracts—it's just making sure the production book is complete in case we get distribution."

"What contracts?"

"Everyone's. Meadors wants a notarized statement from me and Stuts saying that everyone agreed to do the film for SAG plus ten and a point in the back end because Tobey keeps fucking around and threatening Stutman."

Kevin nodded. "Did you talk to them about it?"

"Leo and Tobey?" RD nodded. "Yeah, bro, everybody knows the deal. I'm just trying to keep everybody happy."

"Weren't you supposed to be there at two?" I said.

"Yeah."

I gestured to the wall clock. It read 1:45.

"Fuck. I gotta go now. You gotta come with me, bro. I can't stop at the house. I'm the latest."

"No," I whined. "I got shit to do."

"I'll drop you off at home, no problem," said Kevin.

"Yes! Thank you, Kevin."

"Alright, I guess I'll see you later." RD rushed out the door on his way to the notary.

WE HAD BARELY PULLED AWAY from the curb before Kevin started hitting me with questions.

"Yo, let's talk about the elephant in the room."

I chuckled. "There's an elephant in the room?"

"Leo, bro."

"What about him?"

"He told me he's never gonna release the film, and you guys are out getting contracts certified so Meadors can sell the movie."

"Yeah, well Meadors is preparing for success. You more than anyone should be rooting for us."

"Why's that?"

"Well, for starters, we're friends—"

"That's not what we're talking about."

"And because you're really fucking great in the movie."

"That's a cool thing to hear but... it's not gonna fuckin' matter because Leo's not letting it go."

"I don't believe that. Why not wait and see what happens instead of playing out all the worst possible scenarios in your head?"

"Why, you got some tricks up your sleeve, Wheatley?"

"Just the movie."

"What if everyone loves it except him?"

"If everyone loves it, then so will he."

"What if he doesn't though?"

"We'll deal with it."

"Can an actor just stop a movie they're in? Obviously, Leo can, he's fuckin' Leo, but—"

"I don't even think he can. I don't think anyone can do something like that. I'm pretty sure if you perform on camera, then you've agreed to be in the movie. There might be issues with money or whatever, but I don't think anyone can stop a movie just because they want to—unless it's in their deal of course."

"I doubt Leo would agree with you on that."

"It doesn't matter. I'm telling you, Kevin, this movie is gonna surprise all of you. And if I'm wrong then we'll deal with it."

KEVIN DROPPED me off and I went up to my room to read. I dozed off at some point and was awoken suddenly by RD in a fit.

"What did you say to Connolly?"

Sleep clung to me like a sloth. "What the fuck are you talking about?"

"Leo left a message, bro. Come downstairs." He turned and trampled down the stairs. "We've got problems again, bro! I TOLD YOU TO SHUT YOUR BIG FUCKING MOUTH!"

I followed RD to his desk downstairs. He hit speakerphone and played the message.

"RD and Dale, it's Leo. I just heard from Kevin. What the fuck is going on?" He sighed audibly into the receiver. "Why is Kevin telling me to watch out, that you guys are going to stab me in the back? Call me at my hotel as soon as you get this."

RD glared at me. "What did you say, bro?"

"Nothing like *that*, RD."

"I told you not to talk about the film with them."

"You're the one who told them about the notary—that's what he's freaking out about. He kept calling it a court document. I told him it was no big deal. That's it, that's all I said."

"FUCK!" RD slammed his fist on the table.

"Call him. Right now. I didn't say fuck-all to Connolly."

RD dialed the hotel and asked for his room. Leo picked up right away.

My heart raced.

"What's up, guys?" said Leo over speakerphone. He sounded exhausted.

"What the fuck is going on now, bro?"

"You tell me, RD."

"I have no idea. What did Kevin say?"

"He said I should watch my back—that you guys have a knife poised to stab me in the fuckin' back."

My jaw hit the floor. "That is the most ridiculous thing I've ever heard—why would he say that?"

"He said that you, RD, went with Stutman to court or something, and got some legal papers certified for Don's Plum—something about my and Tobey's contract. I don't have a contract. And what's this shit Stutman sold points in Don's Plum to get fucking liposuction? I haven't agreed that the film can be released and I'm probably not going to. He's stealing that money, bro."

"I don't know what to tell you about the lipo, Stutman's a disaster. But it wasn't court, that's fuckin' crazy. I went to a notary public at a strip mall in Venice. Meadors just wanted something in the books that said all the actors agreed to a favored nation's deal, that's all it fucking was. It's a piece of paper."

"Are you sure?"

"Dude, if I were being shady, why would I tell Connolly in the first place? Think about it."

"Do I have to get my lawyers involved?"

"Do whatever you want, but there's nothing shady going on. Jerry just wanted something in writing because Tobey keeps saying he's gonna fuck over Stutman to get all his points and that's bad for business."

"Dale, Kevin said that you told him that you guys can release the film regardless of what I say."

"I didn't say anything like that." I must have raised my voice because RD held up his hand to calm me. I took a breath before continuing. "I told him I didn't think there was going to be an issue with Don's Plum because the movie is turning out great and that everyone, including you, will be proud of the film. He asked me if actors can legally stop films from coming out and I said I didn't think so, but I wasn't talking about you. You're going to approve the film or not, nothing has changed."

"I really don't need this shit in my life, guys. I don't. I just wanted to do you guys a favor."

"You have nothing to worry about," said RD. "We're just making the best film we can."

"Do I have your word, both of you, that this film isn't going anywhere unless I agree to it."

"Yes," we said.

"What about Stutman?"

"I have just as much say in Don's Plum as he does," said RD. "He can't do anything without me."

"I just want to know I can trust you guys."

"We're your friends," I said. "You can trust us."

"Yeah, bro. Do you really think I'm trying to fuck you over?" said RD. "Why would I do something like that?"

"I don't know what's going on," said Leo. "I'm in fucking Mexico making a movie right now. I'm just going by what people are telling me."

"People are fucking tripping," I said. "There was no reason to get you all worried about dumb shit while you're working on a film. I don't know what Kevin is thinking."

"As long as we understand each other, that's all that matters. I'll be home in a few weeks. We'll hang out then."

"Fuck you, Wheatley," said Kevin. His scratchy voice sounded small and irritated over speakerphone.

"You're either lying or you're a star-fucker," I said. "That's the way I see it."

"I don't understand, bro," said RD, totally exasperated. "You guys are my friends, I'm not gonna stab anyone in the back. You're just disrupting everything."

"I saw something I thought was shady going on behind Leo's back, and I thought he should know about it."

RD shook his head. "That makes no sense. Why would I tell you I'm planning on fucking over Leo?"

"Look bro, everyone thinks you guys are being shady. You don't include any of us in any decisions. You guys have all these meetings behind closed doors. This was supposed to be a film we made together. Meaning all of us, not just you and Dale."

"There's nothing to talk about right now. Dale and I are cutting it together. It's looking good, but there's a lot of work to do. We're not going to pile the entire cast into these editing sessions, and if we let you in, or Sups, or anyone, then we gotta let everyone in, and that ain't gonna work, bro. Post is a long, tedious process... I'm passed out on the couch half the time while they reconfigure the RAID twice a day."

"Maybe some of us want to hear all the details and the ins and outs of what's going on," said Kevin. "Maybe we have thoughts about some of the decisions you guys are making— that's the problem, RD. This was supposed to be about us, and it turned into this big thing with a bunch of people we don't even know."

RD threw up his arms, befuddled. "You guys wanted to make this film. We were supposed to make Last Respects, remember?

You guys literally chose this movie and now all you're doing is talking shit."

I butted in. "What kills me, Kevin, is that Don's Plum will probably benefit you more than any other cast member."

"Yeah, you keep saying that, Dale, and it sounds like a sales pitch to me. I don't need any favors, bro."

I threw my head back and laughed. "Are you sure about that?"

"Fuck you, bro."

"Look at you, though. You're sabotaging your own work. Why?"

"I told you a hundred times already. I saw some shady shit—I would do the same thing for either one of you."

"Please don't," I said. "You're not helping at all, Kevin. You're being destructive."

The argument went on and on, and it would be weeks before I felt like Kevin was anything other than a two-faced traitor. He eventually apologized. He said he was acting out of fear or something to that effect. It was enough to patch things up between us and, after some time passed, the scab fell away but the scar never faded.

———

LEO GOT BACK from filming *Romeo + Juliet* sometime in late April or early May. We were at Formosa for happy hour. It had been a while since we were all together, so spirits were high.

Leo tapped the tabletop between the drinks. "Listen for a second. I need some advice from you guys. I gotta make a choice between two movies—"

"Fuckin' rub it in, why don't you?" Kevin chuckled.

"I'm not bragging, it's my situation." Leo held up one finger. "Paul Thomas Anderson is doing a movie called Boogie Nights, and the script is incredible—"

"He did Hard Eight, right?" said Scott. Leo nodded and Scott continued. "I liked it. What's this about?"

"It's loosely based on the life of John Holmes."

"Oh, dude, that's gonna be awesome," said Kevin.

"Who's John Holmes?" I said.

"You don't know who John Holmes is?" said Kevin with a stunned look on his face.

"No."

"Johnny fuckin' Wadd?"

"Is that the same person?" I chuckled.

Kevin chuckled. "John Holmes had the biggest dick in porn in the 70s."

"It was absurdly large," said Scott.

I turned to Leo. "So, would you use a prosthetic, or—?"

"Haha, very funny."

"It's not a bad question," said Kevin. "You can't make a movie about the biggest dick in show business and not fucking show it, right?"

"That's what I'm saying." I said.

"Can we stop talking about penises, please?" said Leo.

Kevin scowled, "You're the one who brought it up!"

"The other film is with James Cameron." Leo flared his eyebrows.

"Just take that one," said Kevin. "It doesn't even matter what it's about, it's already a massive hit."

"It's a movie about the Titanic, he's calling it 'Titanic,' actually."

"That doesn't sound good," said Scott. "We already know how it ends. How's the script?"

Leo shook his head. "Not good. It's not the worst thing I ever read, but it's not nearly as good as Boogie Nights. The problem with Boogie Nights is it's so small, and I'm bombing with the small movies. Titanic is a huge studio movie, which I've never done before. Should I do the film with the much better screenplay? Or go with James Cameron who never misses at the box office?"

"Take Boogie Nights," said RD.

"Why?" said Leo.

"The script's great. Hard Eight was great—he's obviously up and coming. You don't want Schwarzenegger's career, bro. You want Pacino's, De Niro's, Joe Dain's."

"Who the fuck is Joe Dain?"

"You know Joe Dain, my mom's client. He redid our floors."

"He did a pretty good job," muttered Kevin.

Leo shook his head. "You're so fuckin' random, RD."

"I would go in the other direction," said Kevin. "James Cameron is a proven genius. You can't top movies like the Terminator and Aliens. This is an easy decision if you ask me."

Scott nodded at Kevin. "You really don't think he should do the movie with the best script?"

Kevin shook his head. "He doesn't know if Paul Thomas Anderson is going to make a good movie, but we all know James Cameron will. That dude knows what he's doing."

Leo nodded in my direction. "What about you?"

I shrugged, "If you want to be in a movie that makes two-hundred million dollars, do Titanic. If you want awards and prestige, then do the other one—what's it called again?"

"Boogie Nights."

"Incredible title," I said. "Why can't I think of cool shit like that?"

"What's your gut telling you to do?" said RD.

Leo smirked. "Boogie Nights."

"Follow your gut, bro," said RD. "Boogie Nights all the way."

Despite most of us favoring *Boogie Nights*, including Leo himself, Leo chose *Titanic* and filming was set to start almost immediately in Mexico.

———

WE SPENT one of Leo's last nights in LA at his house, drinking and smoking by the pool. It was a small gathering, just me, RD, Ethan, Kevin, Leo's girlfriend, Kristen Zang, and a couple of her hot model friends. Everyone but me and Suplee were in swimming trunks or bikinis. Leo sported a pair of skintight blue and red Speedos, and a ratty t-shirt with the sleeves cut off.

At one point I was bullshitting with someone when I felt the distracting, almost foreboding feeling of someone's eyes on me.

Like a magnet, I was drawn to Leo, and it was him. His gaze was intimidating. "What?" I said through an uneasy grin. He didn't say anything, but he kept staring.

I knew what it was of course. Don's Plum was taking its toll on our friendship. He had two giant movies happening in his life and the prospect of a bad, no-budget indie coming out of nowhere and fucking up his plans probably made him feel uneasy. Which meant that RD and I made him feel uneasy. The rumor milling by Ethan, Kevin, and Tobey didn't help either. I wanted to get rid of all his doubt. I wanted to make him feel better about everything and assure him that there was nothing to worry about, that we would honor our agreement, but I was terrified to mention anything because he could decide in an instant to stop everything on the spot if he didn't like something I said. That would haunt me for the rest of my life.

"What?" I repeated.

"Nothing, bro," he said. "Just thinking about a lot of shit, that's all. You want another beer?"

I tilted my can. "Yeah, sure. Thanks."

He got up and disappeared into the house, walking on his tippy-toes as he went.

I've long said that Leo was one of the funniest people I've ever known. His vulgar, physical humor was second to none. He emerged from the house with a six-pack of beer in one hand and the front of his Speedos bunched up in the other like he was holding carrots by the greens. He had pulled his Speedos up to his navel, until they became a front-facing thong, dividing his exposed scrotum into two distinct sacks, one testicle dangling on either side of the fabric like a marble in a deflated balloon.

Everyone erupted in laughter.

Leo said in a lisp, "Who wantsss beersss?" He walked toward us, swinging his hips like a runway model, his dangling balls knocking into one another with every swing.

"Whatsssup, Supsss, would you like a beverage?"

Ethan laughed and took a beer.

Leo pranced from one person to another, handing out cold

beers, making us all cry with laughter. Then he put his nuts away and fired up the hot tub. Leo, Kristen, and the other models slipped into the steamy, bubbling water. They tried to goad the rest of us in with them, but I wasn't interested.

Kristen got out and took Ethan's hand. "Come in with us," she said seductively, and led him from his deck chair to the hot tub. Ethan stripped down to his boxers and undershirt and got into the tub, displacing the water to its brim. Kristen whispered in the ears of her model friends, and they both waded toward Ethan, mounting him from both sides like seductive Greek sirens. Ethan's eyes caressed their bodies as he stretched his arms around the tub's edge like a king. Leo looked on like a proud father.

I sat back, sipped my beer, and watched everything like it was an episode of *The Real World*.

35

JERRY ARRANGED for a test screening of Don's Plum at Cal State-LA for more than a hundred students. The audience was split equally between males and females, and everyone was under twenty-one years old. It was surreal to see so many people streaming into an auditorium to watch something we had created together.

It's difficult to describe how it felt when the lights went down and the opening credits to Don's Plum flickered to life. It felt a lot like that moment on a rollercoaster just as it's about to drop into its steepest, scariest dive. We must have watched Don's Plum a hundred times during the course of post-production, but never once did it make me feel like it did in front of those kids. It was as if the movie belonged to them in some spiritual or metaphysical way and they had just reclaimed it.

When the credits rolled, the room burst into vigorous applause. The end credit scene sequence kept everyone in their seats laughing all the way until the lights came up. Volunteers distributed and later collected short questionnaires that Jerry had prepared for the audience.

JERRY COMPILED the test screening data back at the office and was delighted with the results. We scored an impressive 87% "recommend see" score.

"I haven't seen a score that high since Forrest Gump," said Jerry.

"Let's not get nutty," said RD.

"I'm not delusional, RD. I know what Don's Plum is. But on a few hundred screens, it could easily grow into an arthouse hit. Tobey also outscored Leo and everyone else with the women, which was entirely unexpected."

"Really!" I said. "That's almost unbelievable."

"I'm not surprised," said RD. "Leo's a fuckin' dick in the movie."

"It's still wild," I said. "So what's next, Jerry?"

Jerry shrugged. "Screen it for Leo, right? Any word on when he's back from Titanic?"

"Mid to late June," said RD.

"Find out exactly when, will you? I need to book the theater soon if we're going to get a good date. Let's invite a few distributors to the screening and see what kind of reaction we get. I know we can't look at offers yet, but there's nothing wrong with getting distributors excited, don't you agree?"

"Absolutely," said RD. "As long as we don't make any deals until after Leo's cool with everything, we're good."

"We should also make a small announcement in Variety as well."

"I don't know about that, Jerry," said RD. "That could create problems."

"Am I totally handcuffed here? Distributors aren't going to show up just because we booked a theater. An announcement in the trades will fill the seats with buyers. You gotta let them know you're there."

"I think it could cause trouble," said RD.

"Why? We're not breaking a story about Leo, if that's what you're worried about. We're announcing a small independent film to the industry. What possible harm can it cause? Do you want to ask him first?"

"Leo? Absolutely not."

"Why not?"

"Because I just want to show him the movie when it's finished and then whatever happens, happens."

Jerry nodded at me. "What about you?"

"I don't see a problem. Leo's gonna love the movie. It's got his best friends in it and they're all amazing. I think we're fine."

"I don't know that I can even get the article to run by the time we screen the film for Leo anyway," said Jerry. "Don's Plum isn't news. That's why I want it to run in the first place. I'm pulling another favor from a very good friend so we can start working the town now, not weeks from now."

RD shrugged. "Look, if you guys want to put out an announcement, be my guest, but I think it could come back to bite us in the ass."

LEO CONFIRMED his availability for the last Friday in June. Jerry booked the screening room at MGM for June 21st and began working on the guest list while John Schindler helped with the logistics and planning. We called Leo in Mexico to make sure the day worked for him, and he re-confirmed. Jerry spoke with his source at the *Daily Variety* and the article had been submitted, but she could not say when it might run.

Meanwhile, I chewed my fingernails around the clock.

"FUCK!" RD trampled up the stairs to my room. I put my book down just as he arrived in my doorway, breathless. "You're not going to fucking believe this shit, bro, Leo just canceled!"

"Canceled what?"

"He fuckin' canceled Friday—he's not coming to the screening."

"No! He can't do that!"

"He just did."

"Why?"

408

"He's going to Juliette Lewis' birthday party in Vegas."

"No, that's not true. You can laugh now, RD—haha."

"I'm serious, bro. A fucking birthday party."

"Let's call him." I stood up and walked past RD and down the stairs.

RD hit the speakerphone button for a dial tone and called Leo's number. Leo picked up.

"What the fuck, Leo?"

"I'm sorry, R. I fucked up and forgot about Juliette's birthday."

"You can't do this to us. We set up this whole thing for you."

"It's cool. I'll watch it as soon as I get back."

"No, bro, the whole cast and crew will be there. It's at MGM for fuck's sake."

"I'm sorry, guys, but I promised Juliette—"

"You promised us," I said.

"Three fucking times," snapped RD.

"I know. I'm sorry. I really am…"

"Just go to Vegas on Saturday morning," I said. "Or late Friday night."

"I'm not gonna miss her party, bro. I'll be back on Sunday. Set it up for Monday, or anytime next week. I promise I will be there this time. One hundred percent. I'm sorry, guys. I gotta go."

"WHAT DO YOU MEAN HE CANCELED?!" Jerry sounded livid over speakerphone.

"He's going to Juliette Lewis' birthday party in Vegas," said RD.

"You can't be serious! I can't just cancel MGM studios days before the screening is scheduled to happen, RD. Did you tell him we have the entire cast and crew coming?" RD tried to say yes, but Jerry spoke over him. "That distributors are coming and are expecting to see him and the rest of the cast, save Tobey Maguire? What am I supposed to do? Tell the head of acquisitions for Fox Searchlight, 'I'm sorry, but Leonardo DiCaprio can't come to the screening because he has to go to a fucking birthday party?' How old is he?"

RD balled up his fist and shook it. "FUCK!"

"Who cancels like this?" said Jerry.

I shrugged. "I told you—he thinks Don's Plum is nothing."

"How? He hasn't even seen it."

"Can we just move it to Monday?" said RD.

"No, RD. I just told you I can't push the screening on two days' notice. It's ridiculous and totally unreasonable. Besides, how do we know it's not someone else's birthday on Monday?"

"Let's just try and fix it," said RD.

"I guess I'll call and see if I can book the room for Monday. We'll have two screenings, but there won't be anyone there on Monday. Everyone's already RSVP'd for Friday. What an absolute disaster."

I WOKE up on the morning of the MGM screening with a belly full of fear and a voice message from Jerry Meadors saying the article on Don's Plum would be out in that afternoon's *Daily Variety*. The paper didn't hit the stand until noon so RD and I just milled around the condo aimlessly, our nerves so shot we couldn't even eat.

Noon arrived and we ventured to the newsstand on the corner of Laurel Canyon and Moorpark to grab the latest issue of *Variety*. We had to flip through the newspaper a few times before finding the blurb tucked away in the bottom third of a slim section called "Insider Moves."

RD read the article aloud, "DiCaprio, Maguire Ice Indie Pic. Leonardo DiCaprio and Tobey Maguire, who is wrapping production on Ang Lee's Ice Storm at Fox Searchlight, have quietly shot an indie feature film called Don's Plum with first-time director RD Robb. The project, which also stars Kevin Connolly and Scott Bloom, was shot in black and white and in real time. The story is about a night in the life of four guys who are hanging out in a coffeehouse. The project was Executive Produced by Jerry Beckman and Jerry Meadors, who is a former marketing VP at Paramount."

I smiled at RD. "You're in the trades, bro."

RD looked ill. "I got a bad feeling about this."

We bought all the copies they had and headed back to the condo.

The message light on the phone was blinking when we got home. RD hit the speakerphone and dialed the password. He pressed the number one to listen to the new message, and Leo's voice came through loud and extremely agitated.

"What the fuck is an article doing in Variety, RD and Dale?" He sounded like he was talking through gritted teeth. "I told you nothing happens unless we agree to it. I'm coming to the fucking screening tonight. We'll talk afterward." A loud crack ended the call.

RD hit the button and then staggered to the sofa, "We're fucked." He collapsed onto it. "We're totally fucking fucked."

I had no words.

RD looked at me with wide, terrified eyes. "What are we going to do?"

"Let's go to the mansion and talk to Meadors."

RD and I sped over Laurel Canyon to our office in the mansion. We told Jerry everything and he didn't seem to grasp the gravity of the situation at first.

Jerry chuckled. "Well, at least he's coming to the screening tonight."

"This isn't funny, Jerry," said RD. "We're pretty much fucked right now. He's furious."

"Why? What's the big deal?"

"Because we should have waited until Leo saw the film before making any announcements. I told both of you that."

"A lot of good that would have done. He stood you up, RD. The only reason he's coming to see the movie tonight is because of the article. He'll calm down. It's a harmless blurb in the trades. The only people who're going to care are distributors."

"He cares, Jerry," said RD. "And that's all that matters."

"He's overreacting. When he cools down, he'll realize the article is meaningless, and if he doesn't, I'll explain it to him myself. It's not a big fucking deal. I had to pull favors to get it to run in the first place. He's acting like all anyone in the media wants to do is write about him."

"We should have waited until he saw the film before making any announcements."

"Need I remind you, RD, that I suggested you fly to Mexico months ago when your friends were acting anxious and screen the same cut for Leo that we screened for Tobey, and you refused? Both of you did as I recall."

"Yeah, I did, Jerry. It was a bad idea—Tobey would have already convinced him to shelve it by now if we did that."

"He can't just shelve it," said Jerry. "No one gave him that power."

"We did."

"You told me the only requirement was that the film had to be good. The film is good."

"Yeah, well, he hasn't seen it yet."

"He will tonight! But let me be clear, RD, I didn't agree to Leo having unilateral kill rights to Don's Plum. The agreement has always been based on the quality of the film and we have delivered that in spades."

"Jerry, with all due respect, I don't think Leo gives a fuck what you, or me, or any one of us thinks."

"Well, if he's going to go beyond the scope of our agreement, if he's going to play a heavy hand over a harmless blurb in the trades, then at least he knows we have a voice in the press."

RD rolled his eyes. "Yeah, I'm sure he's fuckin' terrified."

"What he ought to be is grateful. It was me who lobbied the powers that be at Paramount to push for Leonardo's Oscar nomination for Gilbert Grape. It wasn't even on their fucking radar until I showed them a path to his nomination. I have been nothing but helpful and have worked in good faith, so yes, RD, I will take full fuckin' exception if he tries to stop this film for personal, petty fucking reasons. And so should the both of you. That was not the spirit of our agreement, correct?"

"What?" said RD.

"That he could stop Don's Plum for personal reasons, even if the film is good."

"No," I said. "It was always about the quality of the movie."

"Then if he has a problem with any of us individually, step up and let's talk about it, but threatening the work of everyone involved is totally out of line."

"I agree," I said.

"But look, we're screaming about something that hasn't happened and isn't going to happen. I pulled Wunjo this morning when I asked about the screening tonight. It's the Nordic Rune of wins, gains, and joy!"

RD squinted. "What the fuck does that mean?"

"It means, RD, that Leo's coming to the screening tonight and he's gonna love Don's Plum!"

RD shook his head. "This is a disaster, Jerry."

"We don't know that. Stay positive!"

A GOOD-SIZED CROWD had already gathered in the MGM theater lobby by the time RD and I arrived.

Jerry spotted us and glided over to us jovially. "Hello, boys! Quite a turnout so far. John said they're about to test the print, if you want to check it out ahead of the screening."

"I do," I said.

RD's eyes searched the lobby. "I gotta piss first. I'll meet you in there." He scurried away.

"Dale, you go on ahead," said Jerry. "There are a few more people I'd like to say hello to before the screening begins."

I approached the entrance to the theater and was stopped by a strange, shorter man with a patch over one eye. He was wearing a three-piece suit that was at least one size too big for him, and his slow, strange smile revealed crooked, yellow teeth.

"I'm so sorry," he said, "but we're not letting anyone in the theater just yet. It won't be too long now."

"It's cool, I'm one of the producers. I'm just gonna check out the print." I stepped forward, but he blocked my path with his arm. "What are you doing?"

"What's your name, sir?"

"My name? Dale Wheatley."

"Dale, I can't let you in right now. I'm so sorry."

"What's your name?"

"My name is irrelevant. The doors will be opening soon, and everyone will be allowed in then."

I held up my finger. "I'll be right back."

I turned and scanned the crowd until I found John Schindler standing off in the distance, drinking a beer and mingling with a beautiful woman. I hurried over to him.

"Yo," I said, interrupting them.

"Oh, hi," said John. "Have you met Phoenix?"

"Phoenix? No. I haven't." The red-headed woman offered her hand and I accepted. "I'm Dale. Good to meet you."

"Dale was one of my main creative guys on the film."

I laughed out loud. I couldn't help it. I wasn't John's writer. He was my line-producer. I asked him who was guarding the theater.

"Oh, that's Jack."

I blinked. "Are you serious?"

"Yeah. Why?"

"He's got one eye."

"Yeah, so what?"

I waved my hand. "Never mind. I want to get in there and take a look at the three-quarter."

"Yeah, I asked him not to let anyone in until it's time. I'll talk to him." John excused himself from Phoenix, and I followed him over to the One-Eyed Jack.

"Jack, this is Dale," said John. "He's one of the producers."

"Oh!" Jack reacted as if I hadn't just told him that very same thing a minute earlier. "Nice to meet you, Dale." He stuck out his hand and I took it.

"Nice to meet you too, Jack." I gave him a firm handshake.

John excused himself and returned to his muse.

With a slight bow of his head and a graceful hand gesture, Jack permitted my entrance to the theater.

The theater was a nice size, probably 200 seats or more. The best seats were taped off for the cast. Additional seats on either side of the cast were reserved for distributors. I drew a deep breath and took it all in.

"Yo," said RD as he strolled down the aisle. "Who the fuck is the pain in the ass guarding the door?"

"That's the One-Eyed-Jack."

"The what?"

"He's got one eye, and his name is Jack."

"Oh, yeah? That's pretty funny. Did I miss the test?"

"I don't know. I just got here."

"Bro, feel this." He put his cold, clammy hand on my cold, clammy hand. I yanked mine back.

"Dude! That's disgusting."

He chuckled, "I'm fucking terrified."

"I'm fine."

"Really?"

I took his hand and held it to my thudding chest.

His eyes popped open. "Jesus!"

"Can you see it in my neck, bro?" I tilted my chin upward.

He leaned in for a closer look. "Holy shit, bro, you're worse than me. Don't have a fuckin' heart attack."

"I should sit down."

The projectionist finally threw Don's Plum up on the screen. It was absolutely massive, and beautiful.

RD looked over at me, smiling pridefully. "That's our film, bro. We made that shit."

It felt amazing. Everything I ever wanted was happening right before my eyes. "No matter what happens tonight, we pulled it off, RD."

RD jostled me by the shoulder. "We made a fucking movie."

I smiled, "And a pretty good one."

. . .

415

LEO WAS among the last to arrive. Seeing him was hard on my nerves, but I did my best to conceal it.

"What's up guys?" Leo's face was hardened and unpleasant.

"What's up, Leo," said RD cautiously.

"What's up?" I said. "Sorry about Variety. We didn't know it was gonna run today."

Leo looked at me sternly. "There never should have been an article in the first place."

"You're right. We fucked up... For whatever it's worth, I'm really fucking glad you're here tonight."

He sighed, "We'll talk about it after. Where am I sitting?"

We walked Leo to his seat and then took ours a few rows back. Fifteen minutes later, every seat in the house was filled. Nearly our entire cast and crew were present. I was worried about all the drama, but I was also lifted by the tremendous buzz and excitement in the room.

RD stood before the crowd and delivered a memorized speech that he and Jerry had written a few days prior. I wish RD had spoken from his heart rather than from something prepared. It didn't sound like him, and it felt disconnected from his friends and from the true inspiration behind Don's Plum. He referred to our friends as cast members and actors and to himself as director, but Don's Plum was about our friendships and about our creative collaboration. It should have been a selfless moment, but I got the veiled sense that RD was taking credit for the vision of the film, or believed that he should because he held the title of director. RD knew as well as anybody that it was the unhindered collaboration between many ferociously talented people that made Don's Plum what it was, and not any one person's vision. Don's Plum was its own thing, separate from all of us. We merely had the privilege of ushering it into existence, and I wish RD's words had focused on that rather than industry tropes about relationships between directors and their cast and crew. Everyone deserved praise, but not for their service to RD, the director. Upon finishing, RD got a round of applause. He took his seat next to me just as the lights dimmed to black.

I closed my eyes and said a prayer in my head to a god I didn't believe in, and then sunk deeper into my seat.

Don's Plum takes a few minutes to get going, but it wasn't long before the audience started warming up to it. I tried not to stare at Leo, but it was impossible not to. My entire future was playing out before his eyes, one frame at a time, and I just needed to see a sign, any sign, that he liked what he was watching. He was rather stoic through most of the opening sequence, even a little uncomfortable, but after a few minutes, he seemed to relax. He was in his element after all. Leo genuinely loved going to the movies.

A giant smile opened on his face when Jerry Swindall, playing Leon, appeared on the screen, jawing on his mobile phone. Leo shifted in his seat when his character Derek entered the scene and grabbed Leon's phone from him. Leo and the rest of the crowd laughed loudly when Derek hung up on whomever it was Leon was talking to and began dialing for chicks.

I felt a rush of excitement and then RD's hand squeezing my knee. I took a deep, elated breath and exhaled months of tension all at once. Don's Plum was about to do its magic.

I expected the scene between Leo and Jerry Swindall to play well, but by the end of it the audience was roaring! Leo jumped out of his seat and smacked the carpet in front of him. He turned to Jerry Swindall and high-fived him so hard I could hear the slap from my seat.

RD pinched my arm and mouthed, "Holy fuckin' shit!"

When Leo first arrived, he was visibly angry over the *Variety* article and probably a bunch of other shit he'd been harboring, and within the first twenty minutes of Don's Plum, he was laughing his ass off without a care in the world. That's why I love movies, they have the power to change the way we feel.

Don's Plum played better than it did at Cal State. It didn't matter if it was all because the room was filled with the people who made the movie—the night was golden. When the end titles began, the room erupted in applause with hooting, hollering, and whistling, and it continued like that through the entire end title sequence. It was a breathtaking moment.

After the lights came up, most of the crowd filed out of the auditorium, but the cast lingered. I noticed Leo and Jenny embracing, and I could see tears on Jenny's cheeks. He was telling her how proud he was of her.

When Leo and I finally spoke, his demeanor toward me had totally changed. His eyes were warm and friendly again and the tension in his face was gone.

"So that's what we've been doing, dude." I smiled.

"It's really fuckin' good," said Leo. "I'm very surprised."

"Well, you guys were incredible. Like I've been saying."

"I'm still not happy about Variety at all..."

I shook my head. "We made a mistake, I'm sorry, bro."

RD dipped in between us, and he and Leo hugged. "Pretty good, right?"

"Really fuckin' good, bro. I need my agents and Rick to see it, but you guys really surprised me tonight."

RD smiled. "That's such a relief, bro."

Leo looked at me. "What are you guys doing now?"

"After party at El Compadre," I said. "You should come."

"Nah, I'm jumping on a plane to Vegas. We'll talk when I get back. Congratulations, you guys."

THE FIRST THING that hit me when I walked inside El Compadre was the bounty of delicious fragrances. Meats, onions, garlic, and cumin hung in the air, teasing my stomach until it moaned. The restaurant was warm and charming, with big red leather booths, each with a unique tin lantern casting a dim light from above.

The long, dark bar was crowded with folks from the screening. RD and I were greeted by dozens of people, friends and strangers, every one of them raving about Don's Plum and congratulating us. It was wonderful. I grabbed a cold Pacifico and we found a booth where RD, Jerry, and I could talk.

"Did you see Leo jumping out of his fucking seat?" said RD.

Jerry guffawed. "The whole place saw him jumping out of his seat, RD."

"What a fucking night!" I said.

"Tell me what Leo said again?" said Jerry. "I could barely hear you at MGM through all the excitement."

RD shrugged and smiled. "He said he really liked it. He wants us to screen it for his agents, of course, but he said he liked it a lot."

"Well, we're getting offers. TriMark and First Look Pictures have both committed to having something for us within a week."

"Slow down, Jerry. Leo's not officially on board—"

I waved my hand dismissively. "Come on, RD."

A giant grin stretched across RD's face. "We still don't know *for sure*, bro."

I spotted Kevin Connolly and Nikki Cox enter the restaurant. Nikki was cradling a bouquet of flowers. Once they spotted us, they beelined for our booth.

"Holy fuck, bro!" Kevin's face was lit up like Christmas.

"You liked it?!" said RD.

"Are you fucking kidding? Of course! I fucking loved it. We all did. The whole theater loved it. That was incredible."

"Congratulations to you, bro," I said. "You're so good in it."

"I mean, I don't even know what to say, you guys. This is far beyond anything I thought either of you were capable of—I think we're all in a state of shock. That this is your first film completely blows me away."

Nikki stepped forward with the flowers. "These are for you." She handed them to RD and kissed his cheek.

"Wow. Thanks, guys." RD opened the card and smiled. "This is really nice." He handed it to me.

It read, *"Congratulations! You did it!"*

"Leo's done a complete one eighty, bro."

"Really?" said RD smiling.

"One-hundred and eighty degrees, bro."

"I should think so," said Jerry.

"I think you guys did it." Kevin chuckled and looked at each of us. "I think you guys actually pulled this shit off."

"What did he say exactly?" said RD.

"First of all, he said he loved me in it. How fucking cool is that?

I know we're friends, but still—he's an Oscar nominated actor, and he's never said anything like that about my work before, it's a big fuckin' deal."

"Did he say anything about it being too long?" said RD.

"Not at all. Not one word. He just—he said he loved it, dude. I can't speak for the guy, obviously, but I think everything is gonna be fine. I hope so."

"Holy shit," said RD.

Kevin chuckled. "Complete one-eighty, bro."

My grin was so big my cheeks hurt.

"I'm a lead in an independent feature film with Leonardo DiCaprio." Kevin raised his eyebrows. "It's pretty unreal."

"The first of many great performances by you, I'm sure," said Jerry.

"Thanks, Jerry. So, what's the plan? Sundance?"

Jerry chuckled. "Oh, I've already packed my bags for Park City."

Kevin looked at RD. They were both stunned and jubilant. "RD, are we going to the Sundance Film Festival?"

RD shrugged his shoulders, but the look on his face was unquestionable. "I think probably... yeah..."

The rest of the night was like being the groom at a gala wedding. We were showered in praise and congratulations. People I've never seen before were telling me how the film moved them deeply, how it made them laugh, even though they found it deeply disturbing at times. I was living in a dream come true. I felt limitless.

―――――

LEO SET up a screening of Don's Plum for all his representatives at CAA headquarters in Beverly Hills. RD and I rode there with Jerry. David was waiting for us outside the building when we arrived.

The exterior of CAA looked like something carved out of a giant iceberg, beautiful but cold and foreboding. The interior felt sanitized and aggressively corporate. It looked more like law firm out of a John Grisham novel than the world's leading creative talent agency. We were greeted by a lovely receptionist. She called us Messrs, Robb, Stutman, Meadors, and Wheatley, which was a first for me. She escorted us to the theater where we were greeted warmly by Leo's agent, Adam Venit, Leo's manager, Rick Yorn, and Leo's personal attorney, Steve Warren. There were two other agents present, Beth Swofford, a notable literary agent, and Ken Hardy, who represented directors for the agency.

Rick Yorn's mobile phone rang and he took a seat a few rows away to answer it. "This is Rick... Hi there... Uh–huh. Well, that's a problem. He's going to have to address it somehow... No, they are Leo's concerns. It's too cheesy, those are Leo's words... I understand. I understand. He agreed to look at Leo's notes... No, not at all. Leo just wants Jack to have a little more substance, something more than a love story. He thinks he's one-dimensional... I sent them over. Sure, I can fax them again. Sure... OK... OK, thanks. Bye." He flipped the phone closed and apologized.

After all the introductions, the lights went down like magic, and the first frames of Don's Plum flickered to life.

This screening was a very different experience from those at Cal State LA and MGM. The laughs came and went quickly, like chuckles in church. There were moments when the room was disturbingly quiet. Rick Yorn was constantly fielding calls, scooting in and out of the auditorium causing distractions. Don's Plum is a voyeuristic piece, it requires immersion to really work. When the movie ended, I had no idea what to expect, so I braced for the worst.

But Don's Plum delivered again and delivered huge this time. All of them loved it, particularly Beth Swofford. She went on about how unique it was and how affected she was by the rawness of the performances and production. She said it drew her deeper into the characters and made her want to know more about them. Adam Venit's sentiments were similar. They asked for a moment to discuss it briefly among themselves, and so we stepped out into the hall. We just stood there, too afraid to speak but we couldn't stop smiling. A couple of minutes later, they invited us back in the room.

"We're on board," said Adam Venit. "Really nice work, guys."

"Yeah, we're good," said Rick Yorn. "I think it's a great little movie. I'm so sorry, but I gotta run. Really good work, guys. Congrats."

Jerry huddled up with Adam Venit and Beth Swafford to get them up to speed on distribution while RD and I boiled in excitement. They started dropping names and territories, sales agents, stuff of that nature, but it was the talk of Don's Plum getting into the upcoming Sundance Film Festival that sent me to the fucking moon.

"We'd love to be involved," said Beth Swofford. "We represent Robert Redford, so we're confident we can get Don's Plum into Sundance. Our colleague, Manny Nunez, reps projects for producers, I'm sure he'd have a lot of great ideas as well. Can we loop him into the conversation?"

"Yes, of course!" said Jerry. "The more, the merrier."

WE COULD BARELY CONTAIN our excitement long enough to get out of the building.

"CAA wants to rep the film—do you know how huge that is for this project? This is a whole new ball game!" Jerry cackled. "Jesus, look at me. I'm so excited, I'm making sports analogies."

"Guys..." I couldn't get the next word out before the giggles started dribbling out. "We're gonna be in Sundance!"

"In competition!" squealed RD.

I don't think I've ever seen a face so full of joy like RD's. He was blinking away tears that I don't think he even knew were there.

"It's official now, right?" said David.

RD nodded, "Oh it's official, bro. You can pay for that lipo, baby.

David shook his head. "Why you gotta be a dick, RD?"

"Gentlemen," said Jerry in his charming mid-Atlantic drawl. "I think it's time we get Harvey Weinstein on the line."

––––––

"HELLO, this message is for RD Robb. RD, this is Ken Hardy at CAA. I'd like to represent you as a director. I'm going to assume you want to work with us, so give me a call at the office and we can go over some of the details. Congratulations."

RD collapsed into his office chair and swiveled around to face me. "Holy fucking shit! I just got signed by the biggest talent agency in the world."

36

MANHATTAN WAS like a city made by gods. I couldn't get my head around how puny little beings, standing on average five feet and a few inches tall, were able to build a city so magnificent it could touch the clouds. We taxied to an apartment in Greenwich Village that Edie Robb had arranged for us and dropped off our bags. We walked to a restaurant for a quick meal before hailing a cab to the screening Jerry had arranged for Miramax executives. I ogled skyscrapers from my window while the sounds and smells of the city flooded my senses.

Our screening was held in a posh little theater in an inconspicuous office building on the edge of Times Square. Don's Plum played beautifully, and we were approached afterward by Miramax's senior acquisitions executive, Amy Israel, and a couple of her associates.

"What can I say?" said Amy. "We loved it!"

Jerry clapped his hands together. "Wonderful!"

"It's so real. How did you write it?"

"Improv mostly," said RD. "Then me and this guy," he gestured to me with a thumb, "started coming up with the character arcs and story lines—how everything works together."

"It felt like we were eavesdropping the whole time." Amy giggled adorably. "It made me uncomfortable at times."

"In a good way, I hope." I said.

"In a very good way. I didn't know Leonardo DiCaprio was so funny, either!"

"He's the funniest guy I know," I said.

"Well, we're so glad you enjoyed the film," said Jerry. "Miramax would be a lovely home for Don's Plum."

"We think so too," said Amy. "Give us a couple of days. We've got to talk to Harvey. Can we get a screener for him?"

"I'll have one sent over straight away," said Jerry. "Half-inch?"

"Perfect. He's gonna love it. Are you guys screening for other distributors?"

"Yes, of course," replied Jerry.

Amy grinned. "Do you have any offers?"

"I've been told to expect them."

She raised her brow. "Do you mind sharing who you're talking to?"

"I think I'd rather wait until their offers are in, if that's all right."

"Of course. Just thought I would ask."

Jerry chuckled nervously. "Thank you... You know how these things are, people can say they're making offers all day long."

Amy nodded. "Miramax is definitely making an offer."

My heart rolled over in my chest. I nearly yelped.

"That's exciting news," said Jerry.

"I hope you won't accept anything before hearing back from us. I think we can do great things for Don's Plum."

"We'll wait with bated breath!" said Jerry. "We're flattered by your interest, Amy. Thank you."

As soon as we got out on the street, RD and I started clawing at each other like squealing teenagers.

"We're going to be a Miramax film, bro!" said RD.

I couldn't believe my ears. We were about to be in the same company as Quentin Tarantino, Lasse Hallström, Steven Soderbergh, and Jim Jarmusch.

"We'll be a Miramax film if they make the best offer," said Jerry. "I don't mean to shit on your parade, but just because they're interested doesn't mean they're the best option. We have to consider all offers very carefully."

I heard Jerry, and he made perfect sense, but my mind had already been made up. I was going to do whatever was necessary to steer Don's Plum toward Miramax.

WE SPENT the rest of our time in Manhattan partying into the wee hours of the morning in cool little dive bars and clubs. We ate at fancy restaurants and hot spots throughout the city. I saw a rat the size of a cat that scared a cop so badly he drew his gun on it. I heard someone yell "I'm fuckin' walkin' here!" at a cab driver edging his way into an intersection. I got a slice of thin crust pizza that was as big as a newspaper that I had to fold in half to eat. I heard the music of subway buskers that was so amazing I wondered how it was possible they hadn't been signed by a major label. It seemed like every New York City trope played out before us, and I delighted in all of it.

We saw a few Broadway shows. *Rent*, which had just won the Tony for best musical, was utterly jaw-dropping. I barely remained conscious through *Something Funny Happened on the Way to the Forum* with Nathan Lane, that year's best actor on Broadway, but my favorite show of them all was Reg E. Gaines' *Bring In Da Noise, Bring In 'Da Funk*. Savion Glover showed me a side of tap dancing I never knew existed and it touched my soul. I loved New York City.

I COULDN'T SLEEP on the red-eye back to LA. I wondered if I would ever be able to sleep soundly again. Everything that was happening was thudding around my head like sneakers in a clothes dryer. Laughter would just bubble up out of nowhere and I had to suppress it somehow because RD and a half a dozen other passengers were sleeping right next to me. So, I sat there, keeled over, heaving muted laughter into my hands, smothering my joy as much as I possibly could.

37

LEO ENDED up staying in LA longer than expected. He said there were construction issues with the set, but the rumor around Hollywood was that James Cameron had gone way over budget and they needed to bring in another studio to finish *Titanic*. Regardless, Leo remained in town and Jerry thought it would be fun to throw a private party for the cast since Leo and Tobey weren't able to make it to El Compadre after the MGM screening.

Jerry asked his friend Henry Daes to host the party at his house in the hills. Henry was a wonderful friend to Jerry and a huge fan of Don's Plum. He was also a very kind host, with a stocked fridge and plenty of snacks plated throughout the house.

Most of our friends were there, including the cast and key crew members of Don's Plum. Henry had some of his friends over and Jerry invited a bunch of people I never met before. The place was hopping. I spotted Jerry in the mob and walked over to him.

"There you are, Wheatley. How did you get here?"

"Bloom."

"And where is he?"

"On the deck, smoking with the guys."

"Have you seen RD?"

"He's not here yet."

"Dale, is that Marky Mark talking to Tobey Maguire?" He pointed through the crowd until I spotted them.

"Yes," I replied. "Although he goes by Mark Wahlberg now."

"He's much better looking in person. Don't you think?"

"I don't know, maybe. You should talk to him."

"Oh, that reminds me. We heard back from Rivers Cuomo, he won't give us the publishing rights to the Buddy Holly song regardless of how much we offer."

"Oh no, are you serious? That's fucking terrible—it'll ruin the best transition in the movie."

During the second day of filming Don's Plum, the whole cast broke into an impromptu sing-along of the Buddy Holly song by Weezer after their altercation with the greasy mechanic character, played so wonderfully by Brandon Morgan. It was the perfect ending to the scene and losing it meant trouble. "Did he read RD's letter?"

"He did and he declined," said Jerry. "You'll figure out the cut, don't worry."

"That's so fucking bad, Jerry."

"Not all is lost. How would you feel about Mike D and Beastie Boys scoring?"

"Scoring our movie? Seriously?"

"Of course."

"Ecstatic. Insanely ecstatic—RD would lose his fuckin' mind."

"Well, they're interested. Don't say anything to anyone yet, not even RD. CAA is still talking to them, but it looks very promising. Oh, there's Henry Daes, I need to ask him something, Dale. I'll be right back." Jerry waded through the crowd toward our host. I headed to the balcony for another smoke.

Leo, Scott, Kevin, and Ethan were all puffing thick nicotine clouds into the still night when I stepped onto the deck.

"Where the fuck is RD?" said Kevin at the sight of me.

I shrugged. "I don't know—he's been busy."

"He's meeting with fuckin' studio heads and huge producers, huh?"

"I think he's delivering breakdowns for his mom, actually."

"Dude, RD will be a fuckin' multi-millionaire, multi academy award-winning director and Edie Robb will still make him deliver her fuckin' breakdowns." Kevin chuckled. "It's true, bro. She will."

"What's up with Titanic?" I said.

Leo sighed. "They're building an actual replica of the ship."

"Like on a sound stage?"

"No, the whole fucking boat in a giant water tank. It's a scale replica from the original blueprints."

"What the fuck are they gonna do with that afterward?"

"Turn it into a ride at Disneyland," muttered Kevin. "Everyone fuckin' drowns at the end."

I laughed just as RD walked through the sliding door like a prince late for his own ball.

"The man of the hour." said Scott, grinning.

"What's up, dudes?"

"RD Robb!" said Kevin. They clasped hands and pulled each other in for a hug.

"Hey, look who's here," said Leo. "It's the big director man, RD Robb. The big CAA boy has finally graced us with his presence." He gave RD a lazy hug. "Congrats, bro. I'm happy for you."

"It's so crazy," said RD.

"A slight upgrade from Don Buchwald," said Kevin.

"I'm staying at Buchwald."

"CAA's not repping you for acting?"

"No."

Kevin shrugged, "Who cares, you're a legit a director now. Are you gonna even bother with acting anymore?"

"I don't know what's going to happen, bro. There's so much shit going on. But yeah, I love acting."

"Yeah, of course, but directing is your thing now, right?" said Kevin. "You know why I'm asking RD, don't you? Yo, check this out, listen to this. Me and this guy right here made a fucking deal, we put it fucking writing and everything, that when he makes it big as a director he will put me in every movie he ever makes. Ask him."

RD chuckled. "Yes, we did."

"I'm holding you to it, RD. I still have the fuckin' contract."

RD chuckled. "We're putting all you fuckers in our movies, bro."

"What agent did you end up signing with?" said Leo.

"Ken Hardy."

"Never heard of him."

RD shrugged. "I don't know anything about him other than he reps directors."

"I hope they do a good job for you, bro."

———

Tobey Maguire called and asked if he could get a few of his scenes on a tape to show Lasse Hallström, who was directing an adaptation of *Cider House Rules* by John Irving. We were happy to help. Paul Heiman laid off a VHS tape with a few of Tobey's choice scenes. When I heard Tobey arrive at the mansion to pick it up, I stepped out of the editing bay to greet him.

"What's up, bro?" I said, opening my arms to him. "Good to see you." We hugged.

"Good to see you, too."

"Look at you—from Ang Lee to Lasse Hallström. Holy shit, Tobey."

"Yeah, well, I haven't got Cider House, yet. Hopefully, these scenes will help."

"I'm so happy for you, dude. Fucking incredible."

"Look at you guys, too. I feel like everyone is talking about Don's Plum."

"I wish you were at the screening, Tobey. It was magical."

"Yeah, me too. I'm excited to see it though. I kind of gotta run, do you have the—"

"Oh, yeah, sure," I said. "Let me grab the tape."

"Oh hey, is it on VHS?"

"Yeah."

"Shit. I should have told you that I need it on three-quarter. Leslie thinks she may need to send a tape to a few producers, maybe a couple of agents as well, so she wants to run a few copies off."

"Let's ask Schindler." I led Tobey into the kitchen where John and Nabil were hanging out. John said he might have a tape and went to check in another room.

"Hey, Nabil," said Tobey. "Good to see you again."

Nabil smiled. "Yeah man, it's always good to see you in real life." He chuckled. "I'm so used to seeing you on a little screen."

John returned with his wife, Tracy.

"We only have one three-quarter tape, Tobey," said John.

"And it's the master of my acting reel," added Tracy, sharply.

John chuckled. "Yeah, so please don't lose this, or she'll kill me."

"Oh, I'm already going to kill you, John." She laughed, perhaps a little too maniacally.

Tobey chuckled. "I promise I'll take care of it and bring it right back as soon as we're done. Maybe even later today."

We made Don's Plum to boost all of our careers so we were thrilled and proud that scenes from our little movie might help Tobey book such an incredible role.

38

Danny DeVito's production company, Jersey Films, contacted Edie Robb and requested a meeting with RD. One of their executives had attended the June 21st screening at MGM and wanted to talk about RD's future. As RD's partner and co-creator, I was very excited of course, but it was short-lived because RD, or perhaps his mother, decided that I should be excluded from the meeting. It was the same shit he had pulled with Jerry Meadors, only this time it involved the biggest opportunity that had come our way.

RD returned from the meeting glowing, with a big toothy smile. "Dude, Jersey Films wants to make films, bro. They wanna give us three million dollars to make three films."

"Are you serious?"

"Anything we want." He grabbed me by the shoulders and shook me like a toy. "We did it, fucker! We got a three-picture deal!"

I managed to smile, but I wasn't happy.

"What's wrong with you?"

"This is your deal, RD. It's not my deal, It's not Meadors' deal. Maybe you want us to work on your deal with you, but it's not our deal."

"What the fuck are you talking about? We're partners."

"Then why wasn't I in the meeting?"

"My mom set it up, bro. I don't know."

"If we're partners, I would have been in the meeting with you, no? You wouldn't want me taking important meetings without you, would you?"

"Bro, this is for all of us. For you, me, Meadors, all our friends... It's what we've been working for."

I nodded, "Yeah, OK."

"I don't know what's wrong with you."

I grinned. "I'm cool, man. It's amazing news... very exciting."

"I'm gonna call Meadors and tell him—he'll be fuckin' thrilled. He finally gets to make Young Men Dressed in Silver."

———

A COUPLE OF DAYS LATER, RD, David, Jerry, and I gathered at our office at the mansion to discuss our options and opportunities for Don's Plum. TriMark offered 1.5 million dollars and a pretty nice back-end deal for worldwide rights. First Look Studios didn't offer a minimum guarantee, but they had the pedigree with Robbie and Ellen Little running the company, and they offered the best split out of everyone.

"Miramax is coming in under a million," said Jerry. "And the split is mediocre at best."

"That deal makes no sense," said David.

"Shall I call Amy Israel and pass on Miramax then?" said Jerry.

I sighed, "Oh, man, I don't know. This fuckin' sucks." I glanced over at RD.

"Sucks hard, bro." he said.

"Nothing sucks, you two. I'm talking to the two best Japanese distributors in the world, and they both want the movie. CAA is assisting, maybe they can drive up the price and Miramax will make a fair offer, but TriMark is a wonderful home for Don's Plum. We're in great shape, we need to make sure we land the best company and the best offer—"

"Miramax is the best company for Don's Plum," I said.

"Not if they're not willing to pay for it. TriMark released Kids, Dale."

"I don't know why, Jerry, but I just feel like Miramax is where we belong."

"Well, we're not going to lose three-quarters of a million dollars and a much better back-end deal for your feelings. No offense, Dale. We haven't accepted anyone's offer yet so who knows what'll happen, but if Miramax is supposed to be our distributor, then they'll come around and make an offer worth accepting—but make no mistake, Dale, Mark Amin is every bit as talented at putting out a movie as Harvey Weinstein."

———

RD HUNG up the phone after a lengthy conversation with his agent. I was sitting at my desk in our mansion office, so I heard most of RD's side of the conversation.

"Ken Hardy's got me up for two films already, bro." RD began pacing.

"Wow."

"Yeah, bro. Nutty."

"Do you want to tell me what they are?"

"You're not gonna like 'em."

"Why? What are they?"

"The first one is the sequel to Dennis the Menace."

I spat out some coffee when I laughed.

"Told ya."

"That's funny. Why would he even think of you for that?"

"With Walter Matthau, bro."

"Yeah, but... it's a Dennis the Menace sequel. That's—you can't do that."

He raised is eyebrows. "Yeah, but Walter Matthau is a big deal, bro."

"You are not thinking about directing Dennis the Menace two—"

434

"Ken thinks I could get like five, maybe even six-hundred thousand dollars."

"Who fuckin' cares? You cannot follow-up Don's Plum with Dennis the Menace. That would be a terrible decision."

"You think I should turn down a half a million dollars?"

"Yes! Stop fucking with me, RD, please."

"I'm not. I have to think about it, bro. You don't just say no to a half a million dollars."

"Yes, you fuckin' do. What's the other one?"

He shrugged. "It's this thing with Kirstie Alley—something about beauty pageants—I don't know. They want it done docustyle and Ken thinks Don's Plum is the perfect comp. He doesn't think they're gonna offer much more than scale, so that's probably a pass. But that Dennis the Menace money is very tempting."

"I can't believe you would even consider it." I could feel my blood pressure rising.

"Why?" He laughed. "You don't love Dennis?"

"We just made a serious art-house movie that is raw and daring and provocative, and experimental—and you want to follow it up with fucking thoughtless, mass-consumer bullshit? You're about to disappoint everyone that has supported you, bro. Except your mom. She's gonna fuckin' love it."

"We can still make our movies, bro. I can do both."

"I'm not gonna fuckin' wait around for you to finish your little kid's movie, RD."

"Do it with me, and then—

"I'm not working on that film."

"Why not?

"I already told you why."

"Making money is a good thing. You should give it a try sometime."

"You don't have to be a fucking dick, bro. I'll make plenty of money, and I'll have my integrity when I do."

"I want to work with Walter Matthau. Why would I pass that up?"

"It not the Fortune Cookie, bro. It's not The Odd Couple. It's

435

Walter Matthau taking a pension check. You don't have to take the first movie they offer you."

"I can't pass on that kind of money, Dale. I could pay off my mortgage."

"What about Jersey Films?"

"They can wait. We're not going to make any money on those, bro."

I laughed. "Why do you think everyone is going to wait around for you? You're going to ruin all of this... everything we did."

"It's one movie. Let's just see how it goes."

"They're not going want me on Dennis the Menace two, bro. I got nothing to offer that movie."

"What makes you think you're so fucking superior."

"I'm not. I'm an arthouse guy, that's all. It matters to me. I got nothing against entertainment, RD, but that's not what I do, and it's not something I thought you did either. I thought Ken was on board to bring the resources together and elevate the career you wanted, not this fucking garbage. I hate money, bro."

"I don't know what to tell you, bro. The world runs on it."

I was hit hard by the realization that there was a very real possibility RD and I were never partners at all, and that he was not the artist I thought he was. "I gotta go for a walk, bro."

I STROLLED ALONG FRANKLIN VILLAGE, smoking a cigarette and wrestling with my thoughts. I was supposed to be on cloud nine but, instead, I felt tense and alone. I should have taken the co-director credit when I had the chance, but I thought RD and I were establishing a long-term, possibly even career long collaboration. I think there was also a part of me that was afraid of working without RD. He gave me my big break, and we worked together harmoniously. We fed off each other like songwriters do, and I had taken for granted that he had felt that same creative connection. Don's Plum was our first movie, and now we knew how to write, direct, and produce, from top to bottom, an improvisational feature film. Those were highly unique skills to have in

Hollywood in 1996. We had only scratched the surface of what we might discover creatively with our process, and we had already experienced incredible success. I could not fathom why anyone would want to change direction.

As I passed a magazine stand, I noticed Leo was on one of the covers and it triggered a daydream. I pictured Leo, Scott, Kevin, Tobey, and RD all on the cover of the same magazine together promoting Don's Plum. The headline would say something like, "Leonardo DiCaprio is headed for the top and he's taking his friends along with him." It was everything I ever wanted for them and for Don's Plum. But I knew greed was coming because money was coming. I just hoped the art would survive it. We created something more than a movie, we stumbled onto a unique approach to independent film and, more than anything, I wanted to see it evolve.

39

Tobey showed up at our apartment at around 7 or 8 in the evening. He had called earlier and asked if he could make us some dinner and talk. He said he had some issues with Don's Plum that he needed to work through. RD and I both hated the idea, but Tobey didn't take no for an answer.

Ethan was already stretched out and comfortable on his couch when Tobey rang our doorbell. I answered.

"What's up, bro?" said Tobey.

"What's up." We hugged and the plastic Ralph's bag hanging from Tobey's wrist knocked me on the back.

"What's up, RD?"

"Hey, Tobes." RD got up from the sofa and gave Tobey a hug. "You're cooking for us tonight?"

Tobey chuckled. "Yes, I am."

He caught Ethan's eye over RD's shoulder.

"What's up, Ethan?"

Ethan grinned, "Yo."

RD plonked his ass back on the couch. "What's the special occasion?"

"Nothing, I just want to talk with you guys, so I thought, you know..." Tobey grinned and shrugged. "Why not make us some dinner?" He walked over to the adjoining kitchen and set the

Ralph's bag on the counter and looked around. "Bro, this place is small, bro."

"I hate it here," RD said. "I can't wait to move back to the condo."

"How much longer?"

RD shrugged. "Who the fuck knows. It's FEMA, they're gonna take forever."

We had to move out of RD's condo while the government retrofitted the entire complex with structural support in compliance with new earthquake measures following the Northridge quake.

"Where's the pots and pans?" said Tobey.

RD nodded at me. "Wheats?"

I stepped into the kitchen. "What do you need?"

"You know, enough for this." He held up a box of Kraft Macaroni and Cheese.

I chortled, "You really shouldn't have."

"With tofu wieners, bro. Don't tell me you don't like mac and cheese."

"Yeah, it's fine." I grabbed a pot from the bottom shelf. "I loved the first thousand boxes I had, but I'm more of a Tony's Frozen Pizza guy these days."

"Well, trust me, you're going to love the way I make it." Tobey filled the pot with water and placed it on the stove. "So, what's happening with the movie?"

"You know," said RD. "We're out there trying to sell it. Jerry and CAA are."

Tobey nodded. "I heard Miramax wants it."

"Yeah, but I don't know if we'll end up there."

"Why not?"

"The deal's not great."

Tobey salted the water and stirred it pointlessly. "What's the offer?"

"I can't tell you the specifics, but it's not great."

"Why are you guys always so secretive?"

RD laughed. "We don't want everyone knowing we're getting

low-balled by Harvey Weinstein. Obviously."

Tobey sneered. "I'm talking about us, RD. That's what's bothering me about all of this. Don's Plum was supposed to be a movie between friends. And now it's just you and Dale being secretive—"

I held up a hand. "Whoa, whoa, whoa..."

"Yeah, bro. You guys are going behind our backs and making decisions and deals. There's all these points being doled out—"

I shook my head, "What the fuck are you talking about, dude?"

"I'm talking about friendship, Dale. Don's Plum belongs to all of us—"

"Yeah, it does, but you're not the one selling it. RD and I aren't selling it either. Meadors and CAA are, and they want the offers close to the chest. What's the problem?"

"Why do you and RD get to know then?"

"You know exactly why, Tobey, come on. I wrote and produced the movie, RD directed it. Besides, you're too big time for us little shits anymore. You work with the best of the best now." I noticed the water on the stove was about to boil over. "You're boiling over, bro."

"That has nothing to do with it—what I'm talking about is—"

"Tobey..."

"What?"

"Your fuckin' water. On the stove."

He snapped. "I don't give a fuck about macaroni and cheese right now!"

"OK, dude," I said and retreated to the living room. "Jesus fuckin' Christ."

"Well, I'm talking about something important, for fuck's sake." He returned his attention to RD. "We should've been involved in the decisions for this film."

"That's ridiculous," said RD.

"No, it's not. It would have been the right thing to do."

RD shook his head. "We can't have a million fucking people going back and forth with Harvey Weinstein or Robbie fucking Little. Do you want four agents negotiating your deals all at once? No, you don't."

Ethan piped up. "You guys wouldn't even be talking to Harvey Weinstein if it wasn't for Leo."

Tobey pointed at Ethan. "That's a whole other issue."

"First of all, that's not true, Ethan," said RD. "Miramax is interested because they like Don's Plum."

Ethan grunted himself into a seated position. "Oh, come on, RD! How can you sit here and say that?"

RD shrugged. "Leo's an amazing actor, and we're lucky to have him in the film, but he ain't worth shit in the box office. Trust me, we're dealing with that right now. Miramax and everybody else wants Don's Plum, but it's not a sure thing just because Leo is in it. There's a lot more to it than that."

"You're so fuckin' high, bro," said Ethan.

I shook my head. "I thought you liked Don's Plum, Ethan."

"I love it. That's not what we're talking about. You guys are trying to say Leo isn't the reason you guys are talking to companies like Miramax, and I think you're both off your asses."

I shrugged. "What do you know about any of it?"

"Nothing. I'm not pretending to..."

"You just said Leo is the reason why anyone is interested in buying the movie."

"And that's a fact."

I waved him off.

Tobey poured the box of macaroni into the pot of boiling water and stirred with a wooden spoon. "You guys could have had Jerry be the one who talks to the executives, and still have gotten feedback from us the whole time. You're making excuses."

"No offense, but why would Jerry Meadors ask for your feedback?" I said. "You're an actor."

Tobey slapped the countertop, suddenly enraged. "Everything is shady about this fucking movie! And I'm sick of it! Leo is fucking sick of it!"

"Pull yourself together, bro." I said.

The macaroni started to boil over. The foamy head spilled over the rim down into the sputtering gas flames.

"Where the fuck is all of this coming from?" said RD.

"From your secrets and all your lies! From your back-handed-ness!" Tobey started blowing on the foam to prevent it from spilling over again. It didn't work.

RD pointed to the door. "Bro, if you're going to scream and shout at me, you can leave."

Tobey yanked the pot from the flame and blew again until the foam retreated, then put the pot back on the stove and stirred. "I want some answers. I want to know what's been going on behind closed doors."

"Nothing—that's absurd," said RD.

"There are no fucking closed doors," I said.

"You know what I'm talking about. You guys are out there raising who knows how much money—David Stutman is getting liposuction and doing all this stupid shit before Leo has agreed to anything. Neither of you has asked any one of us for our input the entire time."

RD shook his head. "That's not true, bro. We talked to all of you, multiple times. We fucking worked with you on your characters. You weighed in on the casting. And, dude, we screened the film for you and Kranzler—you could have said anything you wanted, but all you said was that you liked the movie and would go along with whatever Leo decided."

"Yeah, because you had to get his approval and you—"

"Then don't say we didn't get you involved because we did. We communicated with you more than anyone else."

"Yeah, well, if I'm unhappy, then how do you think Leo feels?"

RD shouted, "Leo's already on board, fuckface!"

Tobey slammed the wooden spoon again, producing a piercing crack.

"Yo, you gotta stop with that shit, bro." I said.

RD got to his feet and puffed up a bit. "Tobey, if you're not gonna calm down, then get the fuck out of here."

Tobey took a deep breath. "You called me fuckface—what do you expect?"

"I call you fuckface all the time."

"Obviously there's some stuff we need to clear up."

RD sat down. "There is nothing to clear up, Tobey. You just need to fuckin' chill out."

"Bro, I just want to get to the bottom of... I want to..." Tobey fished a noodle out of the pot and sucked it into his mouth. "I want to know the truth, RD. That's all I want." He grabbed the steaming pot and poured all the contents into a strainer in the sink and then followed the standard mac & cheese protocol—a knob of butter, the included pouch of cheese powder, a dash of milk, some salt, all stirred together with cold, chopped-up tofu wieners. "Where's your bowls?"

"I'm not hungry," said RD.

"Me either," I said. "In the cupboard above the toaster."

"That sucks. I made all this food for you guys. What about you, Ethan?"

Ethan took a last drag and butted his smoke out in the ashtray. "Fuck yeah, I'll eat that shit."

Tobey reached up into the cupboard and took down two bowls.

"Are you sure you don't want any?" Tobey asked me.

"Hundred percent."

"RD?"

"Knock yourself out, bro."

Tobey filled two bowls and sat next to Ethan on the Sups couch. They ate side by side.

"I apologize for yelling," said Tobey with a cheek full of macaroni. "I just get upset when I think about Don's Plum sometimes."

"Why?" I said. "I don't understand."

"Because it was supposed to be a small project between friends and you guys turned it into this big thing..."

"First of all, Don's Plum is not a big thing," said RD. "The film you just finished in New York, that's a big thing. Titanic is a huge thing. Don's Plum is tiny, bro..."

"Bigger than it was originally supposed to be—stop pretending you don't know what I'm talking about, RD. It's insulting."

"Don's Plum is a little movie," I said. "There's no exaggerating that."

"It was supposed to be a short film," said Tobey.

"Oh, bullshit," I said. "We did what every filmmaker on the planet would do, we cut our film together after we shot it. What did you think was going to happen?"

"That you would make the movie we agreed on."

"We did." I raised my brow. "That's exactly what we did."

"There was never supposed to be a Showtime, there was never—"

"Tobey—"

"No! Hear me out, Dale." Tobey raised his voice sharply and then just as quickly regained his composure. "This was supposed to be a little film between friends that maybe we could put on our reels or whatever. Not a project that was going to be on TV or in major festivals..."

RD shook his head. "Why would anyone make a movie to not be seen? We didn't agree to that."

I shook my head, "Yeah, I guess your memory is all fucked up or something, because we definitely talked about selling Last Respects to Showtime. That has always been in the conversation. We talked about incorporating documentary footage, which would obviously make it longer—"

"We all believed you were shooting a short," said Tobey.

I sighed. "We're way past that—like a long time ago. You did the fuckin' reshoots, bro, what are you taking about? You've been involved every step of the way. I don't know why you're playing these games—"

"Dale, you know full-fucking-well Don's Plum was never supposed to be a feature film. You're the one playing games."

I shook my head. "Don's Plum was an experiment. That's what everyone liked about it. There was no script, no one could have known how long the movie was gonna end up, it—"

"You are lying to yourself, Dale."

"It exceeded our expectations—" I laughed. "Lying to myself? OK fine, explain how we could have known how long Don's Plum was going to be without a screenplay?"

"I'm not going to explain anything to you."

"You can't. It's impossible."

444

Tobey stood up and walked his bowl to the kitchen sink. "You can cut it to whatever length you want... you're choosing to—"

I shook my head. "Tobey, you don't know what you're talking about."

"You're creating opportunity for yourselves by taking advantage of your friends."

"Bull-fucking-shit, bro," said RD.

"This was for everybody," I said.

"Could we have communicated better? Sure," said RD. "There are a lot of things I want to get better at, but you're off your ass, right now. And we were raising money for Last Respects so that's all bullshit too. Everyone knew what was happening at all times."

"You tricked us—you're both fuckin' lying constantly!"

"You're crazy," I said.

RD laughed. "You're fucking' trippin', dude."

Tobey clenched his fists and screamed, "I WANT DON'S PLUM TO BURN!" Spittle and foam shot from his mouth. The veins in his neck welted up like nightcrawlers. "I WANT DON'S PLUM TO BURN!"

RD was back on his feet, fists ready. "GET OUT, TOBEY!"

I got in between them. "Calm down. Come on guys."

Tobey was trembling. RD turned pale. Ethan froze mid-chew.

My breathing was suddenly shallow. "What are you doing, Tobey?"

"You guys fucked over your friends. You guys are—you *disgust* me."

RD shook his head. "We didn't fuck over anyone. You're losing your mind."

"I know there's more—you guys are hiding shit from us. You've been lying to us this whole time—"

"Lying about what?" I said.

"I know there's more—"

"There's nothing," said RD. "You're just looking for trouble."

I reached for Tobey's arm. "Sit down. You've got this all wrong. Let's work it out, OK? I promise you. We're friends, Tobey, let's just talk it out. Come on."

I managed to get everyone seated again. We tried to talk calmly through Tobey's fragile state. His crazed shouting subsided, but he kept insisting we had done something wrong, using words like betrayal and deceit. We denied it all and he accused us of keeping "secrets" but couldn't name any. "That's why they're called secrets, Dale," he said sharply. Tobey's bullshit went on for what must have been hours. Ethan went home at some point and I hoped Tobey would do the same, but he remained. Tense as ever.

RD stood up. "It's fuckin' midnight, I'm exhausted from all this nonsense. I'm going to bed." He looked over at Tobey. "You should go home and get some sleep, Tobey. We can talk tomorrow."

"I don't believe you would have taken no for an answer, RD."

"What?"

"I don't think you guys would have taken no for an answer. If Leo said no."

"Well, that's a pointless conversation because he said yes."

"It's not pointless. It's about friendship. It's about being a man of your word."

RD rolled his eyes. "Yeah, I know, you haven't shut up about it. I love my friends, bro, you included—even if you're out of your fucking mind right now. I hope you feel better. I'm going to bed." RD looked at me. "You guys should do the same."

I nodded and said goodnight, but I couldn't leave Tobey in the state he was in. He was dangerous. He had Leo's ear and could easily convince him to put the brakes on Don's Plum. So I stayed up with him and mostly listened to whatever he had to say. We talked about a lot. I reminded him how much we had in common, like how we'd both survived very difficult childhoods and came out of it with a deep compassion for people, especially those in difficult circumstances. I pointed out how optimistic we both were, despite living through so much turmoil.

"You know, dude, I'm a friend for life," I said. "I'm never going to have a bad intention toward you or any of our friends."

"Well, I'm not going to just turn my head if I see something happening."

"Yeah, good. But, you know our intentions, Tobey. We're all

extremely close. Even if we were capable of being deceitful people, we wouldn't treat you guys that way."

"Once again, if I see something going on that I don't like, or that I find suspicious, I'm going to say something about it."

"As you should, but—"

"No buts, Dale. No buts. I question everything."

I chuckled. "As do I. But our history and our friendship means something—"

"You wanna know what I think?"

"Yes."

"I think you guys got in over your heads, and I think you were mesmerized by the idea of being directors, writers, and producers and you kind of lost yourselves. I just went through it. You have a chance to be successful in Hollywood, and that's a huge deal, but you have to stay vigilant because, just like that." He snapped his fingers sharply and his lips closed tight. "Just like that, Dale, you can be compromised. There's so much temptation out there, so you have to make sure you're always doing the right thing. And look, that's what friends are for, we have to look out for each other. If I keep doing well, I hope you guys will be there for me to make sure I'm in check, so none of this stuff gets to my head—why are you smiling like that?"

"You're really amazing, Tobey. You came from nothing, and look at you now—"

"It hasn't been easy."

"Of course not. That's why it's impressive."

"Two things made it all happen for me—well, one person and one thing. David Legrant, my acting coach, changed my life forever."

"RD loves the guy. Won't shut up about him. What's the big deal with him?"

"He's an actual fucking genius. It's like he taps into the human condition like no one has before and he teaches in a way that I can absorb almost everything he's saying. I don't know... He can see things that normal everyday people can't. You gotta see him in action."

447

"He sounds cool. Maybe, when I finally get some money from Don's Plum, I'll join the class with you guys."

He chuckled. "You gotta get sponsored in, bro. You can't just walk in and start taking classes with the man."

"Of course. I'm probably not ready for someone like him, anyway."

"No, I think you are. I'll happily sponsor you."

"Really?"

He smiled. "If you want."

"Fuck yeah. Thank you."

"Someone just dropped out—now's a perfect time, actually."

"Well, I gotta wait until Don's Plum sells, or I get a job, which-ever happens first."

"You shouldn't wait, it could take forever for another spot to open. I can pay for it so you can start right away."

"It's cool. It's not gonna be that long before I have some money. A few more months, probably."

Tobey shook his head. "There probably won't be a spot by then."

"I gotta take that chance."

"No, you don't. I can afford it. You can pay me back, if that will make you feel better."

I chuckled. "Why are you pushing it so hard?"

"Because I think it will help you reach your potential. Look what you've done in—how long have you been in LA?"

"Two years."

"That's crazy. I've been at this shit for nearly ten already. I can't imagine what you'll be like after learning from David. You'll be unstoppable. What's the big deal if I pay for it until you've got some cash flow? That's what friends are for. You're gonna pay me back anyway."

"You're not going to let me say no, huh?"

"Why would you? It's an awesome opportunity."

I sighed. "OK, fine. But I am paying you back."

"Great. I'll talk to David tomorrow."

Things seemed to have settled down nicely. Tobey was finally calm.

"You want to know the second thing?"

"Yeah."

Tobey raised his eyebrows and grinned. "AA"

"Oh..."

"Probably weren't expecting that."

"Nope. I was not."

"You thought I was going to say Tony Robbins, huh?"

I laughed.

"Alcoholics Anonymous did more for me than anything or anyone in my life, including David. It literally saved my life. And it's making me a better person."

"I'm a little surprised you'd be down with the whole religious thing."

"That's the tiniest part of it, bro. It's the program and the people who changed my life. My sponsor is my personal fucking hero. There are people who could help you too. I could help you."

"Well, I'm not an alcoholic, so..."

Tobey cringed.

"What?"

"I think you need to look a little harder at the situation, Dale."

"I'm not an alcoholic."

"Are you sure you're being honest with yourself right now?"

I chuckled, "Yes."

"It can be a hard thing to face, but you gotta look at it truthfully. It takes courage because it's often not very pretty. You say you're not an alcoholic, but I've taken care of you when you've been falling-down drunk. People who don't have a drinking problem don't get that wasted, Dale."

"I get too drunk sometimes, that's true."

"You get too drunk a lot."

"I don't drink any more than anyone else. Have you had this conversation with Leo, Jay, or fuckin' Sups? Because they all drink more than me. Don't forget, I'm broke, dude. I can't afford alcohol."

Tobey grinned condescendingly, "Dale, come on."

449

"But I know what you're fuckin' saying, and you're not wrong. Sometimes I lose track and I slam a bunch of beers and shots if they're around, and I get a little too wasted."

"Blackout drunk, Dale."

"Nah, come on. That's not true."

"I'm just telling you what everyone else sees."

I sighed again.

"Do you think you're invisible or something? Didn't you just get into a big fight with someone at the mansion... That dude from Kentucky? Because you fucked his girl or something like that?"

"Who told you that? That's not true."

"Ethan said there was a big fight and you broke all of Meadors' expensive wine glasses."

"Ethan's got a big fuckin' mouth."

"Is he lying?"

"He doesn't know what he's talking about. We didn't have sex... I wasn't pursuing her at all. I got really drunk and she fuckin' jumped me, and yeah, she ended up giving me head in the office— and fuckin' Murray walked in and he tried to beat me up... it was horrible. I feel terrible to this day."

"He was your friend, right?"

"Yeah, bro, and I made a terrible, drunken mistake that I'll always regret, but that doesn't make me an alcoholic. It makes me an asshole."

Tobey smirked condescendingly. "You're an alcoholic and until you realize you are—until you face it, you're just going to continue to hurt more people, bro. Including yourself."

I massaged my tired eyes. I didn't want to listen to him anymore.

"I know you're a good person. I know your heart, Dale, and I want to help you."

I chuckled. "You know my heart? Then you know that I can handle it."

"If you say so, bro. But I've seen you out of your mind. A lot. When you threw RD into the bushes at Formosa—Blake told me about you almost getting shot at Burger King..."

"Dude, I wasn't even drunk at Burger King ..."

"Are you going to tell me you weren't drinking and getting high?"

"I was, yeah, but I was far from wasted. Blake was being the biggest asshole on the planet. I told him numerous times to chill the fuck out, and he wouldn't, so some stupid shit went down."

"Finish the story. You guys fought because you were out of control and some dude pulled a gun on you guys."

"How the fuck do you know all this? I had no idea you guys were talking about me behind my back."

"You could have been shot. This isn't Canada."

"It wasn't as dangerous as it sounds. The dude just flashed his gun to chill us out."

"It's a pattern, Dale. A drinking pattern. Do you really want to risk everything you're accomplishing right now over alcohol?"

"No. And I'm not going to."

"You're fuckin' breaking people up, bro. People who loved each other and who considered you a friend. You're almost getting shot at fast-food restaurants—you gotta open your eyes! It's only going to get worse."

"People make mistakes—"

"You're making a lot of them..."

I took another deep breath.

He smiled gently. "If you were sober, would any of that shit have happened?"

I didn't answer. We both knew it wouldn't have.

"Look, maybe I'm wrong and maybe you're not an alcoholic... or maybe you are, and you don't know it. I know you're someone who cares about people. You owe it to yourself to explore this—to explore getting better. There's no shame, bro."

"I don't think there is."

"I'm serious about how AA has changed my life. You don't have to be an alcoholic for it to help you."

"I'm happy for you, Tobey. I really am. I just don't think it's for me."

"How do you know? Have you ever been to a meeting?"

"No."

"I'm going to one in the morning in Santa Monica. You should come."

"No, Tobey. I'm exhausted."

Tobey smiled. "Please. I'm asking you as a friend to come to AA with me. What do you have to lose? We can go back to Bob's place and hang for a bit. Grab a couple of hours sleep maybe and then head over. I'll bring you back here right after the meeting. Do it to support me if that's the only reason you can come up with. Just try it once."

I sighed. "Yeah, alright," I said. "I'll go with you."

WE LEFT the apartment and headed to his place somewhere in Hollywood. Tobey was still in between rentals so he was staying with his friend, Bob Villard. Bob was a controversial person. He was a talent manager and publicist for child actors and had been publicly accused of improprieties with some of his underage clients. I wondered why Tobey would associate with someone with that kind of reputation, but Tobey just brushed off the stories as rumors.

Bob Villard's house gave me the creeps. It was a small, dark space crowded with furniture. Shelves ran the length of the walls, dense with ornaments and tchotchkes. There was a stale smell, like dust and old bread. Tobey brought me a glass of water while I settled into the lumpy sofa.

I looked up at the clock. It was one of those old cat clocks from the 70s with the tail that wagged the seconds of your life away. "Holy fuck, it's 3:30 in the morning!" I felt exhausted suddenly, like I could pass out in the middle of a sentence.

"Wanna just stay up? The meeting is forty minutes away and I always get there early. We gotta get you a book—"

"No need for a book, Tobey. But yeah, we can stay up if you want to."

Tobey smiled. "The books are free. I'll make a donation like I do every week. I'm really proud of you, Dale. This is a big step. It takes courage."

I wanted to tell him I was only doing these things to placate him—to soothe whatever sores were burning him up, but I didn't. I just smiled, and yawned, and sipped my water.

As the night dragged on, I nodded in and out of consciousness, losing small chunks of time.

"I want to ask you something about Don's Plum," said Tobey.

"No, bro. Please."

"Something's bothering me—something RD said, and I want some clarity."

"Talk to RD then."

"You know what's up. And I don't trust RD right now."

"Why? That's ridiculous."

"I think he's keeping shit from all of us."

"He's not. I can tell you that for sure. You need to get all that shit out of your head."

"Well, I asked him about, you know, what were some of the shitty things that went on with Don's Plum and he said there weren't any at all. I know that's not true."

"It is true, though. He's telling you the truth."

"Come on, bro. I have so much respect for you, don't destroy it all in one night."

"Don't destroy what? Your respect for me? Why would that happen?"

"Do you really expect me to believe that there was never anything at least questionable that you guys haven't told us about? And I get it, you guys were scared that Leo would shut down the film, so it's totally understandable. But you know, I just want you to be honest about everything that happened. Cleanse the bad stuff. You guys are always ready and willing to share all the good stuff, all the positive stuff you guys are hearing from the surveys about me scoring high with women in test screenings, and from Harvey Weinstein, and all these distributors, but nothing is that squeaky clean, bro."

"I don't know what to tell you." I smiled. "Everything is good. Nothing bad happened."

His eyes narrowed. "You're not being truthful with me right now, Dale. I want to get past all this stuff with you guys, but I can't because I know you're not being honest."

"I am. We are. This is stupid."

"Was the Variety article a bad thing that happened, Dale?"

"Yes, that was a mistake."

"See? There were bad things."

"You're right."

"Whose idea was it?"

"Jerry wanted to let distributors know Don's Plum existed. That's all it was about."

"You didn't have Leo's approval yet. That article shouldn't have existed."

"That's true, we messed up. But everything's cool. There was no trouble. We learned from it and we moved on."

"Don't act like you and RD didn't have a say in it because I know otherwise."

"Oh, you do? Interesting. Of course I knew about it—and I had mixed feelings. Who—"

"Why didn't you go straight to Leo and tell him that shit was going on?"

"Because I didn't think it was a big deal... we talked about it and my view was that Jerry is a professional who knows what he's doing. I trust him."

"You didn't think Leo would be pissed about you guys putting announcements in the trades before he had a chance to approve the film? What if he said no?"

"No, I didn't. And I was wrong, but you bring up an interesting point. No one, not Jerry, me, or RD, even knew when the article was going to run, or even if it was going to run at all."

"Please don't start with the bullshit again, Dale."

"We didn't find out until Thursday night that it was running the next day. Variety couldn't care less about Don's Plum. That article was a favor to Meadors."

454

"But you knew ahead of time, and you didn't tell Leo."

"I mean, for a few hours, that's true. We may have found out Friday morning, actually—I really don't remember when exactly, just that it was no more than the night before."

"You should have asked Leo before you even tried but, at the very fucking least, you should have told him it was happening. Do you see how it's deceitful?"

"No. That's ridiculous."

"Is it? You knew Leo was more than skeptical that the movie would be releasable."

"Yes, but we knew otherwise."

"So, it didn't matter what Leo's decision was—you guys were moving ahead with or without him."

"No, nothing like that. We believed Leo was going to support Don's Plum because it's a good movie. And we were right."

"That's not your choice to make though—it doesn't matter if you think Leo is going to do something or not, it's still his decision to make, and until he gave you his decision you guys were supposed to hold off on everything."

"That's not entirely true. But that doesn't really matter right now. I'm trying to explain to you what happened—to answer your question. When Jerry mentioned it—"

"The article?"

"Yes, the article. When Jerry mentioned it, I didn't really think much about it because he's the expert. He said we needed it out there to attract interest in the film, and I was cool with it because I didn't see it as that big of a deal. Like I said, I was wrong and I apologized to Leo for that, but there was nothing deceitful done by any of us. Jerry was doing his job and we didn't interfere with him because we don't know anything about what Jerry does. That's why he's on board."

"But, Dale, Leo didn't approve anything yet. There was no job for Jerry to do. Don't you see how it looks? It looks like you guys are grabbing for fame and money, bro."

"That is so ridiculous. I'm not even mentioned in the stupid article—"

"But don't you see how shady all that nonsense about the article looks? Put yourself in Leo's shoes."

"I did after he blew up. And I apologized to him. What more can I do? There was no malice. It was a mistake. Yes, we assumed and expected Leo would approve, and maybe we shouldn't have, but the blurb was to drum up attention so we could get the best deal possible for the movie, nothing more. If Leo had rejected the film that would have been the end of it, article or no article. It wouldn't have mattered."

Tobey shook his head. "There's more. There's something you're not telling me."

"No. There's nothing, Tobey. When have I ever lied to you? Or to anyone for that matter?"

Tobey didn't respond. The quiet lasted long enough for me to nod off. I don't know how long I was out, but it was Tobey's voice that woke me with a jolt.

"Wake up! You need to be honest with me, Dale. I need to be able to trust you again, man. The more I think about it, the more I know something is off. You're keeping something from me and we gotta clear it up right now."

I was deliriously tired. I could barely focus on his words but I knew they were threatening.

"I want to know the worst thing that happened, Dale. What was the worst thing that you or anyone did or said about Leo or Don's Plum or anything?"

"I don't know what you want."

"I just fucking told you."

"I really don't know, though. Can we talk about this after we get some sleep? I'm nodding off, dude."

"I want the fucking truth now, Dale." Tobey gritted his teeth again.

"Tobey. You have the truth. Fuck, bro. I'm too tired for this shit. Do you want me to make something up? What are you trying to accomplish?"

"I want to clear the air, Dale. You guys are putting shit out in

456

the press. I've heard all this shit about the gay press from Scott and Ethan."

"What? What are you talking about?"

"They said all this shit about Jerry talking to the gay press about Leo."

"No, Tobey." I sighed. "That's not even close to reality... Jerry overheard a gay journalist say some shit about Leo, something about how the gay community is pissed at him or something—I don't even know what the fuck it was. Leo said, like, a bunch of shit about being grossed out by kissing Thewlis, and gay writers took offense to it. Jerry was just trying to give Leo the heads-up to be careful, that—that stuff Leo was saying in interviews was gonna get him in trouble. It was already festering behind the scenes."

"I did not know that."

"Yeah, he was looking out for Leo."

"See what I'm talking about? I didn't know that and I don't think anyone else does. I love Jerry Meadors. Thank you for clearing that up." He smiled. "I just want to feel better about the film and about you guys... about all of it."

"Honestly, Tobey, it's too fucking much, though. You're killing me. All of you are killing me. I don't get it."

"Don't get what?"

"I don't understand why you and the others are talking so much shit. You're putting us through hell, bro. I'm sitting here nodding off instead of sleeping because I'm afraid of you. I'm afraid of all of you."

"You're afraid of us?"

"Terrified. I feel like you guys are talking so much shit all the time—like you're against us for some reason. It makes no sense but look what you're doing right now."

"You sound like you hate us, bro."

"That's so ridiculous. Stop saying shit like that. I don't understand where all this crazy shit comes from. I keep thinking you guys are just going to, I don't know, grow up and stop being so fucking petulant all the time."

"What the hell are you talking about?"

"I'm talking about all the fucking bullshit, Tobey." I gestured to him. "This. What you're doing right now. I'm talking about farting peroxide into your friend's face."

"That was a fuckin' joke."

"Yeah, if you're not Scott Bloom, it's the funniest joke of all time. How would you feel if it happened to you?"

"I'm pretty sure Scott's OK with it, bro."

"Two weeks later, Leo's fucking manipulating Emily into masturbating in front of us on Christmas day."

"I wasn't there for of that."

"Why do you think he would do something like that?"

"You honestly sound like you hate us."

"Because I'm questioning your behavior? That's not hate. That's love. I love you guys. Why is it OK for you to call me and RD out on everything but when I point out the shit you guys are doing, I'm a hater?"

"That's a good point."

"I don't understand what you're doing, or why you're going it. It's like every one of you is going a little bit crazy all at once. Maybe it's because you guys talk so much shit all the time. Just before Bijou Phillips spit in RD's face on New Years, I saw Leo whisper something in her ear. And I mean he whispered in her ear and she immediately walked over and spit right in RD's face. Five days after doing that shit to Emily."

"Now you're accusing Leo of making Bijou spit in RD's face?"

"I don't know. How fucked up is that? Think about it. Because the answer, Tobey, is supposed to be, 'no fucking way in hell would Leo do that to one of his best friends,' but instead it's I don't know."

"I feel like you're just trying to change the topic now. Avoid the issue at hand."

I hissed. "I just want to feel better too, you know? Just like you."

"If you want to feel better, then come clean."

I shook my head. "Fuck. Here we go again."

"I'm serious. If you want to feel better about all of this, then just come clean with your friends. I don't know what Leo said to

Bijou either, but maybe all of this is a sign for you and RD to get everything out in the open. I'm giving you the chance to do that right now."

"Really? That's what this is?"

"Yes. Be honest with all of us and tell us what went on. Don't give me any bullshit, don't sugar coat anything. Tell us what went on and we'll deal with it the way friends do."

"Tobey—" I stopped and took a very deep breath. "I don't know what you want me to say to you."

"You can start by being truthful."

"I am not. Fucking. Lying."

"We both know there was shit said and shit done—"

"No, there wasn't." I shrugged dramatically. "I'm sorry to disappoint you—"

"What about the court document Kevin caught you guys with?"

I laughed. "Kevin didn't catch RD with anything. RD told him about it—it was sitting right on the fucking table in front of him and everybody else. Do you see what you're doing? It's not a court document, it's a notarized sheet of paper saying that everyone in the cast agreed to the same deal. And the only reason it exists is because you were threatening Stutman."

"Except Leo."

"Except Leo what?"

"You said we all agreed to the same deal and Leo didn't agree to anything. Not yet, he didn't."

"Yes, he has. So has Rick, Adam, and Steve Warren. They all agreed. I talked to all of them myself. What do you want, Tobey? Besides Don's Plum being burned to the ground, which obviously isn't going to happen. What do you actually fucking want?"

Tobey didn't answer. He just got up and left the room. I don't know where he went or how long he was gone because the next thing I remember, I was being woken up by him again.

"Dale, we need to talk, come on. I'm making us some coffee."

"What? What are we doing? No, don't."

"I'm making coffee. We have to talk. We have to fix this or our friendships are in trouble. Don't you care? You want cream and sugar?"

"What?"

"Do you want cream and sugar?"

"What the fuck are you talking about right now?"

"The truth. Whatever you tell me can stay between us, but we need to clear the air right now, before we go anywhere else. OK?"

"I don't know what... I don't know what I'm supposed to say. What do you want me to say?"

"Tell me everything, Dale. Everything that was bad. Don't lie, don't hide anything—"

"There is nothing to hide."

"I know that's not true." He handed me a mug of black coffee. "I just want to know everything, including the bad stuff. And we both know there was bad stuff. It'll stay between us. Don's Plum is doing its thing, it's not about that. This is about our relationship. This is about our friendships. If something bad happened, we can deal with it. We can get through it. You know? We can take care of each other, as long as you guys put everything out in the open. You care, right?"

"What do you mean? What is the question?"

"Do you care about your friends?"

"You know I do. Why do you think I'm here right now?"

"Then tell me everything, Dale."

"Why don't you believe me? When did that happen?"

"It's hard to trust you when you keep avoiding my questions. So no, Dale, I don't trust you right now."

"That's so terrible. What do you want me to do?"

"I keep telling you the same thing—I just want to know what was the worst thing you saw, heard, or did during Don's Plum. I want you to come clean and I want you to get it all out in the open —I know there's something, and the more you deny it, the more certain I am you guys did some fucked up shit that you're covering up."

"Tobey—"

"This is your time to air it all out and make everything right. I told you it will stay between us. If someone did or said something they shouldn't have, we'll deal it with it, you and me. We'll figure everything out, but you gotta come clean before we can move on."

"I just..." I giggled maniacally, "There's nothing to say, though."

"You can't help yourself, huh? The lies keep piling up and you can't stop. Of course we can't trust you. Well, I can't. I won't speak for everyone."

"I'm not lying, though. I'm not. There was nothing that was..." I took a deep breath and tried to collect my thoughts. I had to figure out some way to pacify him, but I couldn't think straight.

"That was what?"

I sighed and rubbed my eyes.

"Dale? Nothing that was what?"

"There were stupid things that some of us said, sure. You know, when we were, like, scared and you guys were fucking tripping about everything."

"Yeah, like what?"

"I don't even know—just some bullshit. We knew the film was good and, you know, RD was scared that Leo would shut it down even though Don's Plum is an objectively good film." I paused to correct myself. "Reasonably objectively, I mean."

"And?"

"At one point, RD was freaking or whatever, and I told RD that Leo wouldn't stop the film because—I told you all this stuff already."

"Be more specific."

"I mean, I said that I thought Leo would look like a dick if he stopped a perfectly good art-house film with all his friends in it, you know? I still believe that... I still do."

"What else?"

"That's pretty much it...that's what I said." I yawned like a lion.

"What about the Variety article? Was that, you know, done to try and pressure Leo into saying yes?"

"No. Why would you even ask that?"

"What happened after you found out he was upset?"

"We scrambled. We freaked the fuck out. OK, yeah, there was

461

one thing that I thought was *'bad'* I guess. It was harmless, but it made me cringe a little."

"What was it?"

"Leo was freaking out about not being able to go to Vegas for Juliette Lewis' birthday, you know, because of the Variety article and he was really fucking mad, and we were all terrified he was gonna, you know, no matter how good the film was, he was just going to stop it anyway—just to punish us for fucking up his Friday night, basically. And we were arguing about it—and holy fuck, Tobey, it was so stressful. Jerry was so annoyed at one point because RD and I were basically telling him the article probably destroyed Don's Plum's chance at a release. He did not take it well at all. We were arguing back and forth, and at some point RD said he was sure that Leo was gonna shelve Don's Plum because of the article, and Jerry couldn't believe it and he kind of lost it, you know? He said it was disrespectful and offensive, that one person should not be able to fuck with—I'm paraphrasing of course—but something like Leo should not be able to stop Don's Plum just because he has a personal beef with someone, regardless of who it was. And I agreed with that, but that's besides the point—Jerry was visibly upset at the idea, at the notion that Leo might arbitrarily decide to fuck with the film, and I am quoting Jerry this time—he said it was over 'a harmless fuckin' blurb.' And then he said something like, 'Well, if Leonardo is going to behave like an imbecile over it, at least he knows we have a voice in the press,' or something like that."

Tobey's eyes narrowed. "What did you just say?"

"It was stupid—it was reactionary. We were so fucking upset and feeling defensive. You have no idea how stressful that was."

"You brought it on yourselves."

"That's arguable." I chuckled.

"You were going to pit the press against your own friend so you could keep your movie."

"What? No."

"That's what you just said to me, Dale."

"No. I told you that Jerry had—that we all had a bad reaction.

462

Leo was really upset and we were worried and everything was fuckin' nuts."

Tobey stood abruptly and clenched his fist at me. "Are you gonna start fucking lying again?"

For a second, I thought he might actually strike me, but then he lowered his fist. "What the fuck was that?!"

"You just confessed you guys were going to pit the press against Leo!"

"Tobey, that is not tr—"

"Too late, Dale. You can't change your story now. What did you think was going to happen?"

"I'm not—nothing."

"I can't believe you guys would stoop so fucking low. I'm in shock."

"We didn't. I didn't say anyone was going to pit the press against Leo—I said that it would look like—"

"Look like what, Dale?"

"Nothing bad, Tobey."

"You just said, one fucking second ago, that Jerry Meadors was going to pit the press against Leo—that you guys fucking strategized together—"

"I didn't say anything like that."

"You're not gonna wiggle out of this. I heard every word. You're three fucking feet away from me."

"Tobey, listen to me—"

"WE'RE DONE, DALE! YOU'RE DONE! NO MORE LIES, NO MORE BACKSTABBING YOUR FRIENDS. IT'S OVER. YOU AND RD ARE FINISHED. I CAN'T BELIEVE YOU GUYS. WE'RE YOUR FRIENDS!"

"We didn't do anything! Why are you doing this?"

"You know exactly what's happening right now."

"I really don't. Let's just keep talking, please. This is a... a misunderstanding. There was no threat."

Tobey let out a sigh and then, to my complete shock, he laughed. It was a short, patronizing laugh that hit me like a bullet. "I have to go to Leo with this. I have no choice—"

"What's going on? What is this you're doing here?" I was beginning to shake. I was so stunned, like I had just been hit in the head by something. Everything suddenly felt surreal to me. "Tobey, I don't know what happened tonight..."

"You sure fuckin' do, buddy—" Tobey's eyes were blazing.

"No, I don't. And I want to be clear..."

"Oh, you were crystal clear, Dale. You didn't mince any words at all."

"No, I think you've, you know, you're getting it wrong. The context is—"

"You said that you were going to pit the press against your own friend, Dale. He was trying to help you guys out. Do you realize how vile that is?"

"I didn't say anything like that. We would never do anything like that. Never. You know that, Tobey. You must. We're good fuckin' friends. Nothing like that would ever happen."

"You said what you said. Are you trying to say that Jerry didn't say you guys had a voice in the press?"

"I told you something that Jerry said when he was upset... he didn't mean it. He wasn't being literal, he was being defensive because of Leo. Because of Leo's crazy reaction to the Variety article."

"Dale, we're talking to Leo, today."

"Tobey, don't do this. Please."

"Don't do what? Don't tell the truth?"

"I thought you said this was between us. Was that a lie?"

"I will not keep a plot to destroy Leo's reputation a secret."

"To destr—what the fuck? That's outrageous. I can't believe this is happening right now. What the fuck is happening right now?"

"I'm not going to keep your betrayal from Leo. I've known that kid since forever. This is bad. It's really, really bad. I had no idea. I knew you guys got into some shit with this movie, but I had no idea you had fallen this far."

"Tobey, you know I didn't say that—"

"Dale, you already admitted to it. Now you're gonna have to man up. Take it like a man. Have some fuckin' dignity."

"Why are you doing this?"

"I don't know what's going to happen to you guys, but you gotta own up to your shit and take it like men. And to answer your question, I'm doing it because it's the right thing to do. I'm doing what is right, Dale. What you should have done."

"But it's not right, it's literally wrong."

"Hey, at least you were honest with me. It took you a minute, but you came clean, and that stands for something. RD just bold-faced lied to my face and then went straight to bed. You've got a conscience at least."

"You can't do this, Tobey…"

"I haven't done anything."

"I am telling you right now that you've got this all wrong. Meadors was only reacting. There was no threat, there was no ill intent. Everyone was just fucKING STRESSED OUT BECAUSE YOU GUYS HAVE LOST YOUR MINDS!" I started shaking and sobbing. "You're twisting my words…Why? Why? Please, don't do this—we didn't do anything wrong, Tobey. I swear we didn't. We wouldn't. I'm begging you, bro. Please. This is my whole life."

"I don't know what Leo is going to do, bro, but he has to know what you guys did—what you were planning to do. I'm not going to keep threats from him, I told you that and I meant it. I wouldn't keep them from you, either."

I slouched over, the tears rolled down my nose and dripped to the floor. "No one threatened Leonardo DiCaprio. That's ridiculous."

"I hate to see you like this, Dale. I really do."

"Either you've misunderstood me—which is fine. Happens all the time. Or, Tobey, you're the one not telling the truth."

He laughed condescendingly.

I continued to beg and demoralize myself, but nothing seemed to get through. "You gotta think about everyone's work here. It's not just me and RD."

Tobey nodded slowly, thoughtfully. "Yeah. There's a lot to talk about."

I told him about my fantasy of all of them on the magazine cover together, about how Leo was taking his friends with him to the top. "Please just take some time to think about all of this. If you do, I think you'll realize nothing that I or anyone else said was a threat to Leo, that everything was gonna be fine, and that we were just going through a lot of emotions. On both sides. We were wading through a lot of stress and that was a difficult moment for us but, Tobey, you gotta believe me when I tell you that neither RD or I would ever betray our friendships with you guys. It would never happen. We love you guys, bro." My tears returned. "You're all we have..."

"Let's go to AA and then we'll see what happens, OK?"

I nodded and wiped tears away. My face felt like a tight mask.

"But whatever happens with all of this, I want you to give AA a chance. And I still want you to study with David. OK?"

I nodded.

"We're going to get through this, Dale. Let's just get it all out in the open and work it out. That's what friends do, bro."

I sobbed and nodded, "OK."

"Let me pay for Legrant until you're up on your feet. OK?"

"OK. Thank you, Tobey."

"We're still friends, Dale. The important thing is that you guys are honest from here on out."

"Of course," I said. "Of course."

We left for AA, and I felt hopeful everything would be OK. He said some nice things, and I thought he was starting to realize just how blown out of proportion everything had become.

"I think you and RD should probably be available later because I'm guessing we're all going to want to get together and talk about all of this at some point today."

And just like that, all hope was lost. "You're making a mistake—"

"I don't have a choice, Dale." He grinned. "Just be honest like you're being right now and everything will work out. OK?"

We drove in silence the rest of the way. The stress and fear made me sick to my stomach. I felt like Tobey's captive. I wanted to jump out his car and run away and pretend that this night never happened. I wanted to turn back the clock and not answer the phone, not let him in the apartment with his fucking macaroni and cheese, and certainly not spend the night with him at Bob Villard's creepy house.

WE GOT to the AA meeting and entered the brick building through a side door in the parking lot. The place was dimly lit and smelled like an old library. There were probably a dozen people there, all solemn and tired looking, their eyes searching like light-houses for friends and sponsors. We all had our troubles, but at least none of these people were about to be destroyed by the person standing next to them.

Tobey led me to a table of hardbound books with plain blue covers. An older woman sat behind the table with a tin lock box in front of her. She smiled at Tobey, revealing neglected teeth. Her smile was gentle though, and it softened the moment.

"This is my friend, Dale," said Tobey. "It's his first meeting."

The woman smiled at me gently. "Welcome, Dale."

I said thanks. I clung to Tobey's words to her, "this is my *friend*, Dale"

"Can he take a book?" said Tobey.

"Yes, of course. Please." She lifted a book and handed it to me.

I didn't want the fucking book. I didn't want the fucking meeting or the free coffee. I wanted Tobey to stop whatever it was he was doing and whatever he intended to do. I wanted my words back. I wanted to be back home, alone in my bedroom, where I was safe from all the fucking madness. I inhaled deeply and my breath hitched in my throat. Tears tried to come, but I forced them back. I took the damn book.

"It's OK," she said. "We've all been through it. You got this, Dale."

Tobey reached for his wallet and unzipped it. He pulled out a folded ten-dollar bill and handed it to the lady.

"Thanks," she said as she unfolded it and put it in her tin.

"I'll pay you back," I said.

"No, it's a donation. Make a donation at your next meeting if you want to."

We took a seat with the others. A man with long, unkempt hair and a knotted beard stood up and began speaking. His voice was strong and loud, but I couldn't quite hear him for the screaming madness going on in my own head.

Others took turns talking and as time went on some of my anxiety dulled a little. I didn't want the meeting to end because I knew that as long as we were there, Tobey wasn't out in the wild burning my work and my life to the ground.

The meeting ended rather quickly, or so it seemed, and most of the people got up and left, while others hung around, chatting with each other. Most gravitated to the coffee machine where they poured black-as-tar coffee into white Styrofoam cups like the ones I used to bite into as a kid. Tobey chatted with a few people, some he seemed to know, others he had just met. He introduced me and I feigned interest, shaking hands and nodding, repeating my name and theirs when it was necessary. It occurred to me that my melancholy was welcomed by all these people, and unquestioned, and that was comforting. But I knew soon, in the real world, sharks were circling. My blood was in the water and there would be no one to save me.

We got back into Tobey's red truck and drove away in silence. When we got to my apartment, Tobey insisted he come up and tell RD what was going on.

"Can you just take some time and think about this? Please, Tobey. I thought you were going to do that? What can it hurt? Let the emotions settle because I promise if you—"

"Dale, FUCKING STOP!"

.   .   .

468

THE APARTMENT WAS dark and silent. RD was still asleep in the back bedroom. Tobey called out to him from the living room but didn't get a response.

He called again, but much louder. "WAKE UP, RD! We gotta talk."

There was some muted grumbling before RD finally stumbled into the hallway pitching a morning tent in his plaid boxers. He was rubbing one eye and trying to focus with other. "What the fuck, bro? Why are you yelling?"

"Dale told me everything."

"What are you talking about?"

"He told me about your plan to pit the press against Leo if he opposed the film. He told me everything."

RD's eyes went suddenly wide. "What the fuck did you do, Dale?"

"I didn't do anything, RD. Tobey's out of his mind."

"Dale told me the truth, RD. Unlike you."

"What fuckin' truth?"

"I don't have time for your lying bullshit right now, RD. Just be ready because I'm calling a meeting with all the friends. I'm fucking disgusted with you, bro. Both of you."

"I don't know what the fuck you're talking about."

"I'M TALKING ABOUT ALL OF YOUR LIES AND ALL OF YOUR DECEIT. I'M TALKING ABOUT YOUR BETRAYAL OF ALL YOUR FRIENDS, RD!"

RD looked back at me with eyes blazing. "What did you SAY?"

I couldn't speak. I had become so light-headed I thought I might pass out. I made it to the sofa, collapsed, and dropped my head into my hands. "He's gone crazy, RD. I don't know why."

"You guys should get your fucking story straight," said Tobey. "I'll see you later." He turned and walked out the door.

"What the fuck did you do?"

"RD..." My breath left me before I could utter another word. A great affliction grabbed me by the throat and choked me silent. When I tried to swallow it down, hot, heavy tears pushed out instead.

"Tell me everything you said to him."

40

I DON'T KNOW how much time passed before we heard from Adam Venit at CAA, but he seemed genuinely confused by Leo's sudden issues with Don's Plum. RD told him what he could, and Adam suggested we sit tight until things blow over.

Tobey arranged for a meeting between the friends at Kevin Connolly's house for 9:00 that night.

The knives in my guts turned and twisted.

RD worked the phone for the rest of the day. He talked to all the guys except Leo. He called his mom, Ken Hardy, Jerry Meadors, and others. RD acted like he wasn't a part of what had happened, that the whole conflict was between me and Tobey.

I left RD to his work and collapsed onto my bed lifelessly. I couldn't sleep even though I desperately needed to. I just laid there looking up at the ceiling while the previous night played over and over again in my mind. When it was time to leave, RD called up to me from downstairs and told me to meet him in the car. Dread consumed me.

I COULDN'T SIT STILL in the passenger seat. I rocked, twitched, chewed my nails, and cracked my knuckles until they ached. I felt like I had to piss, even though I had just gone before we left. A migraine twisted up behind my eye, and the pain ran all the way down my neck into my shoulders.

We arrived at Kevin's house on time. My heart raced as we approached the door. Kevin greeted us tentatively at first, but soon after everything felt familiar again, and I took that as a good sign.

Kevin chuckled awkwardly. "What the fuck, you guys?"

"Your guess is as good as mine, bro," said RD.

Kevin looked at me. "What happened, Wheatley? You look like you haven't slept in a month."

"I don't know, man—Tobey lost his shit, completely. I'm so fucking confused right now."

"Well, come in. Ethan's already here."

He led us through the kitchen to his screened sunroom where Ethan and Nikki were hanging out together. Ethan got up and hugged us both, but his hug felt loose and empty, like a Hollywood hug. RD and I sat next to each other on a couple of kitchen chairs Kevin had already put there for us. Ethan sat on a bench at the make-shift tiki bar. Kevin joined Nikki on a loveseat.

Ethan took out a cigarette and lit it up. "What the hell, Dale?"

I sighed, "I don't know. I honestly don't. I mean, you saw Tobey at our place, freaking out over nothing. I don't know where it's all coming from."

Ethan nodded, took a big drag of his cigarette and blew smoke rings into the middle of the room.

"Did you talk to Tobey?" I asked.

"Yeah, obviously. And it sounds bad. I'm not going to lie."

"Yeah, but—"

Kevin interrupted. "Look, it's a free country or whatever, but maybe we should wait until everyone gets here before we start talking about this stuff."

The room fell awkwardly silent.

"So, Kevin and Nikki, how was your day?" Ethan smiled wryly, and the three of them laughed like it was an inside joke.

The doorbell rang and I was immediately paralyzed by the fear of seeing Leo or Tobey, but it was Scott Bloom who stepped in the room. His ice-cold eyes bounced back and forth from RD to me. "What's up, guys?"

"Yo," I said.

"What's up, bro," said RD.

"I'd say it's good to see you, but under the circumstances, maybe not so much."

The room fell silent again while we waited for Leo and Tobey. The fear was agonizing. I wanted to get out of there so bad. I think if there was an open window I would have jumped through it.

The doorbell rang and fear ripped through me again. Leo entered with Kristen Zang on his arm. He flicked a contemptuous look our way. "What's up, fellas," he said.

"What's up," I said. I could barely recognize my own voice from the trembling.

"What's up, Leo," said RD.

"Let's wait for Tobey before we start talking about all this nonsense..."

Nonsense, Leo! That's exactly what this is.

"Nikki, why don't you and Kristen go hang in the kitchen or whatever," said Kevin. "So we can talk."

After the girls left, the stillness was fucking dreadful. There was something terrifying about it, like the calm before a deadly storm.

The final doorbell rang and all my anxiety symptoms kicked in at once; sweaty palms, fluttering heart, gulping and swallowing air. I took a sip of water, but my stomach had soured and it left me nauseous.

Tobey walked into the room carrying his keys, wallet, and a bottle of water. He greeted everyone, including RD and me. I managed a nod in his direction, but I couldn't say anything to him.

Tobey perched himself on the edge of a wicker chair and began the meeting immediately. "OK, so I wanted to get us all together to talk about this conversation I had with Dale—Dale and RD really, but it was Dale who was finally honest with me, and he said some pretty troubling things. I thought we needed to come together as friends and get it all out in the open for one, and also talk about what to do about it. I think this probably changes things and so yeah... that's why we're here."

Leo clenched his jaw before speaking. "I wanna hear what you two have to say. Tobey told me some of what you said, Dale, and it's pretty shocking, to say the least. I want to hear everything from you guys directly before we continue."

"Can I go first?" said RD.

"Go right ahead," said Leo.

"OK, well..." RD adjusted in his seat. "I don't know what's been said, but I just can't believe it's come to this. We set out to make a movie together, you know? As friends. And that's what we did, so this is all a fuckin' shock to me. But if we said or did anything that hurt you, or made you angry, or anything at all, then I'm sorry for that. If you think I did anything wrong personally, you know, I don't think I did—it wasn't my intention to do anything wrong. We set out to make the best movie we could, like we all said we wanted to do. It's something we've all wanted to do for a long time."

Tobey hissed. "RD, stop trying to manipulate us, OK."

"What do mean, Tobey?" RD's eyes got big and teary. "You guys are my best friends."

Tobey played a mini violin and the others laughed. "You're avoiding the fucking question, for a change. Dale already told me everything—stop with this facade. It's embarrassing."

"First of all, there was no question. And I don't give a fuck what Dale told you—"

Tobey bared his teeth, jumped to his feet, and lunged forward to within inches of RD. "You're fucking lying, RD." Tobey's spittle hit RD's face.

"Get the fuck away from me, Tobey."

"You betrayed your friends and you got caught."

"No, I didn't. Get the fuck out of my face, bro."

Leo stood and pulled Tobey back by the shoulders. "Alright, alright, calm down for a minute."

"YOU BETRAYED YOUR FRIENDS!"

Leo chuckled, "Calm down, bro." He sat Tobey down.

I looked around at the rest of their faces and they were all grinning, like menacing strangers instead of my closest friends. They looked like they were enjoying it.

Leo narrowed his eyes on me. "I want to hear what you have to say."

I collected myself as best I could. "I don't know what Tobey told you, but I'm sure there's a misunderstanding."

Tobey shook his head. "There's no misunderstanding. Don't start backpedaling. Tell Leo what you told me this morning about the press."

"You got it all wrong, Tobey. I'm not—"

"Just tell everyone exactly what you said to me, and they'll decide for themselves what to make of it."

"There's nothing there—there's nothing to talk about."

"Oh really? You wanna play games now, huh? I'll just tell everyone what you said—"

"I'm not playing games. It was just some reactive bullshit said in passing. It didn't mean anything."

"You know that's not true," Ethan shouted.

"What the fuck are you talking about?"

Ethan sneered. "I heard you, Jerry, and RD talking about the gay press."

"What the fuck is that about?" said Leo.

I licked my dry lips. "Jerry said he heard some shit about some writers, gay writers, who didn't like what you had said publicly about homosexuality when you were doing press for Total Eclipse, and he tried to warn you about it. He was trying to be helpful." I pointed at Tobey, "I told you that this morning."

Tobey shrugged, "These guys remember it differently."

"Yeah, that's not how Jerry put it to me," said Scott. "He said the gay press were chomping at the bit to expose Leo for any misstep. He said he knew some of them personally—it sounded more like a threat than a warning to me."

I shook my head, "That's absurd. A threat from Meadors? Why? It was a warning. He was trying to help."

"Dale, tell Leo what you told me at Villard's house before we went to AA this morning."

475

"We said a lot. We were up all night."

"About the Variety article..."

"He said he wanted to have something in the trades for distributors."

"The truth, Dale—"

"That's why Meadors ran the article," said RD. "That is the truth."

"RD, you weren't in the conversation, so shut the fuck up. We can fuck around all night if you want to, I don't care, but the truth is coming out. Dale, if you would rather I tell Leo everything you said to me, I will. But this is your chance to speak for yourself, in your own words. What message were you guys sending with the Variety article?"

I tried to swallow, but my throat was dry and cracked. I looked over at Leo. He had murder in his eyes. He lifted his eyebrows at me. "We weren't sending messages," I said. "Jerry was trying to get the attention of distributors, that's all. I'm sorry if you don't like that answer, but it's the truth. Call Jerry right now and ask him."

Tobey sighed heavily. "I'm going to give you one more opportunity to tell Leo what you told me before I do it myself."

"Just tell the truth," said Scott. "So we can get on with our evening."

Ethan yawned and stretched. "Yeah, I got other shit to do tonight."

"Why are you even here?" I said. "This isn't even any of your business."

"Because I'm on the side of right," said Ethan.

Tobey shook his head and turned to Leo, "OK, well, Dale told me that they had private meetings—him, RD, Jerry, and—"

I interrupted him. "No, no, don't... Context matters. It was five in the morning, and you kept asking me over and over again what was the worst thing that happened while we worked on the film, and I kept telling you there was nothing—"

"Which was a lie—"

"And you wouldn't fucking believe me. It was true. There was

476

nothing. There is still nothing, Tobey, but you would not fucking stop—you will not stop."

"Dale..."

"No, these are my fucking words." I turned my attention to Leo. "Tobey was asking what the worst thing any one of us did, you know regarding Don's Plum, and he would not relent so I told him that there were times when we were afraid that you might not approve of the film even though we made a good movie, even though we succeeded, and I said that I thought if you tried to stop a perfectly good film that you would look bad for doing it."

Tobey clenched his jaw. "What else?"

"And I told him that I still believed that to be true..."

"Dale—I swear to fucking god."

"That was the worst thing I ever said or did, Tobey."

"You fucking told me that you guys were planning to pit the press against Leo if he didn't go along with Don's Plum."

Leo cocked his head. "Oh really?"

"I did not say that. That never fuckin' happened."

Tobey continued, "And that the Variety article was a message to Leo..."

"I never said that—"

"It was a message from Jerry that if Leo decides to shelve the film, that you guys have a voice in the press—"

"Not true—"

"You said you HATE LEO!"

"That is a lie!"

Tobey jumped to his feet again, screaming, "You're the fuckin' liar, Dale!"

"What did you say, then?" Leo spoke with such hateful eyes. "Tobey sit down. I want to hear what he as to say." Tobey sat and Leo continued. "If Tobey's lying, then tell me what you said to him."

I swallowed as much fear as I could, "I've never said I hated you in my life. Before the screening you were so furious and it stressed us out so bad. I can't even describe it. We had worked so hard—you saw the movie, Leo. We thought you might kill Don's

Plum even though it's good. You sounded that mad over the stupid fucking Variety article that means nothing... And we told Jerry how mad you were, and RD said you might stop Don's Plum over it, and Leo—Jerry probably won't even remember saying any of this... it was so not a big deal. I only told Tobey this happened to appease him because he was being so brutal and I thought it—"

"I wasn't doing anything," said Tobey. "Do you want me to just tell him? Because you can't seem to get it out."

I let out a big breath because I knew this was as good as holding a loaded gun to my head and pulling the trigger. "We were just reacting to your message—it was so fucking upsetting—"

Tobey hissed. "Dale—"

"And Jerry was ranting, and he said if you were gonna be a dick about the stupid article, at least we had a voice in the press or something like that."

Leo grinned menacingly. "He said what? A voice in the press?"

"It was like saying you're gonna kick someone's ass for double dipping their chips. It was nothing. It was just a bad reaction in a stressful situation."

"You guys wanna go to war with me? Are you that fucking stupid?"

RD held up his hands. "No, no, bro—"

"We're all friends," I said. "Jerry's our friend, it was nothing like that—"

Leo stood and pointed at us. "You fuckers want to go to war with me?'

"No, Leo," I said. "Please. We're your friends, that's fuckin' crazy."

"Do you really think you can fuck with me? You think you can damage me in the press?! Are you CRAZY?"

"No one was fucking with you," said RD.

"YOU WANNA FUCK WITH ME? I'M BRAVEHEART, MOTHERFUCKER. I WILL CHOP FUCKING HEADS!! DO YOU HEAR ME?"

I was hunched over my knees, avoiding his eyes.

"YOU THINK YOU CAN PIT THE PRESS AGAINST ME? MY FUCKING AGENTS OWN THIS TOWN. CAA RUNS THIS FUCKING TOWN. THEY DECIDE WHO GETS INTO THE FESTIVALS. I'M IN A TWO-HUNDRED MILLION DOLLAR MOVIE RIGHT NOW. YOU THINK YOU CAN FUCK WITH ME?!"

"Leo, I swear—none of this is true."

Ethan sprang to his feet and joined in the shouting. "LIAR! TELL THE TRUTH, DALE."

"I've never lied to any of you."

Ethan grinned, "You just lied right there. You're a fuckin' lyin' commi-bastard."

They berated us for the next hour, screaming in our faces, calling us liars, cheaters, and opportunists. RD and I tried to defend ourselves whenever we could get a word in, but they just laughed at us.

"What I'm worried about," said Tobey, "are the repreated denials. Like, how can we ever trust you guys again?"

"We can't," said Scott.

RD and I didn't respond.

"Relationships can heal," said Tobey. "But you gotta take responsibility."

"For what?" said RD.

"We've been friends for what? Six years? How can you just lie to my face like this?

Kevin shook his head and pointed at RD, "I've been friends with that fuckin' guy for more than ten years, and all I can say is I did not see this coming."

"Twelve years for us," said Scott. "It's sad."

RD nodded, "Yeah, you guys are my best friends. I would never fuck any of you over."

Tobey raised his voice, "You got carried away with thoughts of success, RD. GREED! You saw an opportunity and you reached for the stars. Maybe you didn't intend to do it at first, I personally don't believe you did, but you saw the opportunity to be this big direc-tor, and you stepped all over your friends to get it, regardless of the price. You didn't care about the consequences. You just wanted to win. You're a success monger, RD."

RD shook his head and shrugged again. "We made this movie for all of us."

Tobey sighed. "You were reaching for the stars, RD. We all witnessed it. Leo told you and Dale both that Don's Plum would never be a feature film and you didn't listen. You refused to accept reality. You didn't care about who might get hurt along the way. You didn't care about who might get ripped off. You only thought about yourselves and what you were getting out of this situation."

RD chuckled. "You should really see the movie, Tobey"

"You manipulated your friends, RD! You fuckin' reached for the stars and you stepped on your friends—you used us, your closest friends, to get ahead. You're no better than a whore. You're a prostitute. Both of you. You threw away your friendships with all of us for cheap success. I can't figure out what hurts more, your lies, or your bold-faced denial. Do you think we're stupid?"

RD threw up his hand. "I'm not going to admit to something I didn't do."

"YOU'RE A TWO-FACED LIAR, RD." Bloated veins welted up on Tobey's neck.

"You need to calm down, bro," said RD.

"Be a man and admit you stepped on you friends. You were reaching for the stars and you didn't care who you hurt, or who you had to fuck over."

RD shook his head slowly. "That's not true."

"Just admit the things you did wrong," said Scott. "Get it off your shoulders."

Tobey nodded. "That's what's so frustrating for me. We can help you out if you're in trouble with the investors, or with Jerry Meadors—whatever. We can support you guys, we're still your friends, but you have to admit what you did before we can start making this right again."

"That's common sense," said Ethan.

A small, exacerbated laugh escaped RD. "But we don't need your help, we didn't do anything wrong."

Tobey lost it. "STOP FUCKING LYING."

"I'm not lying, Tobey. You're the one who has to stop."

"Admit it, RD."

"Admit what?"

"You're so fucking hopeless. God, I'm so disappointed in you, RD."

"Why? What the fuck did I do to you, bro!"

"ADMIT THE FUCKING TRUTH, RD."

"I DID!"

"You and Dale have done nothing but lie and lie, again and again... We just want the truth."

"I TOLD YOU EVERYTHING I KNOW, TOBEY."

"YOU HAVEN'T ADMITTED THAT YOU STEPPED ON YOUR FRIENDS WHEN YOU REACHED FOR THE STARS."

"ALL RIGHT, FINE! I WAS REACHING FOR THE FUCKING STARS, TOBEY, OK? I STEPPED ON MY FRIENDS. ARE YOU HAPPY NOW?"

Tobey's face lost most of its tension. A smile appeared. "Thank you for telling the truth, RD. I can understand why it's upsetting to admit."

"You don't give a fuck about the truth," I said.

"You know, Dale, I'm really—I'm most ashamed of you, I think. You were very honest with me when we were alone, but all you've been doing tonight is lying and backpedaling."

"I haven't lied once."

"It's over, Dale. You guys got caught. Stop."

Scott shook his head and laughed. "It's over."

RD and I sat there like rejects, both of our heads hung in defeat.

"I almost feel sorry for you guys," said Leo.

Kevin chuckled, "Almost."

I looked up at Leo, and our eyes met.

He snarled. "Don't fuckin' look at me, you tree-hugging Canadian piece of shit."

I looked away.

"What about you, Kevin?" said Leo. "You haven't said much."

"I think I've said plenty." Kevin shook his head and frowned, "It's a damn shame. You guys made a good movie. I can't believe it came to this."

"My agents said Don's Plum would be fine for me, like a 'Welcome to the Dollhouse' kind of thing. If I do this, I'm doing it for him." Leo indicated Kevin. "But you two? I don't want you guys to get anything from this movie. You've already gotten too much."

There was a long dead silence that Kevin broke by throwing our own words from Don's Plum in our faces. "Who knows," he said. "Maybe in ten years we'll all look back at this and laugh."

It was such a vile thing for him to do. They had to destroy everything, even the memory. That moment in Don's Plum was about getting past our petty grievances and embracing the life we had ahead of us, together.

"I'm laughing right now," Tobey said with a heartless grin.

Leo guffawed and he and Tobey high five'd. Then Leo looked back at me and RD, disgusted by the sight of us. "You guys need to get out of here. I don't want to look at your faces anymore. I don't want to feel sorry for you—you're pathetic. We're done here. You can leave."

41

THE NEXT MORNING, Adam Venit called Jerry Meadors and asked us to meet at his office at CAA. Jerry picked RD and me up at the apartment and we headed to Beverly Hills in Jerry's truck.

"What the hell did you tell him, Dale?" said Jerry.

I was drained and didn't want to explain it all over again, but I wanted Jerry to hear it from me first. "I was trying to help," I said as new tears flooded my eyes. "I was trying to calm him down..."

"He was calm when I went to bed," said RD.

"No, he wasn't, RD."

"All you had to do was kick him out and go to fucking bed yourself and we wouldn't be in this situation."

"You can try to convince yourself that's true, but it's not. Tobey was on a mission. He was fucking screaming in our faces that he wanted Don's Plum to burn long before you went to bed, have you forgotten that?"

Jerry's eyes widened. "He said that?"

I nodded. "Yes. Screamed it like a fuckin' crazy person."

"This was before your one-on-one with him?"

"Yes. That's why I stayed with him in the first place. He said he wanted to destroy Don's Plum and I was trying to stop him."

"Is that true, RD?"

"Yes, but by the time I went to bed he was much calmer. Then Dale told him all this fuckin' shit."

"What did you say, Dale?"

"He kept wanting me to tell him the worst thing that happened... the worst thing I saw or heard, or whatever. I kept telling him there was nothing and he started calling me a liar. I was like, fuck you, and then he got into the whole Variety article thing, and I don't know... I wanted to just fucking calm him down and so I told him—and keep in mind that I hadn't slept, so I was practically delusional at that point..."

"Why were you up all night?"

"We were going to AA and we decided to stay up until the meeting."

"Why were you going to AA? You're not an alcoholic."

"I know, I know, I told him that."

"When is the last time you slept?"

"Yesterday... the day before yesterday."

"Oh my God, Dale. Then what happened?"

"I told him that when Leo was freaking out about the article, we were super fucking distressed and, you know, we were arguing back and forth."

"The three of us?"

"Yes. Then he started drilling me about Variety, and I said that RD and I were afraid that Leo was just going to reject Don's Plum because of the article, and that got you upset and you said, in reaction, that if Leo was going to be unreasonable at least he knows we have a voice in the press. Something like that."

"What?"

"I told him it was nonsense, Jerry."

"What the hell were you thinking?"

"I... he convinced me that I was lying by keeping things from him... that it was impossible nothing bad had happened through the course of Don's Plum."

"I don't recall saying we had a voice in the press. I used those words?"

"You did. You clearly didn't mean it—you weren't threatening him, you were just reacting to him and I told Tobey all of that."

"RD, do you recall me saying we had a voice in the press?"

"Yeah, it was something like that—but why the fuck would you tell Tobey? It makes no sense."

"I told you why, I thought it would calm him down."

"How would that calm him down, Dale?" Jerry was rightfully confused.

"I know it sounds crazy. He wanted Don's Plum to burn, and I felt like he needed to know I was being forthright with him. He said that. I told him you weren't serious. I repeated it over and over again. He kept accusing us of being secretive, saying shit like, we've been holding things back and having secret meetings... I thought he could tell I was thinking about it."

"Thinking about what?"

"That you said we had a voice in the press... when he said there had to be something bad that one of us said or did, that moment came to mind, Jerry. I'm sorry it did, but it did." I sighed and tears pushed up again.

"But, Dale, I would never do anything to harm a soul. I was obviously just reacting."

"I told him that, Jerry. I told him that so many times. I don't know what I was thinking... I don't know. I was so tired—it was five in the fucking morning. He wouldn't stop, and I was afraid that he was going to do something bad. Fuck. I was nodding off and he kept waking me up. I'm so sorry, Jerry. I can't believe this happened."

"Well, you were delirious!"

"I was sure that I could help him somehow, and I thought if I said something 'bad' that had happened, he would know I was honest and end his fucking tirade. And it was all fluff, Jerry, everyone fucking loves you, including Tobey. I didn't think for a second he or anyone would believe you would threaten anyone."

"I have no memory of this, but why would you lie about something like that?" Jerry let out an exhausted sigh. "I'm just trying to

485

produce a fucking movie and take it to market. What is wrong with you people?"

We arrived at CAA and Jerry pulled up to a loading zone. "Dale, I think it's best if you wait in the car. Maybe you could park the truck?"

"Why?"

"Because you're a mess. Look at you. You haven't bathed, your eyes are swollen, and, quite frankly, I don't know what you might say at this point."

I shook my head. "That's ridiculous."

"Yeah, bro," said RD. "I don't think you should come up either."

I had no fight left. "Whatever you say."

After they jumped out, I slid behind the wheel, put Jerry's truck in drive, and pulled away from the curb. I spent the next 40 minutes driving in a circle around the agency with my sanity dangling by a thread. With every turn I made, I replayed the night in my head, shouting at myself like a madman. "Why did you tell Tobey what Meadors said, you dumb fuck? WHY?" *Because he questioned your honesty. You wanted him to know he could trust you.* "You're such a fucking idiot!" *It was the right thing to do.* "You should have kept your mouth shut. You've ruined everything!" I slammed my fist into the dashboard. Hot tears ran down my cheeks. I wiped them away and turned the truck back onto Santa Monica, pulling around to the front of the agency.

Jerry and RD were waiting there for me. I pulled over and slid to the middle of the bench. They each got in the truck, and we were off again.

"Well, that went better than expected," Jerry said brightly. "Wouldn't you agree, RD?"

RD shrugged, "Yeah, I guess."

"What did they say?"

"It was just Adam Venit, and he believes Leo will come around," said Jerry. "He thinks this is nothing more than a spat among friends that will surely blow over, and I agree with him completely."

"Did he talk to Leo?"

"He has."

"Did he say what they said?"

"Just that Leo's still quite mad, but that he, Adam Venit, doesn't think it will last." Jerry grabbed my knee and shook it. "It's going to be OK, Wheatley. Adam told us to keep shopping the film. They're still on board." Jerry smiled. "Your friends will get over it."

Tears welled in my eyes. I wanted to believe Adam and Jerry, but I knew better. They crossed the line at Kevin's house. They destroyed us that night, and there was no turning back from that.

"Cheer up, you two. Everything's going to be fine! Let's get an early lunch, my treat."

WITHIN DAYS, our world fell around us like dominoes. RD heard back from Matt Berenson at Jersey Films, and they withdrew their multi-picture offer. Matt had met with Tobey and Tobey told him that the rift between us was major and that we had fucked over Leonardo DiCaprio. Matt said they couldn't afford to get in the middle of a dispute with Leonardo. CAA dropped RD faster than they signed him. Robbie Little, CEO of First Look Pictures, got a call from CAA agent Manny Nunez, who told him that CAA no longer represented Don's Plum and that Leo has not agreed to release the movie. David Stutman received a letter from Steve Warren informing him that we did not have any rights to Leo's likeness, and that he would oppose the release of Don's Plum. We lost CAA, Sundance, First Look, and TriMark, all in the same week.

We were shunned socially. Leo, Tobey, Kevin, Scott, and Ethan all drew a proverbial line in the sand, and our mutual friends were forced to choose a sidea. We lost nearly every friend we had, practically overnight.

In less than a week, it was all gone. We had no friends, no film, and no future.

. . .

RD and I were sitting on the porch at the mansion, staring out at nothing. We had just finished what would be our last meeting with our post-production crew. The looks on everyone's faces when we told them what had happened was heartbreaking.

My voice trembled as I spoke. "I don't know how, or when but the truth will come out one day, RD. And so will Don's Plum—"

"Why would they do this to us?" RD's voice cracked and tears formed and fell heavy from his eyes. "What did I do wrong?"

"Nothing. You didn't do anything."

"Why, then? They were our best friends."

I sobbed and shook my head, "I'm so sorry, RD."

PART IV

42

It was like a bomb went off right next to me and everything but my physical body had been totally obliterated. From one week to the next, my life had become unrecognizable and I would never be the same again.

When I arrived in Hollywood in the summer of '94 I was a wide-eyed dreamer who wanted the same thing as everyone else. I wanted to become a star. I wanted to be an accomplished artist. I wanted to create something that would be revered and remembered. I wanted to inspire people as much as others had inspired me. I wanted to buy my mom and dad a house. I wanted to fix my teeth. I wanted a life and a body of work that could at least attempt to represent the intense love I had for the movies and for the creative process.

Jeremy Sisto warned me on day one that there were destructive people in our midst, and I didn't heed a word of it. I thought I could avoid all that nonsense because I had just spent three years studying the work of Anthony Robbins and among the many skills I learned was the ability to unite people and bring out the very best in them. All I needed were enthusiastic, creative people with a common goal, and we could accomplish anything. I believed in the good in everyone, ignoring all their bad parts, and it came back to bite me in the ass. I believed in abundance. I thrived knowing there was enough in the world for everyone. It eliminated any envy in me. I knew mine would come eventually, so I never had to compete with anyone other than myself. I put all my trust and work into collaboration and reciprocity. I believe dreams come true to those with the audacity to fulfill them, and deliberately destroying or tampering with someone else's dream is nothing short of vile and likely sociopathic.

RD's WORDS kept ringing in my head. *"Why'd they do this to us? They were our best friends."* The whole scenario felt like an altered reality, like they had all suffered from a momentary lapse of reason. I suppose that's why I was still slightly optimistic after leaving Kevin Connolly's house on that dreadful night. Leo said that if he were to "do this thing," meaning not interfere with Don's Plum, he would be doing it for Kevin's sake. It was a pretty insensitive thing to say with Scott sitting right there, but it meant that Leo knew exactly what he was doing, or what he was about to do. He knew that destroying Don's Plum meant destroying Kevin's best work as an actor. It meant destroying Kevin's first and only chance to be a lead in a Sundance film, something that could have launched his career into feature films, which was his dream. What kind of person would do such a thing to a fellow actor, let alone their best friend, just to punish somebody else? I think it's reasonable to believe that if Leo thought about Kevin, then he also thought about others as well, like Scott, and Jenny. I would have never imagined Leonardo DiCaprio, the guy I knew and loved, could be someone capable of willfully destroying the work of other artists, but that's what he did. And he still is.

LEO AND TOBEY weren't happy with destroying our work. They needed to destroy our lives too. There were ridiculous attempts at intimidation. We got a voice message from Leo in a not-so-disguised voice, comparing RD Robb, a Jew, to Adolf Hitler. I heard that a couple of strange men showed up at our head of wardrobe's house and confiscated the Polaroid photograph she took of Tobey exposing himself on set. We had stored the rest of our set photography at Henry Daes house, and we were told there was a fire that had destroyed all of it. There are conflicting stories about whether a fire actually happened, but all our photography went missing, and no one has an explanation for it. David Stutman arrived home one afternoon to discover a decapitated teddy bear on his doorstep, which he perceived as a threat to his dog. RD came out of an audition and found his tires had been slashed.

RD and I were made into an example of what would happen if anyone opposed them. In a matter of days, RD and I went from being at the center of a huge tight-knit network of friends, connected to nearly every corner of Hollywood, to being almost completely ostracized, and everyone just watched as it happened. We were abandoned by our friends and blacklisted in the industry, and it happened in the blink of an eye. And they chose to inflict all this damage after just one single night. Not one of them even attempted to investigate Tobey's outrageous claims. They refused to speak with us ever again, creating a wall of protection around Tobey's lies. Their first and only option was merciless annihilation.

RD and his mother blamed me for everything. They said if I hadn't gone with Tobey to Bob Villard's house that night, none of this would have happened, and Don's Plum would have become a Miramax film, conveniently forgetting that Tobey showed up at our place literally screaming that he wanted Don's Plum to burn.

Jerry thought the hatred had to come from somewhere very deep to justify their actions. He suggest their problem was with RD. There was a long history there and maybe something had been festering a long time, but that didn't ring true for me either. The more I thought about everything that happened, the more I saw a smoke screen.

It wouldn't have taken much effort to dig a little deeper to find massive holes in Tobey's story. Tobey said I confessed to him that RD, Jerry, and I plotted to "pit the press" against Leo if Leo didn't go along with the film. He lied. Leo and his reps had already

493

agreed to move forward with Don's Plum and were actively participating in negotiations to sell the movie on our behalf. I had nothing to gain by confessing to deceit, and everything to lose. I may not be the smartest guy in the room, but I'm not going to reveal an active plot against Leonardo DiCaprio to his best friend, especially when the plot doesn't serve any person. We already had Leo's approval. Tobey's accusation was stupid and it's embarrassing that anyone believed him.

Another obvious problem with Tobey's story is that I had allegedly confessed to a plot that was masterminded by Jerry Meadors, but Tobey didn't seem to have any problem with Jerry Meadors after my confession. Jerry's supposed scheme was so evil that Leo and Tobey lost their minds over it and refused to ever speak to me or RD ever again, but just a couple of weeks after the accusations, Tobey invited Jerry to a lovely lunch in Beverly Hills. That lunch all but confirmed Jerry's theory that, for Tobey at least, there was a mysterious hatred for RD. Tobey said to Jerry, in all sincerity, that if he had the money and connections to the mob, he would have RD Robb killed. In Tobey's version of the story, he "may have been joking" about wishing he had connections to the mob so he could have old friend murdered.

If there was hatred for RD, I don't know where it came from. They trusted him enough to direct them in a movie that was intended to be sold to a distributor like Showtime, that's something everyone including Leo has acknowledged. Tobey's hatred was fierce, but it had no obvious cause. I could think of only two possibilities. Either Tobey wanted to destroy our lives and suppress the careers of some of his best friends for purely egomaniacal reasons, or he needed to stop Don's Plum because it interfered with a sudden change in his career path, and he didn't care if lives had to be destroyed to make it happen. They were both plausible, but the latter seemed more likely to me.

IN LATE JULY 1996, we arranged a screening of Don's Plum for Tobey's agents at The Gersh Agency in the hopes that they would talk some sense into him. When the film ended, legendary agent and founder, Phil Gersh, gave Don's Plum a standing ovation and he shouted fervently, "Avant-garde! Avant-garde!" Phil Gersh was right, if Don's Plum is anything, it's avant-garde. Tobey didn't budge, though. His hatred for all things Don's Plum seemed to be growing.

WEEKS WENT by and the only one of our friends willing to stay in touch was Kevin Connolly. I was pretty sure he was coming around to gather intel and report it back to Leo and Tobey. He was always asking questions about what David Stutman was up to, about whether he was going to sue Leo, but we never told him anything. Occasionally, the conversation would turn to the loss of our friendships and the unfortunate fate of Don's Plum. Kevin was justifiably upset over losing the best performance of his career. He told me that having a role like Jeremy in a feature film was a dream he'd had since childhood, but he said he didn't want a feature film career that was "checkered." He never explained what checkered meant, but he stood by it like some unshakable virtue. Kevin would eventually participate fully and freely in the destruction of the best work of his life. It was as if he had completely forgotten that Leo and his agents had already approved Don's Plum, that Leo had done "a complete 180" after the MGM screening, that Don's Plum was verbally accepted into Sundance, and would be released in theaters. Miramax and three other distributors had offers on the table. Everyone was on board until Tobey created a giant fucking mess out of nothing. Kevin Connolly's most valuable work was stolen from him, and he held open the door for the thieves.

43

DON'S PLUM was invited to screen at a groovy Sundance spin-off called Slumdance. RD and I met with the creator, Brian Flemming, and he pitched the event as: indie film festival meets a slumber party. We both loved it and accepted his invitation. The festival had no money so RD and I would have to get to Park City on our own dime.

We managed to raise just enough money for our plane tickets to Utah and $20 a day for food. Neither of us anticipated that getting to Park City from the Salt Lake City airport was such an expensive pain in the ass. We had exactly $20 a day for food for the both of us, and bus tickets were $20 each, one-way. We couldn't possibly afford two days' of food just to get up the mountain, so I found some cardboard and scribbled a sign that said:

NEED RIDE
MOVIE'S IN MY BAG
DREAM IS IN PARK CITY

We were picked up almost immediately by an agent for William Morris in her rental. She was surprised when she figured out who we were. She had heard all about our story from multiple people at the agency and had been meaning to watch the bootleg. We got to dispel some of the rumors, like the one saying that Leo stopped Don's Plum because it contained gay sex scenes between him and Tobey.

The agent dropped us off in front of the abandoned Mrs. Field's cookie factory that Brian Flemming had rented to serve as the festival's venue. It was a great location right on the strip in Park City. They threw up a bunch of tents in the main area of the space and converted them into little individual screening rooms with TVs, VCRs, and a stack of short movies. Each tent had its own selection of films curated by the festival, a couple sleeping bags, and loads of pillows and cushions. It was cozy. One of the highlights of the festival for me was spending an entire night hopping tents with Tim Robbins and watching every short film in the program.

Tobey Maguire was also in Park City, probably promoting *The Ice Storm*, and when he found out Don's Plum was screening on the strip, he got right back on his warpath. I heard he came stomping into the cookie factory and demanded to see the person in charge. He accused Brian Flemming of engaging in "illegal screenings" of Don's Plum and threatened legal action if they continued. It was an absurd claim, and Brain pretty much laughed in his face and told him to beat it. I was told Tobey left in quite a huff.

A couple of nights later, Tobey ran into Joel Michaely at a crowded Sundance event at The Yarrow Hotel that was packed with Hollywood players. Tobey knew Joel was in Park City supporting Don's Plum and he went totally berserk when he saw him at the party. He stormed up to Joel and screamed obscenities inches from Joel's face for supporting us and Don's Plum. It was a vicious verbal assault witnessed by dozens of influential people in the business. The encounter was so stressful that Joel ended up in the emergency room with hemorrhaging in one eye.

When we caught up with Joel, he was wearing an eye patch that he had to keep on for the remainder of the festival. He was humiliated, and Tobey had completely ruined his trip for no reason. RD's mom would later speak with Hollywood agent Phil Raskind of the Endeavor Agency, who, after declining to meet or represent RD, said that a lot of people, himself included, witnessed what Tobey had done to "that poor man" at the Yarrow, describing Tobey's behavior as psychotic and too much of a threat to risk getting involved with RD.

Slumdance became the talk of Park City. Robert Redford spoke out against it and called for an end to all the "leech festivals." All that did was bring more attention to Slumdance. The place was constantly packed and visited by celebrities like John Cusack and Martha Plimpton. My jaw dropped when John Waters walked through the door on the last day of festival. He was being honored at Sundance for *Pink Flamingos,* and he sauntered into the cookie factory with an entourage of servants that included a professional photographer and a dude holding a bounce board. Don's Plum just happened to be up on the big screen being tested for a showing later that night. The entourage stopped for photos and John Waters struck a few poses before he finally caught sight of Don's Plum out of the corner of his eye. He turned to it slowly, pointed his finger, and said with a snarl, "What the hell is that?" Brian Flemming told him it was Don's Plum, one of the films in the festival, and John Waters waved his hand at it dismissively. "Get it off. I don't want my picture taken with a movie I haven't seen." But it was already too late, the photos had already been taken, and somewhere in some photographer's archive, a picture of a smiling John Waters with Don's Plum lit up behind him exists, and every time I think of it, it makes me smile from ear to ear.

Don's Plum closed Slumdance to a full house. The standing room only crowd howled with laughter, and then fell deep into the drama right on cue, from beginning to end. When the credits started to roll, the room erupted in cheers and applause. RD was beaming. I was beaming. It felt so good to enjoy Don's Plum again.

Afterward, I was approached by a young stoner dude who had been eyeing me from across the room. He went on about how Don's Plum affected him and how the film articulated perfectly what he and his friends were going through. He couldn't look me in the eye for long when he spoke. His reaction was so profound and heartfelt, I almost forgot he was talking about something I had made. He said he wanted to give me a gift, and he unfolded his hand to reveal a fat, sticky nugget of marijuana. It was stunning, with glistening crystals and thick red hairs. He presented it to me like it was a medal of honor and said a few more beautiful things about Don's Plum and why it meant so much to him. I was flattered but I couldn't take the guy's nuggets. He wouldn't let me refuse though, so I insisted we smoke it together. We sat in Slumdance's game room playing "Operation" and got totally fucked up on his stinky weed. We exchanged funny stories about our friends and, during the whole time, we never once spoke about the controversy. It was the perfect ending to a bittersweet festival.

44

DAVID STUTMAN TRIED for months to convince Leo to cooperate and settle our issues amicably, but all Leo did was drag David along with empty promises of reconciliation to avoid legal action. What Leo didn't know was that David couldn't find an attorney willing to work on contingency, so he wasn't going to get sued anyway. There wasn't enough money involved.

We went into limbo.

RD Robb started dating Amy Israel from Miramax, so I saw less and less of him as their relationship grew more serious. He would often fly to New York and stay there for weeks. The stillness in my life was debilitating. I was lonely, but I was also horrible company. I couldn't hold down a conversation most of the time because my mind was in chaos. My writing turned so dark that it made me feel even worse. I wanted answers, I needed them desperately, but I knew they would never come because it would mean that Leo and Tobey, and Scott, Kevin, and Ethan would have to admit their cruelty.

AMY HADN'T GIVEN up on acquiring Don's Plum. She said Harvey Weinstein still wanted it and believed he could work it out with Leo. I clung to every word of it, even though I knew in my bones there was no coming back from what they had done. But if there was one person that could persuade Leo, it would have been Harvey Weinstein. He and Leo were close, and Harvey had the one thing Leo wanted most of all: money. Lots of money.

Amy remained supportive. She even flew us both to New York and set us up with loads of meetings with some of the most important people in the New York indie film scene like John Sloss, Ted Hope, and a few other badass filmmakers. The meetings were cool, but we were damaged goods and I felt it in the rooms. We didn't have a good story. "*Hey, yeah, nice to meet you too. Yeah, we made a pretty cool film but our friends, well, our former friends, accused us of betraying them and so now they hate us and are actively trying to destroy our careers and the film we made together. What's going on with your work?*"

The meetings might have been uncomfortable, but I still loved New York City. I'll never forget walking around in the shadows of those giant buildings, feeling so lost about life, and looking up and seeing a giant comet just kind of hanging in the middle of the sky. It didn't even look like it was moving, but it had a long, thick, blazing tail. I must have stared at it for ten minutes. It was so magnificent framed up in the New York City skyline. I wondered if seeing it meant something, like some kind of major change was on the horizon.

BACK IN LOS ANGELES, I became increasingly reclusive. Running into people I once considered friends was a mostly painful experience for me. I was disgraced and, most of the time, that's how I was treated.

When I did get out, it was to catch a movie or grab a quick bite somewhere, and it was always with RD when he was flying solo, or occasionally with Jeremy Sisto. One night we were hanging out at the Fairfax Theater with Jeremy, Brittany Murphy, and another chick I didn't know but who would not shut up. Anything anyone said, she found a way to make it about her, and blathered on about one mindless thing after another. She was more annoying than a street full of leaf-blowers on a perfect Sunday afternoon. I needed the movie to start so she would stop talking.

We were seeing Lars Von Trier's *Breaking the Waves*, and I had no idea what I was in store for, but it was, by far, the most devastating movie I had ever seen. Never had I fallen more in love with a protagonist only to watch her be so ruthlessly and brutally destroyed. It was agonizing in the most glorious way. And that yapping, self-absorbed, annoying chick who wouldn't shut up before the movie, stumbled out of the theater pale as paper and speechless. It was magnificent. At that very moment, while looking at that pale woman, all my dreams shifted and all I wanted to do was write a movie as profoundly beautiful and capable of rendering someone speechless and physically ill.

AMY INVITED me to tag along with her and RD to Miramax's Oscar party at the Mondrian on Sunset Boulevard. I felt sad and out of place the entire night. I couldn't stop thinking about the guys and what we all might have been doing had our fight never happened. We would have probably been at the party together, celebrating the sale of our movie to Miramax and reminiscing about the premiere of Don's Plum at Sundance. It was so heartbreaking, and all I could do was sooth my sorrows at the open bar.

RD and Amy went their own way and I found myself wandering around, counting the celebrities holding Oscars and eating all the hors d'oeurves I could get my fingers on. I came upon the little kid from the Czechoslovakian movie, *Kolya*. He had fallen asleep while hugging, with both arms, the Oscar they had just won for best foreign language film. I was so moved by the sight of him that it pulled me all the way back to my own childhood and that precious feeling of knowing that any dream can come true.

I lost track of my drink count, but by some miracle woke up in my own bed without incident. The hangover, however, was not so kind.

I was still putting fragments of the night back together when

RD arrived at the condo in a foul mood. He said he and Amy were having a drink at Sky Bar with Salma Hayek, and the place was packed with huge people like Lawrence Bender, Quentin Tarantino, people on that level. Then Leo and Tobey showed up. When Leo saw RD at the bar, he pointed at him and shouted loud enough so everyone could hear, "You see that guy right there? That's RD Robb, he's the guy who fucked me over. Watch out for that guy right there. He fucks over his friends." I could see the humiliation on RD's face as he recounted the experience. Later into the night, at the same Oscar party, he said he and Amy were chatting with Denise Doyle, Harvey Weinstein's personal assistant, and she told them about a conversation she overheard where Leo questioned Harvey about why RD was invited to the Miramax party. She said Leo told Harvey that he shouldn't work with RD, that RD was a liar and betrayer, and that he could not be trusted. She said Harvey responded to Leo by saying he didn't know why RD was there, that he was not invited by Miramax, and that Miramax was not working with RD Robb or Don's Plum. That was how we learned that Miramax had officially passed.

IN THE SUMMER OF '97, I made the trip to San Diego to see my brother, Doug, at Comic-Con. He was making solid strides as an illustrator after releasing *Blade: Vampire Hunter,* and it was nice to see him getting established so well in his industry.

Doug was curious about what was going on with me, and I did my best to explain what I could, but the more I spoke, the more incredible the whole thing sounded. When he asked why Tobey would do the things I had claimed, I didn't have a good answer for him, and I wondered how that made me look to him. I think it was easier for people, maybe even my own brother, to believe that we had made a bad movie and were fucking over a movie star than it was to believe that we were the victims. The worst thing about being a victim is that as soon you try and talk about what happened to you, you sound like a victim and people dismiss your pain as exaggerated or made up. It's a lonely place to live.

I ran into Jay Mewes again while he was hanging out with Kevin Smith at Comic-Con. I lit up when I saw him. I don't know why I thought he wouldn't have been affected by all the bullshit with Don's Plum, I guess I was just delusionally hopeful that someone might choose not to believe the rumors. But Kevin Smith treated me like utter trash, even though he and I had only met a couple of times before, and Jay blew me off like I was a stranger. I asked Jay why he was dissing me, and he shrugged and said he talked to Ethan, and that was all he had to say about it.

45

TITANIC WAS my own personal hell. I couldn't step foot outside without being stricken with debilitating stress. I didn't want to watch TV, listen to the radio, or talk to another living soul because Leo was every-fucking-where. Even the girl I was dating went to see *Titanic* five fucking times because she had to see it with every one of her friends. Leo was on every billboard, on buses, taxis, trains, on the cover of every magazine in every grocery store, corner store, liquor store, every kind of fucking store ever constructed. I wish I could have plucked my eyes from my skull, but even that wouldn't have saved me from "My Heart Will Go On."

David Stutman started getting calls from lawyers. Leo went from being a "that guy" in movies to the biggest star in the world, overnight and, just as quickly, lawyers who had passed on our case were now interested. Among them was arguably the most feared and respected litigator in entertainment, Bert Fields. Bert said he thought Leo and Tobey were in bad shape simply because they appeared in the film, and because Tobey had returned to shoot additional scenes months later fully aware he was in a feature film. Bert seemed quite sure Leo would do the smart thing and settle before the dispute had any chance of becoming reputationally damaging. I wasn't so sure.

I HEARD rumors that Leo was talking about turning me into immigration officials. If that was true, federal agents could have come crashing through my door at any moment and taken me away in cuffs. So my girlfriend and I decided the smartest thing to do was to move up our plans and elope.

We drove to Las Vegas on the eve of Valentine's Day and stood in line at the county registrar with a couple thousand other couples from all over the world to get our marriage license. We were married a little after midnight on Valentine's Day at the Little White Chapel wedding drive-thru. We handed our documents to the pastor through the window, she checked them out, and then had us repeat a few simple vows before pronouncing us married. We leaned over the car's center console and kissed and then, after a quick photo outside the car with the pastor, we were back on the strip for crab legs and a few pulls on the triple diamond machines.

My wedding wasn't a happy occasion for me. Instead of feeling like the luckiest man on earth, I thought more about how it would not have happened were it not for Leo and Tobey. I loved my wife, but we wouldn't have been together had those two men not interfered with my life. I would have been too busy with my new career for any serious relationships.

_____

BERT FIELDS WROTE a scathing complaint against Leo and Tobey, and he filed it with the Superior Court of Los Angeles on April 1, 1998. Leo and Tobey lawyered up and filed a counter lawsuit against David Stutman and named me, RD Robb, and Jerry Meadors as co-defendants.

I couldn't afford an attorney and that left me exposed and vulnerable. Unlike the US criminal system, if someone sues you in America and you can't afford a lawyer, you aren't provided one. You are screwed. I couldn't get a lawyer on contingency because I wouldn't likely earn enough to make it worth their time. One of

Bert Field's junior attorneys suggested in a roundabout way that they could represent me jointly with David Stutman if I were willing to sign a conflict waiver. I had no other choice. It was either sign with them or be eaten by wolves.

RD and I threw ourselves entirely into the lawsuit. We spent hundreds of hours prepping the attorneys for every deponent. We were present for the entire depositions of Leonardo DiCaprio, Tobey Maguire, Scott Bloom, Kevin Connolly, Artie Glackin, Ethan Suplee, and others, and we learned so much from their sworn testimony.

Bizarrely, Leo and his pals settled on the story that we deceptively turned a short film into a feature film. It's impossible to overstate how ridiculous this claim is. If it were true, then we would have achieved the impossible and should have been celebrated as groundbreaking geniuses. A filmmaker can't shoot a 20 or 30-page screenplay, and then magically stretch that material into a feature-length film in post-production, it's just not possible. What does make sense, however, and what is also consistent with industry norms, is that we cut together the film we shot, and it ended up running 85 minutes long. We were always open about the success we were having. On the last day of shooting in July 1995, after Blair told us we had just shot over 100 runtime minutes, I couldn't shut up about it, and Tobey testified to that fact under oath in his deposition when he said he knew he was shooting "something longer than a short." That can only be feature. We were vocal about everything because we had no reason to believe our friends would object to our succeeding together as actors, filmmakers, and friends. Success was always our common goal. I could not have imagined in my worst nightmare that any one of them would willfully destroy the movie we made together, regardless of its length. It remains baffling to this day.

. . .

PRODUCERS from the TV news magazine show *Dateline* reached out to our attorneys to do a story on Don's Plum. They pitched Stone Phillips telling our side of the story through a series of interviews and investigative reporting. I was all for it. The truth was on our side, and Leo had already slandered RD in an interview he did for the November '96 issue of *Detour Magazine*, so if anyone was "pitting the press" against someone, it was Leonardo DiCaprio pitting the press against us.

Meanwhile, our lawyers successfully petitioned the judge to compel Leo's deposition. He had been evading the process for months, but his time had finally run out. The first day of his deposition took place at our attorney's office. There were probably 10 people in the boardroom, including the court reporters. Leo did everything he could to avoid eye contact with me and RD. He looked like shit, like he had been partying much too hard.

Seeing Leo after everything he had done to us filled me with more disappointment than it did anger. He could have been a hero. The story behind Don's Plum should have been about creativity, friendship, and gratitude. Instead, he was sitting across from us with his hand raised, swearing his oath on video, as a defendant.

Leo was combative from the start. He avoided most of our questions with the canned "I don't recall" response most litigators teach their clients when preparing them for their deposition. He wasted our time by pretending not to understand simple establishing questions, or by feigning ignorance about word meanings, or by constantly asking the court reporter to read back questions that had been clearly stated. He was obstructing the process so much, our lawyers threatened to file a motion to compel his testimony.

As we broke for lunch on the first day, I realized there was only one way out of the boardroom. The camera and court reporter were blocking the path on one side of the long table, so the only way out was past Leo's seat, opposite the camera. I waited for Leo to leave, but he didn't move, and I needed to get out of there. I approached him and asked him nicely to let me pass, but he didn't even acknowledge me as I stood right next to him. I asked again and again, and when it became clear he was intentionally ignoring me, I slipped in between him and the table and hip-checked him, the way my buddy Roger Lavoi taught me to back in Winnipeg, right into the drawn blinds behind him. It was loud and instantly chaotic. He cried foul and his lawyers came rushing to his rescue, admonishing me.

"I asked him to move nicely," I said indifferently. "He brought it on himself, just like the rest of this mess."

When we returned from our break, our lawyer asked Leo, while under oath, why he cared whether we were cutting a feature film and Leo's response was probably the only time he gave a full answer to a question. It was almost like a prepared monologue, and beautifully delivered by one of the best actors in the world. Leo was so good I could see the concern growing on our lawyers' faces as he delivered each line.

"Why did I care?" responded Leo sharply. "Because, number one, first and foremost, the agreement had always been that this was a short film. I never had any intention of doing a feature film, whatsoever, and that was the agreement between everybody. Everybody agreed that this was a short film. I also cared because, you know, I'm certainly not going to go in—I mean, it's ridiculous for me to go in for one night, or, you know, uh, a certain number of hours and shoot a feature film, and then rush off to New York. That would be ridiculous. When I do a feature film, I have lots of rehearsal, I have script meetings, it takes weeks and weeks and weeks, and I shoot for months and months, up to six months, up to seven months at a time. I would never go in for one night and improvise with my friends and make a feature film. There's no way I would ever do that. Not only that, I mean, RD is a first-time inexperienced director. He's never directed, as far as I know. This was improvised. I wouldn't do an improvised feature film, completely improvised, especially one that I worked on for one night. I also cared because I felt like, you know, like this was something that came out of thin air. They were just, you know, that they just took it upon themselves to sort of try and edit something that was always intended to be a short into something different. God, there's so many reasons, I mean, it's just, you know, a promise is a promise made among people that something is something, and this was always intended to be a short. You don't just go ahead and decide to try and edit it as something different, which would be a feature. Let me think if there's anything else because I'm sure there is. Why did I care? I felt it was extremely deceptive. It came from left field. As far as any kind of feature film editing process, they kept me in the dark about that idea. You know what I mean? They didn't tell me anything about that, to the best of my recollection, until Mexico City and that was a big shock to me. So, you know, what else can I say... Why did I care? You know, Dale and RD were my friends, and how could they try and change what our word was by editing a feature film? It was a shock to me. This started out as a project that was supposed to be on videotape, I mean, the origins of it was supposed to be a short project on videotape that we would all have fun doing, that we could all use for our, you know, that the other actors could use for their reels to give to casting directors or whoever else. So RD could give it as a director for a short film that he directed—and then it became this much bigger thing as far as, you know, trying to make it into film, which I was, you know, making it into a short film shot on film, which I was stand-offish about and I didn't really respond to very well. And the audacity of them at that point trying to say that it would be a— that they were trying to edit it as a feature film was just ridiculous. I mean, I would never go in for one night and shoot a feature film in less than twelve hours. I mean that it's the most ridiculous thing that I've ever heard in my life, and if they're saying anything differ- ent, I mean, it's just absurd. It's absurdity and they know that. Everyone knows that."

Leo gave a lovely performance but his speech was deceptive. Leo knew damn well, and long before Mexico, that we only cut together the movie we shot. He simply refuses to accept what happened, that we did, in fact, shoot a very good feature film in one weekend. And that wasn't a bad thing, it was an incredibly wonderful thing. Leo also omitted that he watched and loved the full-length movie at MGM. He omitted the screening at CAA that he set up for us, where all his reps unanimously approved Don's Plum as a feature film. If they had said in that meeting that they did not support Don's Plum, we would have accepted that decision, even if we disagreed with it. We knew that was the risk going in. I'm sure we would have tried to change their minds, maybe for the rest of our lives, but RD, Jerry, and I would have kept our word. But none of that was necessary because Leo approved Don's Plum, and we moved forward with his blessing. Our entire dispute was over Leo and his representatives breaking their word, not the other way around.

Leo also took no responsibility for his contributions to the length of the movie. He was probably the single biggest reason why the scenes went so long in the first place. His improvisation was incredible. It was Leo who wanted us to fire Amber Benson, but instead we wrote her departure into the movie, and he loved it. And he was brilliant on the day and, consequently, the movie got longer. Leo lengthened the movie again when he insisted we shoot the scene between him and Jerry Swindall at the very end of day two. These scenes would not exist were it not for Leo's direct influence and involvement. If anyone turned Don's Plum from a short into a feature, it was Leo, and I submit the film and his work in it as my proof.

RD and I did not care how long Don's Plum ended up running. We were thrilled it turned out the way it did but, had Don's Plum turned out to be a great short film, we would have been just as excited. We just wanted to succeed, and we did. We all succeeded together. What kind of person punishes their closest friends for succeeding at the thing they were helping them succeed at in the first place? You don't throw out the work of dozens of awesome artists just because we spilled a little paint on the canvas and it turned out to be cool. That's the majesty of art.

Leo got into trouble in several spots on day two of his testimony. He said that he had never discussed Don's Plum as a feature film with his agent Adam Venit, which was an easily proven lie. CAA literally represented Don's Plum because Leo set us up there.

The problem for Leo was that he agreed to be in the film, he signed a deal-memo agreeing to appear on specific dates, which enabled David Stutman to raise capital from investors to pay for the production, and nowhere in the signed agreement does it specify the length of the film. The length of the movie wasn't something any one of us were concerned about, including Leo. We didn't talk about it. He showed up on the days agreed to in his contract and performed his services. His performance appears throughout the entire feature length film.

There was this insinuation that we were taking advantage of Leo, exploiting his fame to sell our movie, but Don's Plum was very well received with multiple distributors bidding for the rights long before Leo experienced any box office success with *Romeo + Juliet* or *Titanic*. Don's Plum was verbally accepted into Sundance, 1997, and Leo's agents said they thought it was a shoo-in for the audience award. Everyone was excited about our little movie, and Leo and his agents were a big part of creating that excitement and buzz. There were holes all over Leo's testimony, and I couldn't wait for our lawyers to expose them all on videotape for a jury to see.

Leo's attorney must have sensed the danger because he called for an early lunch, and he and Leo never returned to finish the deposition. They just walked out and called our lawyers on the phone and said they had terminated the deposition, in violation of the rules, costing our attorneys a considerable sum of money. I was hammered with questions for five straight days during my deposition but the rich and famous guy, with the big shot attorneys he paid for in cash, could just walk out in the middle of the process without any consequences whatsoever. Our lawyers didn't do anything about it either, the issue never made it to the judge.

Leo wasn't the only deponent on their side to get away with blatant obstruction. Our lawyers asked all witnesses to produce all recordings on any audio and video device. They specifically requested the videotape that Ethan Suplee recorded on Christmas 1995 because there was a very strong possibility we talked about

Don's Plum as a feature with our friends, including Leo, on that Christmas tape. During Ethan's deposition, when asked why he hadn't produced the tape, Ethan freaked out, shouting that he would destroy the tape to avoid turning it over to our attorneys. Our lawyers advised him that destroying evidence in a legal proceeding is a serious crime in the state of California, but Ethan did not give a fuck. He said again, while under oath and on the record, that he would destroy the tape before being forced to turn it over to anybody. Some people might think Ethan was being loyal to Leo, but if that were the case, then why would Ethan record him in the first place? And if it was so dangerous, why hadn't he destroyed the tape in the three years since recording it?

Ethan was a fool. We weren't after the Emily Foster recording. It was irrelevant to the case and wouldn't have been allowed into evidence even if we wanted to get it in front of a jury. We wanted that tape to prove we all had openly discussed Don's Plum with Leo and everybody else and nothing more. Ethan never turned over the tape, so we never got to look at that evidence, and our lawyers, once again, didn't do a thing about it.

Kevin Connolly admitted under oath to recording the whole fight at his house. He said he captured the entire meeting on a couple microcassette tapes, but he couldn't produce them because he claimed his house had been broken into and the tapes were stolen. Who breaks into a house and steals cassette tapes? What thief risks possible incarceration for a few $2 microcassettes? I'm assuming nobody. I believe Kevin still has that recording and I want the whole world to hear it.

LEO'S PEOPLE found out about our upcoming interview with *Dateline* and proposed a settlement conference between the friends if we agreed to pass on doing the interview. They specifically asked for me, Leo, RD, Tobey, Scott, Ethan, and Kevin, and used phrases like, "to finally put the whole thing behind us." That was music to all our ears, so RD and I agreed to the meeting, and we passed on the *Dateline* interview.

The meeting took place in the boardroom of Steve Warren's Beverly Hills office. Leo, Tobey, Ethan, Scott, and Kevin were already in the room when RD and I arrived. There wasn't much small talk before we got onto the topic of Don's Plum.

Leo started things off by noting how famous he had become, and how that probably changed the way we saw him, but he wanted to assure us that it was still him, still good ol' Leo. I almost laughed at him. I couldn't believe he was being serious. We didn't give a fuck about *Titanic* or his fame. We wanted him to stop ruining our lives. They all seemed so affected by Leo's success. Tobey sat next to Leo regally, like his wicked queen, while Scott, Ethan, and Kevin sat at their sides like panting minions. I was actually glad to not be a part of their lives anymore, they were insufferable.

Leo asked what we wanted, and we said for Don's Plum to be released around the world, unobstructed. He said there was no chance that would ever happen. I didn't see any need for the meeting to continue. The release of the film was the only thing that mattered to me. Our friendships meant absolutely nothing anymore, they made damn sure of that. I showed up believing we had a chance at putting all this nonsense behind us, but instead they kept offering deals that made no sense for us. Leo never asked nor even hinted that Don's Plum be edited into a short film. He never cared about the length of the movie. He said he didn't want RD or me to benefit from our movie, and so he decided that no one would.

Communication broke down after Tobey started with his shit about our supposed betrayal of our friends. I wasn't going to sit there and let him lie to everyone's face again, so I shouted right back at him that if we betrayed Leonardo DiCaprio then so did he when he showed up for the second shoot knowing full well we were shooting a feature film. Tobey went fucking berserk and started shouting incoherently, spit flying from his mouth like a rabid dog. I jumped to my feet, hoping he would come at me. I would have loved a little violence between us. Tobey took a step toward me, and I cocked my fist, but people were between us instantly. I shouted that it was him who betrayed all of us and that he was only getting away with it because the rest of them were too fucking stupid to see what he had really done. Everyone else got pissed and they started shouting at me, and the whole thing just spiraled out of control. Within in a minute, lawyers from both sides were in the room breaking up the skirmish.

We were separated into different rooms until our tempers cooled. After about half an hour, RD and I were led back to the boardroom where the guys were again waiting for us. Leo was sitting next to Tobey, coddling him and stroking Tobey's thigh, repeating softly and gently to him that everything was going to be all right, that he would be all right.

The meeting never recovered, and I don't think it was meant to. I believe the whole thing was nothing more than a tactic to stop the *Dateline* story from happening, and it worked. Our lawyers got played. The deal should have been that RD, Jerry, and I were going to do *Dateline* unless the case settled before our interview took place. We had all the leverage. That's when it occurred to me that Bert Fields must not have been working on our case at all. I could not imagine someone with his reputation making a deal that terrible for his clients.

ASSOCIATE ATTORNEYS WERE RUNNING our case, and they didn't appear to have a good strategy. Instead of focusing on getting Leo back in the chair to answer the questions he ran away from, instead of compelling Ethan Suplee to hand over the evidence he threatened to destroy, instead of deposing Adam Venit, Beth Swafford, and Rick Yorn, whose testimony, if truthful, would win our case, they went after Danny Masterson. They wanted to send a message that anyone talking shit or meddling with witnesses will have to testify under oath. We heard Danny was talking a lot of shit and trashing our reputation, so they served him with a subpoena on the set of *That 70s Show* as some kind of intimidation tactic. The move only made us look desperate. And I'm pretty confident Danny wasn't the least bit concerned with any of it.

Shortly after that move, Bert Fields dropped our case. We never heard from him directly, but his associates conveyed that Bert had expected Leo to settle, and because he hadn't, the case was becoming too much of a financial burden to the firm. They said they believed the facts would prove our version of events, but Leo's passionate monologue about why he cared whether Don's Plum was a feature was too compelling, and a jury would likely be star struck watching the testimony of the beloved Jack Dawson just a few feet away from them. Bert didn't think we'd win, regardless of the facts. It was rather convenient to scapegoat a jury he never selected, but at least Bert Fields admitted that he was only in it for a quick cash grab, and that he never intended to go to trial in the first place.

When we first met with all the lawyers, we told them what they were up against. We warned them that Leo would never settle, and they said if we were right, then we would go to trial and Leo and Tobey would have to beat one of the best trial attorneys in the country. So what the fuck happened? None of the facts changed. Our case was getting stronger with every deposition, yet there we were, tossed to the curb. I asked if they would at least finish Leo's deposition since we were about to expose him for perjury, but they wouldn't even do that.

DAVID STUTMAN BEGAN his search for a new attorney, but we were damaged goods, so it was tough. A month or two later, David got a meeting with Henry Gradstein. Henry was a fucking bulldog of a trial attorney with a stellar record. He had just won a 40-million-dollar judgment in a high-profile case that went to trial. The man did not fear Leo, or his celebrity, or his attorneys. He was a brash litigator, and he said if we were telling the truth then he would get it out at trial. I asked him what he thought our best evidence was and he said it was the movie itself.

I loved him. He saw the holes in their case. He knew that actors don't get deceived into making feature films. That's never happened before, and it didn't happen with Don's Plum. I wanted him to represent us so bad, but he didn't take the case right away. He wanted to look things over more closely, so he sent for the full case file from Bert Field's office.

I could not believe my eyes when I saw it all for the first time. Stacks of boxes filled Henry's entire boardroom. I had no idea our case was so massive. After spending more than a week with the case file, Henry called us and offered to take our case. He said he thought a settlement was still possible but that he was prepared to go all the way to trial if he had to. I believed him.

After a few months on the case, Henry had a change of heart. The issue wasn't Leo's celebrity, or the facts of the case, it was money. California requires that all contingency contracts between lawyers and their clients be disclosed to all parties involved in a civil case, so Leo and Tobey's lawyers knew that our lawyers were footing the bill, and that made their strategy simple. They would break our backs under the weight of their great fortune. They filed every motion they could think of, they deposed people for days at a time who had absolutely nothing substantive to do with Don's Plum, and they drained Henry dry. Henry told us that we had to settle the case, or he too would have to move on.

HENRY SET up a mediation between the parties. I was being forced into the meeting, but at least I didn't have to sit in the same room as them. We were in separate offices and the mediator, a judge that I'm assuming was mutually agreed on by both sides, went back and forth between rooms with offers and insight. Our judge was an older man, close to retirement, and he started the proceeding by saying that he watched Don's Plum and "hated it," and that he thought it was a "bad student movie." We were appalled, not because of his opinion of our work but because our judge just revealed a clear bias. Henry said that it shouldn't interfere with the proceeding or in our ability to accept or reject an offer, so the mediation continued.

Their first offer would restore our right to distribute Don's Plum worldwide, excluding the United States, Canada, and Japan.

It was a non-starter. The US and Japan were the first and second largest film markets in the world, and their financial performance would determine the value of Don's Plum throughout the remaining territories. Without a high benchmark from either the US or Japan, Don's Plum would lose most of its value. Jerry already had a Japanese deal in place for over two million dollars with a top Asian distributor, we were not going to walk away from that.

There was no movement well into the night, but then the judge arrived with one last offer. Leo and Tobey conceded Japan, but the US and Canada were off the table. If we declined the offer, the mediation would end without a deal.

Japan was significant. Thanks to the two-million dollar deal Jerry already had in place, Don's Plum was projected to earn between nine and eleven million dollars worldwide, excluding the US and Canada. There was so much money on the table that it was unlikely we would leave without a deal, and that pained me. There would be no trial. No truth. And Don's Plum would not be released in its country of origin.

I didn't give a fuck about the money. Money takes care of itself, eventually. I wanted Don's Plum to play at the Laemmle Sunset 5. I wanted to fly to Winnipeg and watch Don's Plum in a theater with my family and the friends I grew up with. I wanted to share an amazing accomplishment in my life with the people who helped shape me. I didn't want to settle for anything less than the whole world. And Jerry was with me, just as passionately, but we didn't have the leverage to sway the decision our way. That belonged to Henry Gradstein, and he wanted the deal.

It was sometime after one in the morning when the lawyers finished piecing together a workable deal. We signed it and then went to Jerry's Deli to grab a bite and "celebrate." The lawyers were tickled, of course. They were about to get paid. The first two million dollars to hit the escrow account would go straight to Henry Gradstein, Bert Fields, and Leo's lawyers. That meant the entire cast and crew of Don's Plum, almost all of whom had back-end participation, paid for Leo and Tobey's legal bills. The deal

Leo and Tobey put on the table was a fucking offense to everyone who worked on Don's Plum.

There was a silver lining, though. Don's Plum had about three million dollars in bills to pay, including the lawyers, leaving as much as six million to split among all the shareholders. Between me, Jerry, and RD, we would make a little over two million dollars between us, enough to make another movie.

46

RD BOOKED A SUPPORTING role on an indie feature called *Falling Sky* with Brittany Murphy. It was so good for him, and working with Brittany was very lucky. She was one of the most genuine, kind, and infectiously happy people I ever knew in Hollywood. It was impossible to be around her and not smile. We partied a lot together, saw a bunch of movies, and hung around the condo with Joel Michaely, bullshitting about whatever. She brought light to a dark situation, and we could forget our troubles around her.

We were all out one night and Brittany drank too much. She thought she was going to be sick, so we rushed her into the bathroom in a nearby hotel lobby. She stumbled into a stall and got down on her knees and waited. We all waited. She thanked us for helping her, and her voice sounded incredible as it reverberated in the toilet bowl. "Wow," she said. "The acoustics are great in here!" I think that was the most I had laughed since our whole ordeal began.

Her nausea passed and she stumbled out of the stall to the sink and rinsed off her hands. She hopped up on the countertop and immediately began losing her color again, so she closed her eyes, took a long, deep breath, and began singing the most beautiful blues a cappella I've ever heard in my life. Everything stopped.

Time stopped. I had no idea Brittany Murphy had such a beautiful voice and I was completely swept away by it.

After essentially healing herself with her magical voice, she slid off the counter and draped her arms around our shoulders, and as we headed back out into the night, she told us she loved us, and couldn't understand why anyone would feel otherwise. She said she wanted to work with us, and that no one could change her mind. It felt so good to hear. They were just words, but she gave us hope, and I think that's exactly what she meant to do.

———

THERE WERE a few distributors interested in the international rights to Don's Plum, but they all took a back seat to Lars Von Trier's Zentropa, who expressed interest through his international sales company, Trust Film Sales. Fortunately for us, their head of sales and acquisitions, Thomas Mai, had a great reputation with all the biggest buyers in the world from handling Lars' work, and Don's Plum was similar in terms of raw, gritty, indie production value, so it was a perfect fit all around.

It didn't take long to put the deal together, thanks again to the work Jerry had done in Japan. Thomas Mai confirmed that Jerry's two million dollar deal translated to an estimated eight million dollars in advances from the rest of the world. He also thought both Cannes and Berlin were great festivals for Don's Plum, and he was confident Zentropa had the relationships to get Don's Plum into one or the other. We were back in very good hands again and it felt great.

TOBEY AND LEO wanted some edits made to the film as part of their settlement agreement. Tobey wanted Ian's dialogue about how he enjoyed sticking his finger up his ass when he masturbates removed, and Leo cut a few lines of Derek's about gay people that he worried might reflect poorly on his character. I thought Tobey was being ridiculous, but Leo's concerns were valid. He was still dealing with the blowback from the insanely stupid things he said in an interview promoting *Total Eclipse*.

In the interview Leo was asked about the graphic sex scenes between him and his co-star David Thewlis and he said, "Actually, I got very nauseous as it was my first time kissing a guy. It was like slow motion, you know what I mean? I saw his lips coming towards mine and I was like, 'oh Jesus, this is really going to happen?' Nasty. My stomach was seriously turning after this... (Thewlis) kept on saying that if you're scared of it, you're homophobic. Well call me homophobic if you like, but I'm just grossed out by it." He added that he made sure that both of their lips were clean with "disinfectant" before they kissed. Those were the very remarks Jerry Meadors heard were stirring up animosity toward Leo within the "gay press" and he tried to warn Leo about it, but Tobey, Scott, and Ethan twisted Jerry's good intentions into some ridiculous threat by all three of us somehow, even though RD and I didn't even know any of it was going on. It was another instance where Jerry was looking out for Leo, like he did when he lobbied for Leo's Oscar nomination for *What's Eating Gilbert Grape*, only this time Jerry got burned for his good deed.

We completed the settlement edits and sent them over for approval, then prepared the entire project to be shipped to Zentropa Studios in Denmark. I was terrified the negative would get lost or destroyed, but it all arrived safely, and RD, Jerry, David, and I followed soon after.

DENMARK WAS BEYOND WILD. I think if I had been mentally well, and single, it probably would have been the greatest time of my life, but instead I was overly neurotic and had difficulty adapting to Danish culture. I didn't realize it at the time, but I had begun developing a cynical outlook on new friendships and people in general.

Peter Aalbæk Jensen welcomed us to Zentropa with open arms. I found his revolutionary approach to life and art amusing and inspiring. What they had done with Zentropa was remarkable, and I was thrilled they wanted to work with us. When I got the chance to thank him, he smiled with bright, true eyes, and said that it was an easy decision for them to make. He said that Don's Plum was a good film that deserved to be seen, and then he strongly condemned Americans for abandoning us.

Peter took us on a tour of the grounds. The studio was an impressive conversion of an abandoned military base that was, if I'm not mistaken, used or built during World War II. There was an air of darkness to the compound, not in any evil or nefarious sense, but rather like a collective struggle of some kind had taken place, and we were standing among the ghosts.

Don's Plum has always had interesting timing. We just so happened to arrive in Copenhagen while Lars Von Trier was shooting *Dancer in the Dark* with Björk in one studio and, in another, Harmony Korine was finishing up the first American Dogme 95 movie, *Julien Donkey-Boy*. It just seemed like no matter how hard Leo and Tobey tried to kill Don's Plum, it always found its way into amazing company.

Meeting Lars Von Trier for the first time was a sweet experience. He was quite reserved, but very kind. We thanked him for taking on Don's Plum and he said such nice things about our work, likening it to what they were doing with Dogme 95. It was pretty fucking dreamy listening to one my favorite living directors compliment my work in such a way.

They put us in a great apartment in a wonderful neighborhood. They set us up with a humble production office on the lot, with an adorable intern who spoke great English to help us through each day. It was a warm welcome, and we wanted to show our appreciation with a gift for Peter and Lars. Peter had a strange but impressive, even museum-quality, collection of dildos, which he proudly displayed in his office, so he was easy to shop for, but Lars was more of an enigma. Everyone we asked told us to get him a bottle, but we wanted to do better than that, so Jerry, ever the mystic, suggested we wait for the right gift to reveal itself to us.

A day or two later, we were eating lunch in the commissary, and it was cold, so I wore my coat like everybody else. I noticed

Lars Von Trier staring at me rather intensely from a couple of tables over. I had no idea why. Then he stood up, with his eyes still fixed on me, and began walking toward me. I just kind of froze. He didn't look like he was coming over to talk, he wasn't even making eye contact with me. I didn't know what to think. Seconds later, he was standing at my side and examining my coat closely. He didn't say anything—he just bent over me, squinting as he ran his finger along the seam of my coat from my shoulder down to my wrist. He asked where I got the coat, and I told him stiffly that it was a gift from an in-law for my trip to Copenhagen. He folded up the back of my collar, presumably to get a look at the label, said thanks to me, and then went back to his seat to finish his lunch. I had already decided to gift Lars my coat before he got to the label, but I wanted to wait for a better moment.

The following day, I walked over to the Nimbus building where I was told Lars was in a casual meeting with Thomas Vinterberg and a few other filmmakers. I knocked on the door and moments later I was invited in. I apologized for my interruption, and asked if I could give Lars a gift from all of us. I took off my coat and held it open for Lars to try on. He was confused at first, but I helped him out of his old, thread-bare coat and slid his arms into his new coat. I told him I had only been keeping it warm for him all this time. He admired his arms in the sleeves, turning them like hot dogs in a campfire. He had a lovely grin that went all the way up into his eyes, and he thanked me sincerely. I apologized again for my intrusion and left the men to their important work.

Days had passed and I still hadn't found a coat I liked. The weather had been mild, so I could be picky about it. I was eating in the commissary when I noticed Lars enter the building. His eyes quickly found me, and he approached me with a black coat folded over his arm and a generous smile on his face. As he unfolded the coat, he said it was the last *Dancer in the Dark* crew parka they had, and he wanted me to have it. I was stunned of course, I wasn't expecting anything from him, and to be given a gift from his production felt special. The coat was cool too, it was charcoal black with the *Dancer* logo and Lars' name silk-screened on the back along with all the participating production companies' logos along the bottom. I absolutely loved it. We chatted for another minute, then he patted me on the shoulder and thanked me again for my coat, and I thanked him once more for his, and we went about our merry business of filmmaking.

AND THEN A NEW NIGHTMARE BEGAN.

A Japanese distributor came out of nowhere and claimed that they had a signed contract with David Stutman that gave them the Japanese rights to Don's Plum for a paltry $175,000. David never disclosed this agreement to anybody, but if it was valid, Don's Plum would lose at least two million dollars from Japan alone, and the losses wouldn't end there. Don's Plum's value would catastrophically drop in all the remaining territories worldwide.

Zentropa suspended presales for Don's Plum pending the outcome of the arbitration. The shift in their energy toward us and Don's Plum was immediate and unsettling. I couldn't blame them —losing Japan would be devastating to all of us. I'm sure it was embarrassing, too. They were in productive talks with half the world when this contract surfaced. Our lawyers were confident we would prevail in the arbitration, and that helped ease some of the tension, but Zentropa still had a lot of damage control to deal with, and they weren't happy about it.

As confident as our lawyers were, there was still a lot of work to do to rectify the timeline before and after the so-called agreement between David Stutman and the Japanese distributor. I probably knew our timelines better than anyone, so I was designated to help prepare the case with the attorneys.

It was a brutal schedule. I worked all day on the post-production of the film and then into the early hours of the morning with the lawyers back in LA. Our strongest evidence was the so-called contract itself. It was signed only by David Stutman and never by the distributor. There was also a delivery date that had expired more than two years before their claim, without fulfillment or any demand for fulfillment, and there was never any amendment to the delivery date in writing or otherwise. David also stated that he and the distributor spoke via telephone as the deadline approached and David explained to them that he there were issues with the rights and he could not deliver the film. Again, there was no discussion about pushing the deadline, and there was no counter-signed agreement. The deal was dead. The distributor had a weak case factually, and they also had to litigate on our turf. They had to convince an American judge that their unsigned, unfulfilled contract should cost an American company and the dozens of American artists and crew members millions of dollars while undercutting Don's Plum's market value by more than 50% worldwide. Finding for the distributor would ostensibly be a denial of the facts and a sentence to put Don's Plum out of business. Our argument was that the claimant couldn't produce a fully executed document because there was no deal, but even if the judge disagreed, we still hadn't met their deadline requirement clearly stated in the terms of the agreement. We argued that the producers had incurred millions of dollars in legal fees to make the movie available to distributors and therefore should be able to get the current market value for the project in order to mitigate those losses.

A good lawyer would never say you're guaranteed to win your case, but ours came pretty fucking close. The evidence and timelines were overwhelmingly in our favor. I slept well the night before the arbitration.

We lost. In a stunning and inexplicable decision that I still cannot believe, the judge ruled for the Japanese distributor. Don's Plum's cumulative losses would amount to more than six million dollars. My personal loss was almost a half a million dollars. The whole case reeked of corruption.

ZENTROPA CALLED an emergency meeting with their leadership. The four of us sat down with Peter Aalbæk Jensen, Sisse Graum Olsen, Morton Fisker, and Thomas Mai. We were told that our deal with Zentropa had to be reworked immediately. With Japan lost, they were at risk of losing a significant amount of money already invested in our post-production, and they needed their percentage and position improved considerably to ensure they recoup most or all of that investment. It was another sickening moment for Don's Plum. We had no choice. We gave them whatever they wanted.

That night while I laid in bed, unable to sleep, it occurred to me that I must be living a cursed life. I had survived so much shit just to get to Hollywood, never mind what it took to succeed, and then to have it all destroyed by my own friends was too much to bear. I tried to ward off the terrible thoughts, but the darkness was thick, and the bruising went all the way to the bone.

THOMAS MAI DIDN'T GIVE up on Don's Plum, he even pulled off a short-lived miracle in Italy. He negotiated a $750,000 deal with the largest Italian distributor in the business. It wasn't Japan, but a deal of that size out of Italy would help minimize our losses in Europe and other territories affected by the Japan catastrophe.

Not long after, however, the distributor called Thomas and withdrew his offer with regret. The distributor didn't want to harm his good and long-standing relationship with Zentropa, so he told the story in confidence, promising to deny it if he was ever asked about it.

The distributor had also purchased the Italian rights to Martin Scorsese's *Gangs of New York,* which happened to be shooting in Italy at the time. He said he had visited Scorsese's set and when he met DiCaprio, he expressed his excitement over purchasing the Italian rights to Don's Plum. He said Leo became visibly upset about it. Leo allegedly told him that Don's Plum was never supposed to be released, and that if the distributor put Don's Plum out in Italy, Leo would do whatever he could to pull the rights to *Gangs of New York* from him, and he would never distribute another Leonardo DiCaprio movie in Italy or anywhere else in the world. I can't confirm the validity of Thomas' story, but Don's Plum remains the only Leonardo DiCaprio movie never released in Italy.

WE KEPT LOSING and I could feel myself separating from the world spiritually. I began feeling detached from people, especially friends. What kind of life is there without justice? What hope is there when your closest friends are the monsters of your undoing?

MY WIFE, who had been working with RD's mother for seven years by then, called me in a panic because, while I was in Denmark fighting for and ultimately losing Don's Plum, Edie Robb couldn't make payroll and bounced her paycheck. My wife sounded like she was having a nervous breakdown. I was frantic, but I couldn't do anything from Denmark. I wasn't even getting a per diem anymore since we re-worked our contract with Zentropa. My wife's small salary was our only source of income, and it barely kept us afloat. My only option was to return home and get a job as quickly as possible. It was crushing, but RD would have to finish the sound mix without me.

47

I TOOK a job telemarketing bubble gum to convenient stores. It was fucking hell, but it paid the bills. Inexplicably, RD took another four months to finish the sound mix in Denmark. I guess he didn't want to leave, and who could blame him. Life in LA was a drag.

The first month of grinding phone sales might have been the most soul-crushing time of my life. The contrast of having my movie, which had the biggest movie star in the world in it, being posted overseas at one of the hottest European production companies while I was sitting in a cubical pitching bubble gum was almost enough to break me. I could have dealt with my own failure—I would have grown from it. But we succeeded. We beat all the odds, and a fucking lunatic took it all away in one night. I was supposed to be writing and producing indies with Kevin, Scott, Ethan, Jay, Johnny, Blake, Jeremy, Meadow, Marisa, Jenny, and on and on and on. But instead, I was stuck in a cubicle, selling candy to keep a roof over my head while making offhanded jokes about suicide.

DON'S PLUM was accepted into the 2001 Berlin Film Festival, which was wonderful news. Then our lawyers put together a set of instructions on what specifically we should and should not say while at the festival if we wanted to avoid being dragged before the judge and sanctioned. Their prepared statement went something like, "We're happy that we were able to settle our differences amicably and we're excited to finally share Don's Plum with the rest of the world." We were told if we deviated from their statement and it ended up getting back to Leo and Tobey through the press or even word-of-mouth, we risked losing even more. It was a serious threat, Leo and Tobey had already dragged Jerry Meadors before the judge and tried to have him sanctioned for a million dollars. Shortly after we settled, Jerry had taken out an ad in *Variety* in which he thanked Leo and Tobey for their gentlemanly discourse and amicable spirits. Jerry just wanted the distributors in town to feel confident the case was over and that our rights had been restored, but Leo and Tobey took Jerry to arbitration and claimed he was trying to cash in on their fame. The judge agreed with them, even though Jerry wasn't mentioned nor personally attributed to the ad in any way. They didn't get the million dollars they asked for, but their mission was accomplished, we were being silenced by the court. It seemed like every time I turned around, we were losing something else to those petty fucking tyrants.

I wanted to be in Berlin next to RD, watching our finished movie on the big screen for the very first time, more than anything else in the whole world. It was all I could dream about for years. The problem is that I got a big fucking mouth, especially if I think I'm being screwed over. My wife was terrified I would say something that would land me in front of the judge, and we would lose whatever was left of Don's Plum. The thought of skipping my premiere at the Berlin Film Festival was absurd and even infuriating, but the threat of DiCaprio raking me over the coals again was too stressful. I just wanted all the trouble to end.

So the night before I was supposed to get on a plane to Berlin, I called up the hotel and the airline and canceled everything. I didn't tell RD because I didn't want to be talked out of it. I knew he would be hurt if I wasn't there and that I didn't tell him I wasn't coming, but I needed to protect myself.

The thought of staying home and moping while Don's Plum

made its debut was as unappealing as getting sued again. I had already taken the time off work to travel to Germany, and it was much cheaper to switch our flights to, say, Italy than it would have been to get a refund, so I said fuck it and booked two tickets to Rome.

While being pulled through the cobblestone roads of Rome by horse and carriage, sitting next to my glowing wife, Don's Plum premiered at the Berlin Film Festival to mostly good reviews, and I pretended not to care.

WE RETURNED from Rome before the Berlin Film Festival ended. There were dozens of messages from RD, Edie, and the organizers, and I felt terrible for ditching them at the last minute, but at least I didn't have the feeling of impending doom because of something I may have inadvertently said to a stranger at a party.

Jerry Meadors got word that NPR's *All Things Considered* was airing a spot on the premiere of Don's Plum in Berlin, so I went on a quick drive and tuned into KCRW, LA's NPR affiliate, to listen in. David D'Arcy did the piece and, like most reporters on this story, got almost all his facts wrong. He may have even been the original source for decades of misinformation, like for instance that we had tried to release Don's Plum after Leo got famous from *Titanic*. D'Arcy did manage to get an amazing quote from renowned *Village Voice* critic J. Hoberman who spoke right after seeing Don's Plum in Berlin. Hoberman said, "I thought that DiCaprio gave an extremely relaxed and credible performance, [Derek's] not a sympathetic character, but he certainly seemed to be enjoying himself. It was not only the strongest performance in the movie by far, but probably one of the best performances he's ever given in a film." I laughed so hard I had to pull over. Hoberman was right, Don's Plum is one of DiCaprio's best performances of the '90s, second only to Arnie in *What's Eating Gilbert Grape* and I just loved that listeners all over the country were hearing about it.

J. Hoberman's quote was gold, but it was Peter Aalbæk Jensen's statement at the Don's Plum presser that got me fired up. Peter said, "We from Europe had to save an American film from the worst kind of American imperialism: the studio system, the star system that was going to kill these two young guys. These nationalists used every fucking power play to squeeze these young guys that just made a film together with their friends. So that's a disgrace, really, for the business in America that treats young artists like that."

Maybe Peter understood more about Hollywood corruption than I did, but the bad guys he was talking about, the "star system" as he put it, were all on board with Don's Plum until Leo and Tobey told them not to be. Don's Plum was destroyed by cannibals, not capitalists.

As I had predicted, RD was upset over my absence from Berlin. He said he understood my position, but things were strained between us. Missing Berlin didn't help, but it was the whole ordeal that damaged our relationship. RD went on to form a company with Thomas Mai producing indies under an American–Danish Zentropa company they called ZentAmerica, and I continued to sell candy to corner stores over the telephone.

DON'S PLUM had about three million dollars in bills to pay, two thirds of which was to be split by the lawyers on both sides, and the remaining million dollars would cover all deferments and any outstanding invoices incurred during post-production. When it was all counted, Zentropa produced roughly three million dollars in total sales from the entire world. Six million short of their original projection. Losing Japan crushed us, but it was difficult to believe it was a coincidence that at the exact point in which RD, Jerry, and I would start earning money, all sales stopped, even with territories like Italy, France, and the UK remaining unsold. I guess we were supposed to believe that foreign distributors didn't want a Leonardo DiCaprio movie for any form of distribution, not rentals or cable or any kind of TV. Every single movie distributor in several major territories had no interest in a Berlin Film Festival selection, with the biggest star in the world, and who had just broken every box office record around the world. Maybe all these things were just the result of oversights and coincidences, or maybe it's compelling evidence of grand theft and an international collusion to suppress Don's Plum and disenfranchise its makers. I don't know because I can't afford the lawyers I need to help me find out.

Three years after Don's Plum premiered in Berlin, Zentropa would produce the Danish film *Brothers* to rave reviews on the festival circuit. The film was produced by Peter Aalbæk Jensen and Sisse Graum Olsen. Tobey Maguire would go on to star in the US adaptation of Brothers, directed by the great Jim Sheridan. In 2021, Leonardo DiCaprio optioned the US remake rights for Zentropa's hit *Another Round,* also produced by Sisse Graum (Olsen) Jørgensen. Projects with stars like DiCaprio can easily take a decade or more to create and set up, so I find it quite intriguing that they're in business with both Leo and Tobey, despite Zentropa's involvement with Don's Plum, and Peter's harsh public statements condemning Leo and Tobey's attack on me and RD and on our film. Working with Zentropa was quite a reversal by Leo and Tobey who, by their own admission, have bullied and intimidated individuals and production companies who had shown any interest in working with us or with Don's Plum. Their threats were public knowledge. In an article by Maximillian Potter that appeared in the February 1998 issue of Premiere Magazine, Jason Blum, Amy Israel's acquisitions partner at Miramax, stated on the record that Leo's manager Rick Yorn warned Harvey Weinstein that "there would be certain implications" if Miramax went ahead with a deal for Don's Plum. Leo and his crew were committed to making sure RD and I didn't benefit from Don's Plum and they succeeded. Approximately seven years after we shot Don's Plum, and after Zentropa deposited about three million dollars into the court ordered escrow account, I received a check in the mail for $187.00 after taxes for my role as the Little Bum in Don's Plum. I haven't made a dime since, despite the film selling all over the world for decades.

I SLID into what I can only describe as a nine-year walking coma. I pretended I had friends, pretended to be married, pretended to be a "team player." I pretended to be alive like everyone else around me, but I was dead and rotting on the inside. I had lost all sense of purpose and belonging. My life felt more like a prison sentence, and that's how I lived it every day. I did my time and I hoped for an early release.

I WAS at a Best Buy one afternoon for something unmemorable and, as always, I wandered over to the TV section to see what current technology I was missing out on. The store was absolutely massive. I had never seen so many TVs in one room before. There was a thirty-foot wall at the back of the store that must have had a hundred screens synchronized into one giant TV. It was so cool. There were several aisles of smaller TV's lined up, also synced up to the same content playing on the giant, synchronized display in front of me.

Suddenly all the screens when gray, and then, in a blink, an extreme close-up of Tobey Maguire as Peter Parker appeared on the giant wall and on the hundreds of other TVs throughout the store. I stopped breathing. I could not inhale. My head started to spin, my heartrate increased, my mouth dried, I staggered for a couple steps. The room started to spin but I could still see Tobey's face grinning at me from every direction. I thought I was going to collapse so I took a knee and an employee rushed to my aid. I told her I was OK, that it was just a panic attack. When I got back to my car I wept in my hands.

A COUPLE OF YEARS LATER, I moved to South Jersey so my wife could be closer to her family. I decided I wasn't going to waste away anymore. I immersed myself in the study of writing and storytelling. I read every book I could find. I broke down dozens of movies into beats and paradigms. I started feeling creative again and a couple of ideas and characters came through that I fell in love with. I spent years crafting those ideas into two mind-bending movies that I can't wait to someday bring to life. It's those stories that keep my dreams alive even today.

In 2010, after returning to the United States from spending months in Canada with my mother while she battled ovarian cancer, my wife and I had our final argument. There was nothing left between us except the house, the car, and all the other stuff that meant absolutely nothing to me. I asked her one question. I said, if she knew she could keep it all, would she want a divorce? She said yes, so I gave her everything except one of the cars. I left Jersey a few weeks later in our Scion XB stuffed with clothes and a few other personal belongings and, at 40 years old, I headed back to Hollywood for another round.

48

I REUNITED with RD Robb at his and Edie's talent management company. RD wanted me to try and improve the company culture, which he said was reeling after one their managers was let go on less than amicable terms. After spending some time in the office, I saw a different problem. RD was miserable. He was supposed to be making films, not co-managing his mother's company. He was the talent, not a talent manager. What Edie should have done, from the very beginning, was fund RD to direct experimental microbudget films with her money and clients, and actually help her son's directing career instead shelving it for her own purposes.

The opportunity at the company wasn't all that great for me, but it felt good to work with RD again. We started talking creatively, and that familiar spark of imagination reignited between us and it got me believing for a minute that maybe we could capture lightning in a bottle one more time. Before long, we were sitting on RD's porch in Silverlake, developing a new feature film—our first together since Don's Plum.

———

RD and I were walking along Selma and Cahuenga Blvd. after lunch when I noticed some dude slow his car and lean his head out of his window to get a look at me. It took me a second or two before I recognized Scott Bloom.

We set up a lunch for the three of us the following day, and it didn't go well at all. Scott sat across from me and acted as if he hadn't taken part in the total annihilation of everything that mattered to me. I guess I wanted an apology from him, but all I got was arrogance. When I asked him why he thought I was capable of betraying all of them so easily, he couldn't give me an answer. I asked if he actually believed we had betrayed them and he said the situation was more complicated than that. Then I asked if he had any regrets, and he said he didn't, so I finished my beer, left some money on the table, and said a final goodbye to Scott Bloom.

———

EDIE WASN'T PAYING us to develop an arthouse film for her son to direct. She should have been, but she wasn't. Instead, she insisted we find ways to generate income to justify keeping the LA office open. One of our production partners had a relationship with John Legend that had intriguing potential. We took a meeting with John and learned that he wanted to expand out of music and into production. Over the next few weeks we collaborated with John and eventually came up with a cool music show in the vein of the BBC's *Later... with Jools Holland*. Our show would filmed live at Capitol Records with a couple of unique twists to the format that I think music fans would have loved. We packaged it up and sold the pilot to Showtime. John Legend was so impressed that we started talking about forming a formal partnership. It was a solid opportunity that could have opened up a lot of possibilities, but sadly "assholes are everywhere"and John Legend's buddy got greedy and tried to get rid of me so he could improve his position. RD said he stood up for me but said that his mom was losing patience and it was only matter of time before things would implode.

———

ABOUT A YEAR into my Hollywood return, I met and fell in love with a barista from my neighborhood coffee bar, The Bourgeois Pig. Her name was Angela, and she took my breath away. I nicknamed her "the mayor of Franklin Village" because no matter where we went, she would run into someone who knew her from The Pig. Her shifts were always packed with a diverse crowd of regulars. Some of us were there for her beauty, but most were there for her music and the great vibe she cultivated on every shift. Three months into our relationship, Angela moved into my apartment with her one-eyed dog, Clarence, and we've been together ever since.

DON'S PLUM wasn't something I talked about often. It was a sore subject for me and easy enough to avoid since the movie had never been released in the United States. One afternoon, I was sitting at the coffee bar during one of Angela's shifts and I was talking with a regular customer who was a TV writer. He had recently made his feature film directorial debut with Amber Benson in the lead role, and that inevitably led to a conversation about Don's Plum. He knew about our movie because he was a fan of Amber's, and so he made a bit of a scene with Angela about why she hadn't told him I had written and produced DiCaprio. I'll never forget the look on Angela's face, it was the first time she'd heard of it. We had been living together for a few months by then, but I had never even mentioned the movie or that part of my past.

She wanted to watch Don's Plum, naturally, but I didn't own a copy. I jumped on eBay and bought a ripped, lo-res DVD out of Mexico for thirty bucks. As soon as it arrived, I set her up in our bedroom with my laptop so she could watch it alone. I hadn't been that nervous over a screening of Don's Plum since our very first one in 1996. I was crazy in love with Angela, and I was terrified, however irrationally, that Don's Plum would find a way to ruin our relationship like it had all the others.

But Angela loved the movie. She went on breathlessly about how we had captured a way of life that doesn't exist anymore but was such a huge part of our lives and social development. She talked about waiting tables when she was younger at a 24-hour diner in Burbank called the Coral Cafe. Groups of friends and nightly regulars would hang out into the wee hours of her graveyard shifts, doing the very same shit we captured on film. She said Don's Plum was hilarious, unsettling, and unexpectedly poignant. It was one of the best reviews of our film I ever heard. I could hardly believe it had been almost 20 years since shooting the first scenes, and Don's Plum was still so relatable.

And then Angela got pissed about it. Really pissed. She said that '90s indie films were defining experiences for her and her friends. Right around the time Don's Plum should have been released, she worked at a video store just so she and her friends could see as many movies as possible. "Do you understand what it would have meant to us to see our lives up on the screen like that? How validating it would have been? That was us—that was our life. I can't believe you were gonna put us all up on the silver screen, Dale, and they fucking stole that from us. I'm sick over it."

She asked about my other projects, so I pitched her two of my favorites. She loved them both, but the story called *Never Say Goodbye*, affected her the most. It's about an old man living with the regret of accidentally killing his fiancé when they were young. It was almost intoxicating to have someone interested in my stories again. It felt like she was breathing life into them.

RD ROBB CALLED and fired me. He blamed it on his mom and Don's Plum. I told him I was sick and tired of his mom using Don's Plum as a scapegoat.

He sighed. "Everybody uses Don's Plum as a scapegoat. I had lunch with Sisto a couple of weeks ago and he's convinced his feature career was killed by Tobey because he supported us after everything went down."

"Oh really? He doesn't think playing Jesus in a network miniseries had anything to do with it?"

"Who knows—they fucked everyone over, bro. My mom is

probably going to leave you a shitty message, just ignore it. She's off her ass for a change."

Edie's message was very colorful. She said she was sorry she had to fire me but, "I'm not paying you to go home and fuck your new girlfriend during lunch hour." Apart from my relationship and lunch hour being none of her business, I wondered what I had done to make her so hostile. The only thing that made sense to me was that she couldn't get over that her son's career had been deliberately and maliciously destroyed without any form of justice, and she needed someone to punish. Maybe I was just easy pickings. I'm not sure who has damaged my reputation more, DiCaprio and Maguire, or Edie Robb, but I've heard that she trashes my name pretty much every opportunity she gets.

I was heartbroken all over again. When RD invited me to work with him, I felt so sure we were going to revive our chemistry from the '90s and do some special things together. Looking back, it was probably never going to happen because Edie didn't want it to, and she still had a strong influence on what RD did with his life. Realizing I had just thrown away another two precious years chasing shadows, I spiraled into a very dark place mentally. I don't know if I would have survived had Angela not been in my life.

WHEN CHRISTMAS ROLLED AROUND, *The Wolf of Wall Street* blew up at the box office, and Leo was every-fucking-where again. Normally, "Leo season" was more of an emotional nuisance that came around every couple of years, but after the most recent fiasco with the Robbs it felt more like a salted wound. To sprinkle a little more on there, Leo was nominated for an Oscar for his performance in *The Wolf of Wall Street* days before my 44th birthday.

A week or so after Leo's nomination, Angela and I were at home enjoying some wine on a Saturday night, and she thought it would be fun to watch *Saturday Night Live*, have a few laughs, and forget about our problems. The episode happened to be hosted by Jonah Hill who was there promoting *The Wolf of Wall Street*, so she turned it off. I wanted to watch it. Jonah Hill had nothing to do with my past, and I was sick of running from everything just because Leo or Tobey might be involved. She was worried Leo might make an appearance and ruin our mood. I assured her there was no chance Leonardo DiCaprio would be on *Saturday Night Live*. That's why Jonah Hill was there—to do what Leo would not. Leo loathed doing TV appearances after having a bad experience on Letterman. I remember a conversation with him about it. I was absolutely safe.

She turned the show back on, and not one damn minute into Jonah Hill's monologue, Leo walked out on the *SNL* stage for the first time in his nearly 30-year career, to gasps and screams from the audience. I just laughed. It was the only thing to do. Angela went for the remote again, but I stopped her. Their two-person sketch was this bizarre pantomime surrounding Jonah's fear of Leo's power and his dysfunctional fealty to him. The whole thing was a parody of power-posturing in Hollywood and the fear of reputational damage. They finished the bit with Leo embracing Jonah as if they were on the bow of the Titanic. Leo looked blissfully happy in the embrace. And why wouldn't he be? He had the perfect life.

"I think I finally figured it out. I think I finally understand what's going on between me and that dude right there." I pointed at the TV where the audience cheered for Leo and Jonah Hill.

Angela grinned. "Oh yeah, what's that?"

"I am Leonardo DiCaprio's sadness."

Angela laughed. "That's hilarious."

"What if it's true? What if Leo's life is too perfect for the expression of sadness? Like, he can't actually be sad because his life is too great, you know? Sadness is inside of him, and it needs to get out, but it can't because it's all trapped under the crushing weight of his immense joy... so it gets metaphysically funneled to me."

"Why you?"

I shrugged. "Probably cos I'm tree-hugging Canadian piece-of-shit, I don't know."

"That explains everything!" She jabbed tickling fingers into my

541

ribs. I screeched and flinched, nearly spilling our wine all over the place.

———

ANGELA ASKED me to write a treatment for *Never Say Goodbye* so she could pass it on to a film producer friend of hers. She wasn't sure anything would come of it, but he was successful and might offer some advice or make a few introductions.

I wrote a decent two-pager, and she sent it over. The producer got back to her a couple of weeks later, saying he loved the treatment and wanted to help get it made. When Angela told me who this guy was, I was floored. He produced massive tent-pole movies for a major studio. He got his start producing independent films and then hit it big with a billion-dollar franchise. But his first love was mind-bending indies, and my story resonated with him. I felt like I won the lottery.

I kissed Angela's face a thousand times. She gave all the credit back to me and called me her golden goose. I tossed my head back and laughed. I was middle-aged, unemployed, flat broke, and blacklisted in the industry where I do my best work. I was not laying golden eggs.

"That's the thing about a golden goose," she said with her perfect smile. "If it's mistreated, nobody gets anything at all. You just need a little love and support and you'll make all the gold you'll ever need."

I got busy refining the treatment and working on how to pitch my unconventional approach to filmmaking.

Angela and the producer met to talk about the project at the producer's favorite spot on Sunset, El Compadre, the very same restaurant we chose to celebrate with the cast and crew after the MGM screening in June of '95. I thought it was a good omen, but I barely made it home from dropping Angela off before she called to be picked up again. Not a good sign.

She started telling me the story before she got the car door closed. The producer wanted to discuss getting a screenplay written, and Angela explained how I work improvisationally and told him about Don's Plum. He knew the movie, and she said the mention of it made him visibly uncomfortable. He said he couldn't afford to get involved with me and risk pissing off the biggest star in Hollywood.

"I couldn't believe it," she said. "I said to him, what do you mean? You're a hugely successful producer—you're more powerful than Leonardo DiCaprio. And he kinda laughed at me and said, 'no one is more powerful than Leo.'"

I sighed. "I'm so fucked."

"No. He wanted to make it, Dale. That's amazing."

We got back to our apartment, and I collapsed onto the sofa. I kept replaying what the producer said in my head. *"No one is more powerful than Leo."* Eighteen years had gone by since our dispute and nothing had changed. I was banished for life.

"I'm gonna get a regular job," I said.

Angela sat beside me and draped her arm around my shoulder. "No, c'mon..."

"There's no other choice."

"Yes, there is. You're just gonna end up miserable, and years will go by, and you'll remember this moment when you could have decided to continue."

"What can I do? It's been twenty years. They control the media, they control the town. I can't get a film made, and even if I did, no one will buy it."

"Don't give up. Don't let them win."

"There's a difference between giving up and accepting defeat. You heard your friend—"

"Forget about him. Forget about Hollywood. We'll go someplace else."

"But I love this town. That's my problem, isn't it? I'm in an abusive relationship. I love Los Angeles, but she keeps kicking the fucking shit out of me. I don't even know why I love it so much. Probably because I figured out who and what I really was in this place. And, as cruel as this town is, it's also filled with the most incredible people I have ever met in my life... There's magic here. Real magic."

"What do you want to do, then?"

"I want to fight back. They should never have gotten away with trashing my reputation and work over nothing."

"I'm glad you're angry about it. You should be. But, how do you fight the most powerful person in Hollywood?"

"With the truth. It's not the '90s, I can tell my side of the story now. They destroyed art and careers, and then they convinced half the world to hate a movie just so they could get away with it. They can lie all they want, but they can't change the facts."

"How would you do it? A blog?"

"Yeah, a blog is perfect... You know what I should do? I should release the movie while I'm at it."

Angela laughed. "Yes! That would be amazing."

"I think I could pull it off." I stood up and started pacing. "I'm gonna fuckin' do it!"

"How? It's banned."

"I'll upload it to Vimeo and embed it on Tumblr. If they want to take down the movie, let them. At least some people will see my work and we'll see where it leads. Maybe I should do some crowd-funding for Never Say Goodbye. Some people out there might want to see what else I can do."

"Let's not do crowdfunding. It's a whole big thing... you need a network, and marketing skills. Yuck."

"Whatever. People will get to see the movie, and then we'll see what happens, we'll see what comes together."

"What can they do to you?"

"They can't put me in jail, and I'm already broke. I'm the fucking writer, don't I have any rights to my own work? I produced the movie. I'm not charging any money. It's on my fucking reel, like Leo wanted."

"They could sue you."

"Go right ahead! I got a car worth three grand. They already destroyed my life and the one thing that was most valuable to me."

"Don's Plum is not destroyed. I just watched it and I loved it."

"This is my point. People need to see the movie. Maybe that's what this whole thing is about. Don's Plum is unfinished business and maybe I gotta make things right before the universe will let me take the next step. I gotta right the wrongs."

Angela smiled, but she looked tired.

"This is a lot," I said. "You didn't sign up for this shit. So if you don't want to be involved—"

"Hey, hey, he, stop right there. You don't need to say any of that."

"I just... I don't know how long it will take, or what I'm even doing. And I don't know what's going to happen."

"I don't care. I believe in you so much. I think you're so damn talented. Besides, you're my golden goose, babe."

I laughed, and tears welled in my eyes.

She took me in her arms. "I'm gonna support you. OK? I don't care what happens. If they come for you, then they'll have to clobber us both."

"Angela—"

"Don't worry about me, I'm tough."

"I love you so much."

"This is my fight too, don't forget that. You made Don's Plum for everyone."

ON SEPTEMBER 5, 2014, I published a lengthy open letter on Tumblr admonishing Leo for destroying the work of dozens of artists. I called for an end to the suppression of Don's Plum and embedded a video link to the lo-res rip from my Mexican DVD I got on eBay for anyone to see for free on my blog, which we aptly named Free Don's Plum. I announced the letter on Facebook and decided to launch an indiegogo campaign simultaneously to fund Never Say Goodbye.

It was all a disaster. Angela was right about everything. I got in way over my head. We raised a little more than $500 with very little engagement. Within a few hours, the letter and the campaign were completely buried.

I guess I was embarrassed. I guess I was sad. I was definitely exhausted. We had so many problems that I wasn't counting on. I can't help but dream big, it's just who I am. Everything I try to do sells a million copies in my mind, wins a cabinet full of awards, and makes boatloads of money, and when none of it happens, I'm usually standing in the rubble of a self-made shitstorm, stunned that my plan didn't work.

Angela was not deterred. She suggested we leave California and find a cheaper place to live so that I could write and develop *Never Say Goodbye* into a novel. I didn't have a lot of confidence I could pull off a novel, but it sounded better than giving up.

We looked at a lot of places and finally settled on Athens, Georgia, where Angela's sister found us a cheap little house to rent that had a backyard for Clarence and our newest rescue, Trucker, who we named after my truck-driving dad because they both had thick paws.

A COUPLE of weeks after settling into our new place, Angela and I attended a filmmaker's meetup hosted by a local non-profit and we met some cool people. The conversations got me romanticizing the idea of moving to a small city that I had never even heard of and producing a badass independent movie, working almost exclusively with local talent. I made myself available to anyone interested in being produced and suddenly found myself developing a handful of writers. Within a year, I was producing a million-dollar faith-based feature called *Small Group* with a first-time writer/director that I developed from page one. It wasn't a movie I would have normally made, I'm not religious and not interested in the genre, but helping a couple of local aspiring filmmakers achieve their dream of making their first feature film was rewarding. And it was so nice to be working with a great crew again. *Small Group* has done well. It won best picture at the largest faith-based festival in the country and is widely considered one of the best faith-based films of 2018.

I also got a chance to create and teach a course at the University of Georgia based on my approach to filmmaking and I discovered a new love and passion for teaching. I hoped that my class would inspire at least one person to risk it all and make an independent movie before the capitalists snatched them into some 50-year plan. As for the rest of the students, I hoped they would connect more deeply with the movies they enjoy and embrace and encourage experimental film in their own lives and community.

I had a local businessman actively raising money to produce *Never Say Goodbye*, with an expectation to be in production in a matter of months. I was teaching and producing, and I was falling more and more in love with Angela with each passing day. My life was great on paper, but I could not shake the deep depression I was in, or the pervading sense of loss in my life. I battled aggressive bouts of suicidal ideation daily. The thoughts were terrifying at first but, after a while, they blended into the never-ending arguments rolling around in my troubled mind. My mental health took an unexpected and terrifying turn for the worse, and I began calmly planning the end of my life.

RD and I started talking again out the blue. There was something different about him, he seemed less cynical than usual. He used to send me scores of articles about filmmakers like the Duplass brothers who had success working experimentally, and say things like, "That should have been us," and "We got so fucked." He was obsessed with what we had lost, and so was I, but I still had hope, whereas RD's seemed lost forever. But something had changed, and we were suddenly talking about working together again. He had recently renegotiated his deal with *A Christmas Story* and offered up a hundred grand to produce a microbudget film. It was a big deal for me. We had talked about making another film for years, but never came remotely close to getting anything off the ground, and we could do a lot with a hundred grand.

I dusted off an old screenplay I had been writing for us back in LA, and within a few months I had a good, workable draft. We got after it just like old times, RD giving copious notes and engaging in long discussions about the different directions we could take the concept. The project started to get a little heartbeat going, and that made my days considerably brighter. RD even sent the script to a few well-respected actors, and we got incredible feedback along with solid interest. We were jamming again.

I woke up one morning after a restless sleep, worried to death that Don's Plum was about to disappear forever. I had no idea of the whereabouts of Don's Plum's assets, including over 300,000 feet of developed negative and reels upon reels of gorgeous nagra recordings from all six days of our shoot. Those tapes are precious, our entire process is on them. The negative was last at Zentropa, but I had no clue if it was still there. If so, that would be unsettling because Zentropa has a relationship with both DiCaprio and Maguire.

RD said he didn't know where the raw materials were, and he didn't think David Stutman knew either. It's entirely possible that RD owns the only 35mm print of Don's Plum in existence. He kept the Berlin festival print, and the last time I saw it, it was stored carelessly at his office, exposed to fluctuating temperatures and vulnerable to being damaged. I did some research and presented RD a plan to get his 35mm print digitized into a digital cinema package. RD agreed to cover the costs, which were substantial, and I set everything up. RD delivered the print to Burbank, where the great folks at Fotokem did an amazing job capturing the print in a crisp 2K DCP. It isn't flawless, but it dramatically increased the odds of Don's Plum's survival.

Fotokem shipped me a drive and holding that digital print in my hands for the first time felt so fucking liberating. These so called giants tried to erase Don's Plum from history and I made sure they failed.

I couldn't wait to see Don's Plum on the big screen again. I had become friends with a professor in the film program at UGA, and when I told him I got my hands on a print of Don's Plum, he set up a screening at the local arthouse theater for his graduating class as a part of their annual student film festival. More than a decade after skipping out on our premiere in Berlin, I finally watched the finished print of Don's Plum on the big screen in a packed American theater.

WE WERE LIVING in Athens for about a year when Leo was nominated for *The Revenant*. I braced myself for another gnarly "Leo season" because they released the movie in December, which meant the studio had budgeted tens of millions of dollars to lobby for awards. They got the nominations, but I was not prepared to witness Leonardo DiCaprio literally beg for an Oscar for two straight months in every form of media. He even went on Ellen, for fuck's sake. I know how much that hurt him.

The begging paid off, though. Leo won the Golden Globe and SAG awards for *The Revenant*, which made him a shoo-in to win the Oscar next. In his SAG Awards speech, Leo encouraged young actors to watch the history of film to learn from the giants who came before them. He said this while, at that very moment, doing everything he could to alter the history of film by blocking the release of Don's Plum. I sincerely hope that young actors do not follow in the footsteps of Leonardo DiCaprio. Throughout his career, Leo has hypocritically proclaimed himself an environmentalist and, at the same time, destroyed prehistoric beaches with his production company, sailed super yachts for his pleasure, and flown in private jets all over the world causing an unbelievable amount of unnecessary pollution. He has perpetuated outrageous wage disparities in Hollywood, playing a key role in the insane inflation of production budgets. And to top it all off, he had the fucking audacity to stand before his fellow actors and give them advice on how to honor the integrity and history of film while simultaneously destroying an innovative indie film in real time. Don's Plum was the work of Leo's peers, they were all members of the same worker's union that was honoring him, and he deliberately destroyed their work over a personal grudge. We'll never know many actors in Don's Plum might have climbed further up "on the shoulders of giants" had Leo not purposely blocked their work from ever being seen and recognized.

ONE OF THE benefits from all that exposure was a modest spike in traffic to freedonsplum.com. I was grateful for the hundreds of people who got to see Don's Plum thanks to all the extra press Leo was doing. One night, about a half a bottle of wine into the next day's hangover, I got a text from my buddy BigHank420 back in Jersey. He wrote, "Dude! You're on the front page of Reddit!"

I immediately jumped onto my laptop and logged into Reddit, and there it was on the front page of my feed with nearly ten thousand upvotes: "TIL that Leonardo DiCaprio blocked a film he was in from being released in the US and Canada. The producer of the film has released it on the internet and drafted a letter to Leo about it."

The entire post was focused on my open letter to Leo. The top comment with thousands of upvotes was simply, "Wow" written above the following quote from my letter: "This letter is about so much more than just a movie. It's about bullying, censorship, and abuse of power. You and Tobey Maguire spat in the face of independent film and the community that helped get you where you are today. You are not bigger than art, Leo. You are not bigger than the films in which you act." It was glorious! I logged onto Vimeo and Don's Plum had been watched more than 30,000 times in just a few hours. People all over the world were suddenly watching and talking about our movie!

Over the next several days freedonsplum.com got a lot of press. Nearly 100,000 people, mostly Americans and Canadians, watched the movie on my Tumblr alone. I was in a state of bliss and disbelief all at once. I thought Free Don's Plum had been a terrible failure but, with a single post by a random stranger on Reddit, the whole thing blew up bigger than I ever imagined, and two decades after it all went down, the truth about Don's Plum finally began to seep into the broader conversation.

.   .   .

I WAS SITTING on my couch answering hundreds of emails when my phone buzzed. It was RD, and I just assumed he was enjoying all the attention Don's Plum was getting as much as I was.

"Thank you for calling freedonsplum.com," I joked. "How may I direct your call?"

"That's not funny, bro. What the fuck is all this shit?" RD was as mad as I've ever heard him. "I don't need these fuckers coming after me again."

"It's a good thing, RD."

"No. No, it's not."

"Yes, it is. I'm getting emails from people all over the world who love our movie. I'll forward them to you—"

"No, don't. I don't want to see any of that shit. I don't want any part of this."

"Relax. I'm the one who wrote the letter, you're fine. I don't think anyone's gonna sue you for reading an email."

"I don't need these fuckers trashing my name all over town again! Amy doesn't need this shit either."

"This is important, RD. I'm fighting for what's right. I'm fighting for the fucking truth."

"How do you not understand this? These fucking people ruined my life, Dale. You need to leave them alone. We were doing fine. We were going to make a fucking movie!"

"And we still can... we should. We absolutely must, RD. You're not involved in this stuff. I'll do my thing with those fuckers—and we'll do our thing totally separate."

"Why the fuck did you do this?"

"Because they ruined my life too. Stop acting like I'm the one to blame. They caused all of this—they should have never gotten away with it."

RD sighed audibly, "Just keep me out of it."

About a week later, I received a letter from RD's lawyer, who admonished my actions and denied any involvement with Free Dons Plum. They formally requested that I stop talking about

Don's Plum, per our settlement agreement. I wondered if RD had his lawyer send a similar letter to David Stutman after he shut down our settlement-compliant escrow account and split to Europe, or if he sent anything to Leo when Leo continued to interfere with the distribution of our film, or for embarrassing RD publicly with totally false accusations.

While RD was busy paying lawyers to rebuke me, my work had led to an outpouring of support for the film and for my fight to preserve it. I emailed RD and Edie a link to a glowing review of Don's Plum that described our work as visionary. I wanted them to see the positive things that were happening because they were the things we had all dreamed about before all the shit went down. RD never replied but his mom did and I think her response demonstrates how people in Hollywood enable monsters to do whatever they want, and also how disturbingly effective intimidation is within Hollywood culture.

Edie: [I] read the article, but everything you touch goes down the drain and I dont know why. so please Dale stay out of our lives. I do wish you much luck

Me: I'll stay out of your life Edie, but you're wrong. It's Tobey who destroys everything he touches. This is my life too. Goodbye.

Edie: I agree with that, but he is a star, so gets away with it. remember you have a gag order and if they come after us, I will come after you and that mouth.

Me: That article I sent you talks about your son as a director with a vision. It praises his work and condemns those men for destroying it. You son's career was destroyed by these people Edie. A career you began working on when he was a baby. They destroyed my career and my dreams too. I've done nothing but love you guys. Year after year... I have never turned my back on you or RD. And I will always defend him and our work. Before I opened my mouth all they wrote about your son is how he got kicked out of the pussy posse. Now they're writing about him as a director. People are coming over to our side Edie... They can't do anything to him that they haven't already done.

There is an unspoken agreement in Hollywood that enables powerful people to abuse others and even commit crimes with impunity. And nearly everyone in proximity to them is complicit. Edie Robb was complicit just by falling in line and accepting that Tobey gets away with ruining our lives because "he is a star." She wanted me to stop telling the truth because she was afraid that they would come and take her precious money and interfere with RD's presently destroyed career. When behavior like hers is repeated by the majority of people in the industry, it allows for people like Harvey Weinstein and Tobey Maguire to ruin people for selfish purposes.

We were destroyed because everybody, even our own friends and family, allowed it to happen. All it took was the love and support of one person in my life for me to gain the courage to begin taking back what those men stole from me.

DON'S PLUM was suddenly getting a lot of attention and apparently Leo's people didn't like it because they contacted Vimeo and had Don's Plum taken down from freedonsplum.com. Leo didn't provide Vimeo any proof of copyright, he doesn't have any, but Vimeo took my work down anyway. The little power move backfired. Everyone suddenly wanted to know why, after 20 years, Leo still wanted to keep Don's Plum from US and Canadian audiences. Why block a movie that's already been released around the world, especially in the age of the torrents and crackstreams? Something was off and people were picking up on it.

I have never said Leonardo DiCaprio is a smart man. All he had to do was shut up and continue campaigning for his Oscar. Most people would have given Free Don's Plum a cursory glance at most, but Leo had to be The Don of Hollywood and block the movie again. It was the stupidest thing he could have done. Let can't seem to grasp that Don's Plum is the thing that is permanent here, not him or his delusions of power.

Consequently, Leo ended up pitting the press against himself. Entertainment Weekly, The Guardian, FOX, Nylon, The Decider, and Vulture were just a few of the media outlets that covered Leo's active suppression of Don's Plum. My inbox blew up with supporters. I didn't expect my story to resonate with so many cultures, but I was hearing from people from all over Asia, Europe, Australia, and the Americas.

I responded to Leo's latest effort to suppress Don's Plum, on freedonsplum.com, and I offered a free, private link to anyone who asked for it. Within days, I had thousands of emails. I responded to all of them, sending five hundred a day, the maximum allowed by Gmail. I was excited to connect with everyone who took the time to write me. Filmmakers, actors, writers, and producers from all over the world reached out to express their compassion, outrage, and support. Complete strangers were genuinely angry that these guys would desecrate art the way they had. There was a zeitgeist feel to the moment. People were tired of the rich behaving like tyrants instead of showing basic kindness and gratitude for their good fortune. I could feel the tides turning, not only on Leo and Tobey, but on elite culture as a whole.

A YouTuber uploaded Don's Plum to their channel, and in the description wrote, "posting because leo and tobey dont want it seen." In a matter of days, just under 100,000 people had watched Don's Plum on that channel alone. When the views hit 350,000, YouTube suspiciously stopped indexing it on searches for Don's Plum. A sped-up and almost unwatchable version of the movie, with an even worse resolution, was uploaded by another account and indexed in its place. It was a nightmare to see our work in such deplorable condition, but at least YouTube didn't take it down. The sped-up version of Don's Plum had just shy of half a million views at the time of this writing.

LEO ENDED up winning his pointless trophy and the world didn't change one bit. His fans rejoiced and his critics debated whether he deserved it for that particular performance. I didn't give a fuck, but the story followed me around like a hungry dog.

. . .

DAYS LATER, Angela and I were at a friend's house for dinner when my phone started blowing up with notifications. Emails were streaming in by the hundreds per minute like coins spilling out of a slot machine. I didn't know what to do with myself, I couldn't even think. I struggled trying to explain to our hosts what was happening. We apologized and ended the night early, rushing home with my chirping phone in my pocket.

Apparently, George Takei shared an article on Facebook and said, "I want to talk about Leo." The article's headline read something like, "Eight Things You Didn't Know About Leonardo DiCaprio," and my open letter was one of them. Hundreds of thousands of visitors hit freedonsplum.com in just a couple of hours. I didn't have a form to fill out on my website, so anyone who wanted to reach out had to use their own email client, and I still ended up with thousands of emails within a few hours of Mr. Takei's post.

Power is almost always an illusion that we accept on its face. I don't care about their so-called power anymore. They can't stop me.

49

I WAITED decades for Leo and Tobey to straighten out the mess *they* made. I truly believed they would all grow up and make this right, but instead I heard stories about members of the "Pussy Posse" assaulting Elizabeth Berkley's boyfriend, and Tobey Maguire trying to get Molly Bloom to bark like a seal for a thousand dollar tip just to humiliate her in front of his influential friends. It's as if hurting and humiliating people became some kind of twisted pastime for them. Maybe that explains why it was so easy for them to turn on indie film the way they did, even though it was that community of creators that helped launch both of their careers.

IF ANYONE WANTS to know why indie film is in dire straits, look no further than Leonardo DiCaprio, and I'm not even referring to his obstruction of Don's Plum. For his work on *The Wolf of Wall Street,* Leo was paid 25 million dollars, which was reportedly one of the highest salaries ever paid to an actor. Leo's salary for that one movie could have fully financed 25 to 50 independent film productions, each with a budget as much as ten times larger than ours was for Don's Plum. That's hundreds of people working and earning union wages for years. That's 25 to 50 dreams come true and possibly hundreds of new, exciting careers launched. But 25 million dollars wasn't even enough for Leo. He was also "gifted" original Picasso and Basquiat paintings valued at 11 million dollars, or up to 20 more fully financed independent feature film productions. The only reason to take 36 million dollars, or more than one-third of the entire budget of the project, is because you are greedy. And it's that greed killing the independent film scene and making movies unaffordable for people to see in theaters. Leo leaves paths of destruction on the way to his good fortune. Pristine, prehistoric beaches were irrevocably damaged to make *The Beach*. Our lives and careers were destroyed just because we made Don's Plum. And a sovereign nation was pillaged for money and precious art, just to pay for Leo and the making of *The Wolf of Wall Street,* and that's just the shit we know about. Leo could have been a hero for independent artists, but he chose to get paid in Picassos instead. What a shame.

NINE YEARS after shooting Don's Plum, Kevin Connolly finally hit it big on TV, playing a character whose identity was defined by his friendship with a movie star. I heard it's a good show, but I can say with certainty that it was not the career Kevin was working toward. And I believe it pales in comparison to the career he would have had if Don's Plum had been released in 1997 unobstructed by him and his buddies. Almost 30 years later, Don's Plum remains Kevin's best performance of his career in a feature film. In 2018, Kevin Connolly released his feature film directorial debut, *Gotti,* to horrid reviews. *Gotti* went on to receive a historic seven Razzie nominations, including one for worst director. I'm not dissing on Kevin, I'm genuinely sorry his movie didn't work. It was his dream project even back when we were hanging out, and so I'm sure it was very painful when it failed. Making a feature film is a hard thing to do, but at least *Gotti* was released without interference and allowed to succeed or fail on its own merits.

. . .

TWO OF SCOTT BLOOM'S four total acting credits since his awesome performance in Don's Plum include the roles of "Desk Guard" and "FBI Agent #3." The others were bit parts, including an appearance in a short directed by his friend, Kevin Connolly. When RD told me that Kevin directed a short film starring Robert Downey Jr. and cast Scott as a featured extra, I laughed out loud, I couldn't help it. These guys betrayed themselves when they went on their little witch hunt, and look what they ended up with. Scott earned himself a senior membership position in the "Pussy Posse" getting thrown bit parts like scraps to an alley dog. I was going to write him into every movie I ever made. I loved the guy and thought he was brilliant. I knew that we had only scratched the surface of what we could do with his talent when we made Don's Plum. He should have had a successful acting career but instead, Scott ran a nightclub that Leo would attend to attract high rollers and more celebrities. With his acting career completely off the table, Scott turned to writing. It was a good choice. He landed his screenwriting debut, penning a biopic on Theodore Roosevelt for Martin Scorsese, with Leo set to star. Twenty years after completing Don's Plum and about one year after my open letter to Leo made headlines and publicly accused Leo of ruining Scott's career by desecrating his work in Don's Plum, it appears as though Leo finally made good. I sincerely hope Scott knocks it out of the park.

ETHAN SUPLEE IS NOW a father of four and famously fit and healthy. He has appeared on my Reddit front page more than once for shedding all the weight and getting in great shape. I'm very happy for him, and I hope he has a long, healthy life. Ethan recently wrote a heartfelt letter to a Los Angeles Superior Court judge supporting his close friend and convicted serial rapist, Danny Masterson. Ethan asked the judge to consider all the good things Danny had done before sentencing him to 30-years to life. Ethan clearly values his friends, even after being convicted by a jury of unthinkable crimes, which made me wonder what it was

RD and I did that Ethan would consider worse than forcible rape. Maybe if Ethan had stood beside us like he did Danny, even if he had initially believed RD and I had done something wrong, and asked Leo to consider all the good things we had done in the past, maybe our lives, art, and careers wouldn't have been so ruthlessly destroyed. It sure would have been nice if he had tried.

I WAS WRITING one afternoon when a memory came back to me out of the blue. Back in 1995, I read an article in the trades about James Cameron and something to do with *Spider-Man*. I did some searching online, and sure enough, in March 1995, MGM announced it had purchased the rights to James Cameron's *Spider-Man* scriptment. In the article James Cameron said he believed that CGI technology had finally reached the point where a live-action *Spider-Man* was possible. In a 2021 Polygon article, I learned that Leo said in an interview with Empire Magazine that he and James Cameron had briefly talked about Leo playing a gritty version of Peter Parker in the mid 90s. This was the first I had ever heard of it, but I'd bet Leo told Tobey, even if he had been under an NDA.

I always sensed a professional tension between Leo and Tobey over *This Boy's Life*, that's probably been there since Leo had famously beat out Tobey for that highly coveted role when they were just 15 years old and already buddies. Tobey got a smaller part in the movie, but instead of any resentment or jealousy the two friends became even closer. Probably the most common pact made between young friends in Hollywood is the one where the first person to make it in the business promises to help the other. In fact, Kevin Connolly and RD Robb made such a pact in the '80s. I think it's highly likely Leo promised Tobey that if he made it big first, he would help Tobey so they could be at the top together.

Leo would not have been excited about playing a superhero. I'm sure it was tempting because it was James Cameron, but I believe Leo would have passed and if he did, I think he would have done whatever he could to help Tobey land that life-changing role.

It is entirely plausible that, not long after shooting Don's Plum, Tobey and his manager began strategizing, with or without Leo's involvement, to land the role of Peter Parker and *Spider-Man*.

You gotta strike while the iron is hot in Hollywood, and with Tobey's career gaining momentum, the only thing standing between him and the role of a lifetime was a little gritty arthouse movie in which his character confesses to enjoying anal masturbation. For a little perspective, Tobey didn't seem to care what anyone thought when he pulled his penis out on our set just for a continuity photograph, or when he dipped it in Aaron's morning beverage in some grotesque act of dominance. Surely, Tobey knew witnesses to these acts would talk about them. So it seems to me that Tobey's desire to destroy our film was career motivated rather than morally motivated. All his bullshit about me and RD "reaching for the stars" and "trampling on our friends to get ahead" was projection. Tobey used Leo to end Don's Plum for his own benefit and together they trampled on the work and careers of their friends and peers in the process.

I believe that, had Don's Plum been released and experienced a similar success as *Kids* or *Clerks*, Tobey would have been passed on for the role of Peter Parker. *Spider-Man* is a family franchise. In the moral climate of the '90s, I don't think Ian's dialogue would have helped Tobey land a character so beloved by children around the world. Whether it would have been James Cameron himself, another producer, or a random studio executive making the decision, there would have been at least some risk that Tobey would have been a pass because of his performance in Don's Plum, and I believe he knew that. They certainly wouldn't want to risk losing tens of millions of dollars because of some dumb micro budget indie that Tobey made with his stupid friends. Whatever the reason, Don's Plum had to go, and I believe after Leo approved Don's Plum and got CAA involved, Tobey needed to improvise fast to make that happen, so he turned RD and me into villains and manipulated Leo into believing he was going to war so he would blow the whole thing up.

The final mystery for me was why Tobey had to be so wicked.

Once Don's Plum was out of the way, why continue to inflict so much damage? It's truly frightening behavior because Tobey knew RD and I hadn't done anything wrong, but he still made damn sure our reputations and every aspect of our Hollywood existence was irreparably and irrevocably harmed. Tobey was void of reason, empathy, and decency, and it's a pattern he has repeated at least once since Don's Plum with Molly Bloom, as told in her memoir, *Molly's Game*. I am not a mental health professional, but all that stuff sounds like antisocial personality disorder to me.

My *Spider-Man* theory is just that, a theory I can't factually prove any more than I can diagnose someone with a mental disorder, but the puzzle pieces I propose fit together effortlessly and they reveal a compelling picture that, in my opinion, offers a plausible explanation as to why Tobey Maguire would go to such terrible lengths to get rid of a perfectly good arthouse film that he willingly participated in with his friends.

50

NOBODY CAN FIX what happened to Don's Plum. Leo and Tobey can never undo the damage they have caused us personally or professionally. Don's Plum can never be released in the summer of 1997, at the height of one of the greatest eras in American independent film. Kevin Connolly will never be the lead in an edgy, experimental feature making its debut at the Sundance Film Festival. Scott Bloom will never know what his career could have been like if it had taken its natural course. I know with certainty that he would have been the lead in at least one more feature film because I was writing it, and we already had a deal to get it made. Don's Plum was supposed to be the beginning of our collaboration, not the end of it.

I've spent decades trying to understand what happened to us, and I don't know that I've gotten any closer, but I take solace in the truth. We were just a group of close friends living in Hollywood who decided to make a movie together and it turned out to be pretty good.

It took a few years, but I finally gave Leo his sadness back. None of those guys get to control the narrative of my life anymore and they can't affect the way I feel. This sort of thing never has to happen again. In reality, Hollywood has far more good people than bad. They just need to come together and find a way to put an end to the abuses of power that stain the industry. And maybe next time around I'll find my way into some of their good company and we'll get a chance to make something beautiful together.

I wake up every day grateful to be alive. My depression is firmly behind me. I live creatively and I keep growing and learning more about myself every day. Angela and I enjoy slow mornings together talking about growing gardens and all the creative ideas we have for the new book we're working on. After my writing sessions, I usually jump on my Free Don's Plum email account and send out links to curious film fans and every time I do, I'm reminded of the true power of art and how it can bring people together in ways that extend beyond the work itself.

For years, I have been emotionally and spiritually lifted by these complete strangers who believe Don's Plum should be available to anyone who wants to see it, and I owe them everything. I've been especially moved by young writers and filmmakers, with their lofty dreams in front of them, who tell me how Don's Plum and what I'm doing to preserve it inspires them. They understand that these things we love and create become a part of us, and perhaps by fighting for Don's Plum I'm in some symbolic way, protecting their work as well. Filmmaking is the hardest thing I've ever done. There are thousands of battles and ridiculous obstacles to overcome, so I tell everyone that it's critical to not only embrace every creative moment and collaboration with unwavering love and trust, but to also be fearless in the face of adversity because making their first feature film might become the single most defining experience of their life.

As for me, I'm back to my old form. I've learned the hard way that my voice is my power and I'll never let anyone fuck with it again. I won't ever stop fighting for Don's Plum, not until it's released, but at least I can finally move forward on my own terms.

ACKNOWLEDGMENTS

I want to start by thanking my wife, my closest friend, and my phenomenally gifted editor, Angela Carvalho. Angela's thousands of insightful and inspiring notes can be read and felt throughout the entire book. Her unflinching love and support kept me on the rails and got me to the finish line in what was by far the most difficult project I have ever done. I could not have completed this work without her patience and faith in me. Angela is my golden goose and dream come true, and I am the luckiest man I know because of her.

I want to thank my most ardent supporter and friend, Tom Elliot who patiently listened while I sat on his couch and read out loud the early, less than entertaining drafts for far too long. Tom provided me with invaluable support and insight through some of the most vulnerable periods, without his contributions Too Real would not be the book it is today.

I was extremely fortunate to have a handful of people who voluntarily read my early drafts, and whose feedback I used to write a better book and become a better writer. Thank you, Jerry Meadors, Andras Jones, Samanta Carvalho, Micah Hudson, Stephanie Holcombe, Jason Boswell, and Sandy somewhere in Greece, for your honesty, wisdom, and your constant encouragement.

I'd like to thank some of my family and friends who were there for me through some of my darkest days. I know I wasn't the best company or the best friend, but you mean everything to me, and I think about you every day. Thank you, Trevor Lawrence, Amie Moore, and Keaton Moore. Thanks to my oldest friends on this earth, Mark May, Dennis Cooper, and James Comeau. Thanks to my mom and dad and to my brother Doug, his wife Angela, and their wonderful children Sky and Ryan. I miss and love you all.

I want to acknowledge all the fans of Don's Plum who have taken time out of their busy lives to reach out to me in support of the work and the fight to keep the film alive. When I was at my absolute lowest, it was your encouragement that kept me believing that art truly is bigger than life, and that it's worth fighting for. Whenever I felt like giving up, like angels, you would appear and say the perfect thing to keep me going. Your love and support saved my life and my work, and I will forever be in your debt. I love you all. May all your dreams come true.

Made in the USA
Coppell, TX
25 October 2024

39182278R00333